INSPIRING QUOTATIONS

CONTEMPORARY & CLASSICAL

COMPILED BY
ALBERT M. WELLS, JR.

DIRECTOR OF
NATIONAL PERIODICAL LIBRARY
P.O. Box 47
Flint, MI 48501

THOMAS NELSON PUBLISHERS
Nashville

The wisdom of the wise and the experience of
the ages may be preserved by quotations.

Isaac D'Israeli

Published in Nashville, Tennessee, by Thomas Nelson
Inc., and distributed in Canada by Lawson Falle, Ltd.,
Cambridge, Ontario.

Printed in the United States of America.

Some Scripture quotations are from THE NEW KING JAMES VERSION.
Copyright © 1979, 1980, 1982, Thomas Nelson, Inc., Publishers.

Some Scripture quotations are from *The New English Bible.* © The Delegates of the Oxford
University Press and the Syndics of the Cambridge University Press 1961, 1970. Reprinted
by permission.

Some Scripture quotations are from the King James Version of the Bible.

Library of Congress Cataloging-in-Publication Data

Inspiring quotations.

1. Quotations. I. Wells, Albert M., 1931–
PN6081.I55 1988   082   87-34776
ISBN 0-8407-7563-6

2 3 4 5 6—92 91 90 89

CONTENTS

PREFACE

Gerald Kennedy once said that the only way a man can speak or converse with any profit to others is to lean heavily on the work of other persons. The purpose of *Inspiring Quotations* is to expedite this process and provide its readers with some excellent and stimulating food for thought. And one might dare hope that this linear table will be an occasion for feasting.

I have found that quotations often enable one to draw a sharp focus on a given subject and sometimes assist in making a particular view perceptible where an abundance of words may only muddy the waters.

The short succinct statements that make up many quotations are seldom meant to be absolute or completely definitive. They are simply brief declarations that emphasize a particular point, often with explosive and exclamatory language. They frequently awaken and always alert the mind to become aware of new suppositions. This awareness may accept or reject the stated position. But in either case, good "classified information" comes through with color and clamor, impact and intensity, giving insights that will help you feel deeply and think clearly.

It will be interesting and sometimes helpful to check the Source List which indicates where a particular entry was encountered. It is hoped that the Author Index will also enhance the utility of this book.

The information set forth in these pages is a collection of slightly less than 3,000 items, classified by subject, which I have collected from my professional reading and research activities. Some will edify, some will entertain, and others may provoke. It is hoped that each one will bless and enrich your life.

I wish to thank my mother, Nina I. Wells, and my late father, Albert M. Wells, Sr., for their encouragement and support in my work as a writer and editor. Even more importantly, I am grateful for their Christian influence and spiritual nurture.

I also wish to thank Joanne Holland, an education/language arts specialist and a long-time friend for her assistance in the preparation, revision, and correction of manuscript materials.

Finally, I want to thank each of the writers whose quotations have contributed to this book's profound and interesting insights.

Albert M. Wells, Jr.

ABORTION

1. You can scrape the baby out of the womb but you cannot scrape the baby out of the mind. —**Frank J. Ayd**

2. It has not been the purpose, in this short essay, to attempt to prove that personhood exists before birth or at any particular point in the developing process. . . . I merely wish to suggest that the converse cannot be proved and it is far better to err on the side of life. If we are not sure whether it is a man or a moose, we dare not shoot. —**Wayne Dawes**

3. Abortion must be seen as the interruption of a process that would otherwise have produced a citizen of the world. Denial of this reality is the crassest kind of moral evasiveness. —**Bernard M. Nathanson**

4. Prevention of birth is premature murder, and it makes no difference whether it is a life already born that one snatches away or a life that is coming to birth that one destroys. The future man is a man already. The whole fruit is present in the seed. —**Tertullian**

5. The Bible says that Mary was "great with *child*" (Luke 2:5). An expectant mother is a woman "with child." To terminate the life of that child is murder.

ACCOUNTABILITY

6. When we are given our rewards, I would prefer to be found to have erred on the side of grace rather than judgment; to have loved too much rather than too little; to have forgiven the undeserving rather than refused forgiveness to that one who deserved it; to have fed a parasite rather than to have neglected one who was truly hungry; to have been taken advantage of rather than to have taken undue advantage; to have believed too much in my brothers rather than too little; having been wrong on the side of too much trust than too much cynicism; to have believed the best and been wrong, than to have believed the worst and been right.

—**Gerald Boyer**

7. We are all weaving rope. Most of it is made away from the scrutiny of others, but we can be sure that what we do in the darkness will be tested in the light.

—**George Holmes**

8. The fact that when we are "in Christ" there is no condemnation for our sins does not mean there is no examination of our works. —**Samuel Leith**

ACHIEVEMENT

9. I am only one, but I am one. I cannot do everything but I can do something; and what I can do, that I ought to do; and what I ought to do, by the grace of God I shall do. —**Edward Everett Hale**

10. The only people who achieve much are those who want knowledge so badly that they seek it while the conditions are still unfavorable. Favorable conditions never come. —**C. S. Lewis**

ADMINISTRATION

11. The best executive is the one who has sense enough to pick good men to do what he wants done, and self-restraint enough to keep from meddling with them when they do. —**Theodore Roosevelt**

AGRICULTURE

12. The agricultural population produces the bravest men, the most valiant soldiers, and a class of citizens the least given of all to evil designs. —**Cato**

ALCOHOLIC BEVERAGES

13. Drinking alcoholic beverages is deceptive; tolerance for alcohol increases, giving the drinker a false assurance. But the increased tolerance merely indicates the body and its nervous system "require" more alcohol for the same effect—the first and certain step toward addiction.
—**Fred H. Baker, Sr.**

14. Drink has drained more blood, hung more crepes, sold more homes, plunged more people into bankruptcy, armed more villains, slain more children, snapped more wedding rings, defiled more innocence, blinded more eyes, twisted more limbs, dethroned more reason, wrecked more manhood, dishonored more womanhood, broken more hearts, driven more to suicide and dug more graves than any other poisonous scourge that ever swept its death-dealing waves across the world.
—**Evangeline Booth**

15. No man ever drank lard into his tub, or flour into his sack, nor meal into his barrel, nor happiness into his home, nor God into his heart. —**Benjamin Franklin**

16. I have rarely met a young person who drinks in moderation. Experience tells me that from age thirteen to sixteen, one either abstains from alcohol or gets roaring drunk. There is very little middle ground.
—**Robert L. Gram**

17. Beverage alcohol has many defenders but no defense. —**Abraham Lincoln**

18. O God, that men should put an enemy in their mouths to steal away their brains. —**William Shakespeare**

19. I'm going to fight the liquor business till hell freezes over, and then I'll put on ice skates and fight it some more.
—**Billy Sunday**

20. The name of every saloon is *bar*,
The fittest name by far;
A bar to heaven, a door to hell,
Whoever named it, named it well.

A bar to manliness and a bar to
    wealth,
A door to sorrow and broken health;
A bar to honor, pride and fame,
A door to sorrow, grief and shame.

A bar to hopes, a bar to prayer,
A door to darkness and despair;
A bar to useful, manly life,
A door to brawling, senseless strife.

A bar to heaven, a door to hell,
Whoever named it, named it well.

—Written by a twenty-five-year-old
inmate while in prison
at Joliet, Illinois

AMBITION

21. If you believe in Christ, you lead to love; outside of Christ you love to lead.

—Howard Butt

22. The poor man is not he who is without a cent, but he who is without a dream.

—Harry Kemp

23. Scripture does not prohibit anyone from reaching for the heights; it only specifies that it be done for the glory of God.

(see also: Achievement)

AMERICA

(see: United States)

ANGELS

24. The dispensers and administrators of the divine beneficence toward us; they regard our safety . . . and exercise a constant solicitude that no evil befall us.

—John Calvin

25. An angel is a spiritual creature created by God without a body, for the service of Christendom and of the Church.

—Martin Luther

ANGER

26. Hot heads and cold hearts never solved anything.   —Billy Graham

27. Anger is momentary passion, so control your passion or it will control you.

—Horace

28. Anyone who angers you conquers you.   —Sister Kenny

29. No matter how much someone deserves your anger, the anger itself does not hurt that person as much as it hurts you.

—Nina Walter

30. Unholy tempers are always unhappy tempers.   —John Wesley

31. When a man's temper gets the best of him it reveals the worst of him.

(see also: Interpersonal Relations)

ANTICHRIST

32. One of the chief differences between the church of our age and that of the Book of Revelation is that instead of fighting the Beast we stroke it and pet it and say, "Nice pussy!"   —Halford Luccock

33. What will finally destroy us is not communism nor fascism, but man acting like God.   —Malcolm Muggeridge

ANXIETY

34. Anxiety is the natural result when our hopes are centered in anything short of God and His will for us.   —Billy Graham

35. Anxiety is not only a pain which we must ask God to assuage, but also a weakness we must ask Him to pardon.

—C. S. Lewis

36. Charles H. Davis tells of a man who was hiking on a mountain. Caught up in the wonder of the landscape he lingered on the trail and darkness overtook him. Feeling his way down the mountain side, he slipped and fell over a cliff. As he fell he managed to grab a tree limb and he hung on for what seemed like hours, hoping someone would happen along and give him a hand. Finally, no longer able to hold his grip, he turned loose and plunged down—a full six inches to the ground. Only six inches from safety, yet he suffered in terror. Why do we hang in fear when we can trust God for safe keeping? When things look tough, look up and trust.

37. Anxiety springs from the desire that things should happen as we wish rather than as God wills.

(see also: Worry; Fear; Peace of Mind)

APATHY

38. Truth is violated by falsehood, but it is outraged by silence.

—Henri Frederic Amiel

39. When they are asleep you cannot tell a good man from a bad one.   —Aristotle

40. I only did what you have done
A thousand times or more
When Joseph came to Bethlehem
And knocked upon my door.

I did not turn the Christ away
With alibi so deft.
Like you I simply gave to Him
Whatever I had left.

—B. P. Baker

41. I'm afraid the more organized and specialized we become—the more we cop out, and move away from our personal involvement. And the result is, our religion becomes a one-way street—one of only coming and not going.

—Lawrence Balleine

42. A Christian never falls asleep in the fire, or in deep waters; but he is likely to grow drowsy in the sunshine.

—W. G. Burns

43. The death of religious faith is seen in nothing so much as in the fact that, in general, it has lost its power to move anyone to die for it.   —Whittaker Chambers

44. The Christian faith has not been tried and found wanting. It has been found difficult and left untried.

—G. K. Chesterton

45. We Christians have given "Calvary" to the Communists. They accept deprivation and death to spread their gospel, while we Christians reject any gospel that does not major on healing and happiness.

—George E. Failing

46. We have vivid religious interest, but no decisive experiences. We have fine sympathies but not a more fearless conscience; a warmer ethic, but a poorer courage; eloquence about morals, silence about holiness, much about criticism, little sense of judgment.   —Peter Taylor Forsyth

47. The average American lets his boss think for him at work, his television for him at home, and his pastor thinks his theology for him on Sunday. The most he taxes his brain is trying to figure out the next play his favorite football team will run.   —David Gillespie

48. Some people today listen to an evangelical preacher and to a liberal preacher with equal satisfaction, so long as they hear the name of Jesus mentioned every once in a while.   —Vance Havner

49. Waking up is not getting up. In the average so-called revival, the local church wakes up only to turn over and go back to sleep.   —Vance Havner

50. The work of God is held back not by bad men and women, but by good ones who have stopped growing.   —M. P. Horban

51. We are losing our Christianity because Christianity is a creed for heroes while we are mainly harmless, good-natured people who want everybody to have a good time. **—W. R. Inge**

52. E. Stanley Jones described slightly religious people by saying they had been inoculated with a mild form of Christianity and thus rendered immune from the real thing.

53. There is nothing sinful about . . . consumption of food, commercial transactions, consignment of seed to the soil, and construction projects. But to proceed in the face of imminent moral destruction as if life will continue undisturbed demonstrates a distorted view of priorities and a regrettable degree of immaturity.
—W. Carl Ketcherside

54. Too many of us are on the sidelines, keeping a safe distance from the fray—content, apparently, to watch others run the risks, take the losses, sustain the injuries. Too many of us are AWOL from the Lord's army; some have left for lunch and linger long into the afternoon, allowing the business of the King to go lacking.
—George S. Lauderdale

55. It is since Christians have largely ceased to think of the other world that they have become so ineffective in this one. **—C. S. Lewis**

56. We often excuse our own want of [involvement] by giving the name of fanaticism to the more ardent zeal of others.
—Henry Wadsworth Longfellow

57. While Samson slept in the lap of Delilah he was shorn of his power to act for God. A church that sleeps in the lap of the world will be a contributor to its evil when it should have been a disturber of its conscience. **—W. E. McCumber**

58. Cooling down a fanatic is easier than warming up a corpse. **—W. E. McCumber**

59. There is nothing that can so lock the lips of a Christian as an inner life which is not right. **—Kenneth L. Miles**

60. To live adventurously for God
　　We have not dared,
　　When there were needs that we
　　　　might fill
　　We have not shared.

But all our wrong in thought and
　　deed
　　Has sprung up from this poisonous
　　　　seed—
We have not cared!
—Belle Chapman Morrill

61. In Germany the Nazis came for the Communists and I didn't speak up because I was not a Communist. Then they came for the Jews and I didn't speak up because I was not a Jew. Then they came for the trade unionists and I did not speak up because I was not a trade unionist. Then they came for the Catholics and I was a Protestant so I did not speak up. Then they came for me. By that time there was no one left to speak up for anyone. **—Martin Niemoller**

62. In any moment of decision the best thing you can do is the right thing, the next best thing is the wrong thing, and the worst thing you can do is nothing.
—Theodore Roosevelt

63. Most people in the pews are like people sitting in an airline terminal. They hear announcements of arrivals and departures, watch all the hurry and bustle, and imagine they are really in on the action,

9

yet they never purchase a ticket or board the plane. —Samuel M. Shoemaker

64. Even fanaticism is to be preferred to indifference. I had sooner risk the dangers of a tornado of religious excitement than see the air grow stagnant with a dead formality. —Charles H. Spurgeon

65. Men are accomplices to what leaves them indifferent. —George Steiner

66. The real corrupters of society may be, not the corrupt, but those who have held back the righteous leaven, the salt that has lost its savor, the innocent who have not even the moral courage to show what they think of the effrontery of impurity—the serious, who yet timidly succumb before some loud-voiced scoffer—the heart trembling all over with religious sensibilities that yet suffers itself through false shame to be beaten down into outward and practical acquiescence by some rude and worldly nature. —J. H. Thomb

67. That this world is a playground instead of a battleground has now been accepted in practice by the vast majority of fundamentalist Christians. —A. W. Tozer

68. In the shaker, safely I dwell,
Close to those I love so well,
Secure among each Christian peer,
Supported by each friendship dear;
Fearful to be shaken out,
Lest fear be overcome with doubt
And, meeting with the world's
    disfavor,
I find that I have lost my savor.
—Wanda M. Trawick

69. Small vision in thought
        plus
Low visibility in witness
        equals
Few victories in deed.
—Albert M. Wells, Jr.

70. There are many people who would argue loud and long for the existence of hell while at the same time being reluctant to open their heart and home to rescue some who are going there. —Albert M. Wells, Jr.

71. The depreciation of Christianity by indifference is a more insidious and less curable evil than infidelity itself.
—Richard Whatley

72. If absence makes the heart grow fonder, how some people must love the church!

73. Which disturbs you the most? A soul lost in hell or a scratch on your new car? Your missing the worship service or missing a day's work? Your church not growing or your garden not growing? The church work neglected or housework neglected? Missing a Bible study or missing your favorite TV program? The cry of the multitude for bread or your desire for another piece of cake?

74. I know that God will find me His redeemed child; but I wish it were more evident to the people across the street. Our churches more than ever are religious clubs, blessed with very satisfying fellowship, but awash in endless talk.

75. Apathy is the ally of Satan.

76. Times are especially trying for those who aren't trying.

77. God isn't dead but His public relations staff could stand a good shaking up.

APOSTASY

78. When people stop believing in God, they do not believe in nothing. They believe in *anything*. —G. K. Chesterton

ARROGANCE

79. If we assume that we are 100 percent correct and others are clearly and completely wrong, it is either abysmal ignorance or colossal arrogance—or perhaps a little of each.   **—Kenneth J. Weller**

(see also: Pride)

ASPIRATION

80. Nothing at all will be attempted if all possible objections must first be overcome.
          —**Samuel Johnson**

81. Aim at heaven and you get earth thrown in. Aim at earth and you get neither.   **—C. S. Lewis**

ASSURANCE

82. My religious beliefs teach me to feel as safe in battle as in bed.
          —Thomas (Stonewall) Jackson

83. There are times when I sense such a
          feeling of peace,
     Like the brooding of wings from
          above!
There are times when it seems all
          feeling is gone;
     Then I rest in the *fact* of His love!
Though kingdoms may crumble, His
          Word is secure,
     The plan of salvation intact:
Though it's precious to *feel* His
          presence is near,
     Our hope is not feeling, but *fact*!
          —Alice Hansche Mortenson

ATHEISM

84. There are so few atheists in the world because it takes more credulity to accept the atheistic position than most men can muster.   **—Gerald Kennedy**

85. No one has ever died an atheist.
          —Plato

86. Atheists brag that they can get along without God; this is hardly a distinction in an era where very, very few pay the Lord more than a Sunday call.
          —Dagobert D. Runes

87. An atheist's most embarrassing moment is when he feels profoundly thankful for something, but can't think of anybody to thank for it.   **—Mary Ann Vincent**

ATONEMENT

88. I must die or get somebody to die for me. If the Bible doesn't teach that, it doesn't teach anything. And that is where the atonement of Jesus Christ comes in.
          —Dwight L. Moody

89. O Love divine, what hast Thou
          done!
     Th' incarnate God hath died for me!
     The Father's co-eternal Son
     Bore all my sins upon the tree!
     The Son of God for me that died:
     My Lord, my love, is crucified.
          —Charles Wesley

(see also: Good Friday Theme; Salvation)

ATTITUDE

90. A militant attitude often betrays an inner turmoil.   **—Emile Caillet**

91. More important than the size of a bank account or the lack of it is the attitude of the one who signs the checks—or wishes he could.   **—Raymond L. Cox**

92. One of the most stultifying attitudes for quenching productivity is an absorbing concern over what others may think. There is one person who is totally free from this. He is the man who has discovered that only God matters.

—**Robert B. Hammond**

93. Life is a grindstone. But whether it grinds us down or polishes us up depends on us. —**L. Thomas Holdcroft**

94. Two men look out through the same bars;
One sees the mud and one the stars.

—**Frederick Langbridge**

95. Just as the same sun melts wax and hardens clay, so Christ's presence either softens or hardens our hearts, depending on our attitude. —**Rodrigo Tano**

96. He that hath so many causes of joy, and so great, is very much in love with sorrow and peevishness who loses all these pleasures and chooses to sit down on his little handful of thorns. —**Jeremy Taylor**

97. There are things I can't force. I must adjust. There are times when the greatest change needed is a change of my viewpoint. —**C. M. Ward**

98. Circumstances are like a feather bed: comfortable if you are on top, but smothering if you are underneath.

AUTUMN

99. Why is it that so many of us persist in thinking that autumn is a sad season? Nature has merely fallen asleep, and her dreams must be beautiful if we are to judge by her countenance.

—**Samuel Taylor Coleridge**

Backsliding

100. Do you know what you have to do to backslide? Nothing! —**J. Donald Freese**

101. Vice is a monster of such frightful mien,
That to be hated needs but to be seen,
But seen too oft, familiar with her face,
We first endure, then pity, then embrace.

—**Alexander Pope**

102. Backsliding starts when kneebending stops.

103. If God seems far away, who moved?

104. When you are growing in grace you are critical of yourself, but when you are backsliding you are critical of others.

(see also: Apathy)

BALANCE

105. No man has a right to lead such a life of contemplation as to forget in his own ease the service due to his neighbor; nor has any man a right to be so immersed in active life as to neglect the contemplation of God. —**Augustine**

106. Let nothing good or bad upset the balance of your life. —**Thomas à Kempis**

107. I'm very careful with the cup;
I daren't play the clown.
I know that if I live it up,
I have to live it down.

—**Gertrude Leigh**

BAPTISM

108. I was dead, but because in Baptism I died together with Christ, I received the light of life from Christ. And he who dies in Christ, being warmed by Christ, receives the breath of life and resurrection.

—**Ambrose**

109. Baptism is the declaration of the universal Face of the Sonship of man to God. —**Phillips Brooks**

110. A part of the act of baptism in the Church of India is for the candidate to place his own hand on his head and say, "Woe is me if I preach not the gospel." This is part of the baptismal service of new members, not the ordination of ministers.
—**E. Paul Hovey**

111. When a Baptist was asked about baptism, he replied, "It's all right, but you mustn't hang around the river too long."
—**E. Stanley Jones**

BEAUTY

112. Where there is beauty apparent, we
    are to enjoy it;
Where there is beauty hidden, we
    are to unveil it;
Where there is beauty defaced, we
    are to restore it;
Where there is no beauty at all, we
    are to create it.
—**Robert McAfee Brown**

113. If God took time to create beauty, how can we be too busy to appreciate it?
—**Randall B. Corbin**

114. Though we travel the world over to find the beautiful, we must carry it within us, or we find it not.
—**Ralph Waldo Emerson**

115. A thing of beauty is a joy forever.
—**John Keats**

116. There is beauty in the forest
    When the trees are green and
    fair,
There is beauty in the meadow
    When wild flowers scent the air,
There is beauty in the sunlight

And the soft blue beams above,
Oh, the world is full of beauty
When the heart is full of love.

BENEVOLENCE

117. Benevolence is allied to few vices; selfishness to fewer virtues. —**Henry Home**

118. Benevolent feeling ennobles the most trifling actions.
—**William M. Thackeray**

(see also: Charity)

BIBLE

119. So great is my veneration of the Bible, that the earlier my children begin to read it the more confident will be my hope that they will prove useful citizens of their country and respectable members of society. —**John Quincy Adams**

120. The study of God's Word for the purpose of discovering God's will is the secret discipline which has formed the greatest characters. —**James W. Alexander**

121. The central issue about the Bible is whether we live it. —**John F. Alexander**

122. Man can live by bread alone—if it's the Bread of Life. —**A. J. Amick**

123. Don't leave your Bible on the shelf,
    Where days will take their toll
Of dust and mold and mildew,
    On your poor neglected soul.
—**Winnie Andrews**

124. If you believe what you like in the Gospel and reject what you do not like, it is not the Gospel you believe, but yourself.
—**Augustine**

125. When you find in Holy Scripture

anything you did not believe before, believe it without doubt. —Augustine

126. God used the Scriptural Gospel to bring me to saving faith in Jesus Christ. He has also convinced me that the Scriptures are utterly true, inerrant, if you will; they are "the swaddling clothes in which Christ is laid." Some will call this conviction hopelessly naive or a refusal to look at the findings of twentieth century science. So be it. If the scientist is our final authority, ask him if dead men rise. —Karl Barth

127. When you don't feel like reading the Bible, that's the time to read it.
—Lorna Beall

128. Apply thy whole self to the text; apply the whole text to thyself.
—John Albrecht Bengel

129. Ad fontes was a Reformation motto—back to the fountain, back to God and back to the Bible. This is not a regressive idea; it is the essence of our need.
—Harold Borchert

130. The fate of the Bible is the fate of Christianity. —Emil Brunner

131. The Bible is not only a book which I can understand; it is also a book which understands me. —Emile Caillet

132. Scripture is like a pair of spectacles which dispels the darkness and gives us a clear view of God. —John Calvin

133. No man is uneducated who knows the Bible and no one is wise who is ignorant of its teachings. —Samuel Chadwick

134. Last eve I paused beside a
blacksmith's door
And heard the anvil ring the
vesper chime:

Then looking in, I saw upon the
floor,
Old hammers worn out with
beating years of time.

"How many anvils have you had,"
said I,
"To wear and batter all these
hammers so?"
"Just one," said he, and then with
twinkling eyes,
"The anvil wears the hammers out,
you know."

And so, I thought, the anvil of
God's Word
For ages skeptics' blows have beat
upon,
Yet though the noise of falling
blows was heard,
The anvil is unmarred, the
hammers gone.
—John Clifford

135. This book outlives, outloves, outlifts, outlasts, outreaches, outruns, and outranks all books. This Book is faith-producing. It is hope-awakening. It is death-destroying. And those who embrace it find forgiveness of sin. —A. Z. Conrad

136. Read it to be wise.
Believe it to be safe.
Practice it to be holy.
—Robert C. Cunningham

137. Read it through; pray it in; live it out; pass it on. —George Gritter

138. If you cannot always get the right explanation for some Scripture, be sure you don't miss the application of it.
—Vance Havner

139. The Bible is the rock on which our republic rests. —Andrew Jackson

140. Unless we form the habit of going to the Bible in bright moments as well as in trouble, we cannot fully respond to its consolations because we lack equilibrium between light and darkness. —Helen Keller

141. You can read the Bible as literature only by a *tour de force*. You are cutting the wood against the grain, using the tool for a purpose it was not intended to serve. It demands incessantly to be taken on its own terms: it will not continue to give literary delight very long except to those who go to it for something quite different.
  —C. S. Lewis

142. The less the Bible is read, the more it's translated. —C. S. Lewis

143. I have but to say, the Bible is the best gift God has given to man. All the good Savior gave to the world was communicated through this book. But for it we could not know right from wrong. All things most desirable for man's welfare, here and hereafter, are to be found portrayed in it. —Abraham Lincoln

144. I follow the example of St. Augustine, who was . . . the first and almost the only one who determined to be subject to the Holy Scriptures alone, and independent of the books of all the fathers and saints. —Martin Luther

145. The Bible is alive, it speaks to me; it has feet, it runs after me; it has hands, it lays hold on me. —Martin Luther

146. Read the Bible, not as a newspaper, but as a home letter. If a cluster of heavenly fruit hangs within reach, gather it. If a promise lies upon the page as a blank check, cash it. If a prayer is recorded, appropriate it, and launch it as a feathered arrow from the bow of your desire. If an example of holiness gleams before you, ask God to do as much for you. If the truth is revealed in all its intrinsic splendor, entreat that its brilliance may ever irradiate the hemisphere of your life. —F. B. Meyer

147. Disregard the study of God and you sentence yourself to stumble and blunder through life, blindfolded, as it were, with no sense of direction and no understanding of what surrounds you. —J. I. Packer

148. He who will give the meaning of Scripture, and does not take it from Scripture, is the enemy of Scripture.
  —Blaise Pascal

149. Priests, atheists, skeptics, devotees, agnostics and evangelists are generally agreed that the Authorized Version of the English Bible is the best example of English literature that the world has ever seen. —William Lyon Phelps

150. We have adopted the convenient theory that the Bible is a Book to be explained, whereas first and foremost it is a Book to be believed. . . . There is a world of difference between knowing the Word of God and knowing the God of the Word.
  —Leonard Ravenhill

151. The Christian who is careless in Bible reading will be careless in Christian living. —Max I. Reich

152. I have heard a few Greek scholars say that when they first read Plato, they found it a mirror for their souls. That may be. But they never found in Plato salvation from their sins, nor a sinless Redeemer, nor the absolute assurance of eternal life and of resurrection after death. Only the Bible offers you that. —Wilbur Smith

153. Defend the Bible? I would just as soon defend a lion. Just turn the Bible loose. It will defend itself.
  —Charles H. Spurgeon

154. The overriding reason for accepting the divine inspiration and authority of Scripture is plain loyalty to Jesus Christ.
—John R. W. Stott

155. The Bible does not argue for the existence of God. It reveals Him.
—Roy E. Swim

156. God's Word is an enemy for depression, an escape from temptation, the promise of the future, as well as a guide, hope, and inspiration for now and always.
—Al and Brenda Taylor

157. It matters not what others do,
For God has left a standard true.
I'll search its pages day by day,
And pray for courage to obey.
—Tullett

158. If there be anything in my style to commend, credit is due to an early love of Scriptures. —Daniel Webster

159. The man who doesn't read his Bible has no advantage over the man who has no Bible. —Albert M. Wells, Jr.

160. You who like to play at Bible—
Dip and dabble, here and there,
Just before you kneel, aweary,
And yawn through a hurried prayer;
You who treat the crown of writings
As you treat no other book—
Just a paragraph disjointed,
Just a crude, impatient look—
Try a worthier procedure,
Try a broad and steady view;
You will kneel in very rapture
When you read the Bible through.
—Amos R. Wells

161. I want to know one thing—the way to heaven; how to land safe on that happy shore. God Himself has condescended to teach the way: For this very end He came from heaven. He hath written it down in a book. O give me that book! At any price, give me the book of God! I have it: Here is knowledge enough for me. Let me be a man of one book. —John Wesley

162. Bible study is like eating fish. When you find a bone, you need not throw away the whole fish. Lay aside the bone and eat the meat. —Alex Wilson

163. What the Bible does [in the lives of people] makes what it says believable.
—Kenneth L. Wilson

164. There are a good many problems before the American people today, and before me as President, but I expect to find the solution of those problems just in the proportion that I am faithful in the study of the Word of God. —Woodrow Wilson

165. I am sorry for the men who do not read the Bible every day. I wonder why they deprive themselves of the strength and the pleasure. —Woodrow Wilson

166. Despite the cynic's angry word,
The skeptic's narrow look,
The running ages have not matched
This holy, mighty Book.
—Lon Woodrum

167. Before General Eisenhower died, Billy Graham was invited to visit the former President. He was told he could only stay thirty minutes. But when the time was up, the general asked him to stay longer. "Billy," he said, "I want you to tell me once again how I can be sure my sins are forgiven and that I'm going to heaven, because nothing else matters now." Billy took out his New Testament and read several verses. He pointed out that we go to heaven totally . . . on the merits of what Christ did on the cross. After prayer General Eisenhower said, "Thank you. I'm ready." It is the Word of God, and not man's opinion, that people want when they are stepping into eternity.

—Thomas F. Zimmerman

168. God's Word has been a hammer for nineteen centuries. When other hammers try to break God's eternal anvil of truth, we remember the inscription on the monument to the Huguenots at Paris: "Hammer away, ye hostile hands; Your hammers break; God's anvil stands."

—Samuel Zwemer

169. People do not reject the Bible because it contradicts itself. They reject it because it contradicts them.

170. There are three stages in Bible reading: (1) the cod liver oil stage, when you take it like medicine; (2) the shredded wheat stage when it's nourishing but dry; (3) the peaches and cream stage when it is consumed with passion and pleasure.

171. Whoever heard of a Communist on his death bed asking that Karl Marx's *Das Kapital* be read to him? Or when has an eat-drink-and-be-merry kind of person asked in death for a reading from *Playboy*? But the Christian dies with the words of Scripture on his lips and the Christ of Scripture in his heart, and he's headed for heaven.

172. The Bible contains the mind of God, the state of man, the way of salvation, the doom of sinners, the happiness of believers. Its doctrines are holy, its precepts are binding, its decisions are immutable. Read it to believe, believe it to be safe, practice it to be holy. It contains light to direct you, food to support you, and comfort to cheer you. It is the traveler's guide, the pilgrim's staff, the pilot's compass, the soldier's sword, the Christian's character. Here paradise is restored, heaven opened, and the gates of hell disclosed. Christ is its grand subject, our good its design, and the glory of God its end. It should fill the memory, rule the heart, and guide the feet. Read it slowly, daily, prayerfully. It is a mine of wealth, a paradise of glory, and a river of pleasure. It is given you in life, will be opened at the judgment, and will be remembered forever. It involves the highest responsibility, will reward the greatest labor, and condemns all who trifle with its contents.

173. Fight truth decay! Read your Bible!

174. On September 11, 1777, the Continental Congress approved the outlay of $300,000 to buy Bibles which were then distributed throughout the thirteen colonies.

175. The Bible is God's love letter to His children. If you don't understand it, it's because you're reading somebody else's mail.

(see also: The Gospel)

BLESSINGS

176. There are loyal hearts,
There are spirits brave,
There are souls that are pure and true;
Then give to the world
The best that you have,
And the best will come back to you.

—Madeline Bridges

177. The year's at the spring,
And day's at the morn;
Morning's at seven;
The hillside's dew-pearl'd;

The lark's on the wing;
The snail's on the thorn;
God's in His heaven—
All's right with the world.
　　　　　—Robert Browning

178. There is in man a higher than love of happiness; he can do without happiness, and instead thereof find blessedness!
　　　　　—Thomas Carlyle

179. Reflect upon your present blessings, of which every man has many; not on your past misfortunes, of which all men have some. 　　　—Charles Dickens

180. I am a confirmed believer in blessings in disguise. I prefer them undisguised when I myself happen to be the person blessed; in fact, I can scarcely recognize a blessing in disguise except when it is bestowed upon someone else. —Robert Lynd

(see also: Thanksgiving)

BOOKS

181. Some books are to be tasted, others to be swallowed, and some few to be chewed and digested. 　—Francis Bacon

182. It isn't what people need to know, it's what people *want* that sells books and makes authors popular. —Harold Borchert

183. All that mankind has done, thought, gained or been: it is lying as in magic preservation in the pages of books.
　　　　　—Thomas Carlyle

184. There is no Frigate like a Book
To take us Lands away
Nor any Coursers like a Page
Of prancing Poetry—
This traverse may the poorest take
Without oppress of Toll—
How frugal is the Chariot
That bears the Human soul.
　　　　　—Emily Dickinson

185. If he shall not lose his reward who gives a cup of cold water to his thirsty neighbor, what will not be the reward of those who, by putting good books into the hands of those neighbors, open to them the fountains of eternal life.
　　　　　—Thomas à Kempis

186. I would urge upon every young man . . . to obtain as soon as he can, by the severest economy, a restricted, serviceable, and steadily . . . increasing series of books for use throughout life. 　—John Ruskin

187. No other agency can penetrate so deeply, witness so daringly, abide so persistently, and influence so irresistibly as the printed page. 　　—Samuel Zwemer

188. No man can be called friendless when he has God and the companionship of good books.

(see also: Reading)

BROTHERHOOD

189. When I am with God my fellowmen are not far off and forgotten, but close and strangely dear. 　—Walter Rauschenbusch

190. We all are debtors to our race;
　God holds us bound to one
　　another;
The gifts and blessings of His grace
　Were given thee to give thy
　　brother.
　　　　　—A. B. Simpson

191. Father Taylor of Boston used to say: "There is just enough room in the world for all the people in it, but there is no room for the fences which separate them."
　　　　　—Rita Snowden

192. O brother man, fold to thy heart
　thy brother,

Where pity dwells the peace of
God is there,
To worship rightly is to love each
other,
Each smile a hymn, each kindly
deed a prayer.
—John Greenleaf Whittier

193. I sought my soul—but my soul I
could not see;
I sought my God—but my God
eluded me;
I sought my brother—and I found
all three.

(see also: Love; Charity; Interpersonal Relations)

CALVARY

194. There is something in Calvary that passes our understanding, and the words about the Precious Blood should never be read or sung except on the knees of our spirit. —Amy Carmichael

(see also: Atonement; Good Friday Theme)

CAPITALISM

195. It is just as illogical to suggest abolishing capitalism because it hasn't abolished poverty as it would be to suggest abolishing the churches because the churches haven't abolished sin.
—C. Donald Dallas

196. The natural effort of every individual to better his own condition is so powerful that it is alone and without any assistance, not only capable of carrying on the society to wealth and prosperity, but of surmounting a hundred impertinent obstructions with which the folly of human laws too often encumbers its operation.
—Adam Smith

CAPITAL PUNISHMENT

197. In the decade [of the 1970s] the death penalty has fallen into disuse, our criminals have become the best protected, defended and treated in history; our citizens the most terrorized of any civilized society on earth. —Patrick J. Buchanan

198. Opposition to capital punishment clearly teaches that all who set themselves against society's highest good, and deliberately destroy the person, will not suffer the execution of the judgment they have passed upon themselves.
—Lester De Koster

199. It is the sanctity of life that demands the death penalty for the crime of murder. It is the sense of this sanctity that constrains the demand for the infliction of this penalty. The deeper our regard for life the firmer will be our hold upon the penal sanctions which the violation of that sanctity merits. —John Courtney Murray

CARNALITY

200. Though your old you was actually crucified with Christ . . . it is possible for the dead ego to climb out of the casket and mess up the new you, which is what Paul calls being "carnal or fleshly."
—Rolf L. Veenstra

CENSORIOUSNESS

201. A plumber's commercial says: "Any faucet can turn the water on but only a good faucet will turn it off"—which reminds us of what James has to say about the tongue. —Joel Belz

202. The average critic has more confidence in criticism than in prayer to remedy a situation. —Paul E. Billheimer

19

203. Boys flying kites haul in their
      white-wing'd birds:
    You can't do that way when you're
      flying words.
    "Careful with fire" is good advice,
      we know;
    "Careful with words" is ten times
      doubly so.
    Thoughts unexpressed may
      sometimes fall back dead,
    But God Himself can't kill them
      when they're said.
                        —Will Carleton

204. A cup brimful of sweet water cannot
spill even one drop of bitter water however
suddenly jolted.   —Amy Carmichael

205. If there is any person to whom you
feel dislike, that is the person of whom you
ought never to speak.   —R. Cecil

206. A word is dead when it is said,
      some say.
    I say it just begins to live that day.
                        —Emily Dickinson

207. I don't know what silence does. Is it
a scrub-brush? Is it a detergent? But once
you put it through, what it amounts to is
thinking before you speak—but not thinking with your head, thinking with your
heart! Everything changes. At least I find
it so.   —Catherine Doherty

208. If you are faithful in keeping silence
when it is not necessary to speak, God will
preserve you from evil when it is right for
you to talk.   —Francois Fenelon

209. I realize how dangerous criticism
can be, even when we try to sanctify the
term by calling it constructive criticism. It
is often tainted with personal feelings and
reactions.   —Floyd J. Goins

210. The Lord knows those who are His.
He will determine the saved and the unsaved, and will never ask any man's opinion. So let's not give one. —Virgil Hurley

211. Before you criticize another Christian, tell him how much you love him and
you may have second thoughts about your
first thoughts.   —William J. Johnston

212. We are never more easily offended
than when we behold in others the evil
that is in ourselves.   —Donald Mallough

213. God has not called us to see through
each other, but to see each other through.
                        —Horace Moody

214. Who steals my purse steals
      trash . . .
    But he who filches my good name
    Robs me of that which not enriches
      him,
    And makes me poor indeed.
                    —William Shakespeare

215. I pray to be a guardian
      Over all I say and do,
    Remembering what I sow, I reap,
      That life will soon be through.

    So I will think before I speak
      And put a censor on my tongue;
    And apologize when I have killed
      A song before it's sung.
                —Charles Hastings Smith

216. Freedom to express oneself is a good
thing, but it is a good thing that one can
have too much of.   —John Sparrow

217. It is only at the tree loaded with fruit
that men throw stones.
                    —Charles H. Spurgeon

218. For strength to keep my mouth
      shut, Lord,
    When ugly things I'd say,

For power to chew the words that
cut,
Then swallow them, I pray.

When I am hurt by words so snide
That someone cruelly said,
Please help me not to jeer and
chide,
But smile or laugh instead.
—Barbara Weeks

219. As Christians our role is not to judge and reject each other according to our own convictions. It is rather to cooperate without compromise or conflict. To interact only with people holding our own preferences and convictions is to seldom interact. —Albert M. Wells, Jr.

220. Bigotry is too strong an attachment to, or fondness for, our own party, opinion, church and religion. —John Wesley

221. It's easier to say what someone else should do than it is to be what someone else should be. —Kenneth L. Wilson

222. Judge not, for what to your dim
sight
May seem a stain,
In God's pure light may prove
To be a scar,
Won on some hard-fought field
Where you would only faint or
yield.

223. Most of us would get along very well if we used the advice we give to others.

224. You have to be little to belittle.

225. Fault finding is like window washing. All the dirt seems to be on the other side.

226. It is easy to make a mountain out of any molehill. All you do is add dirt.

(see also: Gossip)

CHANGE

227. When you're through changing, you're through. —Bruce Barton

228. The past is a guidepost, not a hitching post. —L. Thomas Holdcroft

229. The most significant change in a person's life is a change of attitude—right attitudes produce right actions.
—William J. Johnston

230. When the authority of the past is too suddenly and too drastically undermined; wherever the past ceases to be the great and reliable reference book of human problems; wherever, above all, the experience of the father becomes irrelevant to the trials and searchings of the son—there the foundations of man's inner health and stability begin to crumble.

—George Kennan

231. Be not the first by whom the new is
tried,
Nor yet the last to lay the old aside.
—Alexander Pope

232. Barbarians are people without historical memory. Barbarism is the real meaning of radical contemporaneity. Released from all authoritative pasts, we progress towards barbarism, not away from it. —Philip Rieff

233. In a moving world readaptation is the price of longevity. —George Santayana

234. Everybody thinks of changing humanity and nobody thinks of changing himself. —Leo Tolstoy

235. A man who goes out to change the world must be an optimist. But the man who goes out to change the world without some way of changing human nature is an absolute lunatic.

236. Mankind is always changing, but man always remains the same.

CHARACTER

237. The true worth of a man is to be measured by the objects he pursues.

—Marcus Aurelius

238. Life is a grindstone, and whether it grinds a man down or polishes him up depends on the stuff he's made of.

—Josh Billings

239. We talk about our evil world, but actually this is an ideal world for God's purposes—building character.

—J. B. Chapman

240. If adversity develops character, prosperity demands it. —J. D. Eppinga

241. The true test of character is not how much we know how to do, but how we behave when we don't know what to do.

—John Holt

242. I think t'would be lovely to live and
　　do good,
　　To grow up to be the girl that I
　　　should;
　　A heart full of sunshine, a life full
　　　of grace
　　Are beauty far better than beauty of
　　　face.

　　I think t'would be lovely to make
　　　people glad,
　　To cheer up the lonely, discouraged
　　　and sad;
　　What matter if homely or pleasant
　　　to see,
　　If lovely in spirit I'm striving to be.

—Margot Isobel

243. Character is built into the spiritual fabric of personality hour by hour, day by day, year by year in much the same deliberate way that physical health is built into the body. —E. Lamar Kincaid

244. When little men cast long shadows it is a sign the sun is setting.

—Walter Savage Landor

245. I do the very best I know how—the very best I can; and I mean to keep doing so until the end. If the end brings me out all right, what is said against me won't amount to anything. If the end brings me out wrong, ten angels swearing I was right would make no difference.

—Abraham Lincoln

246. Not in the clamor of the crowded
　　　street,
　　Not in the shouts and plaudits of
　　　the throng,
　　But in ourselves, are triumph and
　　　defeat.

—Henry Wadsworth Longfellow

247. The use of money, investment of leisure, and subjects of humor and laughter are a trinity that teach self-knowledge.

—Albert J. Lown

248. Watch your thoughts; they become
　　　words.
　　Watch your words; they become
　　　actions.
　　Watch your actions; they become
　　　habits.
　　Watch your habits; they become
　　　character.
　　Watch your character; it becomes
　　　your destiny.

—Frank Outlaw

249. You are what you are—and not what people think you are. —O. W. Polen

250. A true intellectual is a person who puts a high premium on thinking but an even higher one on thoughtfulness.

—Nathan Pusey

251. The distinguishing mark of the hero is that he does not dwell on the surface of things. —E. Merrill Root

252. One of the rarest things that a man ever does is to do the best he can.

—Henry Wheeler Shaw

253. Man is very much like a barrel of apples. The apples that are seen on the top are his reputation, but the apples that are down below represent his character.

—Fulton Sheen

254. The shortest and surest way to live with honor in the world is to be in reality what we appear to be. —Socrates

255. There is something finer than to do right against inclination; and that is to have an inclination to do right. There is something nobler than reluctant obedience; that is joyful obedience. The rank of virtue is not measured by its disagreeableness, but by its sweetness to the heart that loves it. The real test of character is joy. For what you rejoice in, that you love. What you love, that you are like.

—Henry Van Dyke

256. I hope I shall always possess firmness and virtue enough to maintain what I consider the most enviable of all titles, the character of an honest man.

—George Washington

257. Associate yourself with men of good quality if you esteem your own reputation, for 'tis better to be alone than in bad company. —George Washington

258. It is a great asset to have in one's head a will of steel and in one's breast a child-like heart—both of which form a great combination: sympathy to feel and the determination to act.

—Albert M. Wells, Jr.

259. The way we respond to criticism pretty much depends on the way we respond to praise. If praise humbles us, then criticism will build us up. But if praise inflates us, then criticism will crush us; and both responses lead to defeat.

—Warren W. Wiersbe

260. Nearly all men can stand adversity, but if you want to test a man's character, give him power.

261. True worth is doing, not seeming;
In doing each day that goes by
Some little good and not dreaming
Of great things to do by and by.

For whatever men say in their
blindness,
Whatever the fancies of youth,
There is nothing so kingly as
kindness,
There is nothing so royal as truth.

262. It is hard: to forget, to apologize, to save money, to be unselfish, to avoid mistakes, to keep out of a rut, to begin all over again, to make the best of all things, to keep your temper at all times, to think first and act afterwards, to maintain a high standard, to keep on keeping on, to shoulder the blame, to be charitable, to admit error, to take advice, to forgive. BUT IT PAYS!

263. A horse can't pull while kicking,
This fact I merely mention;
And he can't kick while pulling,
Which is my chief contention.

Let's imitate the good old horse
And lead a life that's fitting;

Just pull an honest load, and then
There'll be no time for kicking.

(see also: Honesty; Integrity; Interpersonal Relations; Self-Examination)

CHARITY

264. The fragrance of what you give away stays with you. **—Earl Allen**

265. Find out how much God has given you and from it take what you need; the remainder which you do not require is needed by others. **—Augustine**

266. The finest gifts are given, not after waiting until need has to ask, but by the man whose eye sees and whose heart feels and whose hand is stretched out even before any request is made. It was while we were yet enemies that Christ died for us. God hears our prayers even before we speak them. And we should be to our fellow men even as God has been to us.

—William Barclay

267. It takes wisdom and discernment to minister to people in need. We must look beyond the apparent and seek to meet the needs of the whole person.

—Richard C. Chewning

268. To feel sorry for the needy is not the mark of a Christian—to help them is.

—Frank A. Clark

269. There is no real religious experience that does not express itself in charity.

—C. H. Dodd

270. Where our bread is concerned, it is a material matter. Where our neighbor's bread is concerned, it is a spiritual matter.

—J. D. Douglas

271. Not what we give, but what we share,

For the gift without the giver is bare;
Who gives himself with his alms feeds three,
Himself, his hungering neighbor and Me.

—James Russell Lowell

272. There is a destiny that makes us brothers;
None goes his way alone.
All that we send into the lives of others
Comes back into our own.

—Edwin Markham

273. Charity may be ignorant of many things but it never forgets one thing. It may flounder in ineffective strategies, but it has a bulldog grip on one reality. . . . Love is more than life or death. **—John Shea**

274. For we must share, if we would keep
That blessing from above;
Ceasing to give, we cease to have—
Such is the law of love.

—Richard C. Trench

275. *Sharing* what you have is more important than what you have.

—Albert M. Wells, Jr.

276. Go share with thy sister and brother thy bread.
For giving is loving, the angel said.
But must I keep giving again and again?
My peevish and piteous question ran.
Oh no, said the angel, piercing me through,
Just give till the Master stops giving to you.

277. Love that is hoarded molds at last,
Until we know someday

That the only things we ever have
Are those we give away.

The kindness that is never used,
But hidden all alone,
Will slowly harden till it is
As hard as any stone.

It is the things we always hold
That we will lose someday.
The only things we ever keep
Are those we give away.

278. The trouble is that too often charity not only begins but ends at home.

(see also: Giving; Stewardship)

CHASTITY

279. Chastity is to have the body in the soul's keeping.   —**Robertson Davies**

280. Saying "yes" to God means saying "no" to things which offend His holiness.
—**A. Morgan Derham**

281. Chastity is the most unpopular of Christian virtues.   —**C. S. Lewis**

282. Chastity is a requisite of Christian singleness. Furthermore, chastity is possible. There will always be somebody to suggest that such thinking is legalistic, unreasonable, and unlikely to succeed. My reply can only be: "When it's bigger than I am, so is God."   —**Rosalie De Rosset**

(see also: Purity; Sex)

CHEER

283. Let me but live from year to year
      With forward face and
          unreluctant soul;
      Not hurrying to, nor turiing
          from, the goal;
      Not mourning for the things that
          disappear
In the dim past, nor holding back
      in fear
From what the future veils; but
      with a whole
And happy heart, that pays its
      toll
To Youth and Age, and travels on
      with cheer.
                    —**Henry Van Dyke**

(see also: Joy)

CHOICES

284. Choices are the hinges of destiny.
                    —**Edwin Markham**

285. Many of life's circumstances are created by three basic choices: the disciplines you choose to keep, the people you choose to be with, and the laws you choose to obey.   —**Charles Millhuff**

286. To every man there openeth
      A way, and ways and a way.
      And the high soul climbs the high
          way
      And the low soul climbs the low,
      And in between, on the misty flats,
      The rest drift to and fro.
      But to every man there openeth
      A high way and a low;
      And every man decideth
      Which way his soul shall go.
                    —**John Oxenham**

287. The roads we take are more important than the goals we announce. Decisions determine destiny.

                    —**Frederick Speakman**

288. The pain of a divided heart is the consequence of knowing what you should do while doing what you shouldn't. The pain of a crucified heart is the result of doing what you should while rejecting what

would seem to be gratifying. Both choices are painful but only one is therapeutic.
—Albert M. Wells, Jr.

(see also: Decisions; Priorities)

CHRIST

(see: Jesus Christ)

CHRISTIAN ACTION

289. Do what you can do and pray for what you cannot yet do. —Augustine

290. Be strong!
We are not here to play—to dream, to drift.
We have hard work to do and loads to lift.
Shun not the struggle—face it; 'tis God's gift.

Be strong!
Say not the days are evil. Who's to blame?
And fold the hands and acquiesce. O shame!
Stand up, speak out, and bravely in God's name.

Be strong!
It matters not how deep entrenched the wrong.
How hard the battle goes, the day how long:
Faint not—fight on! Tomorrow comes the song.
Be strong!
—Maltbie D. Babcock

291. Things alter for the worse spontaneously, if they be not altered for the better designedly. —Francis Bacon

292. In Christianity intellectual effort and emotional experience are not neglected—far from it—but they must combine to issue in moral action.
—William Barclay

293. "Not called!" did you say? "Not heard the call," I think you should say. Put your ear down to the Bible, and hear Him bid you go and pull sinners out of the fire of sin. Put your ear down to the burdened, agonized heart of humanity, and listen to its pitiful wail for help. Go stand by the gates of hell, and hear the damned entreat you to go to their father's house and bid their brothers and sisters, and servants and masters not to come there. And then look Christ in the face, whose mercy you have professed to obey, and tell Him whether you will join heart and soul and body and circumstances in the march to publish His mercy to the world. —William Booth

294. You never become truly spiritual by sitting down and wishing to become so. You must undertake something so great that you cannot accomplish it unaided.
—Phillips Brooks

295. Grant us the will to fashion as we feel,
Grant us the strength to labour as we know,
Grant us the purpose, ribbed and edged with steel,
To strike the blow.

Knowledge we ask not, knowledge Thou has lent,
But, Lord, the will—there lies our deepest need,
Grant us the power to build, above the high intent,
The deed, the deed!
—John Drinkwater

296. To reach the port of heaven, we must sail, sometimes with the wind, and

26

sometimes against it, but we must sail, not drift or lie at anchor.
—Oliver Wendell Holmes

297. If you read history you will find that the Christians who did the most for the present world were just those who thought the most of the next. —C. S. Lewis

298. By the time the average Christian gets his temperature up to normal, everybody thinks he's got a fever.
—Watchman Nee

299. Our business is not to do something for the church, but to do something with it. —Joseph Fort Newton

300. There is a special relationship between thought, word, and action. If we fill our thoughts with acknowledgement of God, with meditation upon His works, if we fill our mouths with words of recounting His benefits and joyfully sing His praises, then the inner sources of human action become attuned with God and they will bring about actions consistent with His nature and will. —Ward Patterson

301. As Christians we are justified in being angry with evil. But with anger goes the responsibility of compassionately loving those whom evil is destroying and giving of ourselves to fight the evil.
—Chip Ricks

302. He who labors as he prays lifts his heart to God with his hands.
—Bernard of Clairvaux

303. Stand against that which is wrong, show why it is wrong, overcome it and plant truth in its place. —A. W. Tozer

304. If I had three hundred men who feared nothing but God, hated nothing but sin, and were determined to know nothing.

among men but Jesus Christ and Him crucified, I would set the world on fire.
—John Wesley

305. Find out what God would have you do,
    And do that little well;
For what is great and what is small,
    'Tis only He can tell.

(see also: Involvement; Service; Conviction)

CHRISTIAN COMMITMENT
(see: Commitment)

CHRISTIAN CONVERSION
(see: Conversion)

CHRISTIAN EDUCATION
306. Which group impressed Jesus—the well educated or the spiritually vigorous? When Jesus started His movement, did He go down to the University of Jerusalem and look up the top twelve Ph.D's and say, "I need some excellent preachers who know how to be relevant?" No, He picked up some bad-smelling fishermen and a midget named Zacchaeus—in short, a spiritual zoo. Jesus was not concerned about the outer credentials. If He was He would have gone to the Pharisees. The Pharisees had the credentials. Instead He took those who society said were nothing, but in whom He saw a potential for surrender to the Spirit. —Anthony Campolo

307. There is an education of the mind
    Which all require and parents only
        start.
    But there is training of a nobler
        kind
    And that's the education of the
        heart.

Lessons that are most difficult to
give
Are Faith and Courage and the way
to live.
—Edgar Guest

308. Educating people to die meaningful deaths is one way to describe the teaching mission of the church. —John A. Harms

309. To keep the faith we must know the faith. —George Sweeting

310. Now we have learned that it is the secular school student who is overprotected. He is protected from the basic facts of right and wrong. He then confronts the slings and arrows of the real world—naked.

(see also: Education)

CHRISTIAN FREEDOM

311. It is absurd to espouse a "freedom of choice" that allows people to do evil rather than good, with no thought given to the consequences. —Harold O. J. Brown

312. There is a slavery which is the essence of freedom. It involves accepting a yoke that is uniquely ours and wearing it faithfully in the toils and triumphs of His service. We are called to put on a beautiful bondage—that of the humble Jesus, whose servants have found the secret to real freedom. —Barry L. Callen

313. Freedom is the ability to self-actualize within the framework of one's relationship with God. —Rosemary Dennis

314. Freedom is the controlled opportunity to move in the direction of what is good. The laws (of nature, society, or God) which enable us to do that are not restrictions; they are aids to freedom.
—Linda Doll

315. Freedom is the name of virtue; slavery, of vice. —Epictetus

316. There are two freedoms: the false where one is free to do what he likes and the true where he is free to do what he ought. —Charles Kingsley

317. We must be anchored in self-discipline if we are to venture successfully in freedom. —Harold Kohn

318. Real freedom means to welcome the responsibility it brings, to welcome the God-control it requires, to welcome the discipline that results, to welcome the maturity it creates. —Eugenia Price

319. To obey God is perfect liberty.
—Seneca

320. Freedom always relates to oughtness. —Fulton Sheen

321. There are several kinds of freedom. There is a freedom that is apparent and one that is real; a superficial freedom, and one that is substantial; a freedom that is temporary and deceptive, and one that is abiding and permanent; one that ministers to the lower appetites and passions, and another that encourages growth in the sweeter things of life. . . . But there is but one kind of freedom that is worth the name, and that is the one embodied in the words spoken centuries ago by the Great Master: "And you shall know the truth, and the truth shall make you free."
—Booker T. Washington

(see also: Freedom)

CHRISTIAN HOME

322. Every Christian family ought to be, as it were, a little church, consecrated to Christ, and wholly influenced and governed by His rules. And family education

28

and order are some of the chief means of grace. If these fail, all other means are likely to prove ineffectual.

—Jonathan Edwards

323. Christian family living is . . . the gospel most intimately made real.

—Nels Ferre

324. Home ain't a place that gold can buy
Or get up in a moment;
Afore it's home there's got to be
A heap o' living in it.

It must be filled with faith and love
From cellar up to dome;
It takes a heap o' livin' in a house
To make it home.

—Edgar Guest

325. What is a home?
It is the laughter of a child,
The song of a mother,
The strength of a father.
Home is the first school,
And the first church
Where they learn about a loving God.

—Ernestine Schumann-Heink

326. In a Christian family, God's name is taken frequently in reverence at the family altar. God's Book is a familiar text to all. God's day is respected, both at church and at home. Such a home is the hope of the world, the pattern of the Church itself and a foretaste of heaven. —G. Aiken Taylor

327. A church-related home is no substitute for a Christian home any more than a church-related person is a substitute for a Christian. —Albert M. Wells, Jr.

328. If your Christianity doesn't work at home, then it doesn't work at all. So don't export it.

(see also: The Family; Parenthood)

CHRISTIAN INFLUENCE
(see: Influence)

CHRISTIANITY

329. Christianity will last as long as the world. Neither savage nor civilized man, without a revelation, could ever have discovered or invented it. —John Adams

330. To be sound in faith and holy in life—this is the kernel of Christianity.

—Augustine

331. Christianity is not a voice in the wilderness, but a life in the world. It is not an idea in the air, but feet on the ground, going God's way. It is not an exotic to be kept under glass, but a hardy plant to bear twelve months of fruits in all kinds of weather. Fidelity to duty is its root and branch. Nothing we can say to the Lord, no calling Him by great or dear names, can take the place of the plain doing of His will. —Maltbie D. Babcock

332. The truth of Christianity is not a secret which is hidden; it is a secret which is revealed. —William Barclay

333. The gospel of God is more than old-fashioned. It is eternal. —George Gritter

334. By its very nature Christianity is enthusiastic; it means living in faith, hope, love and joy. —William H. Hudnut

335. We are losing our Christianity because Christianity is a creed for heroes while we are mainly harmless, good-natured people who want everybody to have a good time. —W. R. Inge

336. Christianity has its creeds, but it is not a creed, has its rites . . . but is not a rite . . . has its institutions . . . but is not an in-

stitution. . . . Chrisfianity is Christ, or rather our response to Him.

—E. Stanley Jones

337. The Christian message begins at the point which no state constitution, no economic, social, or cultural system can really reach; the point at which humanity experiences a change of heart. This is what politicians, economists, and sociologists desire but do not achieve, what Karl Marx demanded in vain: "a new human being."

—Hans Kung

338. To the unbeliever, of course, all this [the Gospel] is foolishness. But around this very foolishness has rallied all the betterment of human society. —Lynn Landrum

339. I believe in Christianity as I believe in the sun—not only because I see it, but because by it I see everything else.

—C. S. Lewis

340. When the microscopic search of skepticism, which has hunted the heavens and sounded the seas to disprove the existence of a Creator, has turned its attention to human society, and has found a place on this planet ten miles square where a decent man can live in decency, comfort, and security, supporting and educating his children unspoiled and unpolluted; a place where age is reverenced, infancy protected, manhood respected, womanhood honored, and human life held in due regard—when skeptics can find such a place ten miles square where the gospel of Christ has not gone and cleared the way and laid the foundations, and made decency and security possible, it will then be in order for skeptical literati to move thither, and there ventilate their views.

—James Russell Lowell

341. A Christian is someone whose concern in life is to do the business of Christ Himself. —James Earl Massey

342. Being a Christian means allowing the interpretation of life found in Christ Jesus to shape one's existence. This becomes a unifying center for one's life. It is the context in which all else is seen. It is, of all life's considerations, the most important and it relativizes all else.

—Vincent McNamara

343. The world is full of fantasy; there must be some reality somewhere, and the only reality that I've found is the reality of the Christian faith. —Malcolm Muggeridge

344. Crack-up conditions are more conducive to the understanding and practice of the Christian religion than ostensible stability and prosperity.

—Malcolm Muggeridge

345. Show the world the fruits of Christianity and it will applaud. Show it Christianity and the world will oppose it vigorously. —Watchman Nee

346. Christianity stands on a book, a Person, and a day. Destroy any one of those and you will destroy the faith.

—Philip Schaff

347. What impresses us about the real Christians is that they seemingly have more patience with trying people, more hope about wicked people, more time for tedious people and—more distinctively— more forgiveness toward their opponents.

—William P. Soetenga

348. Philosopher David Hume in 1776 stated, "I see the twilight of Christianity." I'm afraid that David Hume couldn't tell the difference between a sunrise and a sunset. —George Sweeting

349. The only greater reality than God's judgment of sinners is God's forgiveness of sin. Not until the former is preached and perceived will the latter be pursued and possessed.   —**Albert M. Wells, Jr.**

350. We've done such a lavish job of buttering up the faith that it's sometimes difficult to distinguish it from a Las Vegas spectacular. The Christian faith is indeed attractive, as health is attractive to a desperately ill patient. But the healing process is not usually fun and games.

—**Kenneth L. Wilson**

351. Many are saying that Christianity hasn't kept pace with the times. But the fact is the times haven't kept pace with Christianity. Christianity is concerned with truth and truth is as irreversible and unchanging as are the basic needs of mankind to which it is universally relevant.

(see also: Christian Life; Christian Freedom; Discipleship; The Gospel)

CHRISTIAN LIFE

352. Love God and do as you please.

—**Augustine**

353. Christian agility, when fully developed, enables a person to walk in two worlds—his heart in heaven and his feet in the dust of this earth. We are agents of heaven commissioned to cultivate the earth and subdue it.   —**Marvin Baarman**

354. A saint is not a man who never falls; he is a man who gets up and goes on every time he falls.   —**William Barclay**

355. The Christian life could be described as getting to know God better every day. A friendship which does not grow closer with the years tends to vanish with the years. And it is so with us and God.   —**William Barclay**

356. In the Christian life there must be the courage which will never retreat and the love which will never fail.

—**William Barclay**

357. To know Christ is to become so one with Him that we share His every experience. It means that we share the way He walked; that we share the Cross He bore; that we share the death He died; and that finally we share the life He lives for evermore.   —**William Barclay**

358. To be a Christian is no light thing. . . . It is the hardest thing anyone can do. Yet anyone can do it . . . and in the end it is the only thing that really matters.

—**James Montgomery Boice**

359. I have found something to believe in—Jesus Christ. I have found something to belong to—the church. I have found something to witness for—God's approaching kingdom.

—**Kenneth E. Bomberger**

360. Let me not sink to be a clod;
Make me Thy fuel, Flame of God.

—**Amy Carmichael**

361. Don't waste time asking God to keep you from doing things. Don't do them.   —**Oswald Chambers**

362. To be far from God is better than to be near, if we are not next to God.

—**G. K. Chesterton**

363. When God shows man the evil of sin, He so convinces the soul that no creature-comforts have any sweetness in them; and when He shows man His righteousness and peace in Christ, He so comforts the heart that no outward afflictions have any bitterness in them. —**John Flavel**

364. The only way to live your last day as you would want to, is to live like that all the time.   —Vaughan Garwood

365. We grow spiritually through constant mortification of the natural man and constant renewal of the spiritual man.
                                —Adoniram J. Gordon

366. To walk with God, we must run to God.   —George Gritter

367. Give us a pure heart that we may
          see Thee;
       A humble heart that we may hear
          Thee;
       A heart of love that we may serve
          Thee;
       A heart of faith that we may live
          Thee.
                            —Dag Hammarskjold

368. Lord of us all, when earth you trod,
       The life you led was perfect, free,
       Defiant of all tyranny.
       Now give us grace that we may face
       Our foes with like temerity,
       And glory give to Thee, O God.
                                  —D. Hankey

369. Turn on the smile?
       Turn off the cry?
          Never any place
          For a tear or a sigh?
       I'm not made of granite,
       And I'm not made of steel;
          I'm flesh and blood—
          I hurt and I feel.
       So I turn off the smile
       And I turn on the cry.
          I even admit
          To asking a "why?"
       There's no clear answer—
       Just a sense of release.
          I've spent my tears,
          But I've gained a new peace.

       I can turn on the smile
       As I turn off the cry,
          For I understand better
          That to live I must die.
                              —Beulah Heavilin

370. It is a faith worth having. [Christ] is a Saviour worth loving, and it will be a life worth living when you trust Him here and now.   —R. Norman Herbert

371. All the water in the world, however
          hard it tried,
       Could never, never sink a ship
          unless it got inside.
       All the evil in the world, the
          wickedness and sin,
       Can never sink your soul's fair craft
          unless you let it in.
                                —A. C. Hoffman

372. Grace is what happens to me.
       Faith is letting it happen to me.
       Work is letting it happen through
          me.
                               —Robert Hutnut

373. We learn, on the one hand, that we cannot trust ourselves even in our best moments, and, on the other, that we need not despair even in our worst, for our failures are forgiven. The only fatal thing is to sit down content with anything less than perfection.   —C. S. Lewis

374. Christian religion is, in the long run, a thing of unspeakable comfort. But it does not begin in comfort; it begins in dismay, and it is no use at all trying to go on to that comfort without first going through that dismay.   —C. S. Lewis

375. The bitterest cup with Christ is better than the sweetest cup without Him.
                             —Ian MacPherson

376. Success is neither fame, wealth nor power; rather it is seeking, knowing, loving and obeying God. If you seek, you will know; if you know, you will love; if you love, you will obey. —**Charles Malik**

377. Christian faith has to steer a course between the legalism that trusts in its own righteousness, and the lawlessness that, claiming to trust in the righteousness of Christ, makes the moral quality of one's life an indifferent matter.
—**W. E. McCumber**

378. Give all to God, take all from God, and use all for God. —**F. B. Meyer**

379. To love man you must know him; to know God you must love Him.
—**Blaise Pascal**

380. Let philosophers wrestle with the idea of God, and theologians with the attributes of God, and scientists with the works of God; but as for me, being interested in the inner and sustaining vitality of true religion, nothing can satisfy me short of the realized presence of God.
—**Paul Rees**

381. The gifts of the Spirit are certainly important but none of them will endure. The Christian will take into eternity the fruit of the Spirit, not the gifts. Love, joy, peace, patience, gentleness, goodness, faith, meekness, self-control—these will endure. —**Pat Robertson**

382. Every Christian, sooner or later, must choose one of two pains: the pain of a crucified heart, or the pain of a divided mind. —**Samuel M. Shoemaker**

383. Our love for God is tested by whether we seek Him or His gifts.
—**Ralph Sockman**

384. They are the true disciples of Christ, not who know most, but who love most.
—**Frederick Spanheim**

385. Every Christian should be both conservative and radical; conservative in preserving the faith and radical in applying it.
—**John R. W. Stott**

386. When Jesus cried, "It is finished," He did not take away the conflict, the contest, the fight. No! He took away only your defeat. —**Ira Taylor**

387. Service without devotion is rootless; devotion without service is fruitless.
—**Elton Trueblood**

388. "Growing in grace" . . . is not becoming a better person [though that will naturally follow], but simply making more room for Christ and less for self every day of our eternal life. —**Rolf L. Veenstra**

389. The Hound of Heaven calls me to enter into a relationship with Him through which I will find that service is freedom, weakness is strength, humility is power, obedience is liberty and losing life is finding new life. Such apparent contradictions turn the world's wisdom upside down; but whenever, timidly and tentatively, I respond to this call, I find a rightness, a truth, a congruity and a peace which passes understanding.
—**Mary Frances Wagley**

390. There is a death to be died before we die, so we can live the resurrection life before the resurrection. —**Reuben Welch**

391. Spiritual maturity is the point at which we cease to rationalize our faults and begin to symbolize our faith.
—**Albert M. Wells, Jr.**

392. The reproduction of Jesus Christ on the canvas of everyday life is the finest of the fine arts. —R. T. Williams

393. There is a vast difference between an attraction and an attachment. Many are attracted to Christ, but few are attached to Him.

394. Five blessings that characterize the Christian life are
1. A conscience you can live with
2. A creed you can live by
3. A cause you can live for
4. A company you can live with
5. A consummation you can live toward.

395. Christians are a people with one priority: lifting up Christ.

396. It does precious little good to memorize the prescription if one doesn't take the medicine. A mere knowledge of what the Scriptures say may add to our guilt instead of relieving it. There must be application.

(see also: Christian Action; Christian Witness; Discipleship; Discipline; Faith; Service; Stewardship)

CHRISTIAN SERVICE

(see: Service)

CHRISTIAN WITNESS

397. I am my neighbor's Bible,
He reads me when we meet.
Today he reads me in my home—
Tomorrow on the street.

He may a relative or friend
Or slight acquaintance be.
He may not even know my name,
Yet he is reading me.

To learn if I am living
And walking as I pray.
He is watching closely
Just what I do and say.

Dear Christian friends and
brothers,
If we could only know
How faithfully the world records
Just what we say and do,

Oh, we would write our records
plain,
And come, in time, to see
Our worldly neighbors won to
Christ
While reading you and me.
—Pearl Anderson

398. It is when men see that we are prepared to suffer something for the faith which we say we hold, that they will begin to believe that we really do hold it. If a thing costs us nothing men will value it at nothing. —William Barclay

399. The final proof that a man himself knows Christ is that he can bring others to Christ. —William Barclay

400. Once we become children of God, we must learn to act like it. —Robert W. Battles

401. I guess we just can't get away from the fact that there is always a "package" around our Christianity. Let's just make sure the package doesn't create false impressions or promise more than it should. But most important, we should try to make the wrapper so transparent that the world can see the quality of our faith and feel they can't live without it. —Charles R. Boatman

402. Here is the key to effective Christian witnessing: unquestioning obedience to the commands of the Lord and action based upon that obedience.

—Michael Bolus

403. What the world expects of Christians is that Christians should speak out loud and clear . . . in such a way that never a doubt, never the slightest doubt, could rise in the heart of the simplest man. They should get away from abstraction and confront the blood-stained face history has taken on today. The grouping that we need is a grouping of men resolved to speak out clearly and pay up personally.

—Albert Camus

404. To keep this good news to ourselves would be in effect to repudiate its validity.

—Robert E. Coleman

405. A wick dare not take credit for a flame, any more than a cello can accept praise for a sonata. But it is a joy to realize that a light—not of our making—can shine through us, and that a melody can arise from us, imperfect instruments though we are.

—Martin B. Copenhaver

406. At any cost, Lord, draw me ever nearer,
Emptied of self 'til others truly see
Thy love reflected from me like a mirror,
Attracting hungry souls, my Lord, to Thee!

—Frances B. Erickson

407. Dawn pilgrims are dawn pointers. They seek others looking for the light, and say, "Here comes the sun!"

—Gabriel Fackre

408. You write a sermon, a chapter each day,
By the deeds that you do and the words that you say;

Men read what you write, if it's false or it's true.
Say, what is the gospel according to you?

—Paul Gilbert

409. Witnessing is not a spare-time occupation or a once-a-week activity. It must be a quality of life. You don't go witnessing, you are a witness. —Dan Greene

410. I'd rather see a sermon than hear one any day;
I'd rather one should walk with me than merely tell the way.

—Edgar Guest

411. Among other strange things said of me, I hear it is said by the deists that I am one of their number; and indeed, that some good people think I am no Christian. This thought gives me much more pain than the appellation of Tory; because I think religion of infinitely higher importance than politics; and I find much cause to reproach myself that I have lived so long, and have given no decided and public proofs of my being a Christian. But, indeed, my dear child, this is a character which I prize far above all this world has or can boast. —Patrick Henry

412. Our religion, no matter how orthodox, will be salt to no one unless when it rains, it pours. —Keith E. Huttenlocker

413. The irony is that we could reach more people if we were blunt about what we assume nobody wants to hear. People dissatisfied with themselves and alarmed at the state of the world might be powerfully attracted to a faith that begins with the knowledge of sin. When they dismiss Christianity as too sunny for their sensibilities, the fault is theirs for not finding out the truth—and ours for obscuring it.

—Eric Jorgenson

414. If you believe that blind men are falling into the furnace, is there any conceivable way you can hold your peace?
—D. James Kennedy

415. There is only one answer to man's deepest needs, only one source of life. Therefore, if I know Christ and have studied the Gospels, that makes me either a missionary or a cop-out. —Virginia Larsen

416. We must throw the printer's inkpot at the devil. —Martin Luther

417. A genuine Christian ought to be as distinguishable amongst his fellows as is a civilized man among savages.
—Hugh McIntosh

418. Kindness has converted more sinners than zeal, eloquence, or learning.
—Henrietta Mears

419. It is not open to any layman to say, "I cannot be an evangelist." If he is a Christian, he must be a witness. If he is not willing to be a witness, it is time he gave up calling himself a Christian.
—Stephen Neill

420. Nothing can happen through you which is not happening to you.
—Lloyd J. Ogilvie

421. You must talk to God about people before you talk to people about God.
—C. E. Prosser

422. A small boy was very perceptive when he looked up at the stained glass windows in church and said: "A saint is a person that light shines through."
—Richard Ruble

423. We were not converted to be introverted. —Richard H. Seume

424. We must know people—like them, enjoy them, make friends with them, take

trouble for them—before it may ever be right to "speak" to them about spiritual matters. —Samuel M. Shoemaker

425. I would not give much for your religion unless it can be seen. Lamps do not talk, but they do shine.
—Charles H. Spurgeon

426. It is not enough to give a cup of cold water; it is necessary also to tell why.
—Elton Trueblood

427. You have one business on earth—to save souls. —John Wesley

428. You are a Christian today because somebody cared. Now it's your turn.
—Warren W. Wiersbe

429. You lived next door to me for years;
We shared our dreams, our joys, our tears.
A friend to me you were indeed,
A friend who helped me in my need.

My faith in you was strong and sure;
We had such trust as should endure.
No spats between us e'er arose;
Our friends were like—and so, our foes.

What sadness then, my friend, to find
That, after all, you weren't so kind.
The day my life on earth did end,
I found you weren't a faithful friend.

For all those years we spent on earth
You never talked of second birth.
You never spoke of my lost soul,
And of the Christ who'd make me whole.

I plead today from Hell's cruel fire
And tell you now my last desire.
You cannot do a thing for me;
No words today my bonds to free.

But do not err, my friend, again—
Do all you can for souls of men.
Plead with them now quite
    earnestly,
Lest they be cast in Hell with me.

430. In 1858 a man named Kimball, a Sunday school teacher, led a Boston shoe clerk to give his life to Jesus Christ. The clerk, Dwight L. Moody, became an evangelist and in New England in 1879 awakened an evangelistic zeal in the heart of F. B. Meyer, the pastor of a small church. Mr. Meyer, preaching on an American college campus, brought to Christ a student, J. Wilbur Chapman. Mr. Chapman, engaged in YMCA work, employed a former baseball player, Billy Sunday, to help with evangelistic meetings. Mr. Sunday held a series of services in Charlotte, North Carolina. A group of local men were so enthusiastic as a result of the series that they planned another campaign, bringing Mordecai F. Hamm to town as the preacher. During the meetings, a young man named Billy Graham heard the Gospel and yielded his life to Christ. Billy Graham . . . and the story goes on! Question: Have you started anything lately?

431. The Christ whom we will not share, we cannot keep.

432. The other day my friend's house was on fire. And I don't think he knew it, even though he was inside it. He must have been asleep. I thought about telling my friend his house was on fire, but then I wondered what he would think. He might get embarrassed. Or what if I should get all sooty? And what would my friends who don't believe in fires think? Besides, isn't it the fireman's job? (Any similarity between the above and witnessing for Christ is absolutely intentional!)

433. The "living Bible" people really read, is you.

(see also: Influence)

CHRISTMAS

434. That there was no room in the inn was symbolic of what was to happen to Jesus. The only place there was room for Him was on the Cross.   —**William Barclay**

435. The cuddly, cooing infant in the manger may evoke warm feelings and sentimental thoughts at Christmas time. But the Man of Galilee has a message and a mission which we dare not lose in an ocean of wrapping paper.
—**Erwin A. Britton**

436. Then let every heart keep
        Christmas within:
    Christ's pity for sorrow,
    Christ's hatred for sin,
    Christ's care for the weakest,
    Christ's courage for right.
    Everywhere, everywhere,
    Christmas tonight!
—**Phillips Brooks**

437. Santa Claus is a fat fake, in
        duplicate;
    A petty moralist always asking,
    "Have you been a good boy?" He's
        an ally
    Of greed, teaching kids their
        "gimme, gimme."
    My friend played Santa Claus in
        one store
    For needed cash. Parents tried to
        use him:

"Tell her she won't get anything if she
Doesn't behave." Anything. Any *thing*.
Yet Santa is fun. Face aglow, eyes atwinkle,
His tummy shakes with laughter: "Ho ho!"
He borrows all his joy from Christmas.
Christmas borrows joy from the One who has no
Duplicate. His gift is "once for all." Now
He walks through Christmas stores forgotten,
Lonely: we'd rather feature Santa Claus.

—**George A. Buttrick**

438. Christmas is the gift from heaven
Of God's Son given for free;
If Christmas isn't found in your heart,
You won't find it under the tree.

—**Charlotte Carpenter**

439. Rings and jewels are not gifts, but apologies for gifts. The only gift is a portion of thyself. —**Ralph Waldo Emerson**

440. Whatever difficulties the fact of the incarnation may present to skeptical minds, there can be no doubt that it was and is what the world needs. —**Isaac Errett**

441. Like the Wise Men let us look for a star—not the star of astrology, or the rebirth of paganism. Not the Red Star of Communism, or the idolatry of materialism. Not the Super Star of a secularized Christianity. But the Star of Bethlehem that leads to Jesus. —**George C. Fry**

442. Of course God might have chosen other methods. He might have sent forth His son trailing clouds of glory from the opened heavens with a legion of angels for His bodyguard. Or He might have revealed His presence by one of those strange and startling theophanies which are occasionally recorded in the Old Testament. He might have heralded His coming with earthquake, tempest, or the voice of thunder. But no! A baby is born of a humble girl in the outhouse of a crowded inn; and Love has set forth on His mighty mission.

—**Edward Gibbon**

443. At Christmas, man is almost what God sent him here to be. —**Edgar Guest**

444. To travel the road to Bethlehem is to keep a rendezvous with wonder, to answer the call of wisdom, and to bow the knee in worship. —**John A. Knight**

445. Our trouble is we want the peace without the Prince. —**Addison H. Leitch**

446. The Son of God became man to enable men to become the sons of God.

—**C. S. Lewis**

447. At Bethlehem God became what He was not before, but did not cease being what He always was. —**Paul Lowenberg**

448. Were earth a thousand times as fair,
Beset with gold and jewels rare,
She yet were far too poor to be
A narrow cradle, Lord for Thee.

—**Martin Luther**

449. There are some of us . . . who think to ourselves, "If I had only been there! How quick I would have been to help the Baby. I would have washed His linen. How happy I would have been to go with the shepherds to see the Lord lying in the manger!" Yes, we would. We say that because we know how great Christ is, but if we had been there at the time, we would

have done no better than the people of Bethlehem. . . . Why don't we do it now? We have Christ in our neighbor.
—Martin Luther

450. "Let the little children come unto me," says Jesus. And we reply, "Yes Master, in due time. But first we want them to put their faith in Santa Claus. After all, they're only children once."
—John Mahoney

451. If we were determined to conceal and subvert the Gospel, it would be hard to invent a better device than the Santa myth.
—John Mahoney

452. When He came, the angels sang,
"Glory be to God on high!"
Lord, unloose my stammering
tongue—
Who should louder sing than I?

Did the Lord a man become
That He might the Law fulfill,
Bleed and suffer in my room,
And canst thou, my tongue, be
still?

O my Saviour, Shield, and Sun,
Shepherd, Brother, Husband,
Friend,
Every precious name in one,
I will love Thee without end.
—John Newton

453. It is a pity that the "optimistic humanism" which people so quickly display one day is so quickly forgotten the rest of the year. Christmas cards too often are full of more genuine spirit than their senders.
—Ken Ripley

454. Christmas turns all wise souls from the surface which is time to the center which is eternity.
—E. Merrill Root

455. He who has not Christmas in his heart will never find it under a tree.
—Roy L. Smith

456. In many ways our Christian celebration of Christmas looks very much like the non-Christian's Christmas. We watch the same bowl games on Christmas afternoon and invest in the same temporal gifts—socks, Barbie dolls, and frilly nighties.
—John Stapert

457. Christmas is when God came down the stairs of heaven with a baby in His arms.
—R. Eugene Sterner

458. A Christian should observe Christmas in wonder, worship and witness.
—John Vander Ploeg

459. When we remember the high meaning that has come into human life, and the clear light that has flooded softly down from the manger-cradle in Bethlehem of Judea, we do not wonder that mankind has learned to reckon history from the birthday of Jesus, and to date all events by the years before and after the Nativity of Christ.
—Henry Van Dyke

460. Once the dollars are removed from Christmas gifts, gift giving becomes more loving, more interesting, and more fun for everyone. Gifts can be found on the seashore, created out of scraps, searched for at book sales, or baked in an oven. Dare to be different. Take the dollars out of gifts and wrap them in love.
—D. W. Woodliff

461. The blessedness of Christmas is all wrapped up in the person of Jesus. Our relationship determines the measure of the blessing.

462. "Ready for Christmas," she said
with a sigh
As she gave a last touch to the gifts
piled high.

Then wearily sat for a moment and
read
Till soon, very soon, she was
nodding her head.
Then quietly spoke a voice in her
dream,
"Ready for Christmas, what do you
mean?
Ready for Christmas when only last
week
You wouldn't acknowledge your
friend on the street?
Ready for Christmas while holding
a grudge?
Perhaps you'd better let God be the
judge."
She woke with a start and a cry of
despair.
"There's so little time and I've still
to prepare,
O, Father, forgive me, I see what
you mean!"
To be ready means more than a
house swept clean.
Yes, more than the giving of gifts
and a tree,
It's the heart swept clean that He
wanted to see,
A heart that is free from rancor and
sin,
So be ready for Christmas and
ready for Him.

THE CHURCH

463. We have been offered [in the
church] all too often, a watered-down gospel in willy-nilly fashion, and so we go
through the motions of being faithful
while turning to a secular world for the
stimulus and satisfaction we seek.
—James Armstrong

464. The church has often been more
concerned to prove itself right than to
present the message which by its trans-
forming effect is its own proof.
—Myron Augsburger

465. The church concerns itself with
"come structures" while the Scriptures
dictate a "go structure." Is it any wonder
that to the world, and to most Christians,
the church is merely the building on the
corner of Tenth and Main rather than
God's special people permeating all culture? —Elwood D. Baas

466. The pity is that the church can be so
harmless that it would not be worthwhile
to take the trouble to crucify it.
—William Barclay

467. The aim of the Church for its members is nothing less than perfection. The
Church can never be content that her
members should live decent, respectable
lives; her aim must be that they should be
examples of perfect Christian manhood
and womanhood. —William Barclay

468. The church is not a gallery for the
exhibition of eminent Christians, but a
school for the education of imperfect ones,
and a hospital for the healing of those
needing diligent care.
—Henry Ward Beecher

469. In the midst of the present crisis,
mere organizational . . . efforts are like rear-
ranging the deck chairs on the Titanic.
—Peter Berger

470. The church was once the force for
evangelism. Today it is the field.
—J. A. Blair

471. The church is looking for better
methods; God is looking for better men.
What the church needs today is not more
machinery or better . . . but men whom the

40

Holy Spirit can use. He does not flow through methods, but through men.
—E. M. Bounds

472. The best neighbors I know anything about are my two hands. They have lived on opposite sides of the street for many years, and they have never had a row. If my left hand is hurt, my right hand immediately drops all other business and rushes across the way to comfort it, and help it out of its trouble. If one happens to hurt the other, the [one that is] hurt doesn't get in a huff and say, "Here, I will not stand for that; you can't treat me that way," and get in a fight. No, no, no. They are good neighbors. My two hands are members of one another. And Christians should be like that. They are members of Christ's body. They should be as loving, as forbearing, as sympathetic and helpful toward each other as are my two hands.
—Samuel Brengle

473. The church exists by mission as fire exists by burning.   —Emil Brunner

474. There are no lesser members in the body of Christ—only less obvious members. In God's eyes all members are needed and all ministries are important.
—Joyce Lyon Burkhart

475. A church does not make you a Christian any more than going into a garage makes you an automobile.
—John B. Conlan

476. The church will take three fateful steps if it lapses into spiritual darkness: (1) the minister will lose his power; (2) the church corporate will lose its purpose; (3) its people will lose their penitence.
—Hughes Day

477. A church is all too often judged not by whether God is worshiped there in

Spirit and in truth, or whether the Word is faithfully proclaimed and the sacraments duly celebrated. On the contrary, a church is usually judged by the attractiveness of its ritual, the friendliness of its members and their ability to make me feel at home.
—James J. DiGiacomo

478. With so much apostasy in the church today, it seems that the people heard better when there was less amplification.   —J. D. Eppinga

479. All that is necessary to save established churches is that such pastors as have not yet done so become Christians.
—Medford Evans

480. The most critical time in the life of any church is when the vision is being carried out by those who have not seen it.
—C. William Fisher

481. There are two dangers that the church must avoid. Isolation from the world and imitation of the world.
—Leighton Ford

482. The program of the local congregation is probably least effective when it concentrates on . . . groups of members who are segregated on the basis of age, sex, marital status, or whatever is the latest form of dividing people up. It probably is most effective . . . when it takes advantage of the fact that it is one of the few social groupings in today's society which spans three or more generations, to involve the young with the old who are visible evidence of their history, and the old with the young who embody the future.
—Barbara Hargrove

483. When organization kills organism, as it often does, this is what happens: first you have a man and a message, then a movement, and in the end a monument.
—Vance Havner

484. What the church is doing in heaven is what the church should be doing on earth. Her ultimate style should be her interim mood. —David A. Hubbard

485. Can I be a Christian without joining other Christians in the church? Yes, it is something like: being a soldier without an army, a seaman without a ship, a business man without a business, a tuba player without an orchestra, a football player without a team or a bee without a hive. —Mrs. William P. Janzen

486. No clever arrangement of bad eggs ever made a good omelet. —C. S. Lewis

487. God never intended His church to be a refrigerator in which to preserve perishable piety. He intended it to be an incubator in which to hatch out converts. —Foreman Lincicome

488. Three ingredients surface in the book of Acts to show us God's method of church growth: the inspiration of a Presence, the demonstration of a Power, and the proclamation of a Person. —J. M. MacKnight

489. The poorest church building, a mere wooden shack, with broken windows and a whining organ, and bare benches, and scattered worshippers and a dull preacher, is yet a far more significant part of any community or city than a library with its thousands of volumes, or a bank with its Grecian columns and its vaults bursting with gold and silver. —Clarence McCartney

490. That's one of the jobs of the church—to shake up our present population. To do that you'd have to preach nothing but hellfire. —Marshall McLuhan

491. The strength of a church is not revealed by how many it seats, but by how many it sends. —W. Stanley Mooneyham

492. The church of Christ does not get on the move by pushing itself harder, but only by opening itself up more fully to the Holy Spirit's power. —Alfred E. Mulder

493. The church is not a society of the successful. It is a fellowship of the forgiven. —Robert Munger

494. The trouble with gimmicks in the church is that they too often become ends in themselves. . . . It's okay to be cute now and then if our congregations are being spiritually nourished. But when fizz and frolic decorate an empty stomach, everyone gets sick. —David C. Shultz

495. Before Christ sent the church into the world, He sent His Spirit into the church. The same order must be observed today. —John R. W. Stott

496. There is a lesson for us in the historical fact that the days of the church's greatest advance were also the days of the Roman Empire's final decay. —G. Aiken Taylor

497. God's work done in God's way will never lack God's supply. —James Hudson Taylor

498. The church is the only society in the world which exists for the benefit of those outside its membership. —William Temple

499. We have lost the art of worship. We are not producing saints. Our models are successful businessmen, celebrated athletes, and theatrical personalities. We carry on our religious activities after the methods of the modern advertisers. Our homes have been turned into theatres, our literature is shallow, our hymns border on sacrilege and scarcely anyone seems to care. Christianity is little more than objective truth, sweetened with song and made palatable through religious entertainment. Christ calls men to carry a cross, but we call them to have fun in His name.

—A. W. Tozer

500. It is part of our contemporary tragedy that just when the world is becoming more aware of its need the church is becoming less sure of its mission.

—Elton Trueblood

501. Denominations, as we know them, are not evil; they simply are not important. There is no harm in their continued existence and they may do some good that would not be done otherwise. But they are no longer central in the Christian stream; they occupy the side channels. It is as inept to condemn the side channel as it is to spend one's life limited to it.

—Elton Trueblood

502. Not all bigness is carnal and not all smallness is spiritual. Not even concerning churches. —C. Peter Wagner

503. The church's future today depends, not on its being able to assume a mighty and popular form of dignity, impressiveness, and stability before men, but simply in its being able to utter to the world the same life-giving word Jesus uttered from the cross. —Ronald S. Wallace

504. Churches are sometimes,
Though it's not admitted,
Over-committeed
And under-committed.

—Ruth M. Walsh

505. When the basic democracy of an organized church is compromised, that church loses its authentic (biblical) identity and is in the process of becoming a cult. —Albert M. Wells, Jr.

506. The church does the most for the world when the church is least like the world. —Warren W. Wiersbe

507. I want to wake up to one truth in these last days. It is this: The church that is rich and increased with goods and in need of nothing, is also blind, wretched, naked, and can be an abomination in the eyes of God. —David Wilkerson

508. We find it easier to go to church than to be the church.

509. Most denominations, though wrong perhaps at some points, are the result of honest men, intent on obeying Scripture.

510. A Bible-reading church is an informed church; an informed church is an interested church; an interested church is an acting church; an acting church is a serving church; a serving church is the Lord's church.

(see also: Church and State)

CHURCH AND STATE

511. The First Amendment was not intended to safeguard society from the influence of religion, but to preserve and protect religious liberty from encroachments by the state.

—John Courtney Murray

512. The presupposition that is increasingly being put forth by American courts and trumpeted by other bastions of humanism is: Religion cannot have a legal position contrary to secular authority or secular consensus. —Albert M. Wells, Jr.

(see also: The Nation)

CITIZENSHIP

513. Bad officials are elected by good people who don't vote.　—Edmund Burke

514. Civilization is always in danger when those who have never learned to obey are given the right to command.
　　　　　　　　　　—Fulton Sheen

515. The political and social practices of our civilization derive from their Christian content—and they will not long survive unless they are replenished by faith.
　　　　　　　　　—Arnold Toynbee

516. With a firm reliance on the protection of Divine Providence, we mutually pledge to each other our lives, our fortunes, and our sacred honor.
　　　　　—Declaration of Independence

(see also: The Nation; Politics and Government)

COMMITMENT

517. Anyone who consistently takes the prophetic stance must be prepared to end up on a hill like Calvary, because true prophetic testimony of profound unconformity may arouse the fiercest violence against it.　　　　　　　　　　—Ivan Illich

518. You ought to beware thinking that Christ will achieve things in the earth quietly and softly when you see that He fought with His own blood, and afterward with all the martyrs.　　　　　—Martin Luther

519. My face is set, my gait is fast, my goal is Heaven, my road is narrow, my way is rough, my companions are few, my guide is reliable, my mission is clear. I cannot be bought, compromised, detoured, lured away, turned back, diluted, or delayed. I will not flinch in the face of sacrifice, hesitate in the presence of adversity, negotiate at the table of the enemy, ponder at the pool of popularity, or meander in a maze of mediocrity. I won't give up, shut up, let up, or slow up till I've preached up, prayed up, paid up, stored up, and stayed up for Christ.　　　　　—Robert Moorehead

520. In forty years I have not spent fifteen waking minutes without thinking of Jesus.
　　　　　　　—Charles H. Spurgeon

521. The world has yet to see what God can do with and for and through and in a man who is fully and wholly consecrated to Him.　　　　　　—Henry Varley

522. Christian commitment is without a complex. In sacrifice it feels no sacrifice and in self-giving it feels no loss. Satisfaction is in direct ratio to the negation of self, not for its own sake, but for Jesus' sake.
　　　　　　　—Albert M. Wells, Jr.

523. Lord, give me one hundred men who hate nothing but sin, and desire nothing but God, and I will shake the world.
　　　　　　　　　—John Wesley

524. I sense an attitude in students and even in older Christians . . . to commit themselves to anything as "long as they feel good about it" and are having a "beautiful" experience. Such an approach to life seems as dependable as a roof shored up by a wet noodle.　　—Katie Funk Wiebe

525. It doesn't take such a great man to be a Christian; it just takes all there is of him.　　　　　　　　—Seth Wilson

526. An irate parent phoned her little boy's Sunday school teacher. "Is it true that you told all the kids that they were crazy?" she demanded. "No, I didn't," the teacher replied, "but I did tell them they should all be committed."

527. The prayer of commitment must be a way of life—not just a despairing cry at the end of failure.

(see also: Duty; Self-Denial)

COMMUNICATION

(see: Interpersonal Relations)

COMMUNISM

528. Communism is a diabolical conspiracy and evil religion, and the deadliest enemy Christianity has ever faced.
—Thomas J. Anderson

529. We set out to improve the world; the Communists set out to own it.
—Thomas J. Anderson

530. Communism is the [distorted] vision of man's mind displacing God as the creative intelligence of the world.
—Hilaire Belloc

531. The notion of an earthly paradise in which men shall dwell together in millennial brotherhood is used to justify crimes and depravities surpassing anything the modern world has seen. . . . Such a disaster never happened to humanity before.
—Max Eastman

532. To see Communism as a cure for social decay is like regarding death as the cure for a cancerous tumor. . . . In strict prisons there is no pornography, no narcotics, no thieving; in a word, no decay. But there is also no society. —Thomas Fleming

533. Power over a man's subsistence is power over his will. —Alexander Hamilton

534. The whole gospel of Karl Marx can be summed up in a single sentence: Hate the man who is better off than you are.
—Henry Hazlitt

535. A favorite taunt of the Marxists is that it took Christianity twenty centuries to eliminate slavery. A Christian church historian has rightly noted that it took Communism but one generation to restore it. —Carl F. H. Henry

536. The [Communist sympathizers] in America try to fool all the people all the time, and those they can't fool, they call McCarthyites. —Rael Jean Isaac

537. Society cannot leap into Communism from capitalism without going through a socialist state of development. Socialism is the first stage to Communism.
—Nikita Khrushchev

538. [Wherever it has come to power] the Communist system has turned poverty into a permanent fixture, bureaucracy into a way of life, and the secret police into a supreme moral authority. —Ephraim Kishon

539. When the capitalist world starts to trade with us—on that day they will begin to finance their own destruction.
— V. I. Lenin

540. With us it is not a matter of reforming private property, but of abolishing it.
—Karl Marx

541. It is said that if a Communist regime were to take over in the Sahara, there would in time be a shortage of sand.
—Patrick Moynihan

542. Communism is intrinsically evil and no one who would save Christian civilization may collaborate with it in any undertaking whatsoever. —Pope Pius XI

543. Among enlightened people it is considered rather awkward to use seriously such words as "good" and "evil." Communism has managed to instill in all of us that these concepts are old-fashioned concepts and laughable. But if we are to be deprived of the concepts of good and evil, what will be left? Nothing but the manipulation of one another. We will decline to the status of animals. —Alexander Solzhenitsyn

544. How many concessions, how many sacrifices have been made [by the West] in order to avoid World War III! But there are not many who realize, and who have the courage to admit, that World War III has already taken place—and the free world has irremediably lost it.

—Alexander Solzhenitsyn

545. Within the philosophical system of Marx and Lenin and at the heart of their psychology, hatred of God is the principal driving force, more fundamental than all their political and economic pretensions. Militant atheism is not merely incidental or marginal to Communist policy. It is not a side effect but the central pivot.

—Alexander Solzhenitsyn

546. There is, in fact, a manly and lawful passion for equality that incites men to wish all to be powerful and honored. This passion tends to elevate the humble to the rank of the great; but there exists also in the human heart a depraved taste for equality, which impels the weak to attempt to lower the powerful to their own level and reduce men to prefer equality in slavery to inequality with freedom.

—Alexis de Tocqueville

547. A revolution is not a banquet; it is not like writing a poem or sketching a design or doing embroidery. A revolution cannot be conducted with elegance, tranquility or delicacy; it does not allow the least softness, kindness, courtesy, restraint or magnanimity. A revolution is an up-

heaval, an act of violence in which one class rises against and puts down another.

—Mao Tse-tung

548. A. V. Lunacharski, the first Soviet Minister of Education, who dedicated his life to the struggle against religion, wrote: "Religion is like a nail: if you hit it on the head it will go deeper. We must surround religion, squeeze it up from the bottom and pull it out by the roots."

—G. Christian Weiss

549. At least 90 percent of all human beings, on both sides of the Iron Curtain, do not want Communism. —Robert Welch

550. Joy Davidman quotes a Communist who said to her: "Of course we're imprisoning our opponents and silencing the press and executing hostile elements. But it's only a temporary expedient, necessary to the ultimate goal."

COMPASSION

551. Jesus teaches that human need must always be helped; that there is no greater task than to relieve someone's pain and distress and that the Christian's compassion must be like God's—unceasing. Other work may be laid aside but the work of compassion never. —William Barclay

552. Sinners can set themselves against the most eloquent preaching, stubbornly resist all logic, stay away from revival meetings, and scorn all truth. But true, heartfelt compassion on the part of the Christian releases a power that in time proves irresistible. —Doyle Brannon

553. Why should we Christians give up our nature to be compassionate even when we get stung in a biting, stinging world?

—Henri J. M. Nouwen

554. Pity weeps and runs away;
   Compassion comes to help and stay.
   —Janet Curtis O'Leary

555. When you help someone else up the hill, you reach the top yourself.

(see also: Love)

COMPLACENCY

(see: Apathy)

COMPROMISE

556. Compromise means the loose ends of things unsolved. Compromise, therefore, inevitably means tension, even if a more or less hidden tension. Tension inevitably means a gnawing worry; and therefore compromise is the enemy of peace.
   —William Barclay

557. From U.S. Civil War days comes the story of a soldier who, desiring to play it safe, decided to compromise. He dressed himself to be acceptable to either side, so he thought. But when he tiptoed onto the battlefield he barely escaped being shot by both sides. Such is the danger of compromise.
   —Morris Chalfant

558. Each appeaser hopes if he feeds the crocodile enough, the crocodile will eat him last.
   —Winston Churchill

559. The hottest places in hell are reserved for those who, in a period of moral crisis, maintain their neutrality.
   —Dante

560. The non-theological Christ is popular, he wins votes; but he is not mighty; he does not win souls; he does not break men into small pieces and create them anew.
   —Peter Taylor Forsyth

561. It is better to die for a conviction than to live with a compromise.
   —Vance Havner

562. A compromise is often a deal in which two people get what neither of them wanted.
   —James Russell Lowell

563. At the Devil's booth all things are sold,
   Each ounce of dross costs its ounce of gold.
   —James Russell Lowell

(see also: Cowardice)

CONFESSION

564. Confess your sins to the Lord and you will be forgiven; confess them to man and you will be laughed at.
   —Josh Billings

565. A general confession is good, but in it lurks the danger of "acknowledging and bewailing" humanity's sins and not our own.
   —Georgia Harkness

566. O God, my earth-desires are full of snares:
   Forgive and do not answer all my prayers.

(see also: Repentance)

CONFORMITY

567. It is said that everyone is born an original and dies a copy.
   —Myron Augsburger

568. When we refuse to consciously and deliberately choose specific behaviors, the powerful ocean of society that we live in is ready to wash us out to sea. There we can bob helplessly along with the crowd.
   —Mary Lou Cummings

569. During the past several decades the church experienced little criticism or conflict from the world, not because the world is more Christian, but because the world and church are so much alike. We long to

be loved so much we've lost the desire for a distinctly different life. Most of us would rather be dead than different.
—John Drescher

570. When all think alike, none thinks very much. —Sir Ronald Gould

571. We Christians often have a regrettable tendency to bring into the church what we practice on the outside, instead of taking outside what God has told us to practice within. —Harris Langford

572. They are slaves who fear to speak
For the fallen and the weak;
They are slaves who will not choose
Hatred, scoffing, and abuse,
Rather than in silence shrink
From the truth they needs must think;
They are slaves who dare not be
In the right with two or three.
—James Russell Lowell

CONSCIENCE

573. A good conscience is a continuous Christmas. —Benjamin Franklin

574. What is indubitably certain is our sense of obligation to answer for our conduct. —Abraham Heschel

575. Two things hold me in awe: the starry heaven above me; and the moral law within me. —Immanuel Kant

576. A clear conscience weighs more in the scale of God and time than an empire.
—Nikos Kazantzakis

577. Unless I am convicted by Scripture and plain reason . . . my conscience is captive to the Word of God. I cannot and I will not recant anything, for to go against

conscience is neither right nor safe. Here I stand. I cannot do otherwise. God help me. Amen. —Martin Luther

578. Many a man thinks he has a clear conscience when what he really has is a poor memory. —Morris Mandel

579. Unless controlled by Christ, the conscience is not trustworthy.
—Arlo F. Newell

580. Labor to keep alive in your breast that little spark of celestial fire, called conscience. —George Washington

581. If to the right or left I stray,
That moment, Lord, reprove;
And let me weep my life away
For having grieved thy love.

O may the least omission pain
My well-instructed soul,
And drive me to the blood again
Which makes the wounded whole!
—Charles Wesley

582. The conscience is a three-cornered thing in my heart that stands still when I'm good, but when I'm bad it turns around and around; and the corners hurt a lot. But if I keep on doing wrong, the corners wear off and it stops hurting.

583. The conscience is the sentinel which guards the soul; the granite column which supports the fabric of self and society; the chamber of justice; God's voice in the soul; God's monitor which approves right and condemns wrong.

584. There is no pillow so soft as a clear conscience.

CONSECRATION

585. Jesus needs what we can bring him. It may not be much but he needs it. It may

well be that the world is denied miracle after miracle and triumph after triumph because we will not bring to Jesus what we have and what we are. —William Barclay

586. By one act of consecration of our total selves to God we can make every subsequent act express that consecration.
—A. W. Tozer

587. All my life's plan in His molding,
Not one single choice be mine,
Let me answer, unrepining,
"Father, not my will, but Thine."

(see also: Commitment; Self-Denial; Surrender)

CONTENTMENT

588. O thou, who kindly dost provide
For every creature's want.
We bless thee, God of Nature wide,
For all thy goodness lent.
And, if it pleases thee, heavenly Guide,
May never worse be sent;
But whether granted or denied,
Lord, bless us with content.
—Robert Burns

589. A soul that is capable of knowing God can be filled with nothing else but God. —Jeremiah Burroughs

590. None of us ought to presume to question the circumstances of his existence. Whether good or bad, comfortable or awkward, opulent or Spartan, we may be certain that we live as we were decreed to live by a caring God. Therefore, all is well.
—Charles Doss

591. Recipe for contentment: (1) Health enough to make work a pleasure; (2) Wealth enough to support your needs; (3) Strength enough to battle with difficulties and forsake them; (4) Grace enough to confess your sins and overcome them; (5) Patience enough to toil until some good is accomplished; (6) Charity enough to see some good in your neighbor; (7) Love enough to move you to be useful and helpful to others; (8) Faith enough to make real the things of God; (9) Hope enough to remove all anxious fears concerning the future. —Johann Wolfgang von Goethe

592. Charles Spurgeon tells of a farmer who has on the weather vane of his barn the motto, "God is love." He was asked if the motto was intended to suggest that God is as changeable as the wind. "Oh, no!" said the farmer. "It means that no matter which way the wind blows, God is love." That is the secret of being content, the secret of a quiet heart.
—E. Brandt Gustavson

593. How rich a God our God is! He gives enough, but we don't notice it. He gave the whole world to Adam, but this was nothing in Adam's eyes; he was concerned about one tree and had to ask why God had forbidden him to eat of it.
—Martin Luther

594. Amid the trials which I meet,
Amid the thorns that pierce my feet,
One thought remains supremely sweet,
Thou thinkest, Lord, of me!

Let shadows come, let shadows go,
Let life be bright or dark with woe,
I am content, for this I know,
Thou thinkest, Lord, of me.
—E. D. Mund

(see also: Happiness; Peace of Mind)

CONVERSION

595. What I feared to be parted from, was now a joy to surrender. —Augustine

596. When we accept Christ we enter into three new relationships. (1) We enter into a new relationship with God. The judge becomes the father; the distant becomes the near; strangeness becomes intimacy and fear becomes love. (2) We enter into a new relationship with our fellow men. Hatred becomes love; selfishness becomes service; and bitterness becomes forgiveness. (3) We enter into a new relationship with ourselves. Weakness becomes strength; frustration becomes achievement; and tension becomes peace. —William Barclay

597. It is not culture but conversion that we need first. Not education, but transformation. Not new knowledge, but a new nature. We must become new creations by the regenerating power of the Holy Spirit before we are ready to live Christ's life and bear His image. —Robert C. Cunningham

598. A faith that has not changed your life has not saved your soul. —Bob Jones, Jr.

599. God is a fire and you must walk on it . . . dance on it. At that moment the fire will become cool water. But until you reach that point, what a struggle, my Lord, what an agony! —Nikos Kazantzakis

600. I did not think, I did not strive;
The deep peace burnt my "me" alive.
The bolted door had broken in;
I knew that I had done with sin.
—John Masefield

601. If you have to be reasoned into Christianity, some wise fellow can reason you out of it. But if you come to Christ by a flash of the Holy Ghost . . . no one can ever reason you out of it. —A. W. Tozer

(see also: New Birth; Salvation)

CONVICTION

602. We must set God upon the throne of the human heart and establish there a prior loyalty that not all the legions of hell can shake. —C. Darby Fulton

603. The lions showed no interest in Daniel. Why should they? After all, he was nothing but backbone and grit.
—Max R. Hickerson

604. The fixed determination to acquire the warrior soul, and to have acquired it to either conquer or perish with honor, is the secret of victory. —George S. Patton, Jr.

605. Show me a person who is not an extremist about some things—who is a "middle-of-the-roader" in everything— and I will show you someone who is insecure. G. Aiken Taylor

606. What a man believes, he will die for. What a man merely thinks, he will change his mind about.

607. There was a time when a man [Servetus] was willing to be burned at the stake for the difference between "Christ, the eternal Son of God" and "Christ, the son of the eternal God." The one he would confess. The other he would rather die than confess.

(see also: Christian Action; Commitment)

COURAGE

608. Life is essentially a series of events to be lived through rather than intellectual riddles to be played with and solved. Courage is worth ten times more than any answers that claim to be total.
—George A. Buttrick

609. Without courage, all other virtues lose their meaning. —Winston Churchill

610. Courage conquers more within
Than any foes without,
Never needs to boast or blame
Or raise his voice and shout.

Courage is a quietness—
Not martial music made—
Born of facing up to life
Even when afraid.
—**Emily Sargent Councilman**

611. Courage is the right disposition toward the fear of death.

612. Courage is fear that has said its prayers.

COVETOUSNESS

(see: Envy)

COWARDICE

613. Not seldom we refrain from rebuke because of mistaken kindness, or because of the desire to avoid trouble. But there is a time when to avoid trouble is to store up trouble, and when to seek for a lazy and a cowardly peace is to court a still greater danger.   —**William Barclay**

614. To know what is right and not do it is the worst cowardice.   —**Confucius**

615. Spiritual cowardice is not only weakness but wickedness. —**J. B. Gambrell**

616. To sin by silence when they should protest makes cowards out of men.
—**Abraham Lincoln**

617. They are slaves who dare not be in the right with two or three.
—**James Russell Lowell**

618. There are at least two kinds of cowards. One kind always lives with himself, afraid to face the world. The other kind lives with the world, afraid to face himself.
—**Roscoe Snowden**

619. Silence is not always golden; sometimes it's just plain yellow.

(see also: Compromise)

CREATION

620. Earth's crammed with heaven;
And every common bush afire with
God;
But only he who sees, takes off his
shoes,
The rest sit round it and pluck
blackberries.
—**Elizabeth Barrett Browning**

621. When we take a view of the universe, in its parts, general or particular, it is impossible for the human mind not to perceive and feel a conviction of design, consummate skill, and indefinite power in every atom of its composition.
—**Thomas Jefferson**

622. Nature never taught me that there exists a God of glory and infinite majesty. I had to learn that in other ways. But nature gave the word "glory" a meaning for me. I still do not know where else I could have found one.   —**C. S. Lewis**

623. The author of Hebrews says that it is "through faith we understand that the worlds were framed by the Word of God" (11:3). When the truth of John 3 becomes a vivid reality, the truth of Genesis 1 and 2 will no longer constitute a problem.
—**G. Aiken Taylor**

624. What can be more foolish than to think that all this rare fabric of heaven and earth could come by chance, when all the skill of science is not able to make an oyster.   —**Jeremy Taylor**

625. I met a scientist quite up-to-date
Who said: "My research proves
that God did not,

As Genesis might seem to say,
  create
A man. No, man once shared the
  lowly lot
Of beast—ate grass or meat and
  walked on hands
As well as feet." This educated
  guess
I couldn't accept—the quaint,
  absurd demands
On reason. Was it wisdom to
  profess
That we could trust a mind that
  from a beast
Evolved? To know I know I'd surely
  wish
My head contained the cells or
  seeds at least
Of better stuff than that from
  jellyfish.
I think, because I am a child of
  God;
I am, because He made me from a
  clod.

    —Mike Vanden Bosch

626. There was this professional critic who even found fault with God and His creation. Talking one day beneath a giant oak tree and near a garden, he told a friend how the acorn should be on the end of the pumpkin vine and the pumpkin on the sturdy oak tree. Just then an acorn fell off and hit him a good rap. His friend said, "Now do you still wish the acorn had been a pumpkin?"

(see also: Nature)

CRIME

627. The tendency to blame guns for crime is as ridiculous as blaming pencils for misspelled words.   —Wallace F. Bennett

628. When a murderer is questioned today, the police are beginning to feel they should provide a psychiatrist, a social worker, a psychologist, a public defender, a clergyman, and a barbershop quartet singing, "Jesus Wants Me for a Sunbeam."

    —Steve Mitchell

629. We are restrained from lawlessness chiefly through reverent fear.   —Pericles

630. Were we to pour forth from our homes, to walk our streets, to visit with neighbors over curbstones and steps and grocery packages, there would be no hiding places for muggers and pushers or rapists and con artists.   —Dorothy R. Samuel

631. It is because sentence upon wicked acts is not promptly carried out that men do evil so boldly.   —Ecclesiastes 8:11 [NEB]

632. In the U.S. we keep a child protected by the law. You really can't do anything (inflict any legal punishment on him) until he is eighteen. When he is eighteen he can vote. So he actually has a period here where he receives no correction for his crime; then the next day he's running the country.   —Al Yonally

633. It is cruelty to the innocent not to punish the guilty.

(see also: Capital Punishment)

CRITICISM

(see: Censoriousness)

THE CROSS

634. The Cross is the proof that there is no length to which the love of God will refuse to go, in order to win men's hearts. The Cross is the medium of reconciliation because the Cross is the final proof of the love of God; and a love like that demands an answering love. If the Cross will not waken love and wonder in men's hearts, nothing will. —**William Barclay**

635. Take another look at the Cross and see the revelation: it is a sword that cuts our conscience; it is a key that unlocks our prisons; it is a royal scepter under which we will live eternally with Him in His kingdom. —**Edith Brock**

636. The Cross is God's centerpiece on the table of time. —**Paul C. Guttke**

637. O gracious Lord, how sweet to take
from Thee the daily Cross,
And know I cannot ever separate
its gain and loss.
The daily Cross is daily loss of all
that keeps from Thee.
The daily Cross is daily gain of all
Thou art to me.
—**Bessie Porter Head**

638. Those who preach the Cross of our Lord Jesus are the terror of modern thinkers. In their hearts they dread the preaching of the old-fashioned Gospel, and they hate what they dread.
—**Charles H. Spurgeon**

639. The Cross is not a weight that bears you down, but it is a supernatural symbol that gives you strength and speeds your way.

(see also: Cross-Bearing; Good Friday Theme)

CROSS-BEARING

640. Anyone who consistently takes the prophetic stance must be prepared to end up on a hill like Calvary, because true prophetic testimony of profound unconformity may arouse the fiercest violence against it. —**Ivan Illich**

641. The beginner, moved by fear, patiently bears the Cross of Christ. The one

who has already made some progress on the road to perfection, inspired by hope, carries it cheerfully; the perfect soul, consumed by love, embraces it ardently.

(see also: The Cross; Discipleship; Self-Denial)

DEATH

642. Living close to God is the answer to man's problem. This takes on practical import when we live close to the church, take pleasure in the study of God's Word, and rejoice in purposeful fellowship with the people of God. From that kind of living, death is but shifting into high gear.
—**Marvin Baarman**

643. It is we ourselves and not outward circumstances who make death what it can be, a death freely and voluntarily accepted. —**Dietrich Bonhoeffer**

644. Death is an inexorable, irresistible messenger who cannot be diverted from executing his orders—not by the force of the mighty, the bribes of the rich nor the entreaties of the poor. —**Thomas Boston**

645. So live, that when thy summons
comes to join
The innumerable caravan which
moves
To that mysterious realm, where
each shall take
His chamber in the silent halls of
death,
Thou go not, like the quarry-slave
at night,
Scourged to his dungeon, but,
sustained and soothed
Like one who wraps the drapery of
his couch

About him, and lies down to
pleasant dreams.
—**William Cullen Bryant**

646. If Christians were as distinctive in
their attitudes to death—repudiating, for
example, the practice of embalming the
dead—as are Orthodox Jews, western society would become healthier and saner.
—**James Munro Cameron**

647. Death is not a period
Bringing the sentence of life to a
close
Like the spilling of a moment
Or the dissolution of an hour.

Death is a useful comma
Which punctuates, and labors to
convince
Of more to follow.
—**William Walter DeBolt**

648. Death, be not proud, though some
have called thee
Mighty and dreadful, for thou art
not so;
For those whom thou think'st thou
dost overthrow
Die not, poor Death, nor yet canst
thou kill me.

—**John Donne**

649. Any man's death diminishes me, because I am involved in mankind, and
therefore, never send to know for whom
the bell tolls; it tolls for thee.

—**John Donne**

650. Richard C. Raines once cited the
letter of a child who wrote: Dear God,
what is it like when you die? Nobody will
tell me. I just want to know. I don't want to
do it. —**John Drescher**

651. Death is an offer we can't refuse.
—**Robert M. Fine**

652. Weep not for me in death
For I have just begun!
My soul unbound at last
Speeds homeward toward the Son.

This all too binding earthly cloak
Thrown off eternally—rejoice!
I am set free of mortal chains
To hear my Master's voice.

Go forth, but not with tears.
I am where I belong.
Seek you what I have found,
Proclaim His glory song!
—**Jane M. Grippen**

653. The hardest thing of all—to die
rightly—an exam nobody is spared—and
how many pass it? —**Dag Hammarskjold**

654. Only one person has ever come back
from the dead to tell us authoritatively
what lies beyond and that was Jesus Christ.
—**Carl F. H. Henry**

655. It is important that when we come
to die we have nothing to do but to die.
—**Charles Hodge**

656. A society's image of death reveals
the level of independence of its people,
their personal relatedness, self-reliance
and aliveness. —**Ivan Illich**

657. God is stripping me of everything to
give me Everything. —**E. Stanley Jones**

658. In one of his more extreme moments, George Bernard Shaw said that
every man should be arrested every five
years. He should be asked to justify his
continued existence. If one could not provide such justification, his life should be
terminated. I would not advocate that, but
I would urge upon us the acceptance of the
imminence of death. . . . This is realistic,
not morbid. It could provide the motivation to help us make the most of our time.
—**Jerry W. McCant**

659. If I can get a man to think seriously about death for five minutes, I can get him saved. —**Dwight L. Moody**

660. Here lies a gullible guy with an open heart who saw the ugliness of man-unkind but looked for the loveliness of persons. Some people laughed—knowing that he loved—thinking that he was taken in. Today he was. —**Ruth Naylor**

661. It is a great art to die well, and to be learnt by men in health. —**Jeremy Taylor**

662. There are three important steps to take in preparation for a holy death. And these three principles should be practiced throughout life. (1) Expect that death will come knocking at your gates at any time; this will keep your priorities straight. (2) Value your time for it is the most precious possession you have. (3) Refrain from a soft and easy life; stress the holy life of self-discipline, labor, and alertness. Engage each day in self-examination. —**Jeremy Taylor**

663. The Christian does not consider death to be the end of his life, but the end of his troubles. —**A. Mark Wells**

664. Ninety-five percent of the people who died today had expected to live a lot longer. —**Albert M. Wells, Jr.**

665. Those who are in Christ shall never taste of the second death; but, as to the first death, how art thou freed? I answer, thou art freed from the curse and from the sting of death; so thou mayest step on the back of death and go into endless glory. Therefore this first death is no death to thee who art in Christ, but rather an entry, or passage, or port to eternal life. —**John Welsh**

666. Because the human mind is able to avoid contemplating the future, most men die totally unprepared.

667. For the Christian, death does not extinguish the light. It puts out the lamp because the dawn has come.

668. The saddest thing from birth to sod Is a dying man who has no God.

669. King Philip of Macedon charged one of his slaves with a unique responsibility. The monarch instructed his servant to awaken him each morning with these words: "Philip, remember, you must die."

DECEPTION

670. Truth is not only violated by falsehood, it may be equally outraged by silence. —**Henri Frederic Amiel**

671. When religion grows weak superstition grows strong. —**William Barclay**

672. It's easy to fool other people. Fooling yourself is a little harder. Fooling God is impossible. —**Chris Harrison**

673. Sin has many tools, but a lie is the handle that fits them all. —**Oliver Wendell Holmes**

674. I would rather be the man who bought the Brooklyn Bridge than the man who sold it. —**Will Rogers**

675. The essence of lying is in deception, not in words. A lie may be told by silence, by equivocation, by the accent on a syllable, by a glance of the eye attaching a peculiar significance to a sentence. All these kinds of lies are worse and baser by many degrees than a lie plainly worded. No form of blinded conscience is so far sunk as that which comforts itself for having deceived because the deception was by gesture or silence instead of utterance.   —John Ruskin

676. Oh, what a tangled web we weave,
When first we practice to deceive.
—Sir Walter Scott

677. An excuse is the skin of a reason stuffed with a lie.   —Billy Sunday

678. The nearer a lie to truth the more deceitful it is.

DECISIONS

679. God took humankind very seriously when He gave us the gift of choice; perhaps more seriously than we take ourselves. We frequently and almost carelessly . . . abdicate our autonomy and let the community, the government, or the church decide for us.
—Mary Lou Cummings

680. Once to every man and nation
Comes the moment to decide,
In the strife of truth with falsehood
For the good or evil side.
—James Russell Lowell

681. There is a time when we must firmly choose the course we will follow, or the relentless drift of events will make the decision for us.   —Herbert V. Prochnow

682. When one bases his life on principle, 99 percent of his decisions are already made. That's what makes Christian principles so critical.

(see also: Choices)

DEDICATION

(see: Commitment; Consecration; Self-Denial)

DEFEAT

(see: Backsliding; Failure)

DETERMINATION

683. Nothing is so common as unsuccessful men with talent. They lack only determination.   —Charles Swindoll

(see also: Perseverance)

THE DEVIL

684. Although the devil be exceedingly crafty and subtle, yet he is one of the greatest fools and blockheads in the world.
—Jonathan Edwards

685. When Charles Finney was asked how he could believe in a devil, he retorted: "Why don't you try opposing him sometime and you'll find out whether he exists or not."   —Charles G. Finney

686. A real firebrand is distressing to the devil and when a wide-awake believer comes along, taking the Gospel seriously, we can expect sinister maneuvering for his downfall.   —Vance Havner

687. The Adversary's most successful method of deception has always been imitation. His packaging has always been almost indistinguishable from the Real Thing, with such ethical knee-jerkers as Religion, Piety, The Golden Rule, and Virtue freely used in prominent places. Only a close reading of the small print reveals the missing ingredients—chiefly, everything having to do with sin and redemption, heaven and hell.
—Calvin D. Linton

688. It is certainly true that if God would not defend us against this evil enemy without ceasing, the devil would not leave one kernel of grain, neither fish nor meat, neither water, wine, nor beer without poisoning it. —Martin Luther

689. The devil comes without invitation but leaves only when commanded.
—W. E. McCumber

690. I have found the devil easier to believe in than God; for one thing, alas, I have had more to do with him. It seems to me quite extraordinary that anyone should have failed to notice, especially during the last half century, a diabolic presence in the world, pulling downwards as gravity does instead of pressing upwards as trees and plants do when they . . . reach so resolutely after the light. —Malcolm Muggeridge

691. The devil's greatest asset is the doubt people have about his existence.
—John Nicola

692. It is an unquestionable truth, that the god and prince of this world still possesses all who know not God. [In old time the devil] frequently tormented their bodies as well as their souls, and that openly, without any disguise; now he torments their souls only, (unless in some rare cases) and that as covertly as possible. The reason of this difference is plain: it was then his aim to drive mankind into superstition. . . . But it is his aim [now] to drive us into infidelity; therefore he works as privately as he can: for the more secret he is the more he prevails. —John Wesley

693. Men don't believe in the devil now
As their fathers used to do.
They've opened wide their
broadest creeds,
And let his majesty through.

The devil is voted not to be;
So, of course, the devil is gone—
But simple folks would like to know
Who carries his business on.

694. The devil is to be avoided as a lion, but he is most to be feared as an angel of light.

(see also: Satan)

DEVOTION

695. Satan rocks the cradle when we sleep at our devotions. —Joseph Hall

(see also: Commitment; Meditation)

DISCERNMENT

696. It is assumed that whoever is against [a certain] evil thereby represents Good. The possibility of his representing an even greater evil is [seldom] considered.
—Lev Navrozov

697. Love those who seek the truth, but beware of those who "find it."
—Marcel Proust

698. Nobody likes contention in the church, but obedience to the Gospel *demands* that a Christian be alert against falsehood. It is as important as being receptive to the truth. —G. Aiken Taylor

(see also: Decisions)

DISCIPLESHIP

699. He may try to be a secret disciple; but it has been well said that to be a secret disciple is impossible because either "the discipleship kills the secrecy, or the secrecy kills the discipleship."
—William Barclay

700. Christianity is more than obstetrics. It is pediatrics, public health, internal medicine, diagnostic care, surgery, and geriatrics. In short, it is a life of discipleship. Years after Jesus had gone to be with the Father, His followers were still known as disciples. You never outgrow the need to listen, learn, follow and lead.

—Jamie Buckingham

701. To succeed fully is beyond us, but to attempt less is unthinkable.

—Barry L. Callen

702. If I'm following Jesus, why am I such a good insurance risk?

—Ernest T. Campbell

703. The disciple who abides in Jesus *is* the will of God, and his apparently free choices are God's foreordained decrees. Mysterious? Logically contradictory and absurd? Yes, but a glorious truth to a saint.

—Oswald Chambers

704. It is not what we do that matters, but what a sovereign God chooses to do through us. God doesn't want our success; he wants us. He doesn't demand our achievements; he demands our obedience. The Kingdom of God is a kingdom of paradox, where through the ugly defeat of a cross a holy God is utterly glorified. Victory comes through defeat; healing through brokenness; finding self through losing self.

—Charles W. Colson

705. The Lord promised His disciples three things: they would be entirely fearless, absurdly happy, and always in trouble.

—T. R. Glover

706. If someone's sense of security depends on having all men speak well of him, he can never be secure in following Christ.

—Calvin Miller

707. Lord, give me the desire to follow you joyfully (cross-bearing and all), so I will never walk away sorrowfully.

—Herbert Sennett

708. The man in Roman times who took up his Cross was not going out to have his life redirected; he was going out to have it ended.

—A. W. Tozer

(see also: Christian Life; Self-Denial; Cross-Bearing)

DISCIPLINE

709. We are not here to play, to dream, to drift.
We have hard work to do and loads to lift.
Shun not the battle; face it. 'Tis God's gift.

—Maltbie D. Babcock

710. We are in bondage to the law in order that we may be free.

—Cicero

711. Surrender to all our desires obviously leads to impotence, disease, jealousies, lies, concealment, and everything that is the reverse of health, good humor, and frankness. For any happiness, even in this world, quite a lot of restraint is going to be necessary.

—C. S. Lewis

712. The greatest firmness is the greatest mercy.

—Henry Wadsworth Longfellow

713. Those who limit their own appetites free themselves to follow voices other than the sirens of self-gratification.

—Peter Monkres

714. Make us masters of ourselves that we may be the servants of others.

—Sir Alexander Paterson

715. The secret of discipline is motivation. When a man is sufficiently motivated, discipline will take care of itself.

716. If God believed in permissiveness, He would have given us Ten Suggestions instead of Ten Commandments.

(see also: Self-Denial)

DIVINE GUIDANCE

717. He who, from zone to zone,
Guides through the boundless sky
    thy certain flight,
In the long way that I must
    tread alone
Will lead my steps aright.
      —William Cullen Bryant

718. An eighteen-year-old asked a kindly old missionary, "How can I know God's will for my life?" The reply was, "Follow the gleam; favor the bent; and watch for the open door."
      —William Randolph Davenport

719. In traditional Chinese painting, there is just one outstanding object, perhaps a flower. Everything else in the picture is subordinate. An integrated life is like that. What is that one flower? As I see it now, it is the will of God. I used to pray that God would do this or that; now I pray that God will make His will known to me.
      —Madam Chiang Kai-Shek

720. Sometimes it is dangerous to pray for guidance when we already know what is right.
      —Kenneth Pike

721. We are not told that we cannot plan ahead, just that we should not be dogmatic in our planning.
      —Edith Schaeffer

722. If God can plan a universe
And spin earth's globe in place,
Direct its path, control its course
With regal rule and grace. . . .

He's surely planned a path of life
So man won't be alone!
Yes, He directs and charts life's
    course
Across the vast unknown.
      —Jack M. Scharn

723. If God's will is your will and if He always has His way [with you] then you always have your way also.
      —Hannah Whitall Smith

724. The will of God will not take you where the grace of God cannot keep you.

(see also: God's Will)

DIVINE HEALING

725. To have a curable illness and to leave it untreated except for prayer is like sticking your hand in a fire and asking God to remove the flame. **—Sandra L. Douglas**

726. When praying for healing, ask great things of God and expect great things from God. But let us seek for that healing that really matters, the healing of the heart, enabling us to trust God simply, face God honestly, and live [triumphantly].
      —Arlo F. Newell

727. We should be completely clear about these two facts: God is not obligated to heal, and healing is not His greatest gift.

728. It is more important, more thrilling, more satisfying and infinitely more valuable to know the Healer than to be healed.

DIVORCE

729. Divorce courts are packed with people who tried to base their marriages on "If you do this, I'll do that."
      —Mary Garson

730. When Christians break the marriage vow it is primarily because they fail to accept God's plan for their marriage.
      —Walter Schoedel

731. Tennyson's statement that " 'Tis better to have loved and lost/Than never to have loved at all" is non-Biblical if it refers to marriage and divorce.

—Haldyne Spriggins

732. Failure and the evil inherent in divorce would destroy us were it not for the fact that God keeps His promises and continues to love even when we break our promises and our love fails.

—William H. Willimon

733. The aim of divorce is freedom. But freedom carries a price tag. The question is, "Can you afford it?"

734. Even if divorce should happen to everyone, it is still wrong.

DOCTRINE

735. Doctrine is the necessary foundation of duty; if the theory is not correct, the practice cannot be right. Tell me what a man believes, and I will tell you what he will do. —Tryon Edwards

736. Doctrine is the framework of life—the skeleton of truth, to be clothed and rounded out by the living grace of a holy life. —Adoniram J. Gordon

(see also: Truth)

DOUBT

737. In the midst of your doubts, don't forget how many of the important questions God *does* answer. —Verne Becker

738. Doubters invert the metaphor. They insist that they need a mountain full of faith to move a little mustard seed.

—Webb Garrison

739. Give me the benefit of your convictions if you have any, but keep your doubts to yourself, for I have enough of my own.

—Johann Wolfgang von Goethe

740. Find out how seriously a believer takes his doubts, and you have the index of how seriously he takes his faith.

—Os Guinness

741. Turn your doubts to questions; turn your questions to prayers; turn your prayers to God. —Mark R. Littleton

742. The Christians of an earlier period felt more and did more than those of the present day, not because they were better men but because they *believed* more; and they believed more because they knew less. Doubt is the offspring of knowledge; the savage never doubts at all.

—W. Winwood Reade

DUTY

743. In the time we have it is surely our duty to do all the good we can to all the people we can in all the ways we can.

—William Barclay

744. Observed duties maintain our credit, but secret duties maintain our life.

—John Flavel

745. A duty which becomes a desire will ultimately become a delight.

—George Gritter

746. Duty is the sublimest word in our language. Do your duty in all things. . . . You cannot do more; you should never wish to do less. —Robert E. Lee

747. Let us have faith that right makes might, and in that faith let us to the end dare to do our duty as we understand it.

—Abraham Lincoln

748. No one does his duty unless he does his best. —Billy Sunday

749. I slept and dreamed that life was
beauty;
I woke and found that life was duty.

EASTER

750. Tomb, thou shalt not hold Him
      longer;
Death is strong but Life is stronger;
Stronger than the dark, the light;
Stronger than the wrong, the right;
Faith and Hope triumphant say
Christ will rise on Easter Day.
      —**Phillips Brooks**

751. Easter is not a passport to another world. It is a quality of perception for this one.   —**W. P. Lemon**

752. Our Lord has written the promise of resurrection, not in books alone, but in every leaf of springtime.   —**Martin Luther**

753. The stars wailed when the reed was
      born,
And heaven wept at the birth of
      the thorn;
Joy was pluckt like a flower torn,
For Time foreshadowed Good
      Friday morn

But the stars laughed like children
      free
And heaven was hung with the
      rainbow's glee
When at Easter Sunday, so fair to
      see,
Time bowed before Eternity.
      —**Fiona MacLeod**

754. The resurrection never becomes a fact of experience until the risen Lord lives in the heart of the believer.
      —**Peter Marshall**

755. Jesus was not the only one to rise from the dead. Lazarus did. Dorcas did. But Jesus rose from the dead never to die again.
      —**Ezhamkulam Samkutty**

756. Easter is the New Year's Day of the soul.   —**A. B. Simpson**

757. "The door is closed," I heard a
      woman say
Concerning one for whom the
      earthly way
Had ended and the land of
      shoreless light
Was habitation, glorious and
      bright.

Then I remembered that a hillside
      tomb
Opened as soundlessly as lilies
      bloom.
O loving Father, help our hearts to
      see
The door is open, open timelessly!
      —**Grace V. Watkins**

758. Love's redeeming work is done.
Fought the fight, the battle won.
Death in vain forbids him rise
Christ has opened paradise.
      —**Charles Wesley**

759. We stood not by the empty tomb,
Where late the sacred body lay,
Nor sat within the Upper Room,
Nor met with Thee in open way.
But we believe what the angel said,
"Why seek the living among the
      dead?"

ECONOMICS

760. The trouble with State [welfare] money is that experience shows it is often a bridge to nowhere.   —**Enoch Powell**

761. The best way for the government to raise revenues is to tax beauty. Let every lady rate her own charms and the tax will be cheerfully paid and very productive.
      —**Dean Swift**

762. It may be true that most people can't stand prosperity, but it is also true that most people don't have to.

763. Walter Heller's definition of an economist, as a man who married Elizabeth Taylor for her money, has a bruising quality about it today that did not exist when it was spoken in whimsey

(see also: Capitalism; Communism; Politics and Government; Socialism)

EDUCATION

764. We have succeeded so completely in expelling particularistic religious beliefs from modern schooling and in providing a "dispassionate," "objective," "scientific," "value-free" education, that our success is becoming our demise. For when put into practice, dispassionate value-freedom comes to mean that no institution is worth defending and no idea is of ultimate significance. With no conception of things sacred, we can communicate neither a social vision nor a sense of purpose to our youth.
— **Chanan Alexander**

765. Many people say that education is neutral; we need only facts. . . . But the Bible teaches this: "From him and through him and to him are all things" (Romans 11:36). — **William H. Bell**

766. I am incurably convinced that the object of opening the mind, as of opening the mouth, is to shut it again on something solid. — **G. K. Chesterton**

767. The problems are not in our tools, fellow teachers, but in ourselves. The task is to ascertain how we should order our desires. Until we do that, we will be like wanton schoolboys let loose in a toolshed. We'll only make mischief.
— **Drew Christiansen**

768. [Much of our modern education has created a society that] makes machines which act like men and produces men who act like machines. — **Erich Fromm**

769. Education without [Christian] values, as useful as it is, seems rather to make man a more clever devil. — **C. S. Lewis**

770. The human personality is to be enlightened, not controlled by education.
— **Arthur Lynip**

771. Having bent over backwards to separate church and state in lower schools and maintain academic freedom in higher education, modern man has filled the value-vacuum with secular religion. Its creed is: man is God; reason is truth; values are relative; and means are ends.
— **David L. McKenna**

772. Apathy is decried on all sides, no less by liberals than by conservatives, but apathy is the logical result of an educational practice which finds no emotion appropriate enough to encourage.
— **John A. Miles, Jr.**

773. A general state education is a mere contrivance for moulding people to be exactly like one another; and as the mould in which it casts them is that which pleases the predominant power in the government, it establishes a despotism over the mind, leading by natural tendency to one over the body. — **John Stuart Mill**

774. Voluntary school prayer was constitutionally practiced (in the United States) for 171 years before the two tragic U.S. Supreme Court decisions. Too much emphasis is placed on the first clause of the First Amendment: "Congress shall make no law establishing a religion," and too little on the second: "or prohibit the free exercise thereof." — **Mrs. Bennett G. Miller**

775. Either the university of the future will take hold of the connections between knowledge and human values, or it will sink quietly and indistinguishably into the noncommittal moral stupor of the rest of the knowledge industry.

—Charles Muscatine

776. In many countries today . . . the notion that the Christian faith can have or ought to have any reasonable part in general education . . . is looked upon as ridiculous. —Elton Trueblood

777. Harvard University was founded in 1636 with the training of ministers as its main objective. Until 1700 more than half of its graduates went into the Christian ministry.

(see also: Christian Education)

ENVY

778. Envy does not so much want the things for itself; it merely wants to take them away from the other person. The Stoics defined it as "grief at someone else's good." . . . It is the quality, not so much of the jealous, but rather of the embittered mind. —William Barclay

779. There is . . . only one way to stop covetousness and the destruction of body and soul that spring from it, and that is to want God so much that we can't be bothered with inordinate wants for anything else. —Joy Davidman

780. Every time you turn green with envy you are ripe for trouble.

ERROR

781. It is human to err, it is devilish to remain willfully in error. —Augustine

782. False doctrine does not necessarily make the man a heretic, but an evil heart can make any doctrine heretical.

—Samuel Taylor Coleridge

(see also: Folly)

ETHICS

783. Whenever men abandon their ethics they cease to make sense regardless of their professional degrees and licenses. Perhaps this is why psychiatry is sometimes called "the study of the id by the odd."

—James Dobson

784. Most people are willing to take the Sermon on the Mount as a flag to sail under, but few will use it as a rudder by which to steer. —Oliver Wendell Holmes

785. The Rotary "four-way test" asks the following questions: Is it the truth? Is it fair to all concerned? Will it build good will and friendship? Will it benefit all concerned?

(see also: Interpersonal Relations)

EVANGELISM

786. If we really wish to help and to save men our attitude must not be that of condemnation but that of pleading; our accent must not be that of criticism but of compassion. —William Barclay

787. The possession of the good news of the gospel involves the obligation to share it. —William Barclay

788. I care not where I go, or how I live, or what I endure, so that I may save souls. When I sleep I dream of them; when I awake they are first in my thoughts. . . . No amount of scholastic attainment, of able and profound exposition, of brilliant and stirring eloquence can atone for the absence of a deep, impassioned sympathetic love for human souls.   —David Brainerd

789. Dost thou see a soul with the image of God in him? Love him, love him. Say to thyself, "This man and I must go to heaven together someday."   —John Bunyan

790. We are not to make men converts of our opinions. But we are to make them disciples of Jesus.   —Oswald Chambers

791. If we all become more Christlike, we shall not need any other bait.

—Frank Crossley

792. Jesus said, "Go," but the church through selfishness and indifference has refused to obey. We try to substitute "write," "send," or "give," for "go." We try to salve our conscience by turning over the task of "going" to someone else and giving languidly for their support. Of course, we must send where we cannot go. But because we can't go across the world does not excuse us for refusing to go across the street.   —R. C. Foster

793.   Give me a vision that I may
            respond
      In town, or country, or farther
            beyond;
      Yes, point out the needs of faltering
            men
      That I may lead them to Jesus
            again.
      Show me the city where Satan runs
            wild
      That I may go there to save the
            defiled,
      Show me a valley that's reeking
            with sin
      Then prod me to go to call them
            within,
      Or point out to me a far away land
      That I may sail there to heed Thy
            command;

Give me a vision that I may
      respond
In town or country or farther
      beyond.

—Wally Gardner

794. Apparently it did not occur to the earliest Christians that instructions in techniques of evangelism were necessary. They had all received the good news of salvation in Christ . . . and they went about the business of telling non-Christians about God's mighty act.   —John Greenlee

795. The beginning of compromise in the message occurs when the emphasis is shifted from a concern for the purity of the message to a concern for how the message is received.   —Charles A. Kempf

796. We shall have all eternity in which to celebrate our victories, but we have only one swift hour before the sunset in which to win them.   —Robert Moffat

797. There is not the slightest hint in the New Testament that evangelism is the special prerogative or responsibility of office bearers. We are to be burdened for men's souls not because any office requires it of us but because we are Christians.

—Ian H. Murray

798. People can only be loved into the kingdom.   —J. B. Phillips

799. Upon the primitive evangelism of the early church God set His seal confirming it with signs following and adding to the church daily so that the most rapid and far-reaching results ever known to history were achieved within one generation. With none of our modern facilities of transit and publication . . . the gospel flew from lip to lip until it touched the bounds of the Roman Empire. Within one century such one-by-one evangelism shook paganism to

its center and the priests of false faith saw with dismay their idol shrines forsaken.
—A. T. Pierson

800. Evangelism is not a professional job for a few trained men, but is instead the unrelenting responsibility of every person who belongs, even in the most modest way, to the company of Jesus. —Elton Trueblood

801. If what we win them with is what we win them to, and I suspect this is largely true, then methods are profoundly important and the medium is indeed the message. —Albert M. Wells, Jr.

802. Unless and until . . . the future of the world becomes more important than the future of the church, the church has no future. —Ralph Winters

803. Give us a watchword for the hour,
A thrilling word, a word of power,
A battle cry, a flaming breath,
A call to conquest or to death,
A word to rouse the church from rest,
To heed the Master's high behest!
The Word is given, you host arise!
The watchword is . . . evangelize.

804. The early disciples were fishers of men—while modern disciples are often little more than aquarium keepers.

(see also: Christian Witness)

EVIL

805. All that is necessary for the triumph of evil is that good men do nothing.
—Edmund Burke

806. We cannot do evil to others without doing it to ourselves.
—Joseph F. E. Desmahis

807. The real problem is in the hearts and minds of men. It is not a problem of

physics but of ethics. It is easier to denature plutonium than to denature the evil spirit of man. —Albert Einstein

(see also: Carnality; Sin)

EVIL, PROBLEM OF

(see: Suffering)

EVOLUTION

808. Creationists do not deny that humans and animals share many characteristics in common, but similarity does not prove animal ancestry for humans. It demonstrates only a common Creator.
—John G. Balyo

809. If my mental processes are determined wholly by the motions of atoms in my brain, I have no reason to suppose that my beliefs are true . . . and hence I have no reason for supposing my brain to be composed of atoms. —J. B. S. Haldane

810. If someone can propose a view of evolution that would be consistent with the Biblical demands that man is created in the image of God, that the sexes appeared separately . . . that there was a unique first human individual, Adam, who was punished for his disobedience and who experienced physical death because of his sin, then we might calmly and dispassionately consider that idea in the light of God's Word. To date, however, I have not seen a satisfactory evolutionary view for the origin of man. —Davis Young

811. Once I was a tadpole, grubbing in the mire,
Till I became ambitious and started to aspire,
I rubbed my tail so very hard against a sunken log,

65

It disappeared completely, and I
    became a frog.

I struggled from my puddle and
    jumped upon the land,
And the feeling deep within me
    was glorious and grand;
It made me kind of frisky, so I
    hopped around a tree
Till I landed in the branches as
    happy as could be.

And there I spent some aeons,
    evoluting without fail,
Till I became a monkey and grew
    another tail.
But still I had ambitions, as the
    aeons quickly sped;
I climbed down from the tree and
    walked the earth instead.

My tail got tired with trailing on
    the hard earth everyday.
And twice within my "process"
    that appendage passed away;
Once again I evoluted, and believe
    it, if you can,
I awoke one summer morning and
    found myself a man!

Now, you tadpoles in the mire, just
    think what you may be,
If you'll only in your puddles start
    to climb the family tree;
I'm the genus homo "finished," for
    all the world to see,
For when I told my story I was
    given a Ph.D.

FAILURE

812. I have no formula for success, but I
have a sure one for failure. Try to please
everyone.   **—Rex Dorn**

813. Failure is usually the line of least
persistence.   **—Wilfred Beaver**

814. Those who try and fail are much
wiser than those who never try for fear of
failure.   **—Andre Bustanoby**

815. We must somehow get comfortable
with the reality of periodic failure. That
does not mean we should break out the
pointed hats and throw a party when we
see it coming. But there is no reason to
schedule a wake, either. Like a trip to the
dentist, the thought of occasional reverses
may not make us tingle with joyful anticipation, but then again, it's not the end of
the world.   **—Sam Collins**

816. The wisest person is not the one
who has the fewest failures, but the one
who turns failures to best account.
      —Richard R. Grant

817. To falter before the forces of life
when the power of God is available is unfortunate and above all unnecessary.
      —E. Ray Jones

818. A man may fall many times but he
won't be a failure until he says that someone pushed him.   **—Elmer G. Letterman**

819. He is foolish to blame the sea who
shipwrecked twice.   **—Publilius Syrus**

820. Failure is not sweet, but it need not
be bitter.

821. In every failure is the seed of success.

822. The following chronology shows
how Abraham Lincoln refused to give up,
even in the midst of what appeared to be
continuous failure:
    1831 failed in business
    1832 defeated for state legislature
    1833 failed in business again
    1835 sweetheart died

1836 had nervous breakdown
1838 defeated for speaker
1840 defeated for elector
1843 defeated for Congress
1848 defeated for Congress
1855 defeated for Senate
1856 defeated for vice-president
1858 defeated for Senate
1860 ELECTED PRESIDENT

823. A mistake is not a failure but evidence that someone tried to do something.

FAITH

824. Seek not to understand that thou mayest believe, but believe that thou mayest understand. —**Augustine**

825. Faith is to believe what we do not see, and the reward of this faith is to see what we believe. —**Augustine**

826. It is of the very essence of faith that we should believe that what Jesus says is true. So often we have a kind of vague, wistful longing that the promises of Jesus should be true. The only way really to enter into them is to believe them with the clutching intensity of a drowning man.
—**William Barclay**

827. For John, belief means the conviction of the mind that Jesus is the Son of God, the trust of the heart that everything he says is true and the basing of every action on the unshakable assurance that we must take him at his word. When we do that we stop existing and begin living.
—**William Barclay**

828. A Christian is a person who bets his eternal life on Jesus Christ.
—**Stephen Board**

829. So I go on, not knowing
—I would not, if I might—

I would rather walk in the dark
    with God
Than go alone in the light;
I would rather walk with Him by
    faith
Than walk alone by sight.
—**Mary Gardner Brainard**

830. Faith is putting all your eggs in God's basket, then counting your blessings before they hatch. —**Ramona C. Carroll**

831. Faith never knows where it is being led, but it loves and knows the One who is leading. —**Oswald Chambers**

832. Faith is the daring of the soul to go farther than it can see.
—**William Newton Clark**

833. Holy affections are not heat without light, but ever more arise from some information in understanding, some spiritual instruction that the mind receives, some light or actual knowledge.
—**Jonathan Edwards**

834. Faith is not a storm cellar to which men and women can flee for refuge from the storms of life. It is, instead, an inner force that gives them the strength to face those storms and their consequences with serenity of spirit. —**Sam J. Ervin, Jr.**

835. Faith can gain a person everything, but it sometimes costs that person everything. Still, the loss is only earthly while the gain is heavenly. —**John M. Falkenberg**

836. Christian faith is more than a dogma. It does not just say, "I believe," but says, "I believe and, therefore, I obey!"
—**Leighton Ford**

837. The fable of the mother bear who told her cub, "Shut up and walk!" when he wanted to know which foot to put forward

first is a perfect illustration. . . . Faith in Jesus doesn't wait until it understands; in that case it wouldn't be faith. . . . Real faith is objective, we are taken up with Christ.
—Vance Havner

838. Biblical faith is trusting in God, and the power of faith is putting the matter in God's hands so that He is able to do what He wants to do in that situation.
—Maurice R. Irvin

839. Faith is kind of like jumping out of an airplane at ten thousand feet. If God doesn't catch you, you splatter. But how do you know whether or not He is going to catch you unless you jump out?
—Ann Kiemel

840. Faith is the art of holding on to things your reason has once accepted, in spite of your changing moods.
—C. S. Lewis

841. Faith enables persons to be persons because it lets God be God.
—Carter Lindberg

842. Without Christ, not one step; with Him, anywhere!   —David Livingstone

843. Forgive us our lack of faith, lest ulcers become our badge of disbelief.
—Peter Marshall

844. Believing is as much an integral factor in man as are eating and sleeping. He neither gains nor loses faith; he merely changes the object of it. . . . Man is simply an inveterate, incurable, inevitable believer.   —Samuel Miller

845. I must believe that God is good and that He cares for me. How do I know? Calvary!   —Forrest Nash

846. To believe in God is to know that all the rules will be fair and that there will be wonderful surprises.   —Newbetti

847. The heart has its reasons that reason does not know.   —Blaise Pascal

848. It was . . . not right that Christ should appear in a manner manifestly divine and absolutely capable of convincing all men, but neither was it right that His coming should be so hidden that He could not be recognized by those who sincerely sought Him. He wished to make Himself perfectly recognizable to them. Thus wishing to appear openly to those who seek Him with all their heart and hidden from those who shun Him with all their heart, He has qualified our knowledge of Him by giving signs which can be seen by those who seek Him and not by those who do not.   —Blaise Pascal

849. An agnostic found himself in trouble, and a friend suggested he pray. "How can I pray when I do not know whether or not there is a God?" he asked. "If you are lost in the forest," his friend replied, "you do not wait until you find someone before shouting for help."   —Dan Plies

850. True faith drops its letter in the post office box and lets it go. Distrust holds on to a corner of it and wonders that the answer never comes.   —A. B. Simpson

851. If we cannot believe God when circumstances seem to be against us, we do not believe Him at all.
—Charles H. Spurgeon

852. Passive faith—the fleeting kind that comes and goes in flashes, and during emotional highs and lows—that kind of faith will not save the soul. Saving faith is the kind born out of deep contrition for sin; out of a heart that has repudiated all iniquity and besetting sins; out of a heart totally and daily surrendered to the Lordship of Christ—only that kind of faith guarantees grace.   —David Wilkerson

853. Faith is not a hothouse plant that must be shielded from wind and rain, so delicate that it has to be protected, but is like the sturdy oak which becomes stronger with every wind that blows upon it. An easy time weakens faith, while strong trials strengthen it.
—**Katherine Workman**

854. To walk by faith, not by sight, means that we discipline our actions not by what we see, but by what we believe.

855. For the believer, there is no question; for the non-believer, there is no answer.

856. Faith sees the invisible, believes the incredible and receives the impossible.

(see also: Trusting God)

FAITHFULNESS

857. It may not be given to every man to enter into the fullness of the promises of God, but it is given to him to live with such fidelity and service that he will bring nearer the day when others will enter into it.
—**William Barclay**

858. A little thing is a little thing, but faithfulness in a little thing becomes a great thing.
—**Plato**

859. The final criterion that will be used by God to judge us is not success but faithfulness.

860. Just an ordinary member
Of the church, I heard him say,
But you'd always find him present
Even on a rainy day.

He had a hearty handclasp
For the stranger in the aisle,
And a friend who was in trouble
Found the sunshine of his smile.

He always paid up promptly
And tried to do his share
In all the ordinary tasks
For which some have no care.

His talents were not many,
But his love for God was true;
His prayers were not in public
But he prayed for me and you.

An ordinary member?
I think that I would say
He was extra-ordinary
In a humble sort of way.

(see also: Perseverance)

THE FAMILY

861. A true family consists of two or more people who care unconditionally for one another and share in the collective health and security of the unit as well as in supporting and helping each member to secure his or her full potential and achieve personal fulfillment.   —**Robert Couchman**

862. The problems of America are the family problems multiplied a million-fold.
—**Dwight D. Eisenhower**

863. There has emerged no institution that can replace the family in turning children into civilized human beings or in retrieving the wreckage of our current disorder.   —**George Gilder**

864. There is a crisis in America as crucial as civil rights, dangerous as bureaucracy, insidious as Communism, unpredictable as politics, uncontrollable as inflation. It is the erosion of the home.
—**Curtis Jones**

865. The ancient trinity of father, mother and child has survived more vicissitudes than any other human relationship. In the Gotterdammerung which

overwise science and overfoolish states-
manship are preparing for us, the last man
will spend his last hours searching for his
wife and child. **—Ralph Linton**

866. American families don't seem to
live in the same place. They merely sleep
in the same house. **—Martin Niemoller**

867. If things go well with the family, life
is worth living; when the family falters, life
falls apart. **—Michael Novak**

868. The family is the basic social unit of
our human world; it is a microcosm of the
larger society. In it we see the fundamental
patterns of every human interaction. . . .
The family setting provides the training
ground for learning to live in the larger
world. **—Margaret Sawin**

869. A church within a church, a republic within a republic, a world within a
world, is spelled in four letters, HOME. If
things go right there, they go right everywhere. The doorsill of the dwelling house
is the foundation of the Church and the
State. **—Thomas DeWitt Talmage**

870. Loving relationships are a family's
best protection against the challenges of
the world. **—Bernie Wiebe**

(see also: Christian Home; Marriage;
Parenthood)

FASTING

871. All men who have had spiritual
power to prevail with God and man have
been men who learned to sternly deny
themselves and keep their bodies under.
—Samuel Brengle

872. Fasting alone accomplishes little except perhaps to cause us to eat more at the
next meal. Prayer by itself is often limited

or blocked in some way. But prayer and
fasting together produce miracles.
—Marjorie Cooney

873. Your hunger will serve as a call to
prayer. It will remind you of your physical
life, but your abstinence in the name of
God will declare your avowed belief in the
supremacy of the spiritual over the physical.

FATE

874. Fate is not the ruler, but the servant
of Providence. **—Edward G. Bulwer-Lytton**

875. I do not believe in that word Fate. It
is the refuge of every self-confessed failure.
—Andrew Soutar

FATHERHOOD

876. As the substitute father for hundreds of youths over the past thirteen
years, I have yet to encounter a young person in trouble whose difficulty could not
be traced to the lack of a strong father-
image in the home. **—Paul Anderson**

877. A careful man I want to be,
A little fellow follows me;
I do not dare to go astray,
For fear he'll go the self-same way.
I cannot once escape his eyes;
Whatever he sees me do, he tries;
Like me, he says he wants to be—
That little chap who follows me.
He thinks that I am big and fine,
He believes in every word of mine;
The base in me he does not see—
The little chap who follows me.
I must remember as I go
Through summer sun and winter
    snow,
I'm building for the years to be—
That little chap who follows me.

O Lord, if I his guide must be,
O let the little children see
A teacher leaning hard on Thee.
—Marvin Baarman

878. We can never afford to forget that we teach our children to call God father, and the only conception of fatherhood that they can have is the conception which we give them. Human fatherhood should be moulded and modelled on the pattern of the fatherhood of God. It is the tremendous duty of the human father to be as good a father as God. —William Barclay

879. When the father exercises a leadership role in family worship, the other roles or expectations seem to fall into place.
—Bill and Pat Bouchillon

880. Ten Commandments for Fathers:
1. A father should strive to be a whole person.
2. A father should love his children.
3. A father should love his wife.
4. A father should be creative.
5. A father should raise his children to leave him.
6. A father should spend time with his children.
7. A father should communicate with his children.
8. A father should discipline his children properly.
9. A father should develop a sense of humor.
10. A father should enjoy being a father.
—Harry James Cargas

881. Father is God's special representative in the home. As the family's divinely appointed priest and intercessor he is the spiritual leader. He is responsible for daily intercession for the mother and each individual child. He is also responsible for beginning and maintaining the domestic altar each day, and for adequate Christian education of mother and children.
—Gordon Chilvers

882. While I don't minimize the vital role played by a mother, I believe a successful family begins with her husband.
—James Dobson

883. Each evening that I am home I oversee their bedtime preparations—brushing the teeth, administering baths, putting on Ryan's pajamas, saying prayers, and hauling four to six glasses of water to each little procrastinator. —James Dobson

884. To the child, the father is God's representative; this makes the father's task sacred and serious. We fathers are to deal with our children as God deals with us.
—John Drescher

885. Could I turn back the time machine, I would double the attention I gave my children and go to fewer meetings.
—J. D. Eppinga

886. I see, Lord, from hence, that my father's piety cannot be entailed; that is bad news for me. But I see also that actual impiety is not always hereditary; that is good news for my son. —Thomas Fuller

887. If God's character is to be understood in terms of my life [as a father], what does my child think of God? —Lee Haines

888. A *Newsweek* article reported that middle class American fathers spend an average of fifteen to twenty minutes per day with their children. In many cases even if the fathers are present physically, they are absent relationally. We need men who will place their families as the number one priority in their lives. Men who

will give as much of themselves to their children as they do to their work.

—James A. Harnish

889. We have learned from Freud and others about those distortions in character and errors in thought which result from a man's early conflicts with his father. Far the most important thing we can know about George MacDonald is that his whole life illustrates the opposite process. An almost perfect relationship with his father was the earthly root of all his wisdom. From his own father, he said, he first learned that Fatherhood must be at the core of the universe. He was thus prepared in an unusual way to teach that religion in which the relation of the Father and the Son is of all relations the most central.

—C. S. Lewis

890. He that will have his son have a respect for him and his orders, must himself have a great reverence for his son.

—John Locke

891. To get his goodnight kiss he stood
Beside my chair one night
And raised an eager face to me,
A face with love alight.

And as I gathered in my arms
The son God gave to me,
I thanked the lad for being good,
And hoped he'd always be.

His little arms crept round my neck,
And then I heard him say
Four simple words I can't forget—
Four words that made me pray.

They turned a mirror on my soul,
On secrets no one knew,
They startled me, I hear them yet:
He said, "I'll be like you."

—Herbert Parker

892. What a father says to his children is not heard by the world, but it will be heard by posterity.

—Jean Paul Richter

893. A child is not likely to find a father in God unless he finds something of God in his father.

—Austin L. Sorensen

894. Every father is the world's best father to his children unless he works hard not to be.

—E. Carl Wilson

895. A man never knows how to be a son until he becomes a father. . . . By the time a man realizes that maybe his father was right, he usually has a son who thinks he's wrong.

896. What shall you give to one small boy?
A glamorous game, a tinseled toy,
A fancy knife, a puzzle pack,
A train that runs on a curving track,
A picture book, a real live pet?

No! There's plenty of time for such things yet.
Give him a day for his very own.
Just one small boy and his dad alone.
A walk in the woods, a romp in the park,
A fishing trip from dawn to dark.

Give him the finest gift you can—
The companionship of a grownup man.
Games are outgrown, and toys decay,
But he'll never forget the gift of a day!

897. There are a great many fathers who tie up their hound dog at night and let their boy run loose.

898. It is easier to build boys, than to mend men.

(see also: Parenthood)

FEAR

899. Men who fear God face life fearlessly. Men who do not fear God end up fearing everything.   —Richard Halverson

900. It is only the fear of God that can deliver us from the fear of man.

—John Witherspoon

901. Fear is the dark room where negatives are developed.

(see also: Anxiety; Peace of Mind)

FEELINGS

902. Human nature, if it is healthy, demands excitement; and if it does not obtain its thrilling excitement in the right way, it will seek it in the wrong. God never makes bloodless stoics; He makes passionate saints.   —Oswald Chambers

903. No natural feelings are high or low, holy or unholy, in themselves. They are all holy when God's hand is on the rein. They all go bad when they . . . make themselves into false gods.   —C. S. Lewis

904. The man who screams at a football game but is distressed when he hears of a sinner weeping at the cross and murmurs about the dangers of emotionalism, hardly merits intelligent respect. —W. E. Sangster

FOLLY

905. Young men think old men are fools; but old men *know* young men are fools.
—George Chapman

906. Hate and despise all human glory, for it is nothing else but human folly. It is

the greatest snare and the greatest betrayer that you can possibly admit into your heart.   —William Law

907. Lustful ambition breeds the fools who bid for counterfeit kingdoms. From such preserve us, Good Lord.
—Richard John Neuhaus

908. Nothing is so safe as an abstract idea that shelters me from reality, but nothing is so dangerous.   —Warren W. Wiersbe

909. Some men die by shrapnel,
And some go down in flames;
But most men perish inch by inch
Who play at little games.

910. Man is pretty much a fool—
When it's hot he wants it cool,
When it's cool he wants it hot,
Always wanting what it's not.

FORGIVENESS

911. When a person forgives another, he is promising to do three things about the intended wrongdoing: not to use it against the wrongdoer in the future; not to talk about it to others; and not to dwell on it himself.   —Jay Adams

912. In forgiveness you bear your own anger and wrath at the sin of another, voluntarily accepting responsibility for the hurt he has inflicted upon you.
—David Augsburger

913. Love can go no further than to think more of the heartbreak of the man who wronged it than of the hurt that it itself has received.   —William Barclay

914. Forgiveness is never a case of saying: "It's all right; it doesn't matter." . . . There is nothing which brings a man to his senses with such arresting violence as to see the effect of his sin on someone who loves him in this world, or on God who loves him for ever, and to say to himself: "It cost *that* to forgive my sin." Where there is forgiveness someone must be crucified on a cross. **—William Barclay**

915. Real forgiveness requires a resolution of all feelings to the point of equal honor for both parties. Both must see each other as worthy and good. They must part with equal dignity. True forgiveness leaves the offender with as much innocence as the offended. **—Richard Hanson**

916. Force may subdue, but love gains; and he that forgives first wins the laurel. **—William Penn**

917. Let us go to Calvary to learn how we may be forgiven. And then let us linger there to learn how to forgive. **—Charles H. Spurgeon**

918. A forgiveness which bypasses the need for repentance issues not from love but from sentimentality. **—John R. W. Stott**

919. Forgiveness is the fragrance the violet sheds on the heel that has crushed it. **—Mark Twain**

920. Only God can throw the first stone—but He doesn't. He offers forgiveness and so should we. **—Albert M. Wells, Jr.**

921. To have an unforgiving spirit is to burn a bridge over which you may someday want to travel.

922. One day General James Oglethorpe said to John Wesley, "I never forgive." Wesley replied. "Then I hope, Sir, that you never sin."

923. Blessed is he who forgives without remembering and who receives forgiveness without forgetting.

FREEDOM

924. Free men are not equal and equal men are not free. **—Thomas J. Anderson**

925. The secret of happiness is freedom and the secret of freedom is courage. **—Louis Brandeis**

926. It is ordained in the eternal constitution of things that men of intemperate minds cannot be free. Their passions forge their fetters. **—Edmund Burke**

927. My first act of freedom will be to believe in freedom. **—William James**

928. We have traded the freedom of the robin for the freedom of the canary. The canary is free from hunger. His food is put in his cage every day. He's free from danger. The cat can't get at him. The robin, however, must risk his life to get his food. He doesn't know where his next meal is coming from. **—Walter Judd**

929. Those who deny freedom to others deserve it not for themselves. **—Abraham Lincoln**

930. Fetters for our dear sake,
Is true freedom but to break
And, with leathern hearts, forget
That we owe mankind a debt?

No! True Freedom is to share
All the chains our brothers wear,
And, with heart and hand, to be
Earnest to make others free! **—James Russell Lowell**

931. If a nation values anything more than freedom, it will lose its freedom; and the irony of it is that if it is comfort or money that it values more, it will lose that too. **—Somerset Maugham**

932. The liberty of the individual must be thus far limited; he must not make himself a nuisance to other people.
—John Stuart Mill

933. Give me the liberty to know, to think, to believe, and to utter freely, according to conscience, above all liberties.
—John Milton

934. When we are no longer willing to die for the freedom of others, we shall no longer merit freedom for ourselves.
—John Warwick Montgomery

935. Law without liberty is tyranny. Liberty without law is license. Liberty under the law is freedom.   —William Penn

936. It sometimes costs more to preserve freedom than it does to achieve it in the first place.   —Eldon Rudd

937. I may not agree with a word you say, but I shall defend unto my death your right to say it.   —Voltaire

938. The one thing you can't have unless you give it to others is liberty.
—William Allen White

939. The history of liberty is a history of the limitation of government power, not the increase of it. When we resist, therefore, the concentration of power, we are resisting the process of death, because concentration of power is what always precedes the destruction of human liberties.
—Woodrow Wilson

940. He is the best friend to American liberty who is most sincere and active in promoting true and undefiled religion, and who sets himself with the greatest firmness to bear down profanity and immorality of every kind.   —John Witherspoon

941. Total freedom is total emptiness.

(see also: Christian Freedom; Liberty; Memorial Day Theme; The Nation)

FREE WILL

942. When God made us in His own image, He gave us a mind that we may know, a will that we may decide, and a heart that we may desire and love. What great potential for good, but also what tremendous capacity for evil.
—George Gritter

943. If a man wants God to leave him alone, that is what will happen—forever.
—M. P. Horban

944. All theory is against the freedom of the will, all experience for it.
—Samuel Johnson

945. It should be a cheering thought that before God every man is what he wills to be.   —A. W. Tozer

FRIENDSHIP

946. What a pity that so many people are living with so few friends when the world is full of lonesome strangers who would give anything just to be somebody's friend.
—Milo L. Arnold

947. Oh, the comfort, the inexpressible comfort of feeling safe with a person, having neither to weigh thoughts, nor measure words, but pouring them all out, just as they are, chaff and grain together, certain that a faithful hand will take and sift them, keep what is worth keeping, and with a breath of kindness blow the rest away.   —Dinah Maria Mulock Craik

948. We take care of our health, we lay up money, we make our roof tight and our clothing sufficient, but who provides wisely that he shall not be wanting in the best property of all—friends?

—Ralph Waldo Emerson

949. Go oft to the house of thy friend, for weeds choke the unused path.

—Ralph Waldo Emerson

950. 'Tis the human touch in the world
that counts—
The touch of your hand and mine—
Which means far more to the
sinking heart
Than shelter or bread or wine.
For shelter is gone when the night
is o'er,
And bread lasts only a day.
But the touch of the hand and the
sound of the voice
Live on in the soul alway.

—Spencer M. Free

951. He will never have true friends who is afraid of making enemies.

—William Hazlitt

952. Friendship is the pleasing game of interchanging praise.

—Oliver Wendell Holmes

953. Five years from now you will be pretty much the same as you are today except for two things: the books you read and the people you get close to.

—Charles Jones

954. Friendship may exist between a man and a woman, quite apart from any influence of sex. Yet a woman always looks upon a man as a man, and so a man regards a woman. This intimacy [friendship] is neither pure friendship nor pure love. It is a sentiment which stands alone.

—Jean de La Bruyère

955. True friends don't spend time gazing into each other's eyes. They may show great tenderness toward each other, but they *face in the same direction*—toward common projects, interests, goals—above all, toward a common Lord.   —C. S. Lewis

956. Today a man discovered gold and
fame;
Another flew the stormy seas;
Another saw an unarmed world
aflame;
One found the germ of a disease.
But what high fates my path attend:
For I—today I found a friend.

—Helen Barker Parker

957. Those who cannot give friendship will rarely receive it and never hold it.

—Dagobert D. Runes

958. Against a foe I can myself defend,
But heaven protect me from a
blundering friend.

—D. W. Thompson

959. Be courteous to all, but intimate with few; and let those few be well tried before you give them your confidence.

—George Washington

960. A real friend is one who helps us to think our best thoughts, do our noblest deeds, and be our finest selves.

961. To have a good friend is one of the highest delights of life; to *be* a good friend is one of the noblest and most difficult undertakings.

(see also: Interpersonal Relations)

FULFILLMENT

962. O soul, He only who created thee can satisfy thee. If thou ask for anything else, it is thy misfortune, for He alone who made thee in His image can satisfy thee.

—Augustine

963. If [His presence] is all that God gives me, I am satisfied, but if all that He gave me was the [whole] world, I would not be satisfied. —Jerimiah Burroughs

964. Everyone does have needs which must be met, and there is nothing wrong in having them met. God's Word, however, declares in the life of Christ that seeking to have one's needs met is a disastrous principle by which to set life's priorities and draw its bargains. J. Dean Dykstra

965. Hearts that are open to the love that is God, feel loved in loving and served in serving. —Edward Gloeggler

966. When you have Christ you are rich and have enough. —Thomas à Kempis

967. Fulfillment is not a goal to pursue. It is a by-product of our completeness. —Malcolm Nygren

968. Fulfillment doesn't automatically happen as a result of linking up with the "right" person, job, or even ministry. Fulfillment . . . happens as a result of being in God's will. —Marilyn Olson

969. God is the whole reason we live, and knowing Him is to be our goal, not social approval or glandular satisfaction. He knows our needs; He has sent us a Comforter. And a life developed cheerfully and fully in the way God intended will bring the rewards that only God can give. —Barbara Sroka

970. It is in loving, not in being loved, the heart is blessed;
It is in giving, not in seeking gifts, we find our quest.
Whatever be your longing or your need, that give—
So shall your soul be fed, and you indeed shall live.

971. Wealth lies not in the extent of possessions, but in the fewness of wants.

(see also: Contentment)

THE FUTURE

972. If you do not think about the future, you cannot have one. —John Galsworthy

973. The future is as bright as the promises of God. —Adoniram Judson

974. We should all be concerned about the future because we will have to spend the rest of our lives there. —C. F. Kettering

975. The future is not something we enter. The future is something we create. —Leonard I. Sweet

(see also: The New Year)

GAMBLING

976. Gambling is incompatible with the Christian view of God, with the Christian responsibility to love our fellowmen, with the Christian understanding of stewardship and with a Christian view of the responsible use of time and energy. —John V. Dahms

977. Gambling is robbery by mutual consent. —C. M. Ward

978. Overheard in Las Vegas: I came here in a $25,000 Cadillac. Now I'm going home in a $75,000 bus.

979. People who can afford to gamble don't need money, and those who need money can't afford to gamble.

GENEROSITY

(see: Charity; Giving; Stewardship)

GIVING

980. Give according to your means, or God will make your means according to your giving.   —John Hall

981. "Go break to the needy sweet
        charity's bread;
For giving is living," the angel said.
"And must I be giving again and
        again?"
My peevish and pitiless answer ran.
"Oh, no," said the angel, piercing
        me through.
"Just give till the Master stops
        giving to you."

982. It's not what you'd do with a
        million
If riches should e'er be your lot,
But what are you doing at present
        With the dollar and quarter
        you've got?

983. All we can hold in our cold dead hands is what we have given away.

(see also: Charity; Love; Money; Service; Stewardship)

GLUTTONY

984. Gluttony is an emotional escape, a sign that something is eating us.
        —Peter De Vries

985. There is something incongruous about asking God to bless buttered rolls and pecan pie at 10:30 P.M. when none of us needs them.   —LaVerna Klippenstein

986. The essence of gluttony is not the consumption of enormous quantities of food, although such consumption may betray gluttony. The essence of gluttony is a false and disproportionate interest in eating. It is the elevation of food to a place of consuming interest.   —John Stapert

987. Many a man has dug his own grave with his teeth.

GOD

988. When I look at the glory of the
        heavens,
    At the sun, moon, and stars that
        be—
If I believe that all come from
        nothing,
    Then nothing is the maker of
        me.

When I see the measureless ocean,
    And walk on the sands of the
        sea—
If I believe that God is nothing,
    Then nothing is a god to me.

When I find in the fields and the
        forests,
    That life is in flower and tree—
If I believe life started from
        nothing,
    Then nothing is in life for me.
        —T. M. Anderson

989. God is the sunshine that warms us, the rain that melts the frost and waters the young plants. The presence of God is a climate of strong and bracing love, always there.   —Joan Arnold

990. The very centre of the Christian belief is the approachability of God. H. L. Gee tells a war story. There was a little boy whose father was promoted to the exalted rank of Brigadier. When the little lad heard the news, he was silent for a moment, and then said, "Do you think he will mind if I still call him Daddy?"
        —William Barclay

991. I never climb my hilltop
But I find that God is there,

Nor watch the windblown clouds,
but that
His voice is in the air.

I know I cannot see His face
Nor touch a warming hand,
But God is on my hilltop,
And there's glory in the land.
—Ralph Spaulding Cushman

992. God is holy; He hates sin.
God is just; He condemns sin.
God is sovereign; He punishes sin.
God is gracious; He forgives sin.
—George Gritter

993. God has a thousand ways
Where I can see not one;
When all my means have reached
their end
Then His have just begun.
—Esther Guyot

994. Nationalism is concerned with the nation and socialism with the class. Only God makes a private visit with the individual. —William James

995. A man can no more diminish God's glory by refusing to worship Him than a lunatic can put out the sun by scribbling the word "darkness" on the walls of his cell.
—C. S. Lewis

996. I can see how it might be possible for a man to look down upon the earth and be an atheist, but I cannot conceive how he could look up into the heavens and say there is no God. —Abraham Lincoln

997. God wants our attention and He knows how to get it. —James Earl Massey

998. Only God is permanently interesting. Other things we may fathom, but He out-tops our thought and can neither be demonstrated nor argued down.
—Joseph Fort Newton

999. If there were no God it would be necessary to invent Him. —Voltaire

1000. How Thou canst think so well of
us,
And be the God Thou art,
Is darkness to my intellect,
But sunshine to my heart.

1001. It's just a good thing that God
above
Has never gone on strike;
Because He wasn't treated fair
Or things He didn't like.

If He had ever once sat down
And said, "That's it—I'm
through,
I've had enough of sin on earth
So this is what I'll do.

"I'll give my orders to the sun—
'Cut off your heat supply,'
And to the moon, 'Give no more
light,'
And run those oceans dry.

"Then, just to really make it tough
And put the pressure on,
I'll turn off air and oxygen
Till every breath is gone."

Do you know He'd be justified
If fairness were the game?
For no one has been more abused
Or treated with disdain

Than God—and yet He carries on
Supplying you and me
With all the favors of His grace,
And everything—for free.

Men say they want a better deal,
And so on strike they go;
But what a deal we've given God
To Whom everything we owe.

We don't care whom we hurt or
harm

79

To gain the things we like;
But what a mess we'd all be in
If God should go on strike.

(see also: God's Forgiveness; God's Judgment; God's Laws; God's Love; God's Sovereignty; God's Will; Holy Spirit; Jesus Christ)

GOD'S FORGIVENESS

1002. God gives his forgiveness in a way that will maintain respect for His laws.
—Ruth Copeland

1003. God has cast our confessed sins into the depths of the sea, and He's even put a "no fishing " sign over the spot.
—Dwight L. Moody

GOD'S JUDGMENT

1004. The wrath of God is simply the rule of the universe that a man will reap what he sows, and that no one ever escapes the consequences of his sin. The wrath of God and the moral order of the universe are one and the same thing.
—William Barclay

1005. There is a hard and terrifying side of God which is as much a part of the Bible as His gentleness and kindness. We dare not neglect it because we can't fit it into our theology. Above all we dare not misrepresent the character of God to those who must one day meet Him face to face.
—Monty Ledford

1006. God's anger is not a passion but a principle—the eternal hatred of wrong, which corresponds with the eternal love of right, and which is only another aspect of love.
—A. T. Pierson

1007. We love to play on the silver trumpet of grace rather than on the ram's horn of justice.
—Charles H. Spurgeon

GOD'S LAWS

1008. The laws of God are written in the tissues of our bodies, in the process of our minds, in the avenues of our souls, and in the fabric of society. You can't throw them away. They are part of your very nature.
—R. Eugene Sterner

1009. Every part of this law must remain in force upon all mankind, and in all ages; as not depending either on time or place, or any other circumstances liable to change, but on the nature of God, and the nature of man, and their unchangeable relation to each other.
—John Wesley

1010. You don't really *break* God's laws. You *violate* God's laws and *they break you!*

GOD'S LOVE

1011. God loves each of us as if there were only one of us.
—Augustine

1012. What I have today I have because of His mercy. I did not earn it. I do not deserve it. I did not pay for it. I have no rights to it. I cannot keep it except for one thing—God's mercy.
—David Crosby

1013. There's a wideness in God's mercy,
Like the wideness of the sea;
There's a kindness in His justice,
Which is more than liberty.

For the love of God is broader
Than the measure of man's mind;
And the heart of the Eternal
Is most wonderfully kind.
—Frederick W. Faber

1014. God loves us the way we are, but He loves us too much to leave us that way.
—Leighton Ford

1015. Ever stand by in wonder and look
    on amazed
  As a waif from the lowest of
    people
  Seems to stir, so to speak, in a
    filthy cocoon
  And emerges a spiritual
    steeple?

  Well, my friend, let me tell you
    the terms high or low
  Were unknown to our Christ in
    His yearning:
  He loved folk who were high, and
    the lowest of low—
  All were souls to be plucked
    from the burning.
               —Roy McCaleb

1016. It is the property of love ever to give and ever to receive. Now, the love of Jesus is both avid and generous. All that He has, all that He is, He gives; all that we have, all that we are, He takes. In His hunger He makes of us His very bread, burning up in the fire of His love our vices, defects, and misdeeds. He would absorb our life in order to change it into His own: ours full of sin, His full of grace and glory.
               —Jan van Ruysbroeck

1017. The love of God is one of the great realities of the universe, a pillar upon which the hope of the world rests. But it is a personal, intimate thing too. God does not love populations, He loves people. He loves not masses, but men.   —A. W. Tozer

1018. Life often seems to be at cross-purposes with God's will unless it is perceived through the Cross-purpose of God's love.   —Albert M. Wells, Jr.

1019. The truth about man is that he needs to be loved the most when he deserves it the least. Only God can fulfill this incredible need. Only God can provide a love so deep it saves from the depths.

(see also: God's Forgiveness; Grace)

GOD'S SOVEREIGNTY

1020. I have lived a long time, sir, and the longer I live the more convincing proofs I see of this truth—that God governs in the affairs of men.
             —Benjamin Franklin

1021. If you think you see the ark of the Lord falling, you can be sure it is due to a swimming in your head.   —John Newton

1022. The world could end right now and God's intentions for humanity would have had a fulfillment that a nuclear blast could not deny. That God should at some time allow this human story to end does not destroy its meaning, for it is God's story too.   —Peggy L. Shriver

GOD'S WILL

1023. God's will is not an itinerary but an attitude.   —Andrew Dhuse

1024. The will of God is not something you add to your life. It's a course you choose. You either line yourself up with the Son of God . . . or you capitulate to the principle which governs the rest of the world.   —Elisabeth Elliot

1025. God does not will every circumstance; but He does have a will in every circumstance.   —J. Kenneth Grider

(see also: Divine Guidance)

GOLDEN RULE

1026. The Golden Rule would reconcile capital and labor, all political contention and uproar, all selfishness and greed.
             —Joseph Parker

1027. Our conscience teaches us it is right, our reason teaches us it is useful, that men should live according to the Golden Rule. —W. Winwood Reade

(see also: Interpersonal Relations)

GOOD FRIDAY THEME

1028. Isaac lay wrapped on the altar ready to be slaughtered. Jesus lay wrapped in the manger ready to be offered. For Isaac they found a substitute, for Jesus a cross.
—Edna M. Hook

1029. That the Potter should die for His clay is a stupendous miracle.
—Lynn Landrum

1030. I simply argue that the cross be raised again at the center of the marketplace as well as on the steeple of the church. I am recovering the claim that Jesus was not crucified in a cathedral between two candles, but on a cross between two thieves; on the town garbage heap; at a crossroad so cosmopolitan that they had to write His title in Hebrew and in Latin and in Greek . . . at the kind of place where cynics talk smut, and thieves curse, and soldiers gamble. Because that is where He died. And that is what He died about.
—George MacLeod

1031. The hands of Christ seem very frail
For they were broken by a nail.
But only they reach heaven at last
Whom these frail, broken hands hold fast.

(see also: Lenten Theme; Self-Denial; The Cross)

GOODNESS

1032. The confession of evil works is the first beginning of good works. —Augustine

1033. The greatest pleasure I know is to do a good action by stealth, and to have it found out by accident. —Charles Lamb

1034. No amount of good deeds can make us good persons. We must be good before we can do good.
—Chester A. Pennington

1035. Do all the good you can,
By all the means you can,
In all the ways you can,
In all the places you can,
At all the times you can,
To all the people you can,
As long as ever you can.
—John Wesley

(see also: Service)

THE GOSPEL

1036. There is no such thing as a "personal gospel" or a "social gospel." There is but one gospel . . . and it has two applications, personal and social. Both are necessary; one without the other is incomplete. A purely social gospel is like a body without a soul—it is a corpse. A purely personal gospel is like a soul without a body—it is a ghost. —E. Stanley Jones

1037. Religion is man-made; the Gospel is God-given. Religion is what man does for God; the Gospel is what God does for man. Religion is good views; the Gospel is good news. Religion ends in outer reformation; the Gospel ends in inner transformation. Religion often becomes a farce; the Gospel is always a force—the power of God unto salvation. —Jerry Noble

1038. Theology sometimes makes us sick but the Gospel always makes us whole.
—Helmut Thielicke

(see also: Christianity; The Bible)

GOSSIP

1039. A gossip is a beast of prey who does not even wait for the death of his victim.
—George Meredith

1040. Gossip is always perverse; it commits abortions on people's reputations.
—Calvin G. Seerveld

1041. You can get statistics for practically everything except the number of human reputations tarnished and blackened by evil gossip. So prevalent is this kind of tongue-wagging that Ogden Nash was prompted to claim that the human race could well be divided into two classes: the gossipers and the gossipees.
—Florence Wedge

(see also: Censoriousness)

GOVERNMENT

(see: The Nation; Politics and Government)

GRACE

1042. The word grace emphasizes at one and the same time the helpless poverty of man and the limitless kindness of God.
—William Barclay

1043. There will always be the seeming contradiction . . . that while God's saving grace is always and forever free, it is never, never cheap. —Herman W. Gockel

1044. Grace means primarily the free, forgiving love of God in Christ to sinners and the operation of that love in the lives of Christians. —A. M. Hunter

1045. Salvation is a gift and you can't boast about a gift. You can only be thankful. —D. James Kennedy

1046. God does not give grace freely in the sense that He will demand no satisfaction, but He gave Christ to be the satisfaction for us. —Martin Luther

1047. Man is born broken; he lives by mending. The Grace of God is the glue.
—Eugene O'Neill

1048. To run and work, the law commands
Yet gives us neither feet nor hands.
But better news the gospel brings;
It bids us fly, and gives us wings.

1049. Free grace! But hurry! The offer may expire soon.

(see also: God's Love)

GREATNESS

1050. Nothing can make a man truly great but being truly good, and partaking of God's holiness. —Matthew Henry

1051. We can do no great things—only small things with great love.
—Mother Teresa

1052. There is no greatness where there is no simplicity, goodness, and truth.
—Leo Tolstoy

1053. A solemn and religious regard to spiritual and eternal things is an indispensable element of all true greatness.
—Daniel Webster

GREED

1054. If we get everything that we want, we will soon want nothing that we get.
—Vernon Luchies

(see also: Materialism and Hedonism)

GUIDANCE
(see: Divine Guidance)

GUILT

1055. There is no such thing as pseudo-guilt. You don't feel guilt because of what happened to you. . . but because of something you did, an attitude you took.
—**Hobart Mower**

1056. One of the most distressing signs of contemporary times is the denial of guilt.
—**Fulton Sheen**

Happiness

1057. If Christianity does not make a man happy, it will not make him anything at all. . . . Christianity is the faith of the happy heart and the shining face.
—**William Barclay**

1058. The U.S. Constitution doesn't guarantee happiness, only the pursuit of it. You have to catch up with it yourself.
—**Benjamin Franklin**

1059. O be assured that the top and flower of the soul's happiness consists in union with God and Christ Jesus.
—**Alexander Grosse**

1060. Happiness is a butterfly which, when pursued, is always beyond our grasp, but which if you will sit down quietly, may alight upon you. —**Nathaniel Hawthorne**

1061. There is just one thing more I wish I could give you. It is the religion of our Lord Jesus Christ. With it, if you had nothing else, you could be happy. Without it, though you had all things else, you could not be happy. —**Patrick Henry**

1062. The plain fact is we aren't made for a sense of well-being that rises or falls with what we can get our hands on. We are made for whatever God brings to pass out of the hard soil of struggle, out of the creative effort of our souls. —**Arnold G. Kuntz**

1063. God can't give us happiness and peace apart from Himself because there is no such thing. —**C. S. Lewis**

1064. Happiness is the by-product of helping others. —**Denny Miller**

1065. I never met a rich man who was happy, but I have only very occasionally met a poor man who did not want to become rich. —**Malcolm Muggeridge**

1066. Not what we have, but what we
        use;
Nor what we see, but what we
        choose,
These are the things that mar or
        bless
The sum of human happiness.
—**Joseph Fort Newton**

1067. It is not the life of knowledge, not even if all the sciences are included, that creates happiness and well-being, but a single branch of knowledge—the science of good and evil. —**Plato**

1068. Scatter seeds of kindness
        Everywhere you go;
        Scatter bits of courtesy—
        Watch them grow and grow.
        Gather buds of friendship;
        Keep them till full-blown;
        You will find more happiness
        Than you have every known.
—**Amy R. Raabe**

1069. Man is happy only as he finds a work worth doing—and does it well.
—**E. Merrill Root**

1070. Life becomes harder for us when we live for others, but it also becomes richer and happier.   —Albert Schweitzer

1071. This is true joy of life—the being used for a purpose that is recognized by yourself as a mighty one, instead of being a feverish, selfish little clod of ailments and grievances, complaining that the world will not devote itself to making you happy.   —George Bernard Shaw

1072. Happiness isn't in possessions, education, or sensory ability. Happiness is found in relationships. And life's greatest happiness is found in life's greatest relationship: a personal relationship with God through Jesus Christ. —Kenneth L. Tangen

1073. The happiness of a man in this life does not consist in the absence but in the mastery of the passions.
    Alfred Lord Tennyson

1074. Happiness does not depend on outward things, but on the way we see them.
    —Leo Tolstoy

1075. The only way to happiness is never to give happiness a thought.
    —Elton Trueblood

1076. Happiness without Christ is a highway to hell.   —Albert M. Wells, Jr.

1077. Happiness is the feeling you're feeling when you want to keep on feeling it.

1078. You cannot always *have* happiness, but you can always *give* happiness.

1079. It isn't our position but our disposition that makes us happy.

(see also: Contentment, Fulfillment)

HATE

1080. Hating people is like burning down your house to get rid of a rat.
    —Harry Emerson Fosdick

1081. Hate is a simple emotion while love is a complex one. Love might be compared to the tall and elaborate sand castle, taking many hours of painstaking effort, cooperation, balance and persistence. Hate is the foot that comes along and with one vicious kick destroys what has been built up.   —Sydney Harris

1082. Always remember, others may hate you but those who hate you don't win unless you hate them. And then you destroy yourself.   —Richard M. Nixon

HEALING

(see: Divine Healing)

HEALTH

1083. If you want to live twice as long, eat half as much, sleep twice as much, drink water three times as much, and laugh four times as much.   —John H. Cable

1084. If people learned to team up with God, the human race would soon be able to throw off the 50 percent of its ailments that medical authorities admit are psychological.   —George W. Crane

1085. Ahead of tithing, ahead of witnessing, ahead of "talenting," from the time of birth until the soul leaves the body, a person's first, primary, and nonterminal responsibility before others and God is to breathe. Indeed, all else is dependent upon this. And the quality of one's breathing— that is the general strength of heart, lungs, and blood-vessels—determines how effective any other stewardship responses may be.   —Eugene E. Greer

(see also: Gluttony)

HEAVEN

1086. My knowledge of that life is small,
The eye of faith is dim,
But 'tis enough that Christ knows all,
And I shall be like Him.
—Richard Baxter

1087. To believe in heaven is not to run away from life; it is to run toward it.
—Joseph D. Blinco

HEDONISM

(see: Materialism and Hedonism)

HELL

1088. The perpetual death of the damned will go on without end and will be their common lot, regardless of what people prompted by human sentiments may conjure up.   —Augustine

1089. The reality of hell is revealed beyond doubt or quibble in the New Testament. . . . One either takes Christ at His word or sets up some private version of afterlife.   —Hugh Calkins

1090. When people no longer believe in hell, they promptly make *this world* into a place of torment.   —Edward Coleson

1091. Abandon hope, all ye who enter here.   —Dante

1092. The poor dunce who says, "If I go to hell, I'll have plenty of friends," will be forever shocked to find that in hell nobody will have any friends! Everyone will be the eternal enemy of everyone else.
—William S. Deal

1093. When Walter Hooper reported to C. S. Lewis a gravestone that read, "Here lies an atheist all dressed up with no place to go," Lewis commented wryly, "I bet he wishes that were true."   —Bert Ghezzi

1094. Ungodly people who have no fear of hell use the word profanely, but hell is nothing to laugh about and they will not be laughing when they get there.
—J. Hershey Longenecker

1095. The old time evangelists used to stress the tragedy of men and women individually going to hell. We don't hear very much about that nowadays, because they say people don't believe in hell. But I notice they talk a lot about it in their conversations.   —Peter Marshall

1096. Why should anyone be shattered by the thought of hell? It is not compulsory for anyone to go there.   —Thomas Merton

1097. He should not preach about hell who can not do it without tears.
—Dwight L. Moody

1098. Some say we can have our hell on this earth. We do. We can start it here but it does not finish here.   —Fulton Sheen

1099. There is a real fire in hell, as truly as you have a real body—a fire exactly like that which we have on this earth, except this: that it will not consume though it will torture you. You have seen asbestos lying amid red hot coals, but not consumed. So your body will be prepared by God in such a way that it will burn forever without being consumed. With your nerves laid raw by the searing flame, yet never desensitized for all its raging fury, and the acrid smoke

of the sulphurous fumes searing your lungs and choking your breath, you will cry out for the mercy of death, but it shall never, never, no never, give you surcease.
—Charles H. Spurgeon

1100. I am abandoned by God and man! I shall go to hell! O Christ, O Jesus Christ!
—Voltaire

1101. There are many people who would argue loud and long for the existence of hell while at the same time being reluctant to open their heart and home to rescue some who are going there.

HERITAGE

1102. Some generations are more aware of what they have achieved than of what they have inherited, forgetting that the heritage makes the achievement possible.
—Reginald E. O. White

(see also: History)

HISTORY

1103. It is the Christian conviction that history is a plan, that history has a purpose, that history is the working out of the will of God.   —William Barclay

1104. The history of the world is but the biography of great men. —Thomas Carlyle

1105. There is properly no history, only biography.   —Ralph Waldo Emerson

1106. One lesson, and only one, history may be said to repeat with distinctness, that the world is built somehow on moral foundations, that in the long run it is well with the good, and in the long run it is ill with the wicked.   —J. A. Froude

1107. The history of the world is none other than the progress of the consciousness of freedom.   —Friedrich Hegel

1108. Our present era seems to be an age obsessed with itself. Our sense of history has never been weaker. —Glen A. Mazis

1109. Without retrospect, no real prospect is possible.   —H. Richard Niebuhr

1110. It is a good thing to know, and always to keep turning over in the mind, the things which were illustriously done of old.   —Quintilian

1111. Those who cannot remember the past are condemned to repeat it.
—George Santayana

1112. There is nothing new except the history you don't know. —Harry S. Truman

1113. The worst thing about history is that every time it repeats itself the price goes up.

HOLINESS

1114. To be sound in faith and holy in life—this is the kernel of Christianity.
—Augustine

1115. Grace is not only a gift; it is a grave responsibility. a man cannot go on living the life he lived before he met Jesus Christ. He must be clothed in a new purity and a new holiness and a new goodness. The door is open, but the door is not open for the sinner to come and remain a sinner, but for the sinner to come and become a saint.   —William Barclay

1116. The aim of reconciliation is holiness. Christ carried out His sacrificial work of reconciliation in order to present us to God consecrated, unblemished and irreproachable.   —William Barclay

1117. A holy life . . . must be founded upon truth, must begin personally in conscious peace with God . . . , must grow with the increase of truth and deliverance from error, must be maintained by fellowship with God in Christ Jesus through the indwelling Spirit of holiness.

—Horatius Bonar

1118. Holiness is not a series of do's and don'ts, but a conformity to God's character in the very depths of our being. This conformity is possible only as we are united with Christ.　　　　—Jerry Bridges

1119. God has one destined end for mankind—holiness! His one aim is the production of saints. God is not an eternal blessing-machine for men. He did not come to save men out of pity. He came to save men because He had created them to be holy.　　　　—Oswald Chambers

1120. Saying "yes" to God means saying "no" to things that offend His holiness.

—A. Morgan Derham

1121. True holiness is learning to enjoy friendship with God.　　　—M. P. Horban

1122. The holiness person masters the world, while the carnal person is mastered by the world.　　　　—Ray H. Hughes

1123. How little people know who think that holiness is dull. When one meets the real thing it is irresistible. If even 10 percent of the world's population had it, would not the whole world be converted—and happy—before the year's end?

—C. S. Lewis

1124. Who is a holy person, then? . . . The answer is in the direction of life: one who moves toward God steadily.

—Ladislas Orsy

1125. While the *title* to eternal life is given to us in our justification, the Lord leads us into the *possession* of eternal life along the way of holiness.

—Norman Shepherd

1126. Take time to be holy, speak oft
　　with thy Lord;
Abide in Him always, and feed on
　　His Word.
Make friends of God's children;
Help those who are weak;
Forgetting in nothing His blessing
　　to seek.
　　　　—George C. Stebbins

1127. There are two extremes in lifting a standard [of holiness]. We can put it too high, or we can put it too low. If we put it too high, we drive people to despair; if we put it too low, we drive them to hell.

—John Wesley

1128. The first priority of my life is to be holy, and the second goal of my life is to be a scholar.　　　　—John Wesley

1129. If Christians were afraid of worldliness as much as they are of holiness, they would set the world on fire for Christ.

1130. Holiness is not a place to stop, but a highway to travel.

(see also: Sanctification)

HOLY SPIRIT

1131. Since Christ puts so much emphasis upon the work of the Holy Spirit and the absolute necessity of His power and presence, it is foolish for us not to.

—Nathan Bailey

1132. The Holy Spirit was not given to make you rich; He was given to make you ready.　　　　—Dan Betzer

1133. Just as the fluid in the eye keeps the dirt out of the eyes, so the constant cleansing presence of the Holy Spirit will keep the filth of the world out of the heart.
—Myron Boyd

1134. Being alive to God means that God's Holy Spirit dwells within us to strengthen and develop holiness in us. First, He causes us to see our need. He opens our minds to understand God's moral will revealed in Scripture and shows us specific areas in which we fail to conform to it.
—Jerry Bridges

1135. The Holy Scriptures declare Him to be the revealer of all truth, the active agent in all works of redemption, and from first to last the instrument of grace in the experience of salvation. In Him, and through Him, and by Him, is the power that saves. Illumination and conviction, repentance and regeneration, assurance and sanctification are all the work of God the eternal Spirit. To the church He is the source and supply of wisdom and power. The church is the Body of Christ, indwelt and controlled by the Spirit. He directs, energizes, and controls.
—Samuel Chadwick

1136. Without the power of the Holy Spirit all human efforts, methods, and plans are as futile as attempting to propel a boat by puffing at the sails with our own breath.
—D. M. Dawson

1137. Watches, cars and Christians can all look chromed and shiny. But watches don't tick, cars don't go and Christians don't make a difference without insides. For a Christian, that's the Holy Spirit.
—Tim Downs

1138. There is one inlet of power in life—anybody's life—any kind of power; just one inlet—the Holy Spirit.
—S. D. Gordon

1139. Three things we should seek to avoid:
> Resisting the Spirit.
> Grieving the Spirit.
> Quenching the Spirit.

Three things we should seek:
> Being filled with the Spirit.
> Using the gifts of the Spirit.
> Bearing the fruits of the Spirit.

—George Gritter

1140. If a person is filled with the Holy Spirit, his witness will not be optional or mandatory—it will be inevitable.
—Richard Halverson

1141. The coming of the Holy Spirit at Pentecost was an advent similar in nature and nearly, if not equally, as important as Christ's coming to earth.
—Maurice R. Irvin

1142. Do not pray for *more* of the Holy Spirit. The Holy Spirit is the Third Person of the Trinity and is not in pieces. Every child of God has *all* of Him, but does He have *all* of us?
—Julia Kellersberger

1143. God will not give us the Holy Spirit to enable us to gain celebrity or to procure a name or to live an easy, self-controlled life. The spirit's passion is the glory of the Lord Jesus, and [the Spirit] can make His abode [only] with those who are willing to be at one with Him in this.
—F. B. Meyer

1144. Jesus does not plead with us to be His witnesses. He does not command. He does not threaten. He simply states a promise: "But you will receive power when the Holy Spirit comes on you; and you will be my witnesses. . . ." The church of Christ does not get on the move by pushing itself harder, but only by opening itself up more fully to the Spirit's power.

—Alfred E. Mulder

1145. I do not find in the Old Testament or in the New Testament, neither in Christian biography, in church history or in personal Christian testimonies the experience of any person who was ever filled with the Holy Ghost and who didn't know it.   —A. W. Tozer

1146. The revelation of Christ in His person and work was absolute and complete, but without the gradual illumination of the Spirit, it is partly unintelligible and partly unobserved.   —B. F. Wescott

HONESTY

1147. Honesty was always rare. Diogenes, the Greek philosopher, lighted a candle in the daytime and went around looking for an honest man. Blaise Pascal said he didn't expect to meet three honest men in a century. Honesty is just as elusive today. The Institute of Behavior Motivation has found that ninety-seven out of one hundred people tell lies—and they do it about one thousand times a year.

—M. P. Horban

1148. If you tell the truth, you don't have to remember anything.   —Mark Twain

1149. I hope that I shall always possess firmness and virtue enough to maintain what I consider the most enviable of all titles: the character of an honest man.

—George Washington

(see also: Integrity; Deception)

HOPE

1150. When you say a situation or a person is hopeless, you are slamming the door in the face of God.   —Charles L. Allen

1151. Other men see only a hopeless end, but the Christian rejoices in an endless hope.   —Gilbert M. Beeken

1152. Hope is the thing with feathers
That perches in the soul,
And sings the tune without the
     words,
And never stops at all.

—Emily Dickinson

1153. Hope is one of those things in life you cannot do without.   —LeRoy Douglas

1154. Man can live about forty days without food, about three days without water, about eight minutes without air . . . but only for one second without hope.

—Hal Lindsey

1155. The American dream offers a shining vision of tomorrow. Christian hope, based in the Spirit, holds out meaning for today.   —Thomas E. Porter

1156. The future belongs to those who belong to God. This is hope.

—W. T. Purkiser

1157. Hope is not a dream, but a way of making dreams become reality.

—L. J. Suenens

1158. Hope is patience with the lamp lit.
—Tertullian

1159. I believe in the sun even when it isn't shining. I believe in love even when I am alone. I believe in God even when He is silent.   —Jewish refugee,
World War II, Poland

1160. Hope works in these ways: it looks for the good in people instead of harping on the worst; it discovers what can be done instead of grumbling about what cannot; it regards problems, large or small, as opportunities; it pushes ahead when it would be easy to quit; it "lights a candle" instead of "cursing the darkness."

HUMANISM

1161. Humanism vainly attempts to help people lift themselves by their own bootstraps, but the gains are only illusory. Humanity repeats Lucifer's sin of pride and self-sufficiency with equally tragic results.
—**David R. Chamberlain**

1162. A number of years ago, Harvey Cox argued that the secular city was a concretization of the Kingdom of God and that technology was its messianic instrument. He was convinced that humankind has the capacity to solve the many problems confronting it and to perfect its world. However, the past fifty years of human experience have cast doubt upon Cox's theory. Auschwitz, Hiroshima, political assassinations, a rampant drug culture, . . . an expanding sea of violence and our ever-growing ability to destroy our planet with nuclear weapons all underscore the fact that secular culture is void of ultimate values and cannot provide us with a sense of direction. . . . We who are committed . . . to making this world a better place . . . must seek meaning elsewhere.
—**Norman J. Cohen**

1163. One can think of nothing that is in the worst interest of mankind more than humanism. Man's knowledge is so limited and his vision so myopic that, left to his own knowledge and wisdom, he can only destroy himself. Society can only turn in upon itself in chaotic cataclysm if it insists on the rule of oneself, by oneself, for oneself.
—**W. F. Lown**

1164. Humanism is not wrong in its cry for sociological healing, but humanism is not producing it.
—**Francis Schaeffer**

1165. If humanism were right in declaring that man is born to be happy, he would not be born to die. Since his body is doomed to die, his task on earth evidently must be of a more spiritual nature.
—**Alexander Solzhenitsyn**

1166. Secular humanism offers a fantasy of abundance while denying the reality of spiritual famine.
—**Albert M. Wells, Jr.**

HUMILITY

1167. Should you ask me what is the first thing in religion, I should reply that the first, second, and third thing therein is humility.
—**Augustine**

1168. What makes humility so desirable is the marvelous thing it does to us; it creates in us a capacity for the closest possible intimacy with God.
—**Monica Baldwin**

1169 Humility is the virtue by which a man becomes conscious of his own unworthiness, in consequence of the truest knowledge of himself.
—**Bernard of Clairvaux**

1170. The true way to be humble is not to stoop until you are smaller than yourself, but to stand at your real height against some higher nature that will show you what the real smallness of your greatness is.
—**Phillips Brooks**

1171. The only wisdom we can hope to acquire is the wisdom of humility: humility is endless.
—**T. S. Eliot**

1172. Be grateful as your deeds become less and less associated with your name, as your feet ever more lightly tread the earth.
—**Dag Hammarskjold**

1173. The tumult and the shouting dies,
The captains and the kings
depart;

Still stands Thine ancient
sacrifice,
An humble and a contrite heart.
—Rudyard Kipling

1174. If anyone would like to acquire humility, I can, I think, tell him the first step. The first step is to realize that one is proud. And a biggish step too. —C. S. Lewis

1175. God and you are two things of such a kind that if you really get into any kind of touch with Him you will, in fact, be humble, feeling the infinite relief of having for once got rid of the pretensions which have made you restless and unhappy all your life. —C. S. Lewis

1176. God created the world out of nothing, and so long as we are nothing, He can make something out of us. —Martin Luther

1177. True humility makes way for Christ, and throws the soul at His feet. —John Mason

1178. I used to think that God's gifts were on shelves one above the other and that the taller we grew in Christian character, the more easily we should reach them. I find now that God's gifts are on shelves one beneath the other and that it is not a question of growing taller, but of stooping lower and that we have to go down, always down to get His best ones. —F. B. Meyer

1179. The humble man, because he sees himself as nothing, can see other things as they are. —Iris Murdoch

1180. Humility is perfect quietness of heart. It is for me to have no trouble; never to be fretted or vexed or irritated or sore or disappointed. It is to expect nothing, to wonder at nothing that is done to me, to feel nothing done against me. It is to be at rest when nobody praises me, and when I am blamed or despised. It is to have a blessed home in the Lord, where I can go in and shut the door, and kneel to my Father in secret, and be at peace as in a deep sea of calmness when all around and above is trouble. It is the fruit of the Lord Jesus Christ's redemptive work on Calvary's cross, manifest in those of His own who are definitely in subjection to the Holy Spirit. —Andrew Murray

1181. Humility is like underwear—essential, but indecent if it shows.
—Helen Nielson

1182. Humility is the proper estimate of oneself. —Charles H. Spurgeon

1183. Humility comes from a constant sense of our creatureliness.
—Richard C. Trench

1184. We practice humility not by thinking merely or negatively about ourselves, but by not thinking about ourselves at all. If we go about our earthly business without assuming importance, we'll never lose humility.

1185. If you are willing to admit you're all wrong, when you are, you're all right.

1186. Be willing to face the music now, and one day you may be chosen to lead the band.

HUMOR

1187. The Bible speaks of a time when all tears shall be wiped away. But it makes no mention of a time when we shall cease to smile. —J. D. Eppinga

1188. Laughter is the sun that drives winter from the human face. —Victor Hugo

1189. Serious people laugh. The others only giggle. —Bastian Kruithof

1190. I would have less wish to go to heaven if I knew that God would not understand a joke. —Martin Luther

1191. It is the soul that is not yet sure of its God that is afraid to laugh in His presence. —George MacDonald

1192. Laugh at yourself first, before anyone else can. —Elsa Maxwell

1193. A sense of humor is the pole that adds balance to our steps as we walk the tightrope of life. —William A. Ward

1194. Humor will never destroy anything that is genuine. All it can do is puncture balloons. —Kenneth L. Wilson

(see also: The Lighter Side)

HUSBANDHOOD

1195. Eve was not taken out of Adam's head to top him, neither out of his feet to be trampled on by him, but out of his side to be equal with him, under his arm to be protected by him, and near his heart to be loved by him. —Matthew Henry

1196. Power and strength, as useful as they are, without gentleness and tenderness will result in tyranny.
—Joanne D. Holland

1197. It would be well for some men to note that, among other things, God gave the man a woman because He knew that the man needed help. —Donald L. Reader

(see also: Marriage)

HYPOCRISY

1198. The church spends much of its time trying to make non-Christians act like Christians. —L. Nelson Bell

1199. Of all villainy, there is none more base than that of the hypocrite, who, at the moment he is most false, takes care to appear most virtuous. —Cicero

1200. The oldest trick of a demagogue is to shout that he is a man of action, not of words—and then continue orating for two hours. —Kenneth Hamilton

1201. Confession without interior change is a game. —Thomas Harris

1202. Waffled attitude—patterned to
        your liking;
    The melted butter of your works
    Will not suffice to cover sin.
    Thick honey of your empty praise
    Is bitter to His taste.
    Why waste your life in a worthless
        mold?
    A soul poured out for Him is
        manna for the world.
                —Jean Rasmussen

1203. Some Christians are like Christmas trees. They are decorated on the outside and dead on the inside.
                —Albert M. Wells, Jr.

1204. The worst lies are those that most resemble the truth.

1205. If fool there be then I am he
    To claim another I than me.
    For I am all the I I see,
    The only I that I can be.

1206. Ye call Me Master and obey Me
        not,
    Ye call Me Light and see Me not,
    Ye call Me Way and walk Me not,
    Ye call Me Life and desire Me not,
    Ye call Me wise and follow Me
        not,
    Ye call Me fair and love Me not,
    Ye call Me rich and ask Me not,
    Ye call Me eternal and seek Me
        not,

Ye call Me noble and serve Me
not,
Ye call Me mighty and honor Me
not,
Ye call Me just and fear Me not.

IDOLATRY

1207. We easily fall into idolatry for we are inclined thereunto by nature, and coming to us by inheritance, it seems pleasant.
—**Martin Luther**

1208. I confess I would almost rather be charged with a religion that extenuated murder, than with one that justified idolatry. Murder, great as the offense is, is but the slaying of man; but idolatry is, in its essence, the killing of God.
—**Charles H. Spurgeon**

1209. It's easy to get attached to idols, good things inappropriately adored. But when you have Jesus in the center of a room, everything else only junks up the decor. —**Charles Swindoll**

ILLUSION

1210. We all need enlightenment to see how our thinking has been warped by a foolish culture that learned its ideas from its prince. We believe nonsense like "money makes a man important," or "sex is the route to personal fulfillment and joy," or worse still, "having things go as I want is essential to my happiness." When we live according to such [illusions] our lives become disordered. —**Lawrence J. Crabb**

1211. Since no one *sees* a dying soul, few believe in it and fewer fear it. —**Erasmus**

1212. Most of us desire a little illusion to spice up our reality. But that is itself the greatest illusion—to think that attractive options can serve either to cover the consequences or enhance the prospects of reality. Illusion, however, dies hard and we are mostly self-kidders who continue to seek new life in beautiful but lifeless cut-flowers. To paraphrase C. S. Lewis: seek the benefits of reality and you get some cut-flowers thrown in; seek cut-flowers and you get neither. The Apostle Paul says it all: "Godliness with contentment is great gain" (I Timothy 6:6).

IMMORALITY

1213. Every individual or national degeneration is immediately revealed by a directly proportional degeneration in language. —**Joseph de Maistre**

1214. What were once vices are now the manners of the day. —**Seneca**

1215. The problem is not necessarily X-rated movies; the problem is X-rated minds. —**Raymond C. Wilson**

1216. The path of least resistance is what makes both men and rivers crooked.

(see also: Sex; United States/Moral Climate)

IMMORTALITY

1217. Join thyself to the eternal God, and thou shalt be eternal. —**Augustine**

1218. If there is no hereafter, nothing matters. If there is a hereafter, nothing else matters, and we had better get ready for it. —**J. K. Gressett**

1219. Some people like to think that God is a celestial Holiday Innkeeper who has carefully filled their reservations. But . . . eternal life is to "know you, the only true God, and to know Jesus Christ, whom you sent." —**Robert M. Herhold**

1220. Life is real, life is earnest,
And the grave is not the goal;
Dust thou art and to dust
returnest
Was not spoken of the soul.
—Henry Wadsworth Longfellow

1221. Socrates argued for the immortality of the soul. Jesus did not argue. He simply raised the dead.   —Warren Webster

(see also: Heaven)

THE INCARNATION

1222. The Eternal Being, who knows everything and who created the whole universe, became not only a man but (before that) a baby, and before that a foetus inside a woman's body. If you want to get the hang of it, think how you would like to become a slug or a crab.   —C. S. Lewis

1223. With the Incarnation came the Man, and the addition of a new spiritual dimension to the cosmic scene. The universe provides a stage; Jesus is the play.
—Malcolm Muggeridge

(see also: Jesus Christ; Christmas)

INFLUENCE

1224. No man has any right to claim a right, to indulge in a pleasure, to demand a liberty which may be the ruination of someone else. It may be that he has the strength of mind and will to keep that pleasure in its proper place; . . . but he has not only himself to think about; he must think of the weaker brother. A pleasure or an indulgence which may be the ruin of someone else is not a pleasure but a sin.
—William Barclay

1225. Example is the school of mankind; they will learn at no other.
—Edmund Burke

1226. Our deeds are like children that are born to us, they live and act apart from our will; nay, children may be strangled, but deeds never. They have an indestructible life both in and out of our consciousness.
—George Eliot

1227. When I think of those who have influenced my life the most, I think not of the great but of the good.   —John Knox

1228. A drop in the bucket
Is only a drop,
A minor and moist detail;
For a drop can't change
The color and taste
In a ten-quart watering pail.

But if that drop
Has the color of love
And the taste of tears divine,
One drop dropped into the vessel
of life
Can change the water to wine.
—Helen Kromer

1229. Lives of great men, all remind us
We can make our lives sublime,
And departing leave behind us
Footprints in the sands of time.
—Henry Wadsworth Longfellow

1230. Drop a pebble in the water,
And its ripples reach out far;
And the sunbeams dancing on
them
May reflect them to a star.
—Joseph Morris

1231. If Christ lives in us, controlling our personalities, we will leave glorious marks on the lives we touch. Not because of our lovely characters, but because of His.
—Eugenia Price

1232. Example is not the main thing in influencing others—it is the only thing.
—Albert Schweitzer

1233. In the dark immensity of night
I stood upon a hill and watched
the light
Of a star,
Soundless and beautiful and far.

A scientist standing there with
me
Said, "It is not the star you see,
But a glow
That left the star light years ago."

Men are like stars in a timeless
sky:
The light of a good man's life
shines high,
Golden and splendid
Long after his brief earth years are
ended.
—Grace V. Watkins

1234. When the Romanian pastor Richard Wurmbrandt and his wife were thrown into prison by the Communists, their 9-year-old son was hauled off to a government school to be indoctrinated in Marxism and atheism. Some years later, as a method of psychological torture for his parents, the boy was brought to see his mother for the purpose of denouncing Christianity to her face. As he studied the marks of suffering written on his mother's face together with the joy evidenced in his mother's spirit, he suddenly declared: "Mother, if Christ means this much to you, then I want Him too." Years of intensive brainwashing evaporated with only a single touch of Christlike influence.

INITIATIVE

1235. Poverty is uncomfortable, as I can testify: but nine times out of ten the best thing that can happen to a young man is to be tossed overboard and compelled to sink or swim for himself. —James A. Garfield

(see also: Ambition; Involvement)

INTEGRITY

1236. If the deal isn't good for the other party, it isn't good for you. —B. C. Forbes

1237. Without integrity, there is no freedom. With integrity, freedom will not become license. —Albert M. Wells, Jr.

1238. In our pursuit of righteousness, we cannot be unrighteous. Being on our way home is no justification for tramping through a flower bed.

(see also: Character; Ethics; Honesty)

INTERNATIONAL RELATIONS

1239. Perhaps Solzhenitsyn was right: World War III has already been fought and won by the Communists and the Arabs. The U.S. is weighed in its own balances and found wanting. —George E. Failing

1240. A neutral nation is usually one,
(And brother, it's not funny)
Which always takes the Russians'
side,
And also U.S. money.
—F. G. Kernan

1241. You are told by your leaders that power without any attempt at conciliation will lead to a world conflict. But I would say that power with continual compliance, continual retreat, is no power at all.
—Alexander Solzhenitsyn

(see also: Peace)

INTERPERSONAL RELATIONS

1242. In necessary things, unity; in doubtful things, liberty; in all things, charity. —Augustine

1243. In our dealings with men, however unkind and hurting they are, we must exercise the same patience as God exercises

with us. It is the simple truth that such patience is not the sign of weakness but the sign of strength; it is not defeatism, but rather the only way to victory.
—William Barclay

1244. We must learn to regard people less in the light of what they do or omit to do, and more in the light of what they suffer.
—Dietrich Bonhoeffer

1245. Two great talkers will not travel far together. —George Borrow

1246. To dwell there above
With the saints that we love—
That will be glory.

But to dwell here below
With the saints that we know—
That's another story.
—Henry Brandt

1247. You make more friends by becoming interested in other people than by trying to interest other people in yourself.
—Dale Carnegie

1248. He who trusts men will make fewer mistakes than he who distrusts them.
—Camillo di Cavour

1249. The gravity of offenses against love . . . is not that they outrage some sort of modesty or virtue. It is that they fritter away by neglect or lust the universe's reserves of personalization.
—Teilhard de Chardin

1250. We are all in the same boat in a stormy sea, and we owe each other a terrible loyalty. —G. K. Chesterton

1251. The art of praising is the beginning of the fine art of pleasing.
—George W. Crane

1252. There is nothing to do with men but to love them; to contemplate their virtues with admiration, their faults with pity and forbearance, and their injuries with forgiveness. —Orville Dewey

1253. A gentleman will not insult me, and no man not a gentleman can insult me. —Frederick Douglas

1254. It is one of the most beautiful compensations of this life that no man can sincerely try to help another without helping himself. —Ralph Waldo Emerson

1255. The only gift is a portion of thyself.
—Ralph Waldo Emerson

1256. Many persons, whose manners will stand the test of speaking, break down under the trial of listening.
—Frederick W. Faber

1257. Praise is like sunlight to the human spirit; we cannot flower and grow without it. Mark Twain once confessed that he could live for three weeks on a compliment, and he was not an exceptionally vain man. He was just admitting openly what most of us feel privately—that we all need a lift from time to time. Yet, while most of us are only too ready to apply to others the cold wind of criticism, we are somehow reluctant to give our fellows the warm sunshine of praise.
—Henry N. Ferguson

1258. Doing an injury puts you below your enemy; revenging one makes you even with him; forgetting it sets you above him. —Benjamin Franklin

1259. If you are not with Christ, then you are not with me. But if you are not with me, you may still be with Christ . . . and if you are for Christ, you cannot be my adversary. —Albert H. Freundt, Jr.

1260. To build a relationship, be it with God, a spouse or whomever, means to [experience] hurt, struggle and risk. It means opening up all sides of ourselves, both the victories and the defeats, prayers answered and times of silence in the midst of fervent crying out. I am convinced that often the tougher the struggle in working out a relationship the greater the eventual satisfaction. —Donald W. Fry

1261. If we take people as they are, we make them worse. If we treat them as if they were what they ought to be, we help them to become what they are capable of becoming. —Johann Wolfgang von Goethe

1262. Authentic Christian experience doesn't make things easier, in fact in a way, it makes them harder because it cuts out self-pity and refuses the refuge of resentment and revenge. —Rosemary Haughton

1263. To be arrogant toward man is to be blasphemous toward God.
—Abraham Heschel

1264. If I live by the human equivalents of grace, love, forgiveness and faith with those who occupy space in my life, thinking more of belonging than of owning, seeking to maintain the relationship as a matter of supreme importance, those relationships will never grow "stale," but sweeter every day. —Sandra W. Hoover

1265. The quality of a relationship is in direct ratio to the quality of the selves entering into that relationship.
—Thomas Howard

1266. Faults are thick where love is thin.
—James Howell

1267. To overcome evil with good is productive. To overcome evil with evil is counterproductive and only strengthens the determination to resist. —David Janzen

1268. We should all keep a large mental cemetery in which to bury the faults of our friends. —Ann Landers

1269. Trust him little who praises all, him less who censures all, and him least who is indifferent about all.
—Johann Kaspar Lavater

1270. We are born helpless. As soon as we are fully conscious we discover loneliness. We need others physically, emotionally, intellectually; we need them if we are to know anything, even ourselves.
—C. S. Lewis

1271. To love the world is to me no chore;
My trouble is the man next door.
—Paul Little

1272. If we could read the secret history of our [personal] enemies, we should find in each man's life sorrow and suffering enough to disarm all hostility.
—Henry Wadsworth Longfellow

1273. I will do nothing in this life except what I see is necessary, profitable, and salutary to my neighbor, since through faith I have an abundance of all good things in Christ. —Martin Luther

1274. Be content if thy person be trod upon for peace's sake—thy person, I say, and not thy conscience. —Martin Luther

1275. When you live to give, you're not disappointed if you fail to receive. If you expect nothing from people, all that comes will be a joyous bonus. No matter how horribly people treat you, you are not unduly upset when you realize that far worse treatment was given to Jesus Christ and He endured it all. —Vernon C. Lyons

1276. The only people with whom you should try to get even are those who have helped you.　　—Mae Maloo

1277. The holy heart can be hurt. But it answers injury with love and prayer and forgiveness.　　—W. E. McCumber

1278. Sticks and stones are hard on
　　　　bones
Aimed with angry art,
Words can sting like anything,
But silence breaks the heart.
　　　　—Phyllis McGinley

1279. Don't put people down—unless it's on your prayer list.　　—Stan Michalski

1280. How easy it is to go on reacting in the same old way, because—if we admit we've been wrong or unwise or unkind—we would feel so awful about the damage we've done. So we continue to make it worse.　　—Phyllis Reynolds Naylor

1281. Whether the man is an atheist or a Christian, I judge him by his fruits, and I therefore have many agnostic friends.
　　　　—Reinhold Niebuhr

1282. Win without tyranny. Win without stripping an honest adversary of his dignity. Win without mocking and denying. Win without sanctimonious greediness and selfishness.　　—Carl Sandburg

1283. It's a sad commentary when a Christian gets involved in a controversy with a non-Christian and the onlookers can't tell which is which.
　　　　—G. Roger Schoenhals

1284. This above all: to thine own self
　　　　be true.
And it must follow as the night
　　　　the day,
Thou canst not then be false to
　　　　any man.
　　　　—William Shakespeare

1285. Our praises are our wages.
　　　　—William Shakespeare

1286. I am I and you are you. I am not in this world to live up to your expectations, and you are not in this world to live up to mine. I will do my thing in keeping with God's calling, and you should do your thing in keeping with God's will for you. If in Christ we should meet, it will be beautiful. If not, perhaps both of us should try harder.　　—Donald Sharp

1287. There is no passion of the human heart that promises so much and pays so little as revenge.　　—Henry Wheeler Shaw

1288. I have never fought for my rights that I did not wish afterward that I had not done so.　　—Samuel M. Shoemaker

1289. There's a little secret
Worth its weight in gold,
Easy to remember
Easy to be told;
Changing into blessing
Every curse we meet,
Turning earth to heaven;
This is all: Keep sweet!
　　　　—A. B. Simpson

1290. Nothing else but seeing God in everything can make us loving and patient with those who annoy us. When we realize that they are only the instruments for accomplishing His purpose in our lives, we will actually be able to thank them [inwardly] for the blessings they bring us.
　　　　—Hannah Whitall Smith

1291. Being cared about is something so desperately needed in this depersonalized world that people will crawl across a thousand miles of desert to get it.
　　　　—Wilber Sutherland

1292. If we meet hate with hate, we are dragging ourselves down to the level of the hater. If we meet hate with the balm of forgiveness and love, the enemy is no longer in control.   —Annie Laurie Von Tungeln

1293. If our relationships with other human beings are going to be meaningful, they will cost us something. Relationships are demanding.   —Herbert Wagemaker

1294. I am not salt if I insist on being pepper.   —C. M. Ward

1295. I have learned that assistance given to the weak makes the one who gives it strong; and that oppression of the unfortunate makes one weak.
    —Booker T. Washington

1296. You can't hold a man down without staying down with him.
    —Booker T. Washington

1297. Love can be every bit as blunt as hostility. We beat around the bush, not because we're tactful, but because we're cowards.   —John White

1298. Be careful of the words you say,
Keep them soft and sweet;
You never know from day to day
Which ones you'll have to eat.

1299. When critics get together,
As the critics often do,
To discuss the whys and
    wherefores
Of the plan you're putting
    through;
When they've twisted it and torn
    it,
And have done the worst they
    can,
Just stop and ask them sweetly,
"Do you have a better plan?"

1300. A good listener is popular everywhere. Not only that, but after a while he knows something too.

1301. Don't be troubled if the temptation to give advice is irresistible; the ability to ignore it is universal.

1302. Flowers leave a part of their fragrance in the hands that bestow them.

1303. A chip on the shoulder indicates there is also wood higher up.

1304. We say we are willing to wash each other's feet, but sometimes we make the water too hot!

(see also: Censoriousness; Forgiveness; Friendship; Influence; Kindness; Love; Resentment)

INVOLVEMENT

1305. Even if you are on the right track, you will get run over if you just sit there.
    —Bennie Bargen

1306. The human race is divided into two classes—those who go ahead and do something and those who sit still and inquire, "Why wasn't it done the other way?"   —Oliver Wendell Holmes

1307. Always I tried to be what Giordano Bruno called himself, "an awakener of sleeping souls."   —E. Merrill Root

1308. Looking longingly at the top of the ladder will avail nothing; it's the climb that counts.   —Robert Louis Stevenson

(see also: Christian Action)

JESUS CHRIST

1309. He became what we are that He might make us what He is.   —Athanasius

1310. Jesus is the yes to every promise of God. —William Barclay

1311. I say, the acknowledgment of God in Christ
Accepted by thy reason, solves for thee
All questions in the earth and out of it.
— Robert Browning

1312. Caesar hoped to reform men by changing institutions and laws; Christ wished to remake institutions and lessen laws by changing men. —Will Durant

1313. He is a path, if any be misled;
He is a robe, if any naked be;
If any chance to hunger, He is bread;
If any be a bondman, He is free;
If any be but weak, how strong is He!
To dead men life is He, to sick men, health;
A pleasure without loss, a treasure without stealth.
—Giles Fletcher

1314. Jesus Christ is not a crutch; He is the ground to walk on. —Leighton Ford

1315. If Jesus Christ were not virgin born, then, of course, He had a human father; if He had a human father, then He inherited the nature of that father; as that father had a nature of sin, then He inherited his nature of sin; then Jesus Himself was a lost sinner and He Himself needed a Savior from sin. Deny the virgin birth of Jesus Christ and you paralyze the whole scheme of redemption by Jesus Christ.
—I. M. Haldeman

1316. No critic of Jesus has ever been taken seriously. His life was the epitome of virtue. —Richard Halverson

1317. Since my eyes were fixed on Jesus,
I've lost sight of all beside.
So enchained my spirit's vision,
Looking at the Crucified.
—Mary D. James

1318. Bruised hand, take the scepter; bruised head, take the crown; blessed Son of God, take the throne for "thine is the kingdom, and the power and the glory forever."
—Paul Lowenberg

1319. Whoever sees Christ as a mirror of the Father's heart, actually walks through the world with new eyes. —Martin Luther

1320. One of Jesus' specialties is to make somebodies out of nobodies.
—Henrietta Mears

1321. Alexander, Caesar, Charlemagne, and I myself have founded great empires. . . . But Jesus alone founded His empire upon love, and to this very day, millions would die for Him. Jesus Christ was more than a man. —Napoleon

1322. His humiliation expiates our pride; His perfect love atones for our ingratitude; His exquisite tenderness pleads for our insensibility. —John Newton

1323. The most outstanding record that is graven on the scroll of time is the date of the birth of Jesus Christ. No issued document is legal, no signed check is valid, and no business receipt is of value unless it bears the statistical reference to this great historic event. —Homer G. Rhea, Jr.

1324. If you wish to be disappointed, look to others. If you wish to be downhearted, look to yourself. If you wish to be encouraged . . . look upon Jesus Christ.
—Eric Sauer

1325. There is in the Lord Jesus a perfect evenness of various perfections. All the elements of perfect character are in lovely balance. His gentleness is never weak. His courage is never harsh. Follow Him through all the scenes of insult and outrage on that night and morning of His arrest and trial. Behold Him before Caiaphas, the High Priest, before Pilate, the governor, before Herod, the tetrarch. How His inherent greatness comes out. Not once did He lose His noble bearing or His royal dignity. —C. I. Schofield

1326. "I know not the way!" despairing I cried.

"I am the Way," Jesus kindly replied.

"I'm searching for Truth!" was my heart's plaintive cry.

"I am the Truth," was His gentle reply.

"I'm longing for Life! Oh, where can it be?"

"I am the Life. Thou shalt find it in Me!"
    —Flora Smith

1327. He died not by a single or sudden death, but He was the Lamb slain from the beginning of the world; for He was massacred in Abel; He was tossed upon the sea in Noah; it was He that went out of His country when Abraham was called from Haran, and wandered from his native soil; He was offered up in Isaac, persecuted in Jacob, betrayed in Joseph, blinded in Samson, affronted in Moses, sawed in Isaiah, imprisoned with Jeremiah. . . . He was stoned in Stephen, flayed in Bartholomew, roasted in Lawrence, exposed to lions in Ignatius, burnt in Polycarp, frozen in the lake where stood the forty martyrs of Cappadocia. The sacrament of Christ's death cannot be accomplished, said Hilary, but by suffering all the sorrows of humanity.
    —Jeremy Taylor

1328. Christ has a habit of inserting a corkscrew into one's heart and then pulling back and forth. You soon discover Christ is around! If He is being personal with us, He brings to the surface in our thinking those inner pollutants that need the care of His Cross. —A. W. Tozer

1329. We do not preach Christ with a comma after His name, as though waiting for something else; or Christ with a dash after His name as though leading to something else; but we preach Christ period.
    —A. W. Tozer

1330. Christ's intercession in heaven is a kind of powerful remembrance of His people, and of all their concerns, managed with state and majesty: not as a suppliant at the footstool, but as a crowned prince on the throne, at the right hand of the Father.
    —Robert Traill

1331. There is the stormy North side to Christ. But be sure of this: there is more divine grace in one of Jesus' blizzards than in all the "sunshine" Satan ever tricked you into. —William Vander Hoven

1332. He who has nothing to say about Jesus Christ has nothing to say.
    —H. Vigeveno

1333. Christ's temptations were utter nonsense if He were only a man. What man would ever be challenged to change a rock into a loaf of bread?

1334. In Jesus we discover all of God we can know; in Jesus we have all of God we can need.

1335. Jesus shut within a book
Isn't worth a passing look.
Jesus prisoned in a creed
Is a fruitless Lord indeed.
But Jesus in the hearts of men
Shows His tenderness again.

1336. The great Word of the Gospel is not God is love. That is too stationary, too little energetic. It produces a religion unable to cope with crises. But the Word is this—Love is omnipotent forever because it is holy. That is the voice of Christ—raised from the midst of time, and from time's chaos and convulsions, yet coming from the depths of eternity where the Son dwells in the bosom of the Father. . . . The key to history is the historic Christ above history and in command of it, and there is no other key.

1337. Jesus and Alexander died at
      thirty-three,
    One lived and died for self; one
      died for you and me.

(see also: Atonement; Easter; Good Friday Theme; The Incarnation; Christmas; Second Coming of Christ)

JOY

1338. The one thing that all men need to learn about joy is that joy has nothing to do with material things, or with a man's outward circumstances. It is the simple fact of human experience that a man living in the lap of luxury can be wretched, and a man in the depths of poverty can overflow with joy.   **—William Barclay**

1339. Where does constant joy abound?
    In the restless social round,
    Entertainment in excess,
    Worldly charm or cleverness?
    Fleeting are their seeming gains.
    Joy is found where Jesus reigns.
        —Hallie Smith Bixby

1340. Oh the sheer joy of it!
    Living with Thee,
    God of the universe,
    Lord of a tree,

    Maker of mountains,
    Lover of me.
      —Ralph Spaulding Cushman

1341. If you have a song of faith in your heart, it will be heard by the look on your face.   **—Allan Dykstra**

1342. When the destitute clamor, we can see exactly what they need. But when the rich and the surfeited multiply their demands, what can they possibly be looking for? Perhaps one thing that wealth and prestige can't give: joy.   **—Joseph Folliet**

1343. A country boy was asked what difference Christ had made in his life. He replied: "I feel better now when I feel bad, than I used to feel when I felt good."
        —J. K. Gressett

1344. When I met Christ, I felt that I had swallowed sunshine. **—E. Stanley Jones**

1345. Joy is the serious business of heaven.   **—C. S. Lewis**

1346. If doing God's will is all that counts for you, then no matter what the rest of life brings, you can find joy.
        —Vernon C. Lyons

1347. Life need not be easy to be joyful. Joy is not the absence of trouble but the presence of Christ.
        —William Vander Hoven

1348. Joy is the royal standard floating from the flagstaff of the heart, telling us that the King is in residence.

1349. Joy is the most infallible sign of the presence of God.

(see also: Happiness; Contentment)

JUSTICE

1350. God aims at satisfying justice in the eternal damnation of sinners.

—Jonathan Edwards

1351. We evaluate our friends with a Godlike justice, but we want them to evaluate us with a Godlike compassion.

—Sydney Harris

1352. [What is called] justice is [sometimes] vengeance dressed up in Sunday clothes. —Stephen Hequet

1353. Though the mills of God grind
slowly,
Yet they grind exceeding small;
Though with patience He stands
waiting,
With exactness grinds He all.

—Henry Wadsworth Longfellow

1354. Because we did not fortify justice, now we justify force. —Blaise Pascal

1355. Tenderness is total love, whereas justice is only a part of love, though it believes itself, mistakenly, to be the whole.

—C. F. Ramuz

1356. If the kingdom of God is the true human society, it is a fellowship of justice, equality, and love. But it is hard to get riches with justice, to keep them with equality, and to spend them with love.

—Walter Rauschenbusch

KINDNESS

1357. You cannot do a kindness too soon, for you never know how soon it will be too late. —Ralph Waldo Emerson

1358. Kindness is the golden chain by which society is bound together.

—Johann Wolfgang von Goethe

1359. Do it that very moment!
Don't put it off—don't wait.
There's no use in doing a kindness
If you do it a day too late!

—Charles Kingsley

1360. "What is real good?"
I asked in musing mood.
Order, said the law court;
Knowledge, said the school;
Truth, said the wise man;
Pleasure, said the fool;
Love, said the maiden;
Beauty, said the page;
Freedom, said the dreamer;
Home, said the sage;
Fame, said the soldier;
Equity, the seer;
Spoke my heart full sadly:
"The answer is not here."
Then within my bosom
Softly this I heard:
"Each heart holds the secret;
Kindness is the word."

—John Boyle O'Reilly

1361. I came by night where snow lay
deep,
All was transfixed in frozen sleep,
I felt a sudden small wind blow
And saw a fire burn in the snow.
With tongues of crimson throb
and leap;
Who gave it life I could not know,
Some hand had kindled its brave
show;
I felt its primal laughter steep
My mind in happiness and keep
Me gazing, with no will to go.
Now as I sit and watch you weep,
When knowledge fails and words
are cheap,
I'll make a little smoldering glow
Of tenderness and bid it grow;
When it begins to laugh and leap

I'll light a fire—there in your
snow.
—Winifred Rawlins

1362. Kindness is a language which the deaf can hear and the blind can see.
—Mark Twain

1363. I can live for two months on a good compliment. —Mark Twain

1364. Kindness is the ability to love people more than they deserve.

1365. Life is mostly froth and bubbles;
Only two things stand like stone:
Kindness in another's troubles,
Courage in your own.

(see also: Interpersonal Relations)

KNOWLEDGE

1366. We don't know one millionth of 1 percent about anything.
—Thomas A. Edison

1367. All people are ignorant—only on different subjects. —Will Rogers

1368. When a man's knowledge is not in order, the more of it he has the greater will be his confusion. —Herbert Spencer

1369. We must not expect simple answers to far-reaching questions. However far our gaze penetrates, there are always heights which block our vision.
—Alfred North Whitehead

LABOR

1370. I never knew an early rising, hard-working, prudent man who complained of hard luck. —Joseph Addison

1371. People were once so primitive that they did not know how to get money except by working for it. —George Ade

1372. Work done for love always has a glory. —William Barclay

1373. I wish I were a fish in a way
'Cause all they do is swim and play;
No work to do, no bills to pay—
But I had trout for dinner today.
—Louis O. Caldwell

1374. Work is the grand cure of all the maladies and miseries that ever beset mankind—honest work, which you intend getting done. —Thomas Carlyle

1375. There is no development physically or intellectually without effort, and effort means work. —Calvin Coolidge

1376. Temporary success can be achieved in spite of a lack of other fundamental qualities, but no advance can be maintained without hard work.
—William Feather

1377. Although it may seem
That the process is slow,
Still, work is the yeast
That raises the dough.
—Mary Hamlett Goodman

1378. Labor disgraces no man; unfortunately you occasionally find men who disgrace labor. —Ulysses S. Grant

1379. If we lose the sense of work and of purpose we will become a weak nation, a poor nation, and we will cease to be a happy nation. If we lose the sense of a job to be done, we will cease to be a fighting nation and that will be the end of us.
—Eric Hoffer

1380. Here's a stubborn truth
On which you can bet:
The harder you work,
The luckier you get.

—L. J. Huber

1381. Labor, if it were not necessary for the existence, would be indispensable for the happiness of man.   —Samuel Johnson

1382. To find integrity in our work let us cease to look toward the reward and let us look toward the work.   —E. Merrill Root

1383. Man is happy only as he finds a work worth doing—and does it well.

—E. Merrill Root

1384. When skill and love work together, expect a masterpiece.

—John Ruskin

1385. I ask that work should be looked upon, not as a necessary drudgery to be undergone for the purpose of making money, but as a way of life in which the nature of man should find its proper exercise and delight and so fulfill itself to the glory of God.   —Dorothy L. Sayers

1386. Now I get me up to work;
I pray the Lord I may not shirk,
And if I die before tonight,
I pray my work will be all right.

—Donald Sharp

1387. No race can prosper till it learns that there is as much dignity in tilling a field as in writing a poem.

—Booker T. Washington

1388. Leisure and I have parted company. I am resolved to be busy till I die.

—John Wesley

1389. A stranger came to three workmen all of whom were employed on the *same* job. He asked each worker what he was doing. Growled the first man: "I'm breaking rocks." Said the second: "I'm earning a living." But the third man replied with a smile, "I'm building a cathedral."

1390. I don't mind work if I've nothing
else to do;
I quite admit it's true
That now and then I shirk
Particularly boring kinds of
work—don't you?
But on the whole, I think it's fair
to say,
Provided I can do it my own way,
And that I need not start today—
I rather like work!

LAW

1391. The issue in law is simply this: Who is the Lord?   —R. J. Rushdoony

1392. If he who breaks the law is not punished, he who obeys it is cheated. Punishment is no longer fashionable. Why? Because . . . it creates moral distinctions among men; and, to the "democratic" mentality, this is odious.   —Thomas Szasz

1393. Respect for the law is the cement that binds together the fragile threads of our society.

(see also: Politics and Government)

LAYMEN

1394. Quite often you will hear someone say, "Our preacher never calls in our home." If this is true, you probably have much for which you can thank God. It usually means that death has not paid you a recent visit, that no serious illnesses have laid low the members of your family, that you are not a shut-in, that the surgeon's knife has not lately threatened you, that you have no serious marital problems, and that you are not a spiritual delinquent.

(see also: The Church)

LEADERSHIP

1395. Perhaps the greatest repentance is needed among silly evangelicals who insist on creating celebrities in the name of One who taught that *real leaders* are the *servants* of all. —Neill Foster

1396. A good leader is not the person who does things right, but the one who finds the right things to do.
—Anthony T. Padovano

1397. A good leader inspires other men with confidence in him; a great leader inspires them with confidence in themselves.

1398. The best executive is the one who has sense enough to pick good men to do what he wants done, and self-restraint enough to keep from meddling with them while they do it.

LEGALISM

1399. The idea of living strictly by what the Bible says has been branded as legalism. —Robert D. Brinsmead

1400. When the rules rule us they ruin us. —Paul Rees

LEISURE

1401. Cassian tells a famous story about John. One day he was found playing with a tame partridge. A narrower and more rigid brother rebuked him for thus wasting his time, and John answered: "The bow that is always bent will soon cease to shoot straight." —William Barclay

1402. The Christian should consider his leisure not as an end in itself, nor as the opposite of work, but as a function in his life which contributes to his calling.
—Harold D. Lehman

LENTEN THEME

1403. So long as Jesus was misunderstood He was followed by the crowd. When they came to really understand Him, they crucified Him. —Dan Harman

(see also: Good Friday Theme; Self-Denial; The Cross)

LIBERALISM

1404. Modern theology likes to reign and is little prepared to serve. It is not unlike the maid who deserts her household, runs away from the kitchen to the fair, and returns with paper flowers and a little cotton candy thinking these will cheer and feed the family. —Klaus Bockmuhl

1405. One of the effects of modern liberal Protestantism has been gradually to turn religion into poetry and therapy, to make truth vaguer and vaguer and more relative, to banish intellectual distinctions, to depend on feeling instead of thought and gradually to come to believe that God has no power, that He cannot communicate with us, cannot reveal Himself to us, indeed has not done so, and that religion is our own sweet invention.
—Flannery O'Connor

1406. All liberalism in our society today is a denial of Biblical truth; the liberal leadership of our day—social, political, economic and educational—is dedicated to the destruction of historic Christianity, not necessarily by the Communist method of open force, but by the more subtle method of replacing it with fables of human invention.   —C. Gregg Singer

1407. When you're in the "middle of the road" you're usually in the *left* turn lane.
    —A. Mark Wells

LIBERTY

1408. All who have ever written on government are unanimous, that among a people generally corrupt, liberty cannot long last.   —Edmund Burke

1409. The condition upon which God has given liberty to man is eternal vigilance.   —John Philpot Curran

1410. They that give up essential liberty to obtain a little temporary safety deserve neither liberty nor safety.
    —Benjamin Franklin

1411. Liberty lies in the hearts of men and women; when it dies there, no constitution, no law, no court can ever do much to help it.   —Learned Hand

1412. The God who gave us life, gave us liberty.   —Thomas Jefferson

1413. Liberty, what crimes have been committed in thy name!   —Madame Roland

1414. To obey God is perfect liberty.
    —Seneca

1415. Liberty, when it begins to take root, is a plant of rapid growth.
    —George Washington

1416. Liberty exists in proportion to wholesome restraint.   —Daniel Webster

1417. A republic . . . must either preserve its virtue or lose its liberty.
    —John Witherspoon

(see also: Freedom; The Nation)

LIFE

1418. Life is my university, and I hope to graduate from it with some distinction.
    —Louisa May Alcott

1419. Those who turn back know only the ordeal, but they who persevere remember the adventure.   —Milo L. Arnold

1420. He most lives who thinks most, feels the noblest, acts the best.
    —P. J. Bailey

1421. The awful importance of this life is that it determines eternity.
    —William Barclay

1422. Alone and without love we die. Life itself is as dependent on relationship with others as it is on food.   —M. N. Beck

1423. This is the way to live, that after you are gone people will wish that you were still around to give them comfort and counsel, love and care, understanding and concern.   —Louis Benes

1424. Life is a little gleam of time between two eternities.   —Thomas Carlyle

1425. Your life is like a coin. You can spend it any way you wish, but you can spend it only once.   —Lillian Dickson

1426. Life itself is a fatal disease. None of us is going to get out of it alive! And it happens so quickly too; about the time your face clears up, your mind gets fuzzy.
    —James Dobson

1427. What life have you if you have not
        life together?
    There is no life that is not in
        community.
    And no community not lived in
        praise of God.
    —T. S. Eliot

1428. Though we travel the world over to find the beautiful, we must carry it within us, or we find it not.

—Ralph Waldo Emerson

1429. Until we recognize that life is not just something to be enjoyed but rather a task that each of us is assigned, we'll never find meaning in our lives and we'll never be truly happy. —Victor Frankl

1430. Your perception of life is mostly a reflection of what you look like on the inside. —J. Donald Freese

1431. The measure of your life is the measure of your cravings. —Donald Gee

1432. It is not doing the things we like to do, but liking to do the things we have to do, that makes life blessed.

—Johann Wolfgang von Goethe

1433. Life has many disasters and reversals, but only one true tragedy: to pass from infancy to senility without ever reaching maturity. —Sydney Harris

1434. We live in a pill culture. We have pain pills, sleeping pills, birth control pills, pills to make you grow, pills to stunt your growth, pills to promote sexual potency, and pills to control sexual conduct. [Secular society] has extended life . . . but offered nothing worth living for. —Philip J. Hogan

1435. Ten Rules for Life:
1. Never put off until tomorrow what you can do today.
2. Never trouble another person for what you can do.
3. Never spend your money before you have earned it.
4. Never buy what you don't want because it's cheap.
5. Beware of pride. It will cost you far more than hunger, thirst, and cold.
6. Remember that we seldom repent of having eaten too little.
7. Remember that nothing is troublesome that we do willingly.
8. Remember that worry will cause much pain over things that will never happen.
9. Take things always by the smooth handle.
10. When angry count ten before you speak. If very angry, count to one hundred.

—Thomas Jefferson

1436. Life is our capital and we spend it every day. The question is, what are we getting in return? —Curtis Jones

1437. Two centuries ago the German philosopher, Immanuel Kant, asked three questions about life:
1. What can I know?
2. What should I do?
3. What may I hope?

—Immanuel Kant

1438. Life can only be understood backwards; however, it must be lived forwards.

—Soren Kierkegaard

1439. I affirm life; I challenge problems; I accept responsibility; I believe God; I live today. —Elizabeth Searle Lamb

1440. Life gives to every man a staff and scale of notes.
The song he sings is one of his own fashioning.

—Alma Lonsdale

1441. Life is a leaf of paper white
Whereupon each of us may write
His word or two, and then comes
night.

Greatly begin! Though thou has
time
But for a line, be that sublime!
Not failure, but low aim, is crime.
—James Russell Lowell

1442. Life is short. Plans for each day
should be lived in the realization that it is
God who will decide if we shall live. *Our*
decision is whether or not to do His will.
—Donald A. Miller

1443. Our lives are like waves which
wash up out of the ocean of eternity, break
upon the beach of time and lapse back into
the ocean of eternity. Some are sunlit,
some run in storm and rain, one is a quiet
ripple, another is a mighty breaker. And
once in every generation there is a great
wave which sweeps over the land. But they
all go back to the sea and lie equally level
there.   —Austin O'Malley

1444. By the yard, life is hard; by the
inch, it's a cinch.   —Robert Schuller

1445. The web of our life is of a mingled
yarn, good and ill together.
—William Shakespeare

1446. There are two tragedies in life.
One is not to get your heart's desire and
the other is to get it.
—George Bernard Shaw

1447. Life is a flame that is always burning itself out, but it catches fire again every
time a child is born.
—George Bernard Shaw

1448. There are three kinds of people in
life: those who make things happen, those

who watch things happen, and those who
don't know what is happening.
—James Smoke

1449. Good or evil—you cannot build
your life apart from this distinction.
—Alexander Solzhenitsyn

1450. Sit loosely in the saddle of life.
—Robert Louis Stevenson

1451. Life is a mirror: if you frown at it, it
frowns back; if you smile, it returns the
greeting.   —William M. Thackeray

1452. Life is an education.
Each new day brings its recitation;
Death brings its end—no
vacation.
Then comes the final
examination.
Plan to pass!

1453. We make a living by what we get—
a life by what we give.

1454. Life can't give me joy and peace—
It's up to me to will it.
Life just gives me time and
space—
It's up to me to fill it.

1455. Life is 10 percent what happens to
us and 90 percent how we respond to it.

1456. Three things will make life worth
living: a self fit to live with; a faith fit to
live by; and a purpose fit to live for.

1457. You're not ready to live your life
until you know what you want written on
your tombstone.

1458. The clock of life is wound but
once,
And no man has the power
To tell just when the hands will
stop,

At late or early hour.

To lose one's wealth is sad indeed
To lose one's health is more.
To lose one's soul is such a loss
That no man can restore.

1459. Life is what happens when you've made other plans.

1460. Take time to think, it's the source
of power.
Take time to play, it's the secret of
youth.
Take time to read, it's the fountain
of knowledge.
Take time to be friendly, it's the
road to happiness.
Take time to laugh, it's the music
of the heart.
Take time to give, it's the feeling
of joy.
Take time to work, it's the price of
success.
Take time to worship, it's the
essence of reality,
the fountain of wisdom, and
food for the soul.

(see also: Man)

THE LIGHTER SIDE

1461. Now I lay me back to sleep,
The speaker's dull, the subject's
deep.
If he should stop before I wake,
He'll know I think he's just a
fake.
—Sherwood Anderson

1462. An auctioneer is a man who proclaims with a hammer that he has picked a pocket with his tongue. —Ambrose Bierce

1463. Once a minister and his organist made a plan to expose the inappropriate chatter by the congregation during that period of time just prior to the worship service. The organist was to build the prelude to a loud fortissimo, then stop suddenly. When the music abruptly halted, one lady was heard to say: "I fry mine in lard!"
—Freda Cavendish

1464. An archaeologist is the best husband any woman can have: the older she gets, the more interested he is in her.
—Agatha Christie

1465. There was a pastor who wished his Easter congregation a merry Christmas and a happy New Year. He was certain he wouldn't see many of the attendants again until the following Easter. —Edward F. Cox

1466. Men are like thumbtacks—they are useful if they have good heads and are pointed in the right direction.
—Randall E. Denny

1467. Blessed is the man who, having nothing to say, abstains from giving wordy evidence of that fact. —George Eliot

1468. Church organist's a busy one,
Back row, I sit and muse,
Alert she is (and here's the pun):
She watches keys and pews.
—Edna Elsaser

1469. If you turned the Lord's Prayer over to a bureaucrat to rewrite, the single phrase, "Give us this day our daily bread," would probably come out something like this: We respectfully petition, request and entreat that due and adequate provision be made, this day and the date hereinafter subscribed, for the satisfying of these petitioners' nutritional requirements and for the organizing of such methods of allocation and distribution as may be deemed necessary and proper to assure the reception by and for said petitioners of such

111

quantities of baked cereal products as shall, in the judgment of the aforesaid petitioners, constitute a sufficient supply thereof. —Fred J. Emery

1470. As the years go by, I find that I am definitely growing stronger. A few decades ago I could not easily carry ten dollars' worth of groceries. Today it's a snap!
—J. D. Eppinga

1471. As a laggard letter writer,
One moment brings me glee:
When my letter correspondents
Somehow end up owing me.
—Donna Evleth

1472. "I'll be there in a minute"
Is a phrase one hears aplenty,
When the stated sixty seconds
Are to multiply by twenty.
—Donna Evleth

1473. Although I've seen my puppy eat
His dog food with delight,
Play with a rubber puppy toy,
Shake it with all his might,

And though I've seen him in the sun,
Just sleeping like a log,
I must admit I've yet to see
Him working like a dog.
—Donna Evleth

1474. There will always be prayers in public schools—as long as there are final exams to take. —B. Norman Frisch

1475. Romance is the irresistible desire to be irresistibly desired. —Robert Frost

1476. An optimist is a person who opens a laundromat in a hippy neighborhood.
—Jack Herbert

1477. Boy: "Dad, what's a religious traitor?"

Dad: "Someone who leaves our church and joins another."
Boy: "Then what do we call someone who leaves his church and joins ours?"
Dad: "Oh, in that case, we call him a convert."
—L. Thomas Holdcroft

1478. So here's to the chigger
Who's usually no bigger
Than the head of very small pin!

But when he digs in
And gets under your skin,
That's where the rub comes in!
—Elizabeth Huizenga

1479. When people compliment you on looking young, you can be sure they think you are growing old. —Washington Irving

1480. Most of us know how to say nothing, but few of us know when. —Wes Izzard

1481. Subtlety is the art of saying what you think and getting out of range before it is understood. —F. G. Kernan

1482. My father used to tell me, "When I want your opinion, I'll give it to you."
—Sam Levenson

1483. An old story describes a Boy Scout who, as bedtime approached, suddenly realized that he hadn't done his good deed for the day. There wasn't much time left; but after some thought, he seized on an idea. He took the canary out of the cage and gave it to the cat. —David R. Mace

1484. St. Theresa, the 16th century religious reformer, stood mired in the mud on one of her journeys and cried to God: "If this is the way you treat your friends, no wonder you don't have many."
—Karen Mains

1485. It was Scout Sunday at Durham Lutheran Church in Durham, Pennsylvania, so the front pews were filled with Brownies, Cubs, Boy and Girl Scouts, plus their leaders. The pastor's sermon was entitled, "Where Are You Going?" A small Cub Scout had just started to walk out the center aisle when the pastor began his sermon with the introductory question: "Where are you *going?*" Red-faced, the boy turned around and timidly said: "I'm going to the bathroom." **—Novalene Melchert**

1486. You can always tell when a man is well informed. His views are pretty much like your own. **—Louie Morris**

1487. My nerves are unsteady,
I'm quaking with fright.
I'm limp as spaghetti,
My hair's turning white.
The Lord I'm beseeching;
For patience I strive—
I'll need it . . . I'm teaching
My son how to drive.
—Louise J. Panni

1488. A Texan visiting Niagara Falls admitted that his great state of Texas had nothing to compare with the falls. But he insisted that Texas had plumbers who could fix it. **—Hillery C. Rice**

1489. Aspirin, heating pad, change all the sheets;
Fruit juices, coffee, the pattern repeats.
Up and down stairs till I'm ready to fold—
The head of the house has contracted a cold.
—Elinor K. Rose

1490. A sermon is thirty minutes to raise the dead. **—John Ruskin**

1491. When his earthly work is done,
Look kindly on the work nut.
And in heaven's pasture, Lord,
Leave a little grass to cut.
—Patricia S. Rutter

1492. If everything turns out backward
That you try so hard to do frontward;
Just turn yourself upside downward,
And laugh from the inside outward.
—Elsie Seibel

1493. I have found the best way to give advice to your children is to find out what they want to do and then advise them to do it. **—Harry S. Truman**

1494. The proper office of a friend is to side with you when you are wrong. Nearly anyone will side with you when you're right. **—Mark Twain**

1495. 'Tain't people's ignorance that does so much harm; 'tis their knowin' so much that ain't so. **—Artemus Ward**

1496. In life, as on a crowded bus, you needn't worry about finding your station; sooner or later, someone's bound to tell you where to get off. **—Joan I. Welsh**

1497. The recipe for a good speech includes some shortening. **—Gene Yasenak**

1498. I know you believe you understand what you think I said, but I am not sure you realize that what you heard is not what I meant.

1499. What most employers are looking for today are alert young people between the ages of twenty-two and thirty-five with forty years of experience.

1500. Dwight L. Moody explained his refusal to pray for a certain sick minister: "He does ten days' work in five and eats everything in sight."

1501. Angels that guard you when you drive,
Usually retire at fifty-five.

1502. A lion met a tiger as they drank
beside the pool.
Said the tiger, "Tell me why
you're roaring like a fool?"
"That's not foolish," said the lion,
with a twinkle in his eyes,
"They call me king of beasts
because I advertise."

A rabbit heard them talking and
ran home like a streak.
He thought he'd try the lion's
plan, but his roar was just a
squeak.
A fox came to investigate and had
lunch back in the woods.
So when you advertise, my friend,
be sure you've got the goods!

1503. The Catholic priest invited three Lutheran pastors to Mass so they could see the Catholic liturgy firsthand. The Lutherans got to the church a little late and the place was packed. They had to stand up since no seats were available. The priest, just starting the Mass, spotted his Lutheran friends in the rear of the church and whispered to one of the altar boys, "*Get three chairs* for the Lutherans." The boy looked baffled and didn't move. Finally spurred on by an urgent side glance from the priest, the lad shrugged dutifully, stepped to the altar rail, faced the congregation and loudly proclaimed: "*Give three cheers* for the Lutherans!"

1504. Church council lament: Why, when motions require seconds, and votes are recorded in minutes, do the meetings last for hours?

1505. Adam and Eve had an ideal marriage. He didn't have to hear all about the men she could have married, and she didn't have to listen to him tell how his mother used to cook.

1506. Now I sit me down to study,
I pray the Lord I won't go nutty,
If I should fail to learn this junk,
I pray the Lord I will not flunk.

Now I lay me down to rest,
I pray I pass tomorrow's test.
If I should die before I wake,
That's one less test I'll have to
take.

1507. My neighbor is a faddist
With a little mental quirk—
He jogs five miles with gusto,
Then drives five blocks to work.

1508. The pioneers who blazed trails now have descendants who burn up the roads.

1509. After a young boy had left half the sumptuous lunch his mother had prepared on the plate, she expostulated: "Johnny, how could you leave so much of your food untouched? Don't you know there are millions of people starving to death in India?" Johnny's prompt reply was: "Name two!"

1510. Even a fish would not be caught if he learned to keep his mouth shut.

1511. Eventually we will run out of food to feed ourselves, fuel to warm ourselves and air to breathe. This is something we must learn to live with!

1512. The woman called to the stand was exceedingly handsome but no longer young. The judge gallantly instructed,

114

"Let the witness state her age, *after which* she may be sworn to tell the *truth*."

1513. Every baseball team could use a man who plays every position superbly and never makes an error. But so far, no one has been able to make him lay aside his hot dog and come down out of the grandstand.

1514. Although I'm pushing fifty
    I'm as solid as a rock,
    And the life of every party
    Until almost nine o'clock.

1515. A little boy, when asked what Father's Day was, answered, "It's the same as Mother's Day, only you don't spend as much for the gift."

1516. Speaking to Mark Twain an acquaintance once made mention of a certain wealthy industrialist. "Of course," said the man, "you know his wealth is tainted." Twain responded, "That's right. 'Tain't yours and 'tain't mine."

1517. In school these days the "three Rs" are Readin', Ritin' and Remember— remember to bring your pocket calculator!

1518. Now there is even a "dial-a-prayer" for atheists. You call a number and nobody answers.

1519. Patience is the ability to count down before blasting off.

1520. A romantic's definition of existentialism: I and thou, here and now, wow!

1521. Remember when HIPPIE meant
    big in the hips,
    And a TRIP involved travel in
    cars, planes and ships?
    When POT was a vessel for
    cooking things in,
    And HOOKED was what
    grandmother's rug might
    have been?

When FIX was a verb that meant
    mend or repair,
And being IN meant simply
    existing somewhere?
When NEAT meant well-
    organized, tidy and clean,
And GRASS was a ground-cover
    normally green?
When lights and not people were
    TURNED ON and OFF,
And the PILL might have been
    what you took for a cough?
When CAMP meant to stay
    outdoors in a tent,
And POP was the way that the
    weasel went?
When GROOVY meant furrowed
    with channels and hollows,
And BIRDS were winged
    creatures, like robins and
    swallows?
When FUZZ was a substance
    that's fluffy like lint,
And BREAD came from bakeries,
    and not from the mint?
When SQUARE meant a 90-
    degree-angled form,
And COOL was a temperature,
    not quite so warm?
When ROLL meant a bun, and
    ROCK was a stone,
And HUNG-UP was something
    you did to a phone?
When CHICKEN meant poultry
    and BAG meant a sack,
And JUNK, trashy castoffs and
    old bric-a-brac?
When JAM was preserves that
    you spread on your bread,
And CRAZY meant barmy, not
    right in the head?
When CAT was a feline, a kitten
    grown up,
And TEA was a liquid you drank
    from a cup?

When SWINGER was someone
   who swung in a swing,
And PAD was a soft, sort of
   cushiony thing?
When WAY OUT meant distant
   and far, far away,
And a man wouldn't sue you for
   calling him GAY?
When DIG meant to shovel and
   spade in the dirt,
And PUT ON was what you
   would do with a shirt?
When TOUGH described meat
   too unyielding to chew,
And MAKING A SCENE was a
   rude thing to do?
Words once so sensible, sober and
   serious,
Are making the FREAK SCENE
   quite PSYCHEDELIRIOUS.
It's GROOVY, MAN, GROOVY,
   but English it's not!
Methinks that our language has
   gone straight to POT.

1522. A survey taker asked a young man what he thought was the greatest problem in society—ignorance or apathy. He replied, "I don't know and I don't care."

1523. A camel is a horse put together by a committee.

1524. Wife: "What is the cause of inflation?"

Husband: "Inflation is due to international tensions, economic instabilities, global recessionary phenomena, and inconsistent fiscal policies. The conglomerature cycle is also a factor, Honey Lamb."

Wife: "Look, Sweetie, if you don't know, why don't you just say so!"

1525. Social tact is making your guests feel at home even though you wish they were.

1526. The Sunday school teacher asked the class how Noah might have spent his time on the ark. When no one answered she suggested that perhaps he'd done a lot of fishing. "What?" responded one of her pupils. "With only two worms?"

1527. A diehard is a man who worships the ground his head is buried in.

1528. Some people think a church service is like a convention. So the family sends a delegate.

1529. Lady: "Why should I repent? The devil hasn't been bothering me."

Friend: "That's because you're both going in the same direction."

1530. We are told that the weaker sex is really the stronger sex. This is due solely to the weakness of the stronger sex for the weaker sex.

1531. Too many people adopt as their main interest talking and thinking—in that order.

1532. Diplomacy is the knack of letting someone else have your way.

1533. Substantial exercise after age sixty is apt to be harmful—especially if you do it with a knife and fork.

1534. A beautiful woman is one I notice. A charming woman is one who notices me.

116

LITERATURE

1535. Writing free verse is like playing tennis with the net down. —**Robert Frost**

1536. A classic is a book which people praise and don't read.

(see also: Books; Reading)

LONELINESS

1537. Loneliness is the anxiety that you do not matter at all. —**Joyce Huggett**

1538. A weary hearts! O slumbering
eyes!
O drooping souls whose destinies
Are fraught with fear and pain,
Ye shall be loved again!
—**Henry Wadsworth Longfellow**

1539. People are lonely because they build walls instead of bridges.
—**Joseph Fort Newton**

1540. Loneliness is the surest cure for vanity.

1541. Solitude is intolerable—even in paradise.

THE LORD'S PRAYER

1542. The prayer "Thy Kingdom come," if we only knew, is asking God to conduct a major operation. —**George A. Buttrick**

1543. I desire no other proof of Christianity than the Lord's Prayer.
—**Madame Anne de Staël**

LOVE

1544. Love is the salt that savors the whole [of life] and drives away the mists so that the sun may eternally shine.
—**George Matthew Adams**

1545. It is love that asks, that seeks, that knocks, that finds, and that is faithful to what it finds. —**Augustine**

1546. Love has hands to help others. It has feet to hasten to the poor and needy. It has eyes to see misery and want. It has ears to hear the sighs and sorrows of men. This is what love looks like. —**Augustine**

1547. One loving heart sets another on fire. —**Augustine**

1548. The real meaning of *agape* is unconquerable benevolence. If we regard a person with *agape*, it means that nothing that that person can or will ever do will make us seek anything but his highest good. —**William Barclay**

1549. Love is the forgetting of oneself in the service of another.
—**R. Ainsley Barnwell**

1550. Alone and without love we die. Life itself is as dependent on relationship with others as it is on food. —**M. N. Beck**

1551. A man is only as good as what he loves. —**Saul Bellow**

1552. Love seeketh not itself to please,
Nor for itself hath any care;
But for another gives its ease
And builds a heaven in hell's
despair.
—**William Blake**

1553. For where love is wanting, the beauty of all virtue is mere tinsel, is empty sound, is not worth a straw, nay more, is offensive and disgusting. —**John Calvin**

1554. Love is giving freely, expecting nothing in return. Law concerns itself with an equitable exchange, *this for that*. Law is made necessary by people; love is made possible by God. —**Mary Carson**

1555. Love as "agape," an accepting relationship to others for their own sake and not a passion for another for one's own sake, is the central concept of Jesus and of New Testament Christianity.

—John Ruskin Clark

1556. There is no Christian virtue in being attracted to certain people over others, even if it's poor people over rich. Christ didn't call us merely to modify our tastes. He called people to love. . . . That is why we are *commanded* to love. It is achieved through effort. —Allen Classen

1557. Love is the light that casts a shadow on the sun. —Donald Danford

1558. Time with his old flail
Beat me full sore;
Till: Hold, I cried,
I'll stand no more.

Then I heard a wail
And looking spied
How love's little bow
Had laid time low.

—John Dewey

1559. A loving heart is the truest wisdom. —Charles Dickens

1560. We are all born for love. It is the principle of existence, and its only end.

—Benjamin Disraeli

1561. Love unites without casting off the diversity. —Dobzhansky

1562. The energy of love discharges itself along lines which form a triangle, whose points are God, self, and neighbor.

—C. H. Dodd

1563. The silence of love, the silence that comes from a pure heart, is ready to examine in wisdom what I speak and what I am told. —Catherine Doherty

1564. To love abundantly is to live abundantly, and to love for ever is to live for ever. Hence, eternal life is inextricably bound up with love. We want to live for ever for the same reason we want to live tomorrow. Why do you want to live tomorrow? It is because there is someone who loves you, and whom you want to see tomorrow, and be with, and love back. There is no other reason why we should live on than that we love and are beloved. It is when a man has no one to love him that he commits suicide. So long as he has friends, those who love him and whom he loves, he will live; because to live is to love.

—Henry Drummond

1565. "Do you love me" means "do you see the same truth" [as I do].

—Ralph Waldo Emerson

1566. Love is not deserved; love is. When we love another truly, he does not have to "measure up." We accept and love him as he is. This is the kind of love which Paul says bears all things, believes all things, hopes all things, endures all things (I Cor. 13:7). When we know that we are loved in this way, then and only then, can we dare throw our masks into the corner and reveal ourselves. Only in such an atmosphere of love and acceptance can real trust, intimacy, and openness flourish and grow. —Wynne Gillis

1567. And love in the heart wasn't put
there to stay;
Love isn't love 'till you give it
away.

—Oscar Hammerstein II

1568. We must die to ourselves as we minister in love to others. If the giving gets rough, we can look up to Him and say, "He did it; in His strength so can I."

—Margaret Johnston Hess

1569. Love expects without expecting too much. Love looks for a return in kind without autocratically demanding it. Love focuses on a present relationship while moving forward toward a future goal. Love believes with God in a new day.
—William Hiemstra

1570. The supreme happiness of life is the conviction of being loved for yourself, or, more correctly, being loved in spite of yourself.
—Victor Hugo

1571. Of all the worn, smudged, dog-eared words in our vocabulary, "love" is surely the grubbiest, smelliest, slimiest. Bawled from a million pulpits, lasciviously crooned through hundreds of millions of loud-speakers, it has become an outrage to good taste and decent feeling, an obscenity which one hesitates to pronounce. And yet it has to be pronounced, for after all, love is the last word.
—Aldous Huxley

1572. Lust and desire cannot wait. True love can.
—Walter A. Kortrey

1573. All one can do is leave open a window so the breeze of love . . . may come in. If a window is open, the breeze may still not blow in; there is no guarantee. There is, however, one guarantee: if the window is not open, the breeze will not blow in.
—Joel Kramer

1574. When I have learnt to love God better than my earthly dearest, I shall love my earthly dearest better than I do now.
—C. S. Lewis

1575. They who love are but one step from heaven.
—James Russell Lowell

1576. The love of our neighbor is the only door out of the dungeon of self.
—George MacDonald

1577. One of the great illusions of our time is that love is self-sustaining. It is not. Love must be fed and nurtured, constantly renewed. That demands ingenuity and consideration, but first and foremost, it demands time.
—David R. Mace

1578. There is a destiny that makes us brothers,
None goes his way alone;
All that we send into the lives of others
Comes back into our own.
—Edwin Markham

1579. It is quite clear that the perceptions . . . the intuitions . . . the ability to perceive truth and reality are far healthier and more acute . . . more efficient when one is in love and loving deeply than when not.
—Abraham Maslow

1580. When we love, we give up the center of ourselves.
—Rollo May

1581. Love ever gives,
Forgives—outlives—
And ever stands
With open hands;
And while it lives,
It gives.
For this is love's prerogative—
To give—and give—and give.
—Robert J. McCracken

1582. Love cures people—both the ones who give it and the ones who receive it.
—Karl Menninger

1583. There is no way under the sun of making a man worthy of love, except by loving him.
—Thomas Merton

1584. The way to love someone is to lightly run your finger over that person's soul until you find a crack, and then gently pour your love into that crack.
—Keith Miller

1585. When you know that God loves you, it helps you love yourself. And when you love yourself, you can love somebody else. —**Kari Milton**

1586. Joy is love's consciousness.
Peace is love's confidence.
Patience is love's habit.
Kindness is love's vitality.
Goodness is love's activity.
Faithfulness is love's quantity.
Meekness is love's tone.
Temperance is love's victory.
—**G. Campbell Morgan**

1587. When I love those who return my love, I feel joy because I have pleased them. When I love those who resist my love, I feel joy because I have pleased God.
—**Geraldine Nicholas**

1588. Love for equals is difficult. We love what is weak and suffers. It appeals to our strength without really challenging it.
—**Reinhold Niebuhr**

1589. Love is the identifying mark of Christianity. In a world of hate, envy, and anger, love sticks out like a healthy thumb. When anyone walks away from an encounter with us, that person should remember our love, not our convictions.
—**Rodney Pickett**

1590. When love and skill work together expect a masterpiece. —**John Ruskin**

1591. If thou wishest to be loved, love.
—**Seneca**

1592. Love is not love
Which alters when it alteration finds,
Or bends with the remover to remove:
O no! It is an ever-fixed mark,

That looks on tempests and is never shaken.
—**William Shakespeare**

1593. To love as Christ loves is to let our love be a practical and not a sentimental thing. —**Charles Villiers Stanford**

1594. How sad it is that when we need love most,
We are the most unlovely. If the heart
Is starved for tenderness, the tongue will boast;
While bodies ache for love they hold apart
Stiff and unyielding, flinging in love's eyes
The pepper of apparent unconcern.
And as the stubborn consciousness denies
A need, hot flames of desperation burn.
They storm the frail defenses we construct
To let us face the world and help us cope;
Reserves of vigor crumble, to obstruct
The channels for recovery and hope.
And love, the only thing that could deflect
Disaster, we persistently reject.
—**Dalene Workman Stull**

1595. Thought, purpose, logic, industriousness, but without radiance or love: Isn't it an accurate description of Satan?
—**William L. Sullivan**

1596. Our Lord does not care so much for the importance of our works as for the love with which they are done. —**Teresa of Avila**

1597. There is no greater love than the love that holds on where there seems nothing left to hold on to.   —G. W. C. Thomas

1598. I am convinced that nine out of every ten persons seeing a psychiatrist do not need one. They need somebody who will love them with God's love . . . and they will get well.   —Paul Tournier

1599. There are three principal postures of love. It gives with joy, receives with appreciation and rebukes with humility and hope.   —Albert M. Wells, Jr.

1600. Love can be every bit as blunt as hostility. We beat around the bush, not because we're tactful, but because we're cowards.   —John White

1601. Love is a decision to serve someone.   —Donald E. Whitney

1602. Love does not have to live;
It can afford to die.
It can afford to be
Against a beam on Calvary.
Love does not have to live:
It only has to give.
   —Lon Woodrum

1603. Love has a hem on its garment
That reaches the very dust;
It touches the dirt of the streets
   and lanes
And because it can, it must.

1604. Love does not parade the imperfections of others or taunt people for their weaknesses. Rather love seeks to understand others—their imperfections and weaknesses.

1605. Fulfillment in life comes not by the love of power but by the power of love.

1606. Love is the one business in which it pays to be an absolute spendthrift: give it

away; throw it away; splash it over; empty your pockets; shake the basket; and tomorrow you'll have more than ever.

1607. If you love something, let it go. If it returns to you, it is yours. If it doesn't, it never was. Accepting the reality thus revealed will dislodge worry and send it packing.

1608. Before we can minister in love, we must be mastered by Love.

(see also: Compassion; Interpersonal Relations; Romance)

LOVE FOR GOD

(see: Commitment; Love; Self-Denial; Surrender)

LOYALTY

1609. To have no loyalty is to have no dignity and in the end no manhood.
   —Peter Taylor Forsyth

1610. Loyalty is so fierce and contagious an energy that it is safe only when the object of it is something that we can love or worship when we are alone.
   —William L. Sullivan

1611. If you are ashamed to stand by your colors, you had better seek another flag.

(see also: Patriotism)

Man

1612. There is a God-shaped vacuum in every man that only Christ can fill.
   —Augustine

1613. Left to ourselves we are at the mercy of our passions and fears.
   —William Barclay

1614. Those who deny the existence of God are hard put to explain the existence of man. —**Harold Berry**

1615. The older I grow, and I now stand on the brink of eternity—the more comes back to me that sentence in the Catechism I learned when a child, and the fuller and deeper its meaning becomes: "What is the chief end of man? To glorify God and enjoy Him forever." —**Thomas Carlyle**

1616. Whatever else is or is not true, this one thing is certain—man is not what he was meant to be. —**G. K. Chesterton**

1617. Man is an exception, whatever else he is. If it is not true that a divine [image-bearing] being fell, then we can only say that one of the animals went entirely off its head. —**G. K. Chesterton**

1618. In dismissing the God he cannot understand, man is left to possess the things he cannot enjoy. —**Donald DeMarco**

1619. When man forsakes the fountain of living water, he cannot get rid of the thirst . . . and there is still within him the same absolute necessity for a revelation of God. —**Joseph S. Exell**

1620. Man is like a heat-seeking missile—loaded, fired and looking for action. —**Robert L. Hart**

1621. The deepest principle in human nature is the craving to be appreciated. —**William James**

1622. So great is the depravity of the unregenerate man that, although there is nothing that he needs more than the gospel, there is nothing that he desires less. —**R. B. Kuiper**

1623. When a man is getting better, he understands more and more clearly the evil that is still in him. When a man is getting worse, he understands his own badness less and less. —**C. S. Lewis**

1624. In whatever man does without God, he must either fail miserably, or succeed more miserably. —**George MacDonald**

1625. When men turn away from God, Pascal tells us, they must either imagine they are gods themselves or . . . revert to being animals and seek their satisfaction in their own carnality. Megalomania or erotomania . . . Hitler or Hugh Hefner. —**Malcolm Muggeridge**

1626. God made man a little lower than the angels, and he's been getting lower and lower ever since. —**Will Rogers**

1627. I have insisted that there is something radically and systematically wrong with our culture, a flaw that lies deeper than any class or race analysis probes, and which frustrates our best efforts to achieve wholeness. I am convinced it is our ingrained commitment to the scientific picture of nature that hangs us up. —**Theodore Roszak**

1628. Man's greatest danger is the combination of his increased control over the elements and his lack of control over himself. —**Albert Schweitzer**

1629. Man, proud man! dressed in a little brief authority, plays such fantastic tricks before high heaven as to make the angels weep. —**William Shakespeare**

1630. God does not love us because we are valuable. We are valuable because God loves us. —**Fulton Sheen**

1631. God is not something like us, only better. Rather, we are something like God, only infinitely less. . . . With Jesus Christ as the central evidence and supreme manifestation of that "something like," this likeness is the most wonderful truth in the entire universe. —**Gardner Taylor**

1632. Plastic people crack easily.

1633. Two natures beat within my
breast.
One is foul, the other blest.
The one I love; the one I hate.
The one I feed will dominate.

1634. The old nature knows no law. The new nature needs no law.

1635. We will either obey God as people or as slaves. God establishes the options. If we obey as people we consent that good be done to us. If we seek by self-determination our own welfare, we obey God's order as slaves. The authority of God is final and absolute.

(see also: Free Will)

MARRIAGE

1636. Even after he has stressed the subordination of women, Paul goes on to stress even more directly the essential partnership of man and woman. Neither can live without the other. If there be subordination it is not for the sake of subordination, but that the partnership may be more fruitful and more lovely for both.
—**William Barclay**

1637. Falling in love is easy; growing in love must be worked at with determination as well as imagination. —**Lesley Barfoot**

1638. How often has it been said that a marriage is not truly a marriage unless it is first a friendship? How true this is, and how true that the satisfaction found in friendship lies not so much in achieving interpersonal skills as in developing ways

and times of relating that build meaning upon meaning. —**Lesley Barfoot**

1639. I repeat the marriage vows that say I take my spouse "For better or for worse, for richer or for poorer, in sickness or in health." When I make those vows, I probably hear the parts that say "better," "richer," and "health"; what about the parts saying "worse," "poorer," and "sickness"? Christian marriage isn't just a time for glory and joy; it involves struggle and service. How easily we glamorize . . . and overlook the fine print: marriage is hard work! —**Paul L. Bremer**

1640. It is difficult to make generalizations that will apply specifically to each couple. However, one important idea that applies in nearly all cases is that sex is a barometer of how well other areas of the marriage relationship are going.
—**Barbara Chesser**

1641. Invest your time with each other. If you live to be old, the relationships that result will be far more valuable to you than money; if you don't [live a long time] you'll have fewer regrets when you die.
—**Richard D. Dobbins**

1642. The closer a man and his wife get to Christ, the clearer they see how important it is for them to stay close to each other. —**Richard D. Dobbins**

1643. O Father, all creating, whose
wisdom, love, and power
First bound two lives together in
Eden's primal hour,
Today to these Thy children
Thine earliest gifts renew,
A home by Thee made happy, a
love by Thee kept true.

Except Thou build it, Father, the
house is built in vain;

Except Thou, Savior, bless it, the
joy will turn to pain;
But nought can break the union
of hearts in Thee made one;
And the love Thy Spirit hallows is
endless love begun.

—John Ellerton

1644. Henry Ford was asked on the occasion of his fiftieth wedding anniversary, "What is the formula for a good marriage?" He replied, "The same as for a successful car; stick to one model."

1645. When you marry someone, you become one flesh. If work interferes and disrupts that relationship, then work is as much an enemy as heroin. —Leighton Ford

1646. A good marriage is the union of two forgivers. —Ruth Bell Graham

1647. In marriage you never arrive, you are always on the road. —Patricia Gundry

1648. Living together without any sense of permanency or legality is no more like marriage than taking a warm shower is like shooting a rapids in your underwear.

—Sydney Harris

1649. Freedom to be yourself in marriage doesn't mean freedom to disregard the other. —Margaret Johnston Hess

1650. The most important minutes of the day are the first five minutes when husband and wife awaken and are aware of each other. Those impressions set the tone for the day: the way they look, the tone of voice, and most of all, the attitude.

—M. P. Horban

1651. Marriage is giving. It is a commitment to seek the other's good, not just temporarily, but "till death do us part."

—M. P. Horban

1652. We have a picture of the perfect partner, but we marry an imperfect person. Then we have two options. Tear up the picture and accept the person, or tear up the person and accept the picture.

—J. Grant Howard, Jr.

1653. If wives and husbands would practice giving love instead of waiting to receive it, I doubt if there would ever be a divorce. But when two people choose a mate on the basis of what they expect to get out of their partner, they are bound for divorce, because each is waiting to receive.

—Dave Imbach

1654. Marriage is a commitment—a decision to do, *all through life,* that which will express love for one's spouse.

—Herman H. Kieval

1655. Your love for your spouse is spineless and weak if you do not demand that your spouse remain faithful to you and uphold the vows that will make your relationship mutually beneficial.

—John Kleinheksel

1656. A properly reciprocal sexual relation is impossible so long as each partner is locked up in the modern separated ego.

—Robert Langbaum

1657. Though you intend to marry, yet let the time never come till you find a person who has those perfections which you have been laboring after yourself—who is likely to be a friend to all your virtues, and with whom it is better to live than to lack the benefit of that person's example.

—William Law

1658. Anyone who wishes to make a case for egalitarianism in marriage is free to do so. But when he or she denigrates Scripture in the process, that's too high a price to pay. And if a case for egalitarianism in marriage cannot be made without doing violence to Scripture, maybe the case isn't very strong to begin with.

—Harold Lindsell

1659. Love endures only when the lovers love many things together and not merely each other. —Walter Lippmann

1660. Let the wife make the husband glad to come home, and let him make her sorry to see him leave. —Martin Luther

1661. Marriage may be described as the ultimate form of friendship achievable between sexually attracted persons.

—Daniel C. Maguire

1662. Getting married is the main point in life at which one says, "I have chosen; from now on my aim will be, not to search for someone who will please me, but to please the one I have chosen."

—Andre Maurois

1663. If Christ's love for the church is to be the model for marriage, then this much both partners can learn: You have to put up with a lot, and you have to cherish a lot.

—George McCauley

1664. When you marry, it's not because you've found the best [spouse] in the whole wide world, but because you've found one about whom you care very much, and you [decide] to share your life with [that person], faults included.

—Phyllis Reynolds Naylor

1665. None of the biblical references to marriage hold out the hope that it will be unfailingly romantic—or that it should be.

—Malcolm Nygren

1666. Marriage is not a vacation or a picnic. Rather, marriage is a career that demands the very best of both partners.

Marriage is a testing-ground for one's integrity, courage and character.

—J. Allen Petersen

1667. The highest happiness on earth is in marriage. Every man who is happily married is a successful man even if he has failed in everything else.

—William Lyon Phelps

1668. A Christian marriage . . . serves a threefold purpose: to enrich the lives of the man and woman, to create a family, and to further the kingdom of God.

—Jack Roeda

1669. In the ideal marriage husband and wife are not loyal to each other because it is their duty, but because it is their joy.

—E. Merrill Root

1670. The essential dimension to a marriage is the quality of peace.

—Robin Scroggs

1671. When true love comes, that which is counterfeit will be recognized. For someday, it will rain on the picnic, ants will sting, mosquitoes will bite, and you will get indigestion from the potato salad. There will be no stars in your eyes, no sunsets on your horizon. Love will be in black and white with no piped-in music. But you will say "forever," because love is a choice you have made. —Ruth Senter

1672. When the old guys emphasized "for richer or for poorer, in sickness and in health," they weren't being sentimental; they meant it. A commitment like that takes guts. —Joseph Sittler

1673. The fullest glory in marriage comes when two people—discipled lovers—trust God to lead them through His ultimate curriculum of love and righteousness. The marriage will not be perfect, but the partners will be experiencing the very best of both journeys.

—Merrita Tumonong

1674. Don't need your spouse too much. Only need God that much. Then, maybe, you will have both God and your spouse.

—Robert J. Valentine

1675. To be faithful is to be committed "in spite of." . . . Marriage is the linking of two individuals in a relationship that tests the capacity for fidelity in the most demanding manner. —James M. Wall

1676. Love, common sense, and true Christian character are the three most important ingredients for lasting marriage.

—P. H. Welshimer

1677. For a married person, flirting is never innocent.

1678. Marriage is more than finding the right person. It is being the right person.

1679. To keep a marriage brimming
With love in the loving cup,
Whenever you're wrong, admit it.
Whenever you're right, shut up!

(see also: The Family; Husbandhood; Wifehood)

MASS MEDIA

1680. The printed word can promote thoughtful discussion more effectively than other media. . . . For instance you can put down the paper or magazine and weigh what is said, discussing this with others. With the other media it is not so easy to manage instant replay . . . or put a commentary on hold. —James J. Higgins

1681. While [the multimedia phenomenon] has facilitated the proliferation of the Gospel, it has nonetheless tended to produce a kind of shirt-tail Christianity. Personal prayer and Bible reading have been supplanted by cassette tapes, devotional books and TV programs.

—Ronald A. Iwasco

1682. For the past twenty years you and I have been fed all day long on good solid lies about sex. —C. S. Lewis

1683. The loss of individual and personal meaning via the electronic media ensures a corresponding and reciprocal violence from those so deprived of their identities; for violence, whether spiritual or physical, is a quest for identity and the meaningful.

—Marshall McLuhan

1684. Media and technologies can be considered as the physical, tangible reality of culture; ideologies are largely media trappings. —Marshall McLuhan

1685. The media in general, and TV in particular, are incomparably the greatest single influence in our society today. This influence is, in my opinion, largely exerted irresponsibly, arbitrarily, and without reference to any moral or intellectual, still less spiritual guidelines whatsoever.

—Malcolm Muggeridge

1686. Both public opinion and popular culture are intimately, even essentially, interlocked within the media system.

—John M. Phelan

1687. The unqualified support given by the media to the "anything goes"—in mores, fashion, behavior, styles of life, mass culture—resulted in deranging the social fabric through a reckless pogrom of criteria that heretofore had constituted the American ethos. Although not alone, the media were eager executioners. Never in history has such a scale of reward been extended to youth as it was to the rock-syndrome heroes in exchange for their illiteracy of mind and heart—hustled as innocence and gnosis. And none of this would have occurred without the ardent assistance of the media. —Leopold Tyrmand

1688. The only problem with the press is they never *do* anything. They only report what others do and criticize it.
—Albert M. Wells, Jr.
(see also: Television)

MATERIALISM AND HEDONISM

1689. The poorest man is he who has gathered to himself everything except the Saviour. The unhappiest man is he who knows only the passing pleasures of a Christless life. —Edwin R. Anderson

1690. No man can live without delight, and that is why a man deprived of spiritual joy goes over to carnal pleasures.
—Thomas Aquinas

1691. The danger of prosperity is that it encourages a false independence.
—William Barclay

1692. Theirs is an endless road, a hopeless maze, who seek for goods before they seek for God. —Bernard of Clairvaux

1693. Comforts and syphilis are the greatest enemies of mankind.
—Alexis Carrel

1694. Men are nailed to the things of this life. —Chrysostom

1695. Can anything be more absurd than to make so much the more provision for life's journey, as there is less of that journey left? —Cicero

1696. Will you be satisfied with the fruit of your life's work? Will the efforts you are making now bring you satisfaction when the things of time are receding and eternity looms just ahead? —Raymond L. Cox

1697. So strong is the materialistic climate of opinion today that even Christians sometimes feel compelled to defend Christianity against the charge of "other worldliness"—to slight its value as . . . the passport to heaven in favor of its usefulness as a blueprint for remodeling earth.
—Joy Davidman

1698. When David Garrick showed the godly Dr. Johnson his fine mansion, garden, statues, and pictures at Hampton Court, Dr. Johnson said, "Ah, David, David, these are the things which make a death-bed terrible." —John Drescher

1699. The true measure of life's worth is the ability to worthily suffer and die. Good health and good housing are not salvation; they may only be narcotics that help poor souls to exist, even though they are "dead."
—George E. Failing

1700. He toiled and saved his earnings
    every day
But starved his mind and
    grasped at common things;
His prisoned soul ne'er struggled
    out of clay,
His better nature never found
    its wings.

He hoped to sit with happiness at
    last,
Mansioned sufficient, when he
    would be old;
But he was just a graveyard, and
    the past
Left naught for him but a rude
    pile of gold.
—Alex Louis Frazier

1701. Man becomes the eternal suckling with an open mouth, taking in without effort and without inner activeness, whatever the boredom-preventing industry forces on him—cigarettes, liquor, movies, TV, sports, lectures.　　—Erich Fromm

1702. The difference between Patrick Henry and the average American today is that Patrick Henry said: "Give me liberty or give me death," and the average American today just says: "Gimme."
　　—Vance Havner

1703. Theologically, wealth is a more serious problem than poverty.
　　—Laurens Hogebrink

1704. We don't need to increase our goods nearly as much as we need to scale down our wants. Not wanting something is as good as possessing it.　—Donald Horban

1705. The love of wealth makes bitter men; the love of God, better men.
　　—W. L. Hudson

1706. As the world turns toward the worship of power, we must remember that the first worshipers of the Christ-child were not the great and mighty, not the rich and noble. The oxen and sheep were His company, and the shepherds were His congregation. No power, no sword, no bombs, no guns, no books, no money.　—F. L. Jensen

1707. Pleasure has a place in a Christian's life. But it must be within the framework of the joy God gives . . . always tempered by our uncompromising devotion to obedience.　—Jon Johnston

1708. Things are to be used and God is to be loved. We get into trouble when we begin to use God and love things.
　　—Jay Kesler

1709. We poor humans boast of our freedom, then exhibit our shackles of material enslavement. We insist that nobody can tell us what to do—but the clanking of our chains gives our plight away.
　　—Ralph Larson

1710. You are wise not to join the Communists, but you will still pierce yourself through with many sorrows—to use Paul's figure—and you will take away your own life—to use Solomon's poetry—if you are greedy of gain.　—George S. Lauderdale

1711. All that is not eternal is eternally out of date.　—C. S. Lewis

1712. Riches are the least worthy gifts which God can give man, yet men toil for them day and night, and take no rest. Therefore, God frequently gives riches to foolish people to whom He gives nothing else.　—Martin Luther

1713. It is so difficult for us to transfer our affections [to things above], for we have fallen in love with toyland and our playthings are so dear.　—Peter Marshall

1714. I may, I suppose, regard myself or pass for being a relatively successfully man. People occasionally stare at me in the streets—that's fame. I can fairly easily earn enough to qualify for admission to the higher slopes of the Internal Revenue—that's success. . . . It might happen once in a while that something I said or wrote was sufficiently heeded for me to persuade myself that it represented a serious impact on our time—that's fulfillment. Yet I say to you—and I beg you to believe me—multiply these tiny triumphs by a million, add them all together, and they are nothing—less than nothing . . . measured against one draught of the living water

Christ offers to the spiritually thirsty, irrespective of who or what they are.
—Malcolm Muggeridge

1715. Riches make people decadent and they behave accordingly. When, as in our affluent society, there are many rich, there is much decadence. —Malcolm Muggeridge

1716. Lustful ambition breeds the fools who bid for counterfeit kingdoms. From such preserve us, Good Lord.
—Richard John Neuhaus

1717. Let me hold lightly
Things of this earth,
Transient treasures,
What are they worth?

Moths can corrupt them,
Rust can decay;
All their bright glory
Fades in a day.

Let me hold lightly
Temporal things,
I who am deathless,
I who wear wings!

Let me hold fast, Lord,
Things of the skies,
Quicken my vision,
Open my eyes!

Show me Thy riches,
Glory and grace
Boundless as time is,
Endless as space!

Let me hold lightly
Things that were mine;
Lord, Thou dost give me
All that is Thine.
—Martha Snell Nicholson

1718. He'd gotten the message early that religion's good for health and business: keep the rules, avoid loose girls, righteous-ness has happy rewards, Moses is a good investment.

It hadn't taken long to show a profit, living proof that piety pays: his heart was sound, the family farm blessed, two kids in Little League, a wife who knew her place.

Confident of his claim on the heavenly bonanza, he put it all on display for Jesus.

The dismissing phrase, "you lack one thing," was disappointing, considering the source.

He'd have to find a better rabbi, one who understood and appreciated the finer things of life. —Eugene H. Peterson

1719. Socrates, on looking around the market place containing almost anything an Athenian of his day could want, made this observation: "What a lot of things there are a man can do without."

1720. Do not pursue what is illusory—property and position; all that is gained is at the expense of your nerves, decade after decade, and is confiscated in one fell night. —Alexander Solzhenitsyn

1721. The constant desire to have still more things and a still better life and the struggle to obtain them imprints many Western faces with worry and even depression, though it is customary to conceal such feelings. —Alexander Solzhenitsyn

1722. It is perhaps a more fortunate destiny to have a taste for collecting shells than to be born a millionaire.
—Robert Louis Stevenson

1723. Expend no part of [your money] merely to gratify the desire of the flesh, the desire of the eye, or the pride of life.
—John Wesley

1724. If my financial security rests on what I own rather than on the one who owns me, my wealth has seduced me into unfaithfulness toward God.

—Merold Westphal

1725. The problem is not that you cannot have what you think you want. The problem is that when you get what you think you want, it won't satisfy. In other words, the problem is not acquisition but illusion.

1726. Not all rich men are godly, but all godly men are rich.

1727. Possessions weigh me down in life;
I never feel quite free.
I wonder if I own my things,
Or if my things own me.

1728. We saved money to buy all the things we have accumulated over the years; and now we finally know we didn't need them.

1729. Christian discipleship has got to be more than driving to church once a week in the latest model car while in between times vegetating in front of a thousand-dollar television console.

1730. Americans often spend money they don't have on things they don't need to impress people they don't like.

1731. One who pursues righteousness may get gain, but one who pursues gain will not get righteousness.

(see also: Money; Worldliness)

MATURITY

1732. God isn't so concerned with delivering us out of the mess we're in as He is in seeing us grow out of the mess we are.

—L. Thomas Holdcroft

1733. Real adulthood is the result of the development of two qualities: self-discipline and self-reliance. The process of developing them together in balance is called maturing.   —J. W. Jepson

1734. Maturity begins to grow when you can sense your concern for others outweighing your concern for yourself.

—John MacNaughton

1735. There is no real maturity without the dimension of spiritual maturity.

—Franklin H. Sellers

1736. Christian maturity may be tested in how one answers the following questions. How do I react to trials? How do I resist temptation? How do I respond to truth? How do I restrain my tongue?

—Lehman Strauss

1737. Some people never grow up—they just grow old. Many a woman has a teenage husband and many a long-suffering male has a child bride with wrinkles.

(see also: Character)

MEDITATION

1738. The mightiest works of God are the fruit of silence.   —F. B. Meyer

1739. The word of God penetrates through the thick of human verbosity to the silent center of our heart; silence opens in us the space where the word can be heard.   —Henri J. M. Nouwen

1740. I met God in the morning
When the day was at its best;
His presence came like sunrise,
Like a glow within my breast.

All day long it lingered near,
All day long it stayed with me.
And we sailed in perfect calm
O'er a very troubled sea.

So I think I know the secret,
Learned from many a troubled
way;
You must meet Him in the
morning
If you'd have Him through the
day.

1741. Transcendental meditation is a sought-after end. Christian meditation is a means to an end—the end of communion with God.

MEEKNESS

1742. The man who is meek is the man who is always angry at the right time, but who is never angry at the wrong time.
—**William Barclay**

1743. Meekness is not weakness. It is power under control. —**Warren W. Wiersbe**

(see also: Humility)

MEMORIAL DAY THEME

1744. Posterity! You will never know how much it cost the present generation to preserve your freedom! I hope you will make good use of it. If you do not, I shall repent in heaven that I ever took half the pains to preserve it. —**John Adams**

(see also: Freedom; Patriotism)

MEN

1745. Men are of two kinds, and he
Was the kind I'd like to be.
No door at which he ever
knocked
Against his manly form was
locked.
No broken pledge lost him
respect;
He met all men with head erect.

And when he passed I think there
went
A soul to yonder firmament
So white, so splendid and so fine
It came almost to God's design.
—**Edgar Guest**

1746. Nothing is more dangerous than weak men who think they are tough guys.
—**I. F. Stone**

1747. That men prefer hard-to-get women misses the point. Men really adore women who are hard for other men to get.

(see also: Fatherhood; Husbandhood)

MENTAL HEALTH

1748. A depressed person is one who has given up on his responsibilities because he has given in to his feelings. —**Jay Adams**

1749. Cheerfulness is the best promoter of health, and is as friendly to the mind as to the body. —**Joseph Addison**

1750. Emotions can make you ill. They can make hair fall out . . . bring on splitting headaches, clog nasal passages . . . tighten the throat with laryngitis, make skin break out in a rash . . . plague one's insides with ulcers and itises. . . . Emotions can kill. —**Blake Clark**

1751. Many people become mentally ill because they refuse to see themselves as they really are. They try to maintain a vision of themselves as virtuous persons doing good against unfavorable odds. In this frame of mind they attribute their faults and failures to others. They justify their behavior as good intentions hindered by circumstances over which they have no control. —**Sylvia Doolin**

1752. In their suffering, those who are sick of mind represent the alienation of all humanity. Mental degradation symbolizes the human condition in its fundamental need of redemption. —**Louis Dupre**

1753. Emotions were made to enjoy—but out of control they tend to destroy.

—**Lyle Flinner**

1754. Persistent affective states of a depressive nature, such as sorrow, worry, or grief, reduce the state of nourishment of the whole body, cause the hair to turn white, the fat to disappear, and the walls of the blood vessels to undergo morbid changes. There can be no doubt that the duration of life can be appreciably shortened by depressive affects.

—**Sigmund Freud**

1755. Two conditions are necessary for mental health; to be able to love and to be able to work. —**Sigmund Freud**

1756. I have to live with myself, and so
I want to be fit for myself to know,
I want to be able as days go by,
Always to look myself in the eye;
I don't want to stand, with the
  setting sun,
And hate myself for the things
  I've done.

I want to go out with my head
  erect,
I want to deserve all men's
  respect;
But here in the struggle for fame
  and pelf,
I want to be able to look at myself.
I don't want to look at myself and
  know
That I'm bluster and bluff and
  empty show.

I can never hide myself from me;
I see what others may never see;

I know what others may never
  know;
I never can fool myself, and so,
Whatever happens, I want to be
Self-respecting and conscience
  free.

—**Edgar Guest**

1757. To alleviate distress at its source, the breach with God must be healed.

—**Bruce Howell**

1758. Depression is a partial surrender to death. —**Arnold A. Hutschnecker**

1759. The central neurosis of our time is emptiness. —**Carl Jung**

1760. If you feel insecure, then it must be that you are looking inward at yourself rather than upward at Jesus Christ.

—**Howard A. Kelly**

1761. [Healthy personalities] accept themselves not in any self-idolizing way but in the sense they see themselves as persons of worth; as persons who are worth giving to another and worthy to receive from another. —**William Klassen**

1762. Fifty years ago we died from bacterial and biological reasons. What do we die from today? Stress-related diseases—heart attacks and all those things. We die from emotional hurts. We die easily from someone's remarks. . . . Stress is a gigantic factor in our life. —**Joyce Landorf**

1763. Money-giving is a good criterion of a person's mental health. Generous people are rarely mentally ill. —**Karl Menninger**

1764. The paradox of *human* cure is that in taking away the pain and anxieties of our daily life, we also remove the excuse for not dealing with the ultimate condition of our existence. —**Henri J. M. Nouwen**

1765. I am convinced that nine out of every ten persons seeing a psychiatrist do not need one. They need somebody who will love them with God's love . . . and they will get well. —**Paul Tournier**

1766. A paranoid mental patient is a person who says, "I am persecuted." Because he believes he is persecuted he behaves in a surly, disgruntled manner and is suspicious and unfriendly. Then people begin to maltreat him, and he says, "See, didn't I tell you I'm persecuted?" Thus he fulfills his own prophecy.

(see also: Self-Pity; Suffering)

MIDDLE AGE

1767. If a man's curve of efficiency is ascending at forty-five and keeps on ascending just after that period, it may move upward for his whole life; but if there is a turn downward at forty-five, he will never recover. —**Nicholas Murray Butler**

1768. You know you've reached middle age when it's a doctor and not a traffic cop who warns you to slow down.
—**Anna Herbert**

1769. The long, dull, monotonous years of middle-aged prosperity or middle-aged adversity are excellent campaigning weather for the Devil. —**C. S. Lewis**

1770. You can tell you are getting to be middle aged when the foods you like the most are liking you the least.

1771. Middle age is when you suddenly realize there are more years in your past than there are in your future.

THE MIND

1772. We have to discipline our minds; it is one of the tragedies of life that men refuse to think until they are incapable of thinking. —**William Barclay**

1773. The Wesleyan warmed heart involved the studying mind.
—**Ralph Sockman**

1774. Once John Wesley received a note from a self-appointed evangelist telling him, "The Lord has told me to tell you that He doesn't need your book learning, your Greek and Hebrew." Wesley replied, "Thank you, Sir. Your letter was superfluous, however, as I already knew the Lord has no need of my 'book learning' as you put it. However, although the Lord has not directed me to say so, on my own responsibility I would like to say, the Lord does not need your ignorance either."

1775. He that will not command his thoughts will soon lose command of his actions. —**Woodrow Wilson**

(see also: Thought)

THE MINISTER

1776. A home-going pastor will have church-going members. —**Sarah Clayton**

1777. A preacher should have the mind of a scholar, the heart of a child and the hide of a rhinoceros. His biggest problem is how to soften his hide without hardening his heart. —**Vance Havner**

1778. The modern preacher has to make as many calls as a country doctor; he has to shake as many hands as a politician. He has to prepare as many briefs as a lawyer; he has to see as many people as a medical specialist. He has to be as good an executive as a college president; he has to be as good a financier as a banker; and in the midst of it all, he has to be so good a diplomat that he could umpire a baseball game between the Knights of Columbus and the Ku Klux Klan.   —Gerald Kennedy

1779. [Ministers] who criticize statistics usually have none to report.
—Charles H. Spurgeon

1780. The Lord calls men to shepherd His flock. But nowhere in Scripture does God call His people a herd. They are a flock, and the leaders are called shepherds. There is one distinctive thing about sheep: they cannot be driven. You can drive a herd of cattle . . . but you cannot drive sheep. They must be *led!*

1781.   The parish priest of austerity,
              climbed up a high church
              steeple,
         To be near God, so that he might
              hand His Word down to His
              people.
         When the sun was high, when
              the sun was low, the good
              man sat, unheeding
         Sub-luminary things from
              transcendency, while he
              forever was reading.
         And now and again, when he
              heard the creak of the
              weather vane a'turning,
         He closed his eyes and said, "Of a
              truth from God I am now
              learning."
         And in a sermon script he daily
              wrote what he thought was
              sent from heaven;
         And he dropped this down on the
              people's heads two times one
              day in seven.
         In his age, God said, "Come
              down and die," and he cried
              out from the steeple,

"Where art Thou, Lord," and the
    Lord replied, "Down here
    among my people."

(see also: Preaching)

MISSIONS
(see: World Missions)

MODESTY

1782. We have plenty of people nowadays who could not kill a mouse without publishing it in the *Gospel Gazette*. Samson killed a lion and said nothing about it; the Holy Spirit finds modesty so rare that He takes care to record it. Say much of what the Lord has done for you, but say little of what you have done for the Lord.
—Charles H. Spurgeon

1783. The girl needs to combine attractiveness and modesty at the same time. If she is attractive without being modest, she directs the desire of the boy to her body. If she's unattractive and only modest, she doesn't have the date in the first place. But if she is modest or careful, she directs the desire of the boy to her soul and he's willing to pay the price for getting the girl.
—Walter Trobisch

1784. Christian modesty and worldly pride are like fire and water. When mixed, one destroys the other.

(see also: Humility)

MONEY

1785. One act par excellence . . . profanes money by going directly against the law of money, an act for which money is not made. This act is *giving*. —Jacques Ellul

1786. If you would know the value of money, go and try to borrow some.

—Benjamin Franklin

1787. He that is of the opinion money will do everything may well be suspected of doing everything for money.

—Benjamin Franklin

1788. Money is like sex. Whether it is good or bad depends on how you use it.

—Max R. Hickerson

1789. Money may buy the husk of things, but not the kernel. It brings you food but not appetite, medicine but not health, acquaintances but not friends, servants but not faithfulness, days of joy but not peace or happiness.   Henrik Ibsen

1790. Money is like a sixth sense without which you cannot make a complete use of the other five.   —Somerset Maugham

1791. Jesus taught that money is one of the spiritual powers we fight—not simply green paper or copper-nickel sandwiches. Money is not some *thing*; it is *someone*. And as someone, it tricks us into thinking we master it, when inevitably it masters us.

—David Neff

1792. Our pocketbooks have more to do with heaven and also with hell than our hymnbooks.   —Helmut Thielicke

1793. When I have money, I get rid of it quickly, lest it find a way into my heart.

—John Wesley

1794. Money is an article which may be used as a universal passport to everywhere except heaven, and a universal provider of everything except happiness.

1795. Money is like manure. Stack it up and it stinks; spread it around and it makes things grow.

1796. The love of money is a root
Which causes care and trouble;
And he that hastens to be rich,
He makes his sorrows double.

1797. Money still talks; it usually says "Goodbye."

1798. It is difficult to save money when your neighbors keep buying things you can't afford.

1799. Inflation is when you have money to burn, but can't afford to buy the matches.

(see also: Stewardship)

MORALITY

1800. Morality, like art, consists in drawing the line somewhere.

—G. K. Chesterton

1801. I think of the old story about the man who tried to save Sodom from destruction. The city's inhabitants ignored him, then asked mockingly, "Why bother everyone? You can't change them."

"Maybe I can't change them," the man replied, "but if I still shout and scream it will at least prevent them from changing me!"

—Charles W. Colson

1802. Morality, without religion, is only a kind of dead reckoning—an endeavor to find our place on a cloudy sea.

—Henry Wadsworth Longfellow

1803. There can be no personal integrity that is not based on the integrity of the universe. Integrity within you, the courage to create quality within you and around you, is not based upon the quicksands of relativism but on the granite of morality. . . . Morality is as basic as the truth that two plus two are four; . . . that the seed grows toward the sun. Morality is a decalogue written in stone and star; it is not a conformity to illusion but a confirmation by reality. —**E. Merrill Root**

1804. I am no historian of morals, but it strikes me that "feeling good" deserves some kind of booby prize as a bankrupt argument for social behavior. "Feeling good" is the argument of the jungle, not civilized societies. —**Bruce Shelley**

(see also: Character; Ethics; Truth; United States/Moral Climate)

MOTHERHOOD

1805. Mothers who are confident, proud of their own femininity, and neither jealous of nor in rebellion against their husband's masculinity will be able to do a much better job in helping both their boys and their girls to be comfortable and secure in their own sexual identity.

—**Ruth Tiffany Barnhouse**

1806. I remember a scathing "put-down" popular in my younger years. When you wanted to label a man as spineless you sneered that "he was tied to his mother's apron strings." Come to think of it, though, the way the world seems to be falling apart, I can't think of a more secure place to be tied to. —**Charles M. Davis**

1807. "Children must have their naps,"
    I say;
"It's mother who knows best."
Now what I really mean by that
Is that I need a rest.

—**Donna Evleth**

1808. If mothers would understand that much of their importance lies in building up the father image for the child, the children would turn out well.

—**Samuel S. Liebowitz**

1809. Mothers . . . fill places so great that there isn't an angel in heaven who wouldn't be glad to give a bushel of diamonds to come down here and take their place. —**Billy Sunday**

1810. If a woman remains unmarried, is appointed matron of an orphanage and brings up other people's children to be good Christians, she is called a church worker. But if she marries, becomes the mother of a family and brings up her children to be good Christians, no one calls her a church worker, yet that good mother is a church worker. —**William Temple**

1811. They say that man is mighty,
He governs land and sea,
He wields a mighty scepter
O'er lesser powers than he.
But a mighty power and stronger
Man from his throne has hurled:
For the hand that rocks the cradle
ıs the hand that rules the world.

—**William Wallace**

1812. The most important occupation on the earth for a woman is to be a real mother to her children. It does not have much glory in it; there is a lot of grit and grime. But there is no greater place of ministry, position or power than that of a mother. —**Phil Whisenhunt**

(see also: Parenthood)

MOTIVES

1813. The last temptation is the greatest
    treason:
To do the right deed for the wrong
    reason.

—**T. S. Eliot**

1814. It has been more wittily than charitably said that the road to hell is paved with good intentions; they have their place in heaven also.   —Robert Southey

MOVIES

1815. The current desire for scanty attire
Leaves actors like me in a daze,
To be poised and composed with
    one's bottom exposed
Ain't required in classical plays.

There are movies and plays being
    offered these days
Which look, smell and sound
    much the same
As a basketball team snapping
    towels in the steam
In the locker room after a game.

The language is crude, the
    characters nude,
Their actions I can't bear to
    mention.
The emotions are raw as the ones
    that we saw
At the last Democratic
    convention.

Don't bother gaining professional
    training
And don't even bother
    rehearsing,
Be a star overnight and the critics'
    delight:
Just take off your pants and start
    cursing.
                    —Victor Buono

1816. Christians ruled out the stage and the movies for the first half of this century. Then, as a new evangelical critic has pointed out, we bought television sets and caught up on all those movies we'd missed.
                    —Robert G. Delnay

1817. Martin E. Marty, after not going to a single movie for four years, returned to the cinema for a double feature. Said he, "We came home with what our collegian sons call 'fried brains,' and also gangrene of the rump."

1818. Hollywood is a place where ten million dollars worth of machinery functions to put skin on baloney.
                    —George Jean Nathan

MUSIC

1819. Music is like fire—a devastating scourge or an unspeakable blessing. It's a tool of hell, or it's the very atmosphere of heaven. Music can loose the wild stallions of passion, or it can inspire the purest praises to God.   —H. H. Barber

1820. True religion sings here, and will sing more hereafter. Distrust your religion unless it is cheerful, unless it turns every act and deed to music, and exults in attempts to catch the harmony of the new life.   —Phillips Brooks

1821. [The proper use of the power of music in the church] is to have songs not only honest, but also holy, which will be like spurs to incite us to pray and praise God, and to meditate upon His works in order to love, fear, honor and glorify Him.
                    —John Calvin

1822. Music and religion are as intimately related as poetry and love; the deepest emotions require for their civilized expressions the most emotional of arts.
                    —Will Durant

1823. For many teenagers—and those from Christian homes are not necessarily an exception—rock music has replaced religion. It provides emotional satisfaction and mystical excitement. Few adults understand its pull.   —Cheryl Forbes

1824. Music is God's gift to man. It is the only art of heaven given to earth and the only art of earth we take to heaven.
—Charles W. Landon

1825. Music is love in search of a word.
—Sidney Lanier

1826. The electronic hardware being thrust upon us makes me wonder if the Lord forgot to equip our bodies with earlids to withstand the onslaught of sound. We are witnessing the influence of rock upon Bach—and the courtship and marriage of church music to Hollywood and Nashville—for personal gain. These commercial efforts have invaded the church. It creates a concern that needs to be reckoned with by every serious Christian.
—Earl W. Lehman

1827. Music is the universal language of mankind by which human feelings are made equally intelligible to all.
—Franz von Liszt

1828. Most of us have experienced this phenomenon, where music inhibits any real chance to attend to what another is saying. We are continuously assaulted by it in restaurant, elevator, subway; there is no escape. It is perhaps part of an unconscious urge to flee from confrontation with the baffling mystery of existence; we just try to drown it out. —Robert G. Middleton

1829. You cannot play the piano well unless you are singing within you.
—Arthur Rubinstein

1830. Isn't music merely a matter of taste . . . ? No. There are such things as bad pieces of music. In this fallen world, music does not occupy some unique place which makes it immune to corruption. . . . And even though our critical faculties have also been corrupted by the Fall, we may not use

that as an excuse "to throw in the towel" . . . any more than we may, for example, refuse to wrestle with difficult social, political or ethical problems. —Calvin Stapert

1831. Church music should not be for entertainment, but a worship experience that lifts us to the portals of heaven and leaves us thinking of the greatness and goodness of God. —Alice Tucker

1832. Christian music—God's music—ought to be distinctive. It is deceitful and demeaning to God to try and "sneak His message" over on some unsuspecting sinner as he listens to the music of the world.

1833. The use of bad music for a good goal does not alter the music's character, only the character of those who use it.

THE NATION

1834. What this country needs is a man who knows God other than by hearsay.
—Thomas Carlyle

1835. I am old-fashioned enough to believe, with George Washington, that religion and morality are indispensable supports to the national welfare.
—John Tracy Ellis

1836. I fear for my country when I remember that God is just.
—Thomas Jefferson

1837. If a nation expects to be ignorant and free, it expects what never was and never will be. —Thomas Jefferson

1838. Lessons of history too soon forgot;
Warnings from Heaven by men heeded not.
Doomed is my homeland; God's judgment her lot,

Lest to repentance our people are brought.
—Bob Jones

1839. When the State starts becoming God, the State begins by expelling God from the schools and evicting God's Word from the lives of the people.
—J. Kesner Kahn

1840. In the day of judgment, it will be seen which is worse, the wickedness of the Communists, or the failure of men in the free world to heed God's warnings and arouse themselves and repent! Both are abominable in the eyes of heaven.
—George S. Lauderdale

1841. I recognize the sublime truth announced in the Holy Scriptures and proven by all history that those nations only are blest whose God is the Lord.
—Abraham Lincoln

1842. It is impossible either to produce or sustain a republican form of government of limited powers apart from the theology of the Bible. A Biblical view of man—and this alone—was the essence of America's greatness in the past; this alone is the hope for America's greatness in the future.
—Tom Rose

1843. That nation is worthless which does not joyfully stake everything in defense of her honor.
—Schiller

1844. If I were asked today to formulate . . . the main cause for the ruinous [Russian] revolution that swallowed up some sixty million of our people, I could not put it more accurately than to repeat: "Men have forgotten God."
—Alexander Solzhenitsyn

1845. You can measure a society's life expectancy by its willingness to discipline: to punish those who break its laws, who destroy its integrity, who commit treason against its commitments, yes, even unto death.
—G. Aiken Taylor

1846. While "freedom under God" may sometimes stagger as a result of human frailty, it is infinitely preferable to any secular substitute ever proposed.
—G. Aiken Taylor

1847. Western civilization thrived on the Christian religion. The decline of that religion, brought about by the critical scientific method, has entailed the decline of the civilization. . . . I maintain that a society that does not want to perish must somehow institutionalize the ultimate values of human life. In other words, some "religion," some system of suprapersonal goals and values shared by the majority, is necessary for a healthy society.
—Valentin F. Turchin

1848. Two hundred years after George Washington sent out his order, "Put none but Americans on guard tonight," we might well revise it to say: "Put none but Christians on guard tonight."
—Alba Miller Wahl

1849. Let us with caution indulge the supposition that morality can be maintained without religion. Whatever may be conceded to the influence of refined education on minds of peculiar structure, reason and experience both forbid us to expect that national morality can prevail in exclusion of religious principle.
—George Washington

1850. If we abide by the principles taught in the Bible, our country will go on prospering and to prosper; but if we and our posterity neglect its instructions and authority, no man can tell how sudden a catastrophe may overwhelm us, and bury all our glory in profound obscurity.

—Daniel Webster

1851. If the power of the Gospel is not felt throughout the length and breadth of the land, anarchy and misrule, degradation and misery, corruption and darkness will reign without mitigation or end.

—Daniel Webster

1852. The sum of the whole matter is this, that our civilization cannot survive materially unless it be redeemed spiritually. It can be saved only by becoming permeated with the Spirit of Christ and being made free and happy of the practices which spring out of that spirit.

—Woodrow Wilson

1853. Nothing is more certain than that a general profligacy and corruption of manners makes a people ripe for destruction.

—John Witherspoon

1854. Men will more and more realize that there is no meaning in democracy if there is no meaning in anything, and there is no meaning in anything if the universe has not a center of significance and an authority that is the author of our rights.

1855. The future of our country depends on whether we can take the policeman off the street corner and put him in our hearts.

(see also: Freedom; Patriotism; United States/Moral Climate)

NATURE

1856. Heaven and earth and all that is in the universe cry out to me from all directions that I, O God, must love Thee, and they do not cease to cry out to all so that they have no excuse. —Augustine

1857. If God took time to create beauty, how can we be too busy to appreciate it?

—Randall B. Corbin

1858. The sun is losing mass at an estimated rate of five million tons per second. It is so big, however, that even at this rate it will take about five billion years before it *begins* to cool.

NEGLIGENCE

1859. The greatest waste in the world is the difference between what we are and what we could be. —Ben Herbster

1860. For want of a nail the horseshoe was lost. For want of a horseshoe the horse was lost. For want of a horse the battle was lost. For want of a battle the war was lost.

(see also: Apathy)

NEUTRALITY

1861. The world is rushing to Armageddon where no one sits on the fence.

—Charles R. Hembree

1862. The man who sees both sides of an issue is very likely on the fence or up a tree.

(see also: Cowardice)

NEW BIRTH

1863. There will always be Pelagians and Augustinians in the world; the first birth produces the one, the second birth produces the other. —Blaise Pascal

1864. A socialist once made a speech during which he declared, "Socialism will put a new coat on a man." A person from the audience, recently converted, shouted: "Socialism might put a new coat on a man, but Jesus Christ will put a new man in the coat."

1865. It always seemed absurd to me
    To sing of "such a worm as I,"
    Until I saw an ugly worm
    Become a gorgeous butterfly.

1866. Better never to have been born at all, than never to have been born again.

(see also: Conversion; Salvation)

THE NEW YEAR

1867. With every power for good to stay
    and guide me,
    Comforted and inspired beyond
    all fear,
    I'll live these days with you [God]
    in thought beside me,
    And pass with you into the
    coming year.
              —Dietrich Bonhoeffer

1868. Be at war with your vices, at peace with your neighbors, and let every new year find you a better man.
              —Benjamin Franklin

1869. Good resolutions are like babies crying in church. They should be carried out immediately.   **—Charles M. Sheldon**

1870. Father, let me dedicate all this
    year to Thee,
    In whatever worldly state Thou
    wilt have me be:
    Not from sorrow, pain, or care,
    freedom dare I claim;
    This alone shall be my prayer:
    Glorify Thy name.

    Can a child presume to choose
    where or how to live?
    Can a Father's love refuse all the
    best to give?
    More Thou givest every day than
    the best can claim,
    Nor withholdest aught that may
    glorify Thy name.

If Thou callest to the cross and its
    shadows come,
Turning all my gain to loss,
    shrouding heart and home;
Let me think how Thy dear Son
    to His glory came.
And in deepest woe pray on:
    Glorify Thy name.

If on life, serene and fair, brighter
    rays may shine;
If in mercy Thou wilt spare joys
    that yet are mine;
Let my glad heart, while it sings,
    Thee in all proclaim,
And whate'er the future brings,
    glorify Thy name.
              —Lawrence Tuttiett

1871. You can never change the past. But by the grace of God, you can win the future. So remember those things which will help you forward, but forget those things which will only hold you back.
              —Richard C. Woodsome

1872. I will start anew this morning
    with a higher, fairer creed;
    I will cease to stand complaining
    of my ruthless neighbor's
    greed;
    I will cease to sit repining while
    my duty's call is clear;
    I will waste no moment whining,
    and my heart shall know no
    fear.

    I will not be swayed by envy when
    my rival's strength is shown;
    I will not deny his merit, but I'll
    strive to prove my own;
    I will try to see the beauty spread
    before me, rain or shine;
    I will cease to preach your duty,
    and be more concerned with
    mine.
              —Bonnie Yarnell

1873. God bless thy year!
Thy coming in, thy going out,
Thy rest, thy traveling about,
The rough, the smooth,
The bright, the drear,
God bless thy year!

1874. People laugh at new year's resolutions. But we can all use ten minutes in a chair followed by a humble prayer.

1875. I asked the New Year for some
message sweet,
Some rule of life with which to
guide my feet;
I asked, and paused: he answered
soft and low,
"God's will to know."

"Will knowledge then suffice,
New Year?" I cried:
And, ere the question into silence
died,
The answer came, "Nay, but
remember, too,
"God's will to do."

Once more I asked, "Is there no
more to tell?"
And once again the answer
sweetly fell,
"Yes! this thing, all other things
above:
"God's will to love."

1876. One of the last official acts King George VI performed before his death was to go on the BBC to address the British people. In his address he quoted words that have since become very well known: "I said to the man who stands at the Gate of the Year, 'Give me light that I may tread safely into the unknown.' And he replied, 'Step into the darkness, put your hand into the hand of God, and that will be to you better than a light and safer than a known way.'"

(see also: The Future; Time)

NONCONFORMITY

1877. No task to row where water is still,
To drift along and dream;
But it takes a fellow plus a will
To row against the stream.

Most any frail duck can float at
ease
And drift along and dream,
But it takes persistence, if you
please,
To swim against the stream.
—**H. Atlee Brumbaugh**

1878. We often explain nonconformity with reference to our Amish and Hutterite brethren, while we are at a loss to say how we ourselves are nonconformed to worldly ways. —**S. Roy Kaufman**

1879. If a man does not keep pace with his companions, perhaps it is because he hears a different drummer.
—**Henry David Thoreau**

(see also: Separation)

NOTHING

1880. Nothing is often a good thing to say, and always a clever thing to say.
—**Will Durant**

1881. People tend to look down at *nothing* and ignore its importance; however, it can mean life or death, success or failure, joy or sorrow. Mountain climbers have died when they stepped out on it. Farmers have lost their farms when they grew it. Ball players and coaches have lost their jobs when they scored it. It is good reason for joy when it represents the sum total of your

debts. It's what you earn when you do it. It's often discussed at meetings with arguments and fights starting over it. You may find it in your mailbox or the nearby candy machine. Even the Biblical writer, James, says: "But let him ask in faith, *nothing* wavering." *Nothing* does make a difference.
— **Daniel H. Kelchner**

1882. God created the world out of nothing, and so long as we are nothing, He can make something out of us.
— **Martin Luther**

Obedience

1883. The Christian man must aim at that complete obedience to God in which life finds its highest happiness, its greatest good, its perfect consummation, its peace.
— **William Barclay**

1884. We may shout from the housetops our faith and orthodoxy, but unless they are coupled with obedience to the teachings of God's Word, there will come a time when we will find ourselves rejected from His eternal presence. — **L. Nelson Bell**

1885. The best measure of spiritual life is not ecstasies but obedience.
— **Oswald Chambers**

1886. To know God is to experience His love in Christ, and to return that love in obedience. — **C. H. Dodd**

1887. We are prone to argue with the Lord against an assignment that seems to us difficult, dangerous, and impossible. But our part is to trust Him fully, to obey Him implicitly, and to follow His instructions faithfully. — **V. Raymond Edman**

1888. For right is right, since God is God,

And right the day must win;
To doubt would be disloyalty,
To falter would be sin.
— **Frederick W. Faber**

1889. If God commands something, that is the highest evidence that we can do it.
— **Charles G. Finney**

1890. A religious revival is nothing else than a new beginning of obedience to God. — **Charles G. Finney**

1891. Loving the Lord is not an emotional goosebump; it is a commitment to selfless obedience. — **John MacArthur, Jr.**

1892. For the heart to obey Christ, the heart must be in Christ. — **F. B. Meyer**

1893. To obey God is perfect liberty.
— **Seneca**

OBJECTIVITY

1894. In conducting the oral examination of a Mormon student who was submitting a Ph.D. thesis on a particular period of Mormon history, the historian asked the student if he, being a Mormon, considered himself sufficiently unprejudiced to write a thesis on Mormon history. The somewhat daring student replied, "Yes, if you, not a Mormon, consider yourself unprejudiced enough to examine it." — **Arnold S. Nash**

1895. It is always easier to see both sides of a question if your prejudices and money aren't involved.

OLD AGE

1896. Grow old along with me,
The best is yet to be;
The last of life
For which the first was made;

143

Our times are in His hand
Who saith, "A whole I
    planned,
Youth shows but half; Trust God,
See all, nor be afraid!"
                —Robert Browning

1897. It is very grand to die in harness, but it is very pleasant to have the tight straps unbuckled and the heavy collar lifted from the neck and shoulders.
                —Oliver Wendell Holmes

1898. When grace is joined with wrinkles, it is adorable. There is an unspeakable dawn in a happy old age.
                —Victor Hugo

1899. Winter is on my head, but spring is in my heart.   —Victor Hugo

1900. For age is opportunity, no less
    Than youth itself, though in
        another dress,
    And as the evening twilight fades
        away
    The sky is filled with stars,
        invisible by day.
    —Henry Wadsworth Longfellow

1901. In the central place of every heart there is a recording chamber. So long as it receives a message of beauty, hope, cheer, and courage—so long are you young. When the wires are all down and your heart is covered with the snow of pessimism and the ice of cynicism, then, and only then, are you grown old.
                —Douglas MacArthur

1902. Youth is not entirely a time of life; it is a state of mind. It is not wholly a matter of ripe cheeks, red lips, or supple knees. It is a temper of the will, a quality of the imagination, a vigor of the emotions— nobody grows old by merely living a number of years. People grow old only by

deserting their ideals. You are as young as your faith, as old as your doubt; as young as your self-confidence, as old as your fear; as young as your hope, as old as your despair.
                —Douglas MacArthur

1903. One of the many pleasures of old age is to become ever more sharply aware of the many mercies and blessings God showers upon us.   —Malcolm Muggeridge

1904. Those who age successfully have made a decision to stay in training— physically, socially, intellectually, and emotionally.   —Eric Pfeiffer

1905. I consider that the old have gone before us along a road which we must all travel in our turn and it is good we should ask them of the nature of that road, whether it be rough and difficult or easy and smooth.   —Plato

1906. Old age is the worst time we can choose to mend either our lives or our fortunes . . . and if we neglect . . . it is a hundred to one odds that we shall die both poor and wicked.   —Susanna Wesley

1907. Getting old is a most unpleasant phenomenon, but the alternative is much worse.

OPPORTUNITY

1908. When one door closes, another opens. But we often look so long and so regretfully upon the closed door that we do not see the one which has opened for us.
                —Alexander Graham Bell

1909. Failure is the opportunity to begin again more intelligently.   —Henry Ford

1910. There is one thing stronger than all the armies in the world, and that is an Idea whose time has come. —Victor Hugo

1911. There is a tide in the affairs of
men
Which, taken at the flood, leads
on to fortune;
Omitted, all the voyage of their
life
Is bound in shallows and in
miseries.
On such a full sea are we now
afloat;
And we must take the current
when it serves
Or lose our ventures.
—**William Shakespeare**

1912. Destiny is not a matter of chance;
it is a matter of choice.

OPTIMISM

1913. Somebody said that it couldn't be
done—
But he with a chuckle replied
That maybe it couldn't but he
would be one
Who wouldn't say so till he'd
tried.
So he buckled right in, with a bit
of a grin
On his face—if he worried he hid
it;
He started to sing, as he tackled
the thing
That couldn't be done—and he
did it!

Somebody scoffed, "Oh, you'll
never do that—
At least no one ever has done it";
But he took off his coat and he
took off his hat,
And the first thing we knew, he'd
begun it.
With a lift of his chin, and a bit of
a grin

Without any doubting or "quit it,"
He started to sing, as he tackled
the thing
That couldn't be done, and he did
it!
—**Edgar Guest**

1914. The pessimist sees the difficulty in
every opportunity; the optimist sees the
opportunity in every difficulty.
—**L. P. Jacks**

1915. The future is as bright as the promises of God.   —**Adoniram Judson**

1916. The trouble with being an optimist is that people think you don't know
what's going on.

(see also: Hope)

Pacifism

1917. A consistent pacifist is not even
entitled to the protection of his or her liberties to oppose the government, because
the pacifist says [in effect] that this freedom was and is not worth defending.
—**Andrew Kuyvenhoven**

1918. It requires more moral courage to
carry out nonresistance than to fight, and I
don't please to call the pacifists "fools" or
"molly-coddles." But we haven't reached
the time in the development of civilization
when the example of nonresistance has its
full weight.   —**William Howard Taft**

PARENTHOOD

1919. A sense of belonging, the loving
involvement of parents which creates a
sense of worth, and a sense of purpose are
what every child deserves to receive.
—**Cyril J. Barber**

1920. The chances are that you will never be elected president of the country, write the great American novel, make a million dollars, stop pollution, end racial conflict, or save the world. However valid it may be to work at any of these goals, there is another one of higher priority—to be an effective parent.

—Landrum R. Bolling

1921. Pampering a child is equivalent to teaching him that he is too weak or incompetent to do things for himself. Therefore, he never develops a sense of realistic accomplishment. —T. L. Brink

1922. Children make parents grow up a lot more than parents make children grow up. . . . You're going to be with your spouse through life. Your child is going to walk away from you. In one respect it requires more generosity to dedicate yourself to someone who will walk away. Your child is by definition unresponsive, unthankful. Children get adequately thankful about the time their parents die. I think there are all sorts of features to the love of children which cause personal maturity of a profound sort that dedication to a spouse doesn't do. —James T. Burtchaell

1923. I suspect . . . that more is done to effect, or fix, the moral and religious character of children, before the age of language than after. —Horace Bushnell

1924. Let every Christian father and mother understand when the child is three years old that they have done more than half they ever will do for his character.

—Horace Bushnell

1925. The experts and I
Can never agree.
They say children are ruined
Before they are three.

But I'll keep on trying
I'll valiantly strive
To rehabilitate Junior
Before he is five.

—Louise Darcy

1926. Parents who neglect discipline are their children's worst enemies.

—F. Marion Dick

1927. Religious words have value to the child only as experience in the home gives them meaning. —John Drescher

1928. I am persuaded that if mothers and fathers would earnestly seek to know the meaning of full consecration in God's service, they would have clear guidance in the rearing of their children.

—V. Raymond Edman

1929. Only as genuine Christian holiness, and Christlike love are expressed in the life of a parent, can the child have the opportunity to inherit the flame and not the ashes. —Stephen G. Green

1930. I took a piece of plastic clay
And idly fashioned it one day.
And as my fingers pressed it still,
It moved and yielded to my will.

I came again when days were past;
The bit of clay was hard at last.
The form I gave it still it bore,
But I could change that form no
more.

I took a piece of living clay
And gently formed it day by day,
And molded with my power and
art,
A young child's soft and yielding
heart.

I came again when years were
gone;

146

It was a man I looked upon.
He still that early impress wore,
And I could change him
nevermore!
—Arthur Guiterman

1931. A permissive home is a home where you don't love enough to exercise the authority that Christ gave you. Quit saying you're broadminded and tolerant. You just lack guts! —Ben Haden

1932. If the principle of "warning and striking" were consistently practiced in our homes and churches, much of the need for junior churches and even nurseries would be gone. I do believe the original church was a family-type assembly.
—Burchard G. Ham

1933. If discipline was practiced in every home, juvenile delinquency would be reduced by 95 percent. —J. Edgar Hoover

1934. The proper time to influence the character of a child is about a hundred years before he is born. —Dean Inge

1935. Any parent . . . who comes to terms with God's claim of authority on his life needs little more to qualify as an effective parent. —Earl Jabay

1936. Children want some honest direction. They want a set of sensible rules to live by. The time has come to dust off the rule book. —Jenkins Lloyd Jones

1937. [Good parents are] not afraid to be momentarily disliked by children during the act of enforcing rules. —Jean Laird

1938. A child is a person who is going to carry on what you have started. He is going to sit where you are sitting, and when you are gone, attend to those things which you think are important. . . . The fate of humanity is in his hands. —Abraham Lincoln

1939. Thus it is true, as men say, that parents, although they had nothing else to do, could attain salvation by training their own children. If they rightly train them to God's service, they will indeed have both hands full of good works to do. For what else are the hungry, thirsty, naked, imprisoned, sick, strangers, than the souls of your own children? With them God makes of your house a hospital, and sets you over them as chief nurse, to wait on them, to give them good words and works as meat and drink, that they may learn to trust, believe, and fear God. . . . O what a blessed marriage and home were that where such parents were to be found! Truly it would be a real church, chosen cloister, yea, a paradise. —Martin Luther

1940. Spare the rod and spoil the child—that is true. But, beside the rod, keep an apple to give him when he has done well.
—Martin Luther

1941. What is the bond between parent and child that can make the difference between citizens and criminals? It is the bond with the entwining strands of love, praise and discipline. Love is the emotional warmth that gives us our security; praise is the word of pride or smile of approval that gives us our self-worth; discipline is that consistently applied standard of right and wrong from which we get our moral values. —David L. McKenna

1942. Little children are less and less refused their often wicked or unnecessary requests so that permissiveness has reduced them to uncontrolled and demanding nuisances, only to grow up to being wicked and self-destructive adults making

147

their desire for a full life at home and in business unattainable.

—Robert K. Rudolph

1943. How sharper than a serpent's tooth it is to have a thankless child.

—William Shakespeare

1944. Why do you parents turn and scrape every stone to gather wealth, and take so little care of your children, to whom one day you must relinquish it all.

—Socrates

1945. A child's back must be made to bend, but not be broken. He must be ruled, but not with a rod of iron. His spirit must be conquered, but not crushed.

—Charles H. Spurgeon

1946. The overindulgent and passive parent is acting out of his own felt needs, not the needs of his child.

—Robert L. Stogner

1947. Children are the sum of what parents contribute to their lives.

—Richard L. Strauss

1948. To fail to feed the child spiritually is to create spiritual cripples, unable to walk in the Spirit as free men and women in Christ, unable to stand straight in the outside world.   —Nancy M. Tischler

1949. You can do everything else right as a parent, but if you don't begin with loving God, you're going to fail.

—Alvin Vander Griend

1950. God has chosen suffering as the avenue for perfecting His children. Let us not deny our children this grace.

—Edward L. Vardy

1951. The child you want to raise as an upright and honorable person requires a lot more of your time than your money.

—George Varky

1952. Parenthood is a partnership with God. You are not molding iron nor chiseling marble; you are working with the Creator of the universe in shaping human character and determining destiny.

—Ruth Vaughn

1953. The rules for parents
Are but three . . .
Love,
Limit,
And let them be!

—Elaine M. Ward

1954. I'll lend you for a little while
A child of mine, He said.
For you to love the while he lives
And mourn for when he's dead.
It may be six or seven years,
Or twenty-two or three.
But will you, till I call for him,
Take care of him for me?

He'll bring you charm to gladden you,
And, should his stay be brief,
You'll have his lovely memories
As solace for your grief.
I cannot promise he will stay
Since all from earth return;
But there are lessons taught down there
I want this child to learn.

I've looked this wide world over
In search of teachers true.
And from the throngs that crowd life's lanes
I have selected you.
Now will you give him all your love
Nor think your labor vain,
Nor hate me when I come to call
To take him back again?

I fancied that I heard them say,
"Dear Lord, Thy will be done;

For all the joy this child shall
   bring
The rash of grief will run.
We'll shelter him with tenderness,
We'll love him while we may;
And for the happiness we've
   known
Forever grateful stay.

But should the angel call for him
Much sooner than we planned,
We'll brave the bitter grief that
   comes
And try to understand!"
—John Greenleaf Whittier

1955. Children begin by loving their parents. After a time they judge them. Rarely, if ever, do they forgive them.
—Oscar Wilde

1956. Too often parents give their children only a small "dose" of Christianity which frequently renders them immune to the real thing.

1957. When parents don't mind that the children don't mind, then children don't.

1958. If you do not instill into the minds of your children the truth, someone else will wash their brains with half-truth, untruth, and unimportant truth.

1959. The trouble with parenthood is that by the time you're experienced, you're unemployable.

1960. Father, may we our children lead
   In paths of peace to Thy sweet
      fold;
   May ne'er our sin or sad neglect
   E'er make them hard, perverse or
      cold.

1961. The actions of some children today suggest that their parents embarked upon the sea of matrimony without a paddle.

(see also: Fatherhood; Motherhood)

THE PAST

1962. The past is a guidepost, not a hitching post. —L. Thomas Holdcroft

1963. The past in retrospect holds manifold disenchantments, failures, and even tragedies; and yet the worst may be forgotten and the best held fast.
—W. Robertson Nicoll

1964. Those who cannot remember the past are condemned to repeat it.
—George Santayana

1965. A church which has lost its memory of the past can only wander about aimlessly in the present and despair of its future. Having lost its identity, it will lose its mission and its hope as well.
—David C. Steinmets

1966. The best compliment we can pay our past is to prophetically and bravely face today and tomorrow. —Bernie Wiebe

1967. The past is never completely lost, however extensive the devastation. Your sorrows are the bricks and mortar of a magnificent temple. What you are today and what you will be tomorrow are because of what you have been. Your faith of yesterday is built into your faith today.
—Gordon Wright

(see also: History)

PATIENCE

1968. Some people pray, "Lord, give me patience, and I want it *right now!*"
—Bernard R. DeRemer

1969. Teach us to care and not to care. Teach us to sit still. —T. S. Eliot

1970. People must be able to combine what they desire with what is objectively

possible and with what they can subjectively accomplish. This is a delicate art.
—Jurgen Moltmann

1971. Patience: a bitter plant that produces sweet fruit.

1972. The grace of vital perseverance is that quality of patience which is always equal to the pressure of the passing moment, because it is rooted in that eternal order over which the passing moment has no power.

(see also: Perseverance; Trouble)

PATRIOTISM

1973. Communism flourishes only where patriotism does not.
—J. Kesner Kahn

1974. A people's . . . readiness to make sacrifices isn't an abstract notion . . . but a factor that will determine a nation's future, the decisive factor. A back held straight outweighs armored battalions; a head held high is worth a forest of missiles.
—Ephraim Kishon

1975. Those who expect to reap the blessings of freedom must, like men, undergo the fatigue of supporting it.
—Thomas Paine

1976. These are the times that try men's souls. The summer soldier and the sunshine patriot will, in this crisis, shrink from the service of their country, but he that stands it now deserves the love and thanks of men and women.
—Thomas Paine

1977. To lose patriotism is to lose the very sources of your life, the very fountains of your being, the deep roots of your soul. It is part of the fragmentation that is the curse of modernity.   —E. Merrill Root

1978. Breathes there a man with soul so dead
Who never to himself hath said,
"This is my own, my native land!"
Whose heart hath ne'er within him burned
As home his footsteps he hath turned
From wandering on a foreign strand?
For him no minstrel raptures swell,
High tho' his titles, power and pelf,
The wretch, concenters all in self,
Living, shall forfeit fair renown,
And, doubly dying, shall go down
To the vile dust from whence he sprung,
Unwept, unhonored, and unsung.
—Sir Walter Scott

1979. I vow to thee, my country,
All earthly joys above,
Entire and whole and perfect,
The service of my love.

The love that asks no questions,
The love that stands the test,
That lays upon the altar
The dearest and the best.

The love that never falters;
The love that pays the price;
The love that makes, unflinching,
The final sacrifice.
—Sir Cecil Arthur Spring-Rice

(see also: The Nation)

PEACE

1980. There is a sword approved by heaven. If swords are in the hands only of those who cannot be trusted with them, then the only peace possible between the lion and the lamb is for the lamb to lie down inside the lion. There are present appeasers of evil who would label that arrangement peace. But a peace dictated by unethical force is the peace of slaves.

—Frederick Brown Harris

1981. All men desire peace, but very few desire those things that make for peace.

—Thomas à Kempis

1982. If there is right in the soul, there will be beauty in the person. If there is beauty in the person, there will be harmony in the home. If there is harmony in the home, there will be order in the nation. If there is order in the nation, there will be peace in the world.   —Lao-Tse

1983. It is strange that peace should be the final trap that betrays mankind. He has survived war. He will not survive peace. It is hell's consummate lie: You can have a good feeling by forfeiting—by setting aside—your own convictions.

—C. M. Ward

(see also: Peace of Mind)

PEACE OF MIND

1984. Order your soul; reduce your wants; live in charity; associate in Christian community; obey the laws; trust in Providence.

—Augustine

1985. When we believe that God is Father, we also believe that such a father's hand will never cause his child a needless tear. We may not understand life any better, but we will not resent life any longer.

—William Barclay

1986. The peace is won by accompanying God into the battle.

—Eivind Josef Berggrav

1987. At the foot of my bed, where I can see it on retiring, and the first thing on arising, are these words: "Thou wilt keep him in perfect peace, whose mind is stayed on thee: because he trusteth in thee" (Isaiah 26:3).   —William Gladstone

1988. There may be those on earth who dress better or eat better, but those who enjoy the peace of God sleep better.

—L. Thomas Holdcroft

1989. This is a sane, wholesome, practical, working faith: That it is a man's business to do the will of God; second, that God himself takes on the care of that man; and third, that therefore that man ought never to be afraid of anything.

—George MacDonald

1990. At the heart of the cyclone
    tearing the sky,
And flinging the clouds and
    towers by,
Is a place of central calm;
And so in the roar of mortal
    things,
There is a place where my spirit
    sings,
In the hollow of God's palm.

—Edwin Markham

1991. Dale Carnegie knew the techniques for "positive thinking" and "self-confidence." He could even teach people to overcome worry with his techniques, but in the end, peace eluded him and he committed suicide. In a world filled with causes for worry and anxiety, we need something tougher than "positive thinking" or even "possibility thinking." We need the peace of God standing guard over our hearts and minds.   —Jerry W. McCant

1992. Beneath the waves of the storm-
    tossed sea
There are peace and calm
    tranquility;

151

But none could guess by the
    foaming crest
That deep in the ocean's heart is
    rest.

The continual tides recede and
    flow,
And the white-capped breakers
    come and go.
They toss in fury and never cease;
Still—deep in the ocean's heart is
    peace.

So—deep in the heart where
    Christ abides,
Though swept by currents of evil
    tides,
Though tempest-tossed and wildly
    driven,
There are peace and rest akin to
    heaven.
          —Kathryn Blackburn Peck

1993. Nothing will or can restore order till our hearts make the great decision: God shall be exalted above all else.
          —A. W. Tozer

1994. To be glad of life, because it gives you the chance to love and to work and to play and to look up at the stars; to be satisfied with your possessions, but not contented with yourself until you have made the best of them; to despise nothing in the world except falsehood and meanness, and to fear nothing except cowardice; to be governed by your admirations rather than by your disgusts; to covet nothing that is your neighbor's except his kindness of heart and gentleness of manners; to think seldom of your enemies, often of your friends, and every day of Christ; and to spend as much time as you can, with body and with spirit, in God's out-of-doors— these are little guideposts on the footpath to peace.   —Henry Van Dyke

1995. Forgiving those who hurt us is the key to personal peace.   —G. Weatherley

1996. When at night you cannot sleep, talk to the Shepherd and stop counting sheep.

1997. Peace is not the absence of conflict but the presence of God no matter what the conflict.

1998. Said the robin to the sparrow,
    I should really like to know
    Why these anxious human beings
    Rush around and worry so.

Said the sparrow to the robin,
    Friend, I think that it must be
    That they have no heavenly
        Father
    Such as cares for you and me.

(see also: Contentment; Fulfillment; Happiness)

PENITENCE

1999. Without hatred of sin and remorse for transgressions, no man will taste the grace of God.   —John Calvin

2000. No man ever enters heaven until he is first convinced that he deserves hell.
          —John Everett

(see also: Repentance)

PERSECUTION

2001. There is a danger in goodness, for in the light of goodness evil stands condemned.   —William Barclay

2002. As the Father sent Him, the Lamb, even so, you are to go to the world as a lamb. In the midst of wolves! Will they howl? They'll howl, all right. Will we feel their fangs? You bet we will. Will it hurt?

Of course it will. Even unto death? Even unto death. How else would you prefer to die? How else would you like to live? Oh, to be like Him. Even if it means being a sheep among wolves.   —Elwyn Davies

2003. It is better to enter heaven maimed than to coast into hell. This was Jesus' conclusion and it should be ours.
          —Allan Dykstra

2004. We Americans are living in a paradise of religious liberty which, if we take the long view, probably will be seen as merely a parenthesis in church history.
          —Roger Greenway

2005. A real fire brand is distressing to the devil and when a wide-awake believer comes along, taking the Gospel seriously, we can expect sinister maneuvering for his downfall.   —Vance Havner

2006. Anyone who consistently takes the prophetic stance must be prepared to end up on a hill like Calvary, because true prophetic testimony of profound unconformity may arouse the fiercest violence against it.   —Ivan Illich

2007. Religion is like a nail: if you hit it on the head it will go deeper.
          —A. V. Lanacharski

2008. Bearing wrong is a glorious part of the fellowship with Christ's sufferings; a glorious mark of being conformed to His most holy likeness; a most blessed fruit of the true life of faith.   —Andrew Murray

2009. Wesley got down from his horse and began to pray, asking God to show him if his lack of persecution was due to any unconfessed sin. While he was on his knees before God, an unsaved man passing by recognized him as the preacher he disliked. The man picked up a brick and tossed it at Wesley. It missed the evangelist, but John Wesley saw it as an answer to prayer. "Thank God," he exclaimed, "it's all right. I still have His presence."

2010. If one has not been persecuted for his Christian faith, he has not walked with Christ long enough or close enough.

PERSEVERANCE

2011. William Carey, when asked the reason for his success as a missionary, replied, "I can plod."

2012. We conquer—not in any brilliant fashion—we conquer by continuing.
          —George Matheson

2013. The only sure sign that any man is one of the elect is his perseverance in the Christian life; for he is elected to holiness as well as happiness. Perseverance, like faith, is the gift of God.   —W. G. T. Shedd

2014. Today's mighty oak is yesterday's little nut that held its ground.

2015. One step and then another and
          the longest walk is ended.
One stitch and then another and
          the longest rent is mended.
One brick upon another and the
          tallest wall is made.
One flake and then another and
          the deepest snow is laid.

Then do not look downhearted
          on the work you have to do,
And say that such a task you never
          can get through;
But just endeavor day by day
          another point to gain,
And soon the mountain that you
          feared will prove to be a
          plain.

2016. When you come to the end of your rope—tie a knot and hold on.

(see also: Determination)

PERSONAL DEVOTIONS

(see: Devotion; Meditation)

PERSONALITY

2017. Cheerfulness is the best promoter of health, and is as friendly to the mind as to the body.   —Joseph Addison

2018. Spring is a mood; it pervades the air,
  Sweet as the blossoming peach or pear;
  It can be found near the melting snow
  Or far in the South where the warm winds blow;
  It's in a city or country place;
  Could be in your or a stranger's face;
  Spring is a feeling—O glory be!
  I've just discovered that Spring's in me.

        —Pauline Oates Glenn

2019. You only gave a smile
  Which cost you not a thing,
  And yet it made me rich
  As any ancient king.

  You only gave me a smile
  My name you did not call,
  And yet it made my day
  The brightest day of all.

  But smiles elicit smiles
  And we each won a friend
  For something free, I'd say
  That's quite a dividend.

        —Perry Tanksley

2020. Youth is such a wonderful thing it is regrettable that we waste it on young people.   —Mark Twain

2021. A bore talks mostly in the first person, a gossip in the third, and a brilliant conversationalist in the second.

(see also: Interpersonal Relations)

PESSIMISM

2022. Some people are making such thorough preparation for rainy days that they aren't enjoying today's sunshine.

        —William Feather

2023. Pessimism has an inestimable advantage, after all, of relieving us of a sense of responsibility for the future. If there's not going to be one, why worry?

        —Michael Korda

2024. No matter how bright the sunshine, pious pessimists point to the tunnel at the end of the light.

        —Kenneth L. Wilson

(see also: Doubt)

PHARISAISM

2025. Spiritual pride is the main door by which the devil comes into the hearts of those who are zealous for the advancement of truth. It is the chief inlet of smoke from the bottomless pit to darken the mind and mislead the judgment. —Jonathan Edwards

2026. The greatest sin is to be conscious of none.

(see also: Hypocrisy)

PLEASURE

(see: Materialism and Hedonism)

POLITICS AND GOVERNMENT

2027. If Christians fail to support the government God has ordained, Christians may be forced to submit to the government God has allowed.   —A. Watson Argue, Jr.

2028. Since God created man with certain inalienable rights, and man, in turn, created government to help secure and safeguard those rights, it follows that man is superior to government and should remain master over it, not the other way around.   —Ezra Taft Benson

2029. All who have ever written on government are unanimous, that among a people generally corrupt, liberty cannot long last.   —Edmund Burke

2030. The government of a country never gets ahead of the religion of a country. There is no way by which we can substitute the authority of the law for the virtues of men.   —Calvin Coolidge

2031. We do not want politics in our religion, but we do want Christian standards in our politics.   —Sir Stafford Cripps

2032. The great question of our time is not communism versus individualism, not Europe versus America nor East versus West; it is whether man can live without God.   —Will Durant

2033. Continue to express your dissent and your needs, but remember to remain civilized, for you will sorely miss civilization if it is sacrificed in the turbulence of change.   —Will Durant

2034. Our problem can't be solved by government. Our problem *is* government.   —Milton Friedman

2035. It is the duty of government to make it difficult for people to do wrong, and easy to do right.   —William E. Gladstone

2036. The impersonal hand of government can never replace the helping hand of a neighbor.   —Hubert H. Humphrey

2037. Over in Denmark they excavated the mummy of a man doubled over with one foot in his mouth. A politician, no doubt.   —Wes Izzard

2038. A fine is a tax for doing wrong. A tax is a fine for doing well.   —Wes Izzard

2039. As government grows, freedom recedes.   —Thomas Jefferson

2040. Certainly there is grandeur in politics, but it comes from the importance and not the amount of what is done by government.   —Shirley Robin Letwin

2041. Abraham Lincoln was one of the few politicians who knew how to turn back an accusation with humor. Once when reproached by an opponent for being "two-faced," Lincoln screwed up his homely countenance and replied, "Does anyone imagine that if I had two faces I would choose to wear this one all the time?"

2042. Is there no virtue among us? If there be not . . . no form of government can render us secure.   —James Madison

2043. Watergate was an *uncanny* crisis. There were just too many bodies to be buried too fast, and too many gravediggers digging each other's graves. It was the imperfect crime par excellence.
   —Milton Mayer

2044. The difference between a politician and a statesman is that the politician sees which way the people are going and tries to stay ahead of them, whereas the statesman sees what is best and right and does that even if no one follows.

—Ord L. Morrow

2045. Man's capacity for justice makes democracy possible; but man's inclination to injustice makes democracy necessary.

—Reinhold Niebuhr

2046. Taxpayers are people who don't have to take a civil service examination to work for the government. —Red O'Donnell

2047. Political language is designed to make lies sound truthful . . . and to give an appearance of solidity to pure wind.

—George Orwell

2048. Unity without multiplicity is tyranny, and multiplicity without unity is confusion. —Blaise Pascal

2049. A civil servant is sometimes like a broken cannon—it won't work and you can't fire it. —George S. Patton, Jr.

2050. If men will not be governed by God, then they must be governed by tyrants. —William Penn

2051. Only those who do not desire power are fit to hold it. —Plato

2052. No civilized country in the world has ever voluntarily adopted the extreme philosophies of either fascism or Communism, unless the middle class was first liquidated by inflation. —H. W. Prentiss, Jr.

2053. Governments tend not to solve problems, only rearrange them.

—Ronald Reagan

2054. A conservative is a liberal who was mugged the night before. —Frank Rizzo

2055. In the political appeals which are made, the terms "the poor" and "the weak" are used as if they were terms of exact definition.

—William Graham Sumner

2056. Pilgrims came to America to establish a social order in which the governing principle would be that a man with the Bible in his hand doesn't need a king to tell him what to do. —G. Aiken Taylor

2057. Government never of itself furthered any enterprise but by the alacrity with which it got out of the way.

—Henry David Thoreau

2058. I heartily accept the motto—that government is best which governs least; and I should like to see it acted upon more rapidly and systematically.

—Henry David Thoreau

2059. Politicians, particularly office holders, are the most adulated, flattered, cajoled, sought after, and accommodated—in short, the most tempted people in the world today. —Strom Thurmond

2060. A government which promises everything must pay its bills with everybody's money. —Strom Thurmond

2061. In countries where the fear of God has become a jest, the rights of men have become a joke. —Leonard Verduin

2062. The role of government is to develop the strengths, and not play upon the weaknesses, of the individual citizen.

—James M. Wall

2063. Of all the dispositions and habits which lead to political prosperity, religion and morality are indispensable supports.

—George Washington

2064. If we condemned politicians for opportunism, would any slate be clean?

—Geoffrey Wigoder

2065. The Lord's Prayer has 56 words, Lincoln's Gettysburg Address has 266, the Declaration of Independence has 300; but a government order on cabbage prices contained 26,911 words. —**William Windnall**

2066. Crime wouldn't pay if the government ran it.

2067. The most persistent activity of many political candidates is not to discuss issues, but to gain name recognition.

2068. Reform always comes from below. No man with four aces ever asked for a new deal.

2069. George Washington is the only president who didn't blame the previous administration for his troubles.

2070. How badly a Congressman's political fence needs mending depends on how much he has straddled it.

(see also: Capitalism; Communism; Economics; Socialism)

PORNOGRAPHY

2071. Love is exciting, but sex without it becomes a drag that degrades and stultifies. When will people realize that sexploitation is to abundant living what raw sewage is to Lake Erie? —**Robert L. Cleath**

2072. When three cinemas out of four show pornographic or violent films, one must wonder whether there is freedom of choice. It amounts to a veritable censorship in reverse. —**Francois Marty**

2073. Whatever the risks, local control should be given an opportunity to put the lids on the garbage cans of culture. People should have the right to decide whether they want to have themselves and their children insulated against kinky sex. If they can't function in this fashion, what was 1776 all about? —**Thomas J. Smith**

POWER

2074. The Holy Spirit is God resident on earth. All divine power resides in Him. He is looking for those who are honest enough to be trusted with the power He can give them. They alone will use it for God's glory and not for themselves.

—**Gordon Chilvers**

2075. Watches, cars and Christians can all look chromed and shiny. But watches don't tick, cars don't go and Christians don't make a difference without insides. For a Christian, that's the Holy Spirit.

—**Tim Downs**

2076. Why be content with what one can do in one's own strength when the power of God is available to us? That's worse than having a freezer full of T-bone steaks and living on peanut butter sandwiches. —**Larry McCaw**

2077. Power will come when the way is paved by prayer. —**Harold J. Ockenga**

2078. What God expects us to attempt, He also enables us to achieve.

—**Stephen Olford**

2079. Do you really want to see divine power at work? Then discard your human notions of power and look at the way Christ lived and died.

—**Edmund A. Steimle**

2080. Many Christians estimate difficulties in the light of their own resources, and thus attempt little and often fail in the little they attempt. All God's giants have been weak men who did great things for God because they reckoned on His power and presence being with them.

—**James Hudson Taylor**

2081. There is a fine line between desire to have power for accomplishment and desire to have power for domination.

(see also: Prayer)

PRAISE

2082. Through every period of my life
Thy goodness I'll pursue:
And after death, in distant worlds,
The pleasing theme renew.

Through all eternity to Thee
A grateful song I'll raise:
But oh! eternity's too short
To utter all Thy praise.
—**Joseph Addison**

2083. The Christian should be an alleluia from head to foot. —**Augustine**

2084. Praise is almost the only thing we do on earth that we shall not cease to do in heaven. —**Samuel Brengle**

2085. The unmistakable mark of a living faith is a readiness to praise.
—**Howard H. Jones**

2086. I think we delight to praise what we enjoy because the praise not merely expresses but completes the enjoyment; it is its appointed consummation.
—**C. S. Lewis**

2087. If there were more praise for answered prayer, there would be more answered prayer for which to give praise.

(see also: Thanksgiving)

PRAYER

2088. The purpose of prayer is not to inform God of our needs, but to invite Him to rule our lives. —**Clarence Bauman**

2089. I care not what black spiritual crisis we may come through or what delight-ful spiritual Canaan we may enter, no blessing of the Christian life becomes continually possessed unless we are men and women of regular, daily, unhurried, secret lingerings in prayer. —**J. Sidlow Baxter**

2090. We are all too "busy" to use the mightiest weapon God has given us—prayer! —**J. Sidlow Baxter**

2091. I am accountable to God. That is the immovable lodestar from which we must operate. Prayer keeps that before our minds. —**D. Dean Benton**

2092. God's promises lie like giant corpses without life, only for decay and dust, unless men appropriate those promises by earnest and prevailing prayer.
—**E. M. Bounds**

2093. Do not pray for easy lives. Pray to be stronger men. Do not pray for tasks commensurate with your strength. Pray for strength commensurate with your tasks.
—**Phillips Brooks**

2094. In prayer it is better to have a heart without words than words without a heart.
—**John Bunyan**

2095. A day without prayer is a boast against God. —**Owen Carr**

2096. Prayer is simply believing God to supply what is needed to fulfill His will.
—**Robert E. Coleman**

2097. What isn't won in prayer first, is never won at all. —**Malcolm Cronk**

2098. God has editing rights over our prayers. He will receive them as a teacher does a term paper. He will edit them, correct them, bring them in line with His will and then hand them back to us to be resubmitted. —**Stephen Crotts**

2099. Keep praying, but be thankful that God's answers are wiser than your prayers.
—William Culbertson

2100. Those who pray most in private pray best in public. —R. Edward Davenport

2101. Many people pray as if God were a big aspirin pill. They come only when they hurt. —B. Graham Dienert

2102. True prayer always receives what it asks for—or something better.
—Byron Edwards

2103. Man is never so tall as when he kneels before God—never so great as when he humbles himself before God. And the man who kneels to God can stand up to anything. —Louis H. Evans

2104. Prayer is necessary because everything else is an illusion. —John Garvey

2105. We must move from asking God to take care of the things that are breaking our hearts, to praying about the things that are breaking His heart.
—Margaret Gibb

2106. You can do more than pray—but only after you have prayed. —S. D. Gordon

2107. Your cravings as a human animal do not become a prayer just because it is God you ask to attend them.
—Dag Hammarskjold

2108. When God intends to bless His people, the first thing he does is to set them apraying. —Matthew Henry

2109. Prayer is a kind of calling home every day. And there can come to you a serenity, a feeling of at-homeness in God's universe, a peace that the world can neither give nor disturb, a fresh courage, a new insight, a holy boldness through calling home that you'll never, never get any other way. —Earl G. Hunt, Jr.

2110. The main lesson about prayer is just this: *Do it! Do it! Do it!* You want to be *taught* to pray? My answer is: pray.
—John Laidlaw

2111. We can visit the White House with prayer as many times a day as we think of it, and every single visit makes us a channel between God and the President.
—Frank C. Laubach

2112. Let's move from theology to kneeology! Power for victory in spiritual warfare is found in prayer. —Robert R. Lawrence

2113. There are four ways God answers prayer: (1) No, not yet; (2) No, I love you too much; (3) Yes, I thought you'd never ask; (4) Yes, and here's more. —Anne Lewis

2114. Prayer in the sense of petition, asking for things, is a small part of it; confession and penitence are its threshold, adoration its sanctuary, the presence and vision and enjoyment of God its bread and wine. —C. S. Lewis

2115. I have been driven many times to my knees by the overwhelming conviction that I had nowhere else to go. My own wisdom, and that of all about me, seemed insufficient for the day. —Abraham Lincoln

2116. The less I pray, the harder it gets; the more I pray, the better it goes.
—Martin Luther

2117. My prayers, my God, flow from
    what I am not;
  I think Thy answers make me
    what I am.
—George MacDonald

2118. When you pray, do not encumber the Lord . . . with your thanks for the many

physical blessings He has granted you. A profusion of thanks borders on self-gloating, which is sin. When we pray . . . let us say, "O Jesus, strengthen my faith."
—Charles Malik

2119. In my experience, the deeper one's prayer life is, the deeper one's commitment to Christ and the deeper one's love for others. —Sheila Manchester

2120. If I could hear Christ praying for me in the next room, I would not fear a million enemies. Yet distance makes no difference. He is praying for me.
—Robert Murray McCheyne

2121. Trouble and perplexity drive me to prayer and prayer drives away perplexity and trouble. —Philip Melanchthon

2122. The great tragedy of life is not unanswered prayer, but unoffered prayer.
—F. B. Meyer

2123. Behind every work of God you will always find some kneeling form.
—Dwight L. Moody

2124. Prayer is, above all, fellowship with God and being brought under the power of His holiness . . . until He . . . stamps our entire nature with the lowliness of Christ.
—Andrew Murray

2125. Time spent in prayer will yield more than that given to work. Prayer alone gives work its worth and its success. Prayer opens the way for God Himself to do His work in us and through us. Let our chief work as God's messengers be intercession; in it we secure the presence and power of God to go with us. —Andrew Murray

2126. Thou art coming to a King,
Large petitions with thee bring,
For His grace and power are such
None can ever ask too much.
—John Newton

2127. Only by deep, strong and persistent prayer can we escape the illusion of self-importance. —Henri J. M. Nouwen

2128. A God who filled the prayer-orders of people whose wills were not His own would be no God at all. He would be a heavenly vending machine.
—Malcolm Nygren

2129. Awful things happen to people who pray. Their plans are frequently disrupted. They end up in strange places. Abraham went out, not knowing where he was to go—hardly the picture of someone who has struck it rich on a new power source. —Virginia Stem Owens

2130. Prayer is a sin-killer, a power-bringer, a victory-giver, a holiness-promoter, a dispute-adjuster, an obstacle-remover, and a Christ-revealer.
—Paul Radke

2131. Before we can pray, "Lord, Thy Kingdom come," we must be willing to pray, "My kingdom go." —Alan Redpath

2132. If we are willing to spend hours on end to learn to play the piano, operate a computer, or fly an airplane, it is sheer nonsense for us to imagine that we can learn the high art of getting guidance through communion with the Lord without being willing to set aside time for it. It is no accident that the Bible speaks of prayer as a form of waiting on God.
—Paul Rees

2133. I seldom made an errand to God for another, but I got something myself.
—Samuel Rutherford

2134. No matter how important the prayer, God will not answer:
When you are holding a grudge;

160

When you do not forgive;
When you do not apologize for
your faults or sins;
When you are not making
every possible effort to pay
your debts;
When you do not make your
wrongs right;
When you are not kind and
gentle to all your enemies;
When you are indulging in any
known sin;
When you yield to temptation;
When you are jealous and
critical.

—Julia Shelhamer

2135. Don't pray to escape trouble. Don't pray to be comfortable in your emotions. Pray to do the will of God in every situation. Nothing else is worth praying for. —Samuel M. Shoemaker

2136. We cannot ask in the behalf of Christ what Christ would not ask Himself if He were praying. —A. B. Simpson

2137. One of the elements of real prayer is the readiness on our part to furnish every avenue for its answer that He might ask of us. —William A. Smith

2138. Prayer is the full commitment of human reason to learn, and of human strength to do the will of God.

—David Wesley Soper

2139. I have no small liking to those rare old-fashioned Methodist prayers as made the walls to ring. Oh! For a revival of those glorious, violent prayers which flow like hot-shot against the battlements of heaven. Oh! For more of the prayer of God . . . the body and spirit working together . . . the whole man being aroused to the highest intensity to wrestle with God.

—Charles H. Spurgeon

2140. We cannot all argue, but we can all pray; we cannot all be leaders, but we can all be pleaders; we cannot all be mighty in rhetoric, but we can all be prevalent in prayer. I would sooner see you eloquent with God than with men.

—Charles H. Spurgeon

2141. When I pray, coincidences happen, and when I don't, they don't.

—William Temple

2142. More things are wrought by prayer than this world dreams of. Wherefore, let thy voice rise like a fountain, night and day. —Alfred Lord Tennyson

2143. Prayer is the one approach that can transform drudgery into doxology.

—William Vander Hoven

2144. Three things may cause boldness in prayer: the child of God has a Father to pray to, and the Spirit to help him pray, and an Advocate to present his prayers.

—Thomas Watson

2145. God does nothing but in answer to prayer. —John Wesley

2146. Prayer is the energy that makes us a welcoming place for God's presence.

—Frank M. Wessling

2147. If you find your life of prayer to be always so short, and so easy, and so spiritual, as to be without cost and strain and sweat to you, you may depend upon it, you are not yet begun to pray.

—Alexander Whyte

2148. God may pass by our elaborate programs and outstanding talents, but He will never pass by the prostrate form of an intercessor. —A. A. Wilson

2149. When your day is hemmed with prayer it is less likely to unravel.

2150. Filled with a strange new hope
they came—
The blind, the leper, the sick, the
lame—
Frail of body, spent of soul,
As many as touched Him were
made whole.

The Christ we follow is still the
same,
With blessings that all who will
may claim,
How often we miss Love's healing
touch
By thinking, "We must not ask
too much!"

2151. At the close of a catechetical class
a twelve-year-old girl was called on to pray.
Said she, "O Lord, thank you for all you've
done, and keep up the good work."

2152. Seven days without prayer makes
one *weak*.

2153. God answers *prayer* with certainty.
Wish fulfillment is something else.

2154. A Christian sees more on his knees
than a philosopher on his tip toes.

2155. The only way to pray is to pray, and
the way to pray well is to pray much.

2156. The greatest blessing of prayer is
not in receiving the answer, but in being
the kind of person God can trust with the
answer.

PREACHING

2157. If I knew the Lord was coming in
three years, I would spend two years studying and one year preaching.
—Donald Barnhouse

2158. If preaching is faithful to the Bible,
it cannot be tedious. Scripture is in fact so
interesting . . . that those who listen cannot possibly be overcome with sleep.
—Karl Barth

2159. The saddest moment in any
preacher's life is when he comes down
from his pulpit knowing that he gave the
people not the best he knew, but only what
they expected.   —Henry Ward Beecher

2160. After receiving from a parishioner
generous praise for a sermon I had just
preached, I replied, "Aye, you have no
need to tell me that; for the devil whispered it to me before I was well out of the
pulpit."   —John Bunyan

2161. It is upon preaching that Christianity will stand or fall.
—Peter Taylor Forsyth

2162. Probably the most lasting of all
preaching is with the pen. It continues to
speak after the voice is hushed.
—Reader Harris

2163. I have never yet heard a sermon
that I got nothing out of. But, I've had
some might close calls.   —Vance Havner

2164. It is not the business of the
preacher to fill the house. It is his business
to fill the pulpit.   —Vance Havner

2165. Thomas Carlyle was sitting with
his aging mother once when he complained to her of the conventional Christian ministers of the day: "If I had to
preach, I would go into the pulpit and say
no more than this: 'All you people know
what you ought to do; well, go and do it.'"
His mother calmly replied, "Aye, Tammas,
and will you tell them how?"
—Robert S. Hoagland

2166. Preaching that costs nothing accomplishes nothing. If the study is a

lounge, the pulpit will be an impertinence. —John Henry Jowett

2167. Preaching is not the gathering of a lot of words and sentences into a discourse—it is the overflow of one's devotional life. —D. E. King

2168. When I am angry I preach well and pray better. —Martin Luther

2169. Too many sermons are like Sunday night suppers: the same old stuff served over again, but too long away from the fire. —Cecil May, Jr.

2170. The best cure for sleeping sickness in the pew is some soul-stirring preaching from the pulpit. —William McPhail

2171. Expository preaching is the consecutive treatment of some book or extended portion of Scripture on which the preacher has concentrated head and heart, brain and brawn, and over which he has thought and wept and prayed, until it has yielded up its inner secret, and the spirit of it has passed into his spirit. —F. B. Meyer

2172. One should not rely upon God to fill one's mouth with inspiring utterances when the brain is empty. —Norman S. Ream

2173. What do I preach, then, with all my strength and the power of my voice, but repentance of sin and the mending of our ways, for the sake of our Lord Jesus Christ. —Girolamo Savonarola

2174. Dave Garroway once interviewed H. V. Kaltenborn about Hitler's power to sway and influence people. Kaltenborn said that Hitler followed three rules: "Make it simple; say it often; make it burn." It is a good, succinct course in preaching. —Samuel M. Shoemaker

2175. Outstanding preachers are sometimes able to express their own powerful personalities in their preaching, and they will appear to be very effective. But the question will remain. Is it the power of the preacher or is it the power of God? —Edwin Walhout

2176. The person in the pew wants to know how the preacher "ticks"; is it really "working" for him? Or is he just a funnel for platitudes? —Bernie Wiebe

2177. Lord, fill my mouth with
worthwhile stuff,
And shut it when I've said
enough.

2178. Preach the gospel, brother, preach
it,
Put it high, where men can teach
it;
Put it low, where men can reach
it,
But preach the gospel, brother,
preach it.

2179. His sermon had the usual heads,
And subdivisions fine;
The language was as delicate
And graceful as a vine.

It had its proper opening;
'Twas polished as a whole.
It had but one supreme defect—
It failed to reach the soul.

2180. When the Holy Spirit fills your mouth you'll open it. But merely opening your mouth does not assure that the Spirit will fill it.

THE PRESENT

2181. One of the most tragic things I know about human nature is that all of us tend to put off living. We are all dreaming of some magical rose garden over the horizon instead of enjoying the roses that are blooming outside our windows today.

—Dale Carnegie

2182. Today is God's—
   I face it not alone,
For He who sits upon the throne
Will guide my eager steps
   In paths that He has known.

Today is God's—
   Whatever it may be,
My soul, content, shall rest in
   Him
And take from His own hand
   That which is best for me.

Today is God's—
   And with the wak'ning day
There steals anew within my soul
A longing for His love
   To help me walk His way.

Today is God's—
   The Light probes deep and
     clear;
I yield, submit, embrace Thy will.
Possess me, Holy Ghost,
   Be Thou forever near.

—Dorothy Depew

2183. Escapees into the past and the future have one thing in common: they do not take the present seriously. The past cannot be regained, although we can learn from it; the future is not yet ours even though we must plan for it. . . . Time is now. We have only today.

—Charles Hummel

2184. The present contains all that there is. It is holy ground; for it is the past, and it is the future. —Alfred North Whitehead

2185. No longer forward nor behind
   I look in hope or fear;

But grateful, take the good I find,
   The best of now and here.

—John Greenleaf Whittier

2186. The clock of life is wound but
     once,
   And no man has the power
To tell just when the hands will
     stop,
   At late or early hour.

Now is the only time we own
   Give, love, toil with a will.
And place no faith in tomorrow,
   For the clock may then be still.

2187. You are younger today than you ever will be again. Make use of it for the sake of tomorrow.

2188. With every rising of the sun
   Think of your life as just begun.
The Past has canceled and buried
     deep
All yesterdays. There let them
     sleep.
Concern yourself with but Today;
Grasp it, and teach it to obey
Your will and plan. Since time
     began
Today has been the friend of man.
You and Today! A soul sublime
And the great heritage of time.
With God Himself to bind the
     twain,
Go forth, brave heart! Attain!
     Attain!

(see also: Time)

PRIDE

2189. The big sin is not idolatry or witchcraft, but those hidden kingdoms of the spirit where Jesus is not Lord.

—Linda Beach

2190. Get rid of the idea that we understand ourselves; it is the last conceit to go.
—Oswald Chambers

2191. Sweet praise is like perfume. It is fine if you don't swallow it.
—Dwight D. Eisenhower

2192. The proud hate pride—in others.
—Benjamin Franklin

2193. Not infrequently, we choose our goals to prove our importance.
—Keith Huttenlocker

2194. He who attempts to carry grace in a proud heart carries only dust in the wind.
—William Jenkyn

2195. A proud man is always looking down on things and people; and, of course, as long as you're looking down, you can't see something that's above you.
—C. S. Lewis

2196. The devil is perfectly content to see you becoming chaste and brave and self-controlled, provided all the time he is setting you up in the Dictatorship of Pride.
—C. S. Lewis

2197. God sends no one away empty except those who are full of themselves.
—Dwight L. Moody

2198. Once upon a time a paper kite
Mounted to a wondrous height,
Where, giddy with its elevation,
It thus expressed self-admiration:
"See how the crowds of gazing
people
Admire my flight above the
steeple.
How they would wonder if they
knew
All that a kite like me can do!
Were I but free, I'd take a flight
And pierce the clouds beyond
their sight;
But ah! Like a poor prisoner
bound,
My string confines me to the
ground!
I'd brave the eagle's towering
wing,
Might I but fly without the
string."
It tugged and pulled while thus it
spoke,
To snap the string—at last it
broke.

Deprived at once of all its stay,
In vain it tried to soar away;
Unable its own weight to bear,
It fluttered downward through the
air.
Unable its own course to guide,
The winds soon plunged it in the
tide.
Ah! foolish kite, thou has no
wing;
How couldst thou fly without a
string?

My heart cried out, "O Lord, I see
How much this kite resembles me!
Forgetful that by Thee I stand,
Impatient of Thy ruling hand,
How oft I've wished to break the
lines
Thy wisdom for my lot assigns!
How oft indulge the fain desire
For something more or something
higher!

But for Thy grace and love divine,
A fall this dreadful had been
mine."
—John Newton

2199. Of all the causes which conspire
to blind

Man's erring judgment, and
misguide the mind,
What the weak head with
strongest bias rules,
Is Pride, the never-failing vice of
fools.

—Alexander Pope

2200. A swelled head is one disease that makes everybody sick except the person who has it. —Bud Robinson

2201. The person who piously proclaims, "I am nothing," too often is proud. The statement is an attitude based on the fear that others will evaluate him wrongly.

—Jerry W. Shepperd

2202. Pride grows in the human heart like lard on a pig. —Alexander Solzhenitsyn

2203. Temper is what gets most of us into trouble. Pride is what keeps us there.

—Mark Twain

2204. The only thing that keeps growing without nourishment is the ego.

2205. Those who stare up to admire their own halo are apt to create nothing more than a pain in the neck—somebody else's as well as their own.

2206. Once in a saintly passion,
I cried, with desperate grief,
"O Lord, my heart is black with
guilt;
Of sinners, I am *chief.*"

Then stooped my guardian angel,
And whispered from behind,
"Vanity, my little man;
You're nothing of the kind."

2207. Criticism is often a form of self-boasting.

2208. Some people *grow* under responsibility; others *swell.*

2209. A frog asked two geese to take him south with them. At first they resisted; they didn't see how it could be done. Finally, the frog suggested that the two geese hold a stick in their beaks and this he would hold on to with his mouth. So off they went, and it was really quite a sight. People looked up and expressed great admiration. Someone said, "It's wonderful! Who was so clever to discover such a fine way to travel?" Whereupon the frog opened his mouth and said, "It was I."

PRIORITIES

2210. Always put off until tomorrow that which you shouldn't do at all.

—J. D. Eppinga

2211. Our Father refreshes us on the journey with some pleasant inns, but will not encourage us to mistake them for home.

—C. S. Lewis

2212. I think earth, if chosen instead of Heaven, will turn out to have been, all along, only a region in Hell; and earth, if put second to Heaven, to have been from the beginning a part of Heaven itself.

—C. S. Lewis

2213. Do not have your concert first and tune your instruments afterward. Begin the day with God. —James Hudson Taylor

PROCRASTINATION

2214. God has promised forgiveness to your repentance, but He has not promised tomorrow to your procrastination.

—Augustine

2215. Putting off an easy thing makes it hard. Putting off a hard thing make it impossible. —George Claude Lorimer

2216. Death-bed repentance is like burning the candle of life for the devil and then, when life is over, blowing smoke in the face of God.

(see also: Apathy)

PROVIDENCE

2217. God does not guide history and the destiny of men by continually opposing men in the projects they have taken in hand. On the contrary, He lets them act. To all appearances they are acting simply according to their own plans, and yet they cannot avoid becoming the instruments of God and acting in reality according to His plan. —**Gerhard Van Rad**

(see also: God)

PSYCHOLOGY

2218. He takes the saints to pieces,
   And labels all the parts,
He tabulates the secrets
   Of loyal loving hearts.
He probes their selfless passion
   And shows exactly why
The martyr goes out singing,
   To suffer and to die.

The beatific vision
   That brings them to their
      knees
He smilingly reduces
   To infant phantasies.
The Freudian unconscious
   Quite easily explains
The splendor of their sorrows,
   The pageant of their pains.

The manifold temptations
   Wherewith the flesh can vex
The saintly soul, are samples
   Of Oedipus complex.
The subtle sex perversion

His eagle glance can tell,
That makes their joyous heaven
   The horror of their hell.

His reasoning is perfect,
   His proofs are plain as paint,
He has but one small weakness,
   He cannot make a saint.
      —**G. A. S. Kennedy**

2219. At three I had a feeling of
Ambivalence toward my brothers,
And so it follows naturally
I poisoned all my lovers.

But now I'm happy; I have
      learned
The lesson this has taught;
That everything I do that's wrong
Is someone else's fault.

PURITY

2220. Only a passionate love of purity can save a man from impurity.
      —**William Barclay**

2221. It is safe to tell the pure in heart they shall see God, for only the pure in heart want to. —**C. S. Lewis**

(see also: Chastity; Holiness)

PURPOSE

2222. It concerns us to know the purposes we seek in life, for then, like archers aiming at a definite mark, we shall be more likely to attain what we want. —**Aristotle**

2223. There was a man once, a satirist. In the natural course of time his friends slew him, and he died. And the people came and stood round about his corpse. "He treated the whole round world as his [soccer ball]," they said indignantly, "and he kicked it." The dead man opened one eye. "But," said he, "always toward the goal!"   —Maarten Maartens

2224. Those who have a "why" to live, can bear with almost any "how."
     —Frank Victor

2225. Give me a man who says this one thing I do, and not these fifty things I dabble in.   —Dwight L. Moody

Rationality

2226. If you argue with a madman, it is extremely probable that you will get the worst of it; for in many ways his mind moves all the quicker for not being delayed by the things that go with good judgment. He is not hampered by a sense of humor or by charity, or by the dumb certainties of experiences. He is the more logical for losing certain sane affections. Indeed, the common phrase for insanity is a misleading one. The mad man is not the man who has lost his reason. The mad man is the man who has lost everything except his reason.
     —G. K. Chesterton

(see also: Reason)

READING

2227. Reading is to the mind what exercise is to the body.   —Joseph Addison

2228. Books must be read as deliberately and reservedly as they were written.
     —Henry David Thoreau

2229. The habit of reading, I make bold to tell you, is your pass to the greatest, the purest, and the most perfect pleasures that God has prepared for His creatures . . . ; it lasts when all other pleasures fade.
     —Anthony Trollope

2230. John Wesley had absolutely no faith in the kind of religion that was not informed. He believed a person ought to read, and he offered to give any of his preachers, who could not afford to buy literature, up to five pounds' worth of books.

2231. Don't fail to read between the lines. Some of the greatest reading was never written.   —Glen Williamson

(see also: Books; Literature)

REASON

2232. By reasoning, we cannot add a cubit to our height, love a baby, love ourselves, nor refute the nudist. It is no great loss. Only a few very unwise people try to live by the intellect.   —William H. Davis

(see also: Rationality)

RECONCILIATION

(see: Forgiveness; Interpersonal Relations)

REDEMPTION

(see: Atonement; Calvary; The Cross)

RELIGION

2233. If religion becomes a hit and God becomes a pal, then the world will cancel the one when it becomes boring and snub the other when He becomes demanding.
     —Michael Barton

2234. From Romans 1 to 3 we learn that mankind knows something of the true God, but turns instead to elaborate substitutes. . . . Far from a quest for God, human religion is an evasion of Him.
     —Stephen Board

2235. I want my religion like my tea; I want it hot!   —William Booth

2236. "Religion" is one of those notoriously elastic words that can be called upon to adorn a multitude of virtues and cover an equal number of sins. —John B. Breslin

2237. Many have quarreled about religion that never practiced it.
—Benjamin Franklin

2238. The bane of religion is side issues. Good men waste their time and strength on questions that do not edify, and become absorbed in pretentious messages that do not save souls. —James A. Lord

2239. Tension always exists between religion focused on worship of God and religion focused on meeting our needs. Since God is "for us," worshiping hardly violates our needs. However, when the worship of God recedes into the background and the satisfaction of one's needs moves to the fore, various techniques for "manipulating God" begin to pervert religion into mere superstition. —David Myers

2240. Men despise religion; they hate it and fear it may be true. —Blaise Pascal

2241. There is . . . in many hearts a yearning for the firsthand experience of the presence of God. Many people are tired of religion reduced to social action, group therapy, or theological analysis. They wonder where the wonder went.
—Robert Raines

2242. Religion is not the opiate of the people. Rather, it brings us out of the dream in which we live into the reality of life, into the presence of God.
—John Schultz

2243. Religion is nothing if it is not the foundation of our whole life.
—Robert Thornton

2244. True religion confronts earth with heaven and brings eternity to bear on time. —A. W. Tozer

2245. If your religion hasn't changed you—you had better change your religion.

2246. Some people say it doesn't matter what a man believes about religion. How would they feel if a cannibal moved in next door?

RENEWAL

2247. Has the brook dried up in Cherith?
Is there neither dew nor rain?
Are the cruse and cupboard empty?
Does no oil or meal remain?

Get you up into the mountain,
Put your face between your knees,
Lift your eyes with expectation
Toward the vast and stretching seas.

Send your faith—your willing servant,
Seven times to scan the skies;
In the empty, brassy heavens
See the little cloud arise.

Hear the sound of rain abundant—
'Tis God's pouring-out begun;
Turn you to the greening valley,
Gird, oh, gird your loins . . . and run!
—Ruth Glover

(see also: Revival)

REPENTANCE

2248. A man thinks he is repenting when he says, "I'm sorry. Give me a second

chance and I'll do a lot better." That is not Christian repentance for it is egocentric.
—Handel H. Brown

2249. The bedrock of Christianity is repentance. Strictly speaking, a man cannot repent when he chooses; repentance is a gift of God. The old Puritans used to pray for the "gift of tears." If ever you cease to know the virtue of repentance, you are in darkness. Examine yourself and see if you have forgotten how to be sorry.
—Oswald Chambers

2250. Men who only believe their depravity but do not hate it, are no further than the devil on their way to heaven.
—Charles H. Spurgeon

2251. Repentance is not a thing of days and weeks . . . to be got over as fast as possible. No, it is the grace of a lifetime, like faith itself. . . . That is not true repentance which does not come to faith in Jesus and that is not true faith in Jesus which is not tinctured with repentance.
—Charles H. Spurgeon

2252. The Nineveh story is a tender story telling how a cosmic compassion hovers over mankind, evil though mankind may be. In brief, the story tells us that repentance saved Nineveh. It could still save America—and the world. —Lon Woodrum

(see also: Penitence)

RESENTMENT

2253. If you hug to yourself any resentment against anybody else, you destroy the bridge by which God would come to you.
—Peter Marshall

2254. Those who say they will forgive but can't forget, simply bury the hatchet, but leave the handle out for immediate use. —Dwight L. Moody

(see also: Interpersonal Relations)

RESPONSIBILITY

2255. You cannot help men permanently by doing for them what they could and should do for themselves.
—Abraham Lincoln

2256. Responsibility is my response to God's ability. —Albert J. Lown

(see also: Duty)

THE RESURRECTION

2257. Ghosts, apparitions, and various psychological hallucinations may do a lot of things, but they don't fire up the charcoal grill and cook fish for breakfast.
—Pheme Perkins

(see also: Easter)

REVELATION

2258. We live in a society which does not admit the possibility of God speaking as directly to us as He did to Samuel and Saul. . . . Thus, if God even tries to speak to us, we do not have the ability to hear Him. We have civilized ourselves into spiritual deafness. —Julius Lester

2259. To wrestle continuously with "unanswerable questions" about the economy of God is to falsely assume that God intended for us to know all things or is obligated to tell us.

(see also: Bible; Jesus Christ)

REVENGE

2260. The person who tries to get even by making others suffer for their sins is interfering in God's business.

(see also: Interpersonal Relations; Resentment)

REVERENCE

2261. There is a plant in the corner of my heart called reverence, and it needs watering at least once a week.

—Oliver Wendell Holmes

2262. We are not disembodied spirits, we cannot ignore our bodies when we plan worship services. The call is not to be stylish, but to be prepared for a meeting of great import. This is not said in order to exclude the poor (and thus violate the clear injunctions of James), but in order to rebuke a bad sort of casualness that not only approaches God's throne boldly but proceeds to lounge on it. —Steve Layman

(see also: Worship)

REVIVAL

2263. The poison of rattlesnakes cannot be removed, nor the snakes subdued, by spraying them with perfume. Nothing but the surging tides of revival can cleanse the frontier of human corruption.

—Clarence Autrey

2264. The experience of revival is nothing more than a new beginning of obedience to God. —Charles G. Finney

2265. The Holy Ghost did not fall upon the Upper Room until they had prayed and sought God for ten long days. Daniel did not receive the outline of Israel's history from God's messenger until his twenty-first day of prayer and fasting. Saul, who later became Paul, did not receive sight for his blinded eyes until he had prayed and fasted for three days. There never has been and there never will be such a thing as *spontaneous* revival. Revival did not come like that in Bible times and it will not come like that today. We may never know who prayed the revival down, but if it

comes you can be sure that somewhere a hungry soul sought God. —James Hamby

2266. There never has been a spiritual revival which did not begin with an acute sense of sin. —W. Graham Scroggie

2267. That great religious excitements have occurred apart from gospel truth we admit; but anything which we, as believers in Christ, would call genuine revival of religion, has always been attended with clear evangelical instruction upon cardinal points of truth. —Charles H. Spurgeon

2268. Some say revivals don't last. Neither does a bath, but it helps!

—Billy Sunday

2269. God has never seen fit to make numbers or organization the basis of outpoured blessing. Rather it has again and again been the individual or the small group who are completely surrendered to Him and who undertake their work trusting solely in the power of the Holy Spirit.

—G. Aiken Taylor

(see also: Renewal)

ROMANCE

2270. Love can stand anything but distance. —Allen Dace

2271. How do I love thee? Let me count
    the ways.
  I love thee to the depth and
    breadth and height
  My soul can reach, when feeling
    out of sight
  For the ends of Being and ideal
    Grace.
  I love thee to the level of every-
    day's
  Most quiet need, by sun and
    candlelight.

I love thee freely, as men strive for
    Right;
I love thee purely, as they turn
    from Praise.
I love thee with the passion put to
    use
In my old griefs, and with my
    childhood's faith.
I love thee with a love I seemed to
    lose
With my lost saints—I love thee
    with the breath,
Smiles, tears, of all my life!—and,
    if God choose
I shall but love thee better after
    death.
        —Elizabeth Barrett Browning

2272. I kissed your feet, my Ba, before I
      married you.
    But now I would kiss the ground
      under your feet,
    I love you with so much greater
      love.
        —Robert Browning

2273. I like not only to be loved, but to
be told that I am loved; the realm of silence
is large enough beyond the grave.
        —George Eliot

2274. I love my neighbor out of loving
      kindness;
    Of pity love my poor
      unfortunate brother;
    Of Christian duty manifest a
      fondness
      For even my enemy, which is a
      bother.
    Indeed, because these loves are so
      much trouble,
      Being on intellect, they're
      somewhat noble.
    But you I love for purely selfish
      reasons,

As I love birdsong and the
    smell of rain
The feel of kitten fur, the
    changing seasons . . .
My senses' manna, lotus for my
    brain.
Quite effortless, my love for you,
    and wholly
Foreign to duty, blessed by not a
    ghost
Of altruism. Love, I love you
    solely
For my own pleasure. so I love
    you most!
        —Georgie Starbuck Galbraith

2275. To love is to find pleasure in the
happiness of the person loved.
        —Gottfried Leibnitz

2276.   Eight Ways to Tell If You're In
        Love
  1. True love distinguishes
     between a person and a body.
  2. True love always generates
     respect.
  3. True love is self-giving.
  4. True love can thrive without
     physical expression.
  5. True love seeks to build a
     relationship.
  6. True love embraces
     responsibility.
  7. True love can postpone
     gratification.
  8. True love is basically
     commitment.
        —Erwin Lutzer

2277. Love is the passionate and abiding
desire on the part of two people . . . to produce the conditions under which each can
be, and spontaneously express, his real self;
to produce together an intellectual soil
and an emotional climat‸ in which each
can flourish, far super:or to what each

could achieve alone.   —Alexander Magoun

2278. I hold it true, whate'er befall;
  I feel it when I sorrow most;
  'Tis better to have loved and lost
  Than never to have loved at all.
          —Alfred Lord Tennyson

2279. I love you not only for what you
are, but for what I am when I am with you.
I love you not only for what you are making
of yourself, but for what you are making of
me. I love you for that part of me that you
bring out. I love you for putting your hand
into my heaped-up heart, and passing over
all the foolish, and frivolous, and weak
things that you cannot help dimly seeing
there, for drawing out into the light all the
beautiful and radiant qualities that no one
else has looked quite deep enough to find. I
love you because you are helping me to
make the structure of my life, not a tavern
but a temple; and the words of my every
day, not a reproach but a song. . . . Perhaps
this is what being a friend means after all.

2280. There is beauty in the forest
      When the trees are green and
        fair,
    There is beauty in the meadow
      When wild flowers scent the
        air,
    There is beauty in the sunlight
      And the soft blue beams above,
    Oh, the world is full of beauty
      When the heart is full of love.

(see also: Love)

Sacrifice

(see: Self-Denial)

SALVATION

2281. It is proper for a Christian to say, "I
have been saved, I am being saved, and I

will be saved." The Christian is in a similar
position to a sailor who has fallen overboard, has caught a line thrown to him by
his mates, and is being pulled through the
water to the safety of his ship. He can say,
"I was saved when they threw me the line."
He can also say, "I am being saved as they
pull me through the water." And he can
say, "I will be saved when I stand again on
the deck of the ship."   —Carl Bridge, Jr.

2282. If you fear because you feel your unworthiness, it is a blessed fear. Trust in the
worthiness of Christ and your fear will give
way to faith.   —John T. Clark

2283. I was twenty years old before I ever
heard a sermon on regeneration. I was
always told to be good, but you might as
well tell a midget to be a giant as to tell
him to be good without telling him how.
          —Dwight L. Moody

2284. He that is not saved is under sin.
He that is saved is above sin. And he that is
sanctified is without sin.   —Colonel Ross

2285. The truth about salvation may be
seen in Calvary's three propositions: one
died *in* sin; one died *to* sin; one died *for* sin.
          —Ray H. Sanders

2286. If men had pow'r o'er Him
    To hang Him on a tree,
    Then how could He have pow'r
    To help a wretch like me?

  Calvary was a myst'ry,
    Too great for finite mind;
    But desperate, I was seeking.
    Oh, look what I did find!

  The mercies of God flowing,
    And grace so full and free,
    And somehow I went knowing
    It flowed for even me!

No, I can't explain it.
'Tis too complex for man.
But I can still accept it
As part of God's great plan.
—John A. Thomas

2287. The Father thought it.
The Son bought it.
The Holy Spirit wrought it,
and by grace
I sought it.
—D. H. Walters

2288. At Calvary sin received its mortal wound. There the Victim became the Victor. He fell but crushed the enemy in the fall. He died, but sin was nailed to the cross. His cross becomes the fountain of our life; His tomb, the birthplace of our immortality. —Sim A. Wilson

2289. Let a man go to a psychiatrist and what does he become? An adjusted sinner. Let a man go to a physician and what does he become? A healthy sinner. Let a man achieve wealth and what does he become? A wealthy sinner. Let a man join a church, sign a card, and turn over a new leaf and what does he become? A religious sinner. But let him go in sincere repentance and faith to the foot of Calvary's cross, and what does he become? A new creature in Jesus Christ, forgiven, reconciled, with meaning and purpose in his life and on the way to marvelous fulfillment in God's will.

2290. Spiritual life is a free gift from God whereas spiritual death has to be earned with the wages of sin.

2291. Life is short,
Death is sure.
Sin the cause;
Christ the cure.

(see also: Atonement; Conversion; New Birth)

SANCTIFICATION

2292. To live the sanctified life we must choose to be holy. Sanctification is a life of Christ-centered choices, made evident in loving obedience to God. —Mel E. DePeal

2293. Sanctification does not dissolve personality conflict; it helps one to successfully cope with it. —John W. May

2294. While holiness does not make it impossible for you to sin, the experience does make it possible not to sin.
—Arlo F. Newell

2295. [The word "sanctification"] has three meanings: separation from sin; dedication to God; appointment to ministry.
—George P. Pardington

2296. O sanctifying flame, I pray
Go through my heart, descend
today:
Burn out the sin, make no delay.
Come down, come in, make room
to stay.

O purifying fire, I wait;
Remove the dross, the sin I hate:
My gold refine, thy likeness make
In me, I plead for Jesus' sake.

O holy fire in cloven flame
Descend on me in Jesus' name:
Burn in my heart, let naught
remain
But love Divine, eternal flame.
—W. C. Roberts

2297. In regeneration we pass out of death into life, but in sanctification we pass out of the self-life into the Christ-life.
—A. B. Simpson

2298. Pardon is not enough; we want sanctification. We beseech Thee, let the weeds that grow in the seed plot of our soul be cut up by the roots. . . . We would lead consecrated lives, for we are persuaded that we only live as we live unto God, that aught else is but trifling.

—Charles H. Spurgeon

(see also: Holiness)

SATAN

2299. Is Satan omnipresent? No, but he is very spry. Is he bound? Yes, but with a rather loose rope. —William Ashmore

2300. Satan is an acute theologian.

—John Calvin

2301. The enemy will not see you vanish into God's company without an effort to reclaim you. —C. S. Lewis

2302. For still our ancient foe
Doth seek to work us woe;
His craft and power are great,
And armed with cruel hate,
On earth is not his equal.

—Martin Luther

2303. I believe Satan to exist for two reasons: first, the Bible says so, and second, I've done business with him.

—Dwight L. Moody

2304. If Satan cannot keep you from working for the Lord, he will get you working so hard on so many things that you will end up doing nothing really well, your family is cheated and you are in a state of total frustration. —Lois Oster

2305. Satan, when tempting someone, says that sin isn't very bad, isn't very big and isn't very important. But after the person has yielded to temptation and sinned, and has begun to think about asking God's forgiveness, then Satan reverses his field. And to his victim Satan declares that sin is so big, so bad and so awful that asking forgiveness will hardly suffice.

—John R. W. Stott

2306. Thought, purpose, logic, industriousness, but without radiance or love: Isn't it an accurate description of Satan?

—William L. Sullivan

(see also: The Devil)

SCIENCE

2307. Putting on the spectacles of science in expectation of finding the answer to everything looked at . . . signifies inner blindness. —J. Frank Dobie

2308. Science means exact knowledge. To call by such a name the wild guesses of evolutionists and infidel biologists is but word-prostitution. —H. A. Ironside

2309. Ours is the age which is proud of machines that think and suspicious of men who try to. —Howard H. Jones

2310. What we call Man's power over Nature turns out to be a power exercised by some men over others with Nature as its instrument. —C. S. Lewis

2311. I have insisted that there is something radically and systematically wrong with our culture, a flaw that lies deeper than any class or race analysis probes and which frustrates our best efforts to achieve wholeness. I am convinced it is our ingrained commitment to the scientific picture of nature that hangs us up.

—Theodore Roszak

2312. The [scientific] progress which put a few men on the moon, needs only the pressing of a single button to put the rest of us there. —Leonard Verduin

(see also: Evolution)

SECOND COMING OF CHRIST

2313. Perhaps at cool of morning when
The day is breaking light;
Perhaps at noontide's hour, or
'Midst gathering shades of night:

I'll see a burst of glory, and
The angel's voice I'll hear;
The trumpet's golden throat will
    sound
The summons loud and clear!

Then suddenly—I'll see the Lord!
I'll meet Him face to face . . .
The Lord of all the universe,
The Lord of truth and grace!

My cup of bliss will overflow;
I'll see Him as He is!
What joy to place my hand within
That nail-scarred hand of His!

Perhaps today will be the day
I'll hear His welcomed voice!
Perhaps today I'll see the Lord
And evermore rejoice!
—**Georgia B. Adams**

2314. God's people should plan for a voyage of a thousand years, but be prepared to abandon ship tonight.   —**Joseph Bayly**

2315. Where Christ once bore the world's frown, He is to one day wear the world's crown. And the crown which is now on the false one's brow shall then belong to earth's rightful Heir.
—**Ian MacPherson**

2316. We would be more spiritually thrilled to invest our time in laboring in God's vineyard than in estimating the hour of Sunset. Until that great Day, all of our fervent calculations of times and seasons are little more than childish games played in a pile of sawdust.   —**Jim Sparks**

SECULARISM

2317. Secularism is such full immersion of life in the claims and interests of this world that they assume control.
—**Merrill Abbey**

2318. Perfection of means and confusion of goals seems to characterize our age.
—**Albert Einstein**

2319. The [secular] city symbolizes the supreme work of man—and as such represents man's ultimate rejection of God.
—**Jacques Ellul**

2320. The grey mist of secularism stupefies the sense of holiness, stifles moral outrage, intimidates ethical indignation and questions the worth of purity.
—**Carl F. H. Henry**

2321. He who marries the spirit of his time will soon be a widower.   —**Dean Inge**

2322. When the church undertakes to proclaim the Christian Gospel in a secular idiom, it usually ends up proclaiming the secular gospel in a Christian idiom.

(see also: Humanism; Materialism and Hedonism)

SECURITY

2323. Where is safety to be found?
Underground or overground,
In a square of thickened walls
Or in tunneled mountain halls?
Clear and true the answer rings,
"In the shadow of His wings."
—**Hallie Smith Bixby**

2324. There is more safety with Christ in the tempest than without Christ in the calmest waters.   —**Alexander Grosse**

2325. Since God is wisdom, love, and
    truth

And shows these virtues every
day—
How safe we are who look to Him
To bless and guide us on our way!
        —Esther B. Heins

2326. Security is not the absence of danger, but the presence of God no matter what the danger.

2327. Material abundance should provide no sense of security for the Christian; neither the lack of abundance cause the follower of Christ to be insecure.

(see also: Assurance)

SELF

2328. He who reigns himself and rules his passions, desires, and fears is more than a king.   —John Milton

2329. It's fun to believe in yourself, but don't be too easily convinced.
            —T. Harry Thompson

SELF-CONTROL

2330. Those who wish to transform the world must be able to transform themselves.   —Konrad Heiden

2331. But I will write of him who fights
        And vanquishes his sins,
    Who struggles on through weary
        years
    Against himself and wins.
        —Caroline Begelow LeRow

2332. If you would learn self-mastery, begin by yielding yourself to the One Great Master.   —Johann Friedrich Lobstein

SELF-DECEPTION

2333. A careful study of Christian church history provides endless illustrations of how easy it is to robe Jesus in our own supposed righteousness and then proceed to follow ourselves in His name.
                —Barry L. Callen

2334. There are times when our self-deception rivals that of the legendary unmarried mother who excused her sin on the ground that her baby was a very small one.   —Cornelius Plantinga

2335. You've got to deceive yourself before you can be deceived.

(see also: Illusion)

SELF-DENIAL

2336. We can, if we like, choose the easy way; we can, if we like, refuse the cross that every Christian is called to bear; but if we do, we lose the glory. It is an unalterable law that if there is no cross there is no crown.   —William Barclay

2337. It is not what we take up, but what we give up, that makes us rich.
            —Henry Ward Beecher

2338. When Christ calls a man, He bids him come and die.   —Dietrich Bonhoeffer

2339. We do everything with the cross—except take it up. We sing about it. We preach about it. We make grateful mention of it in our prayers. Some of us even wear it.
            —Handel H. Brown

2340. Hast thou no scar?
    No hidden scar on foot, or side, or
        hand?
    I hear thee sung as mighty in the
        land,
    I hear them hail thy bright
        ascendant star,
    Hast thou no scar?

    Hast thou no wound?
    Yet I was wounded by the archers,
        spent,

Leaned Me against a tree to die,
and rent
By ravening beasts that
compassed Me, I swooned:
Has thou no wound?

No wound, no scar?
Yet, as the Master shall the
servant be,
And, pierced are the feet that
follow Me;
But thine are whole: can he have
followed far
Who has no wound nor scar?
—Amy Carmichael

2341. From prayer that asks that I may
be
Sheltered from winds that beat on
Thee,
From fearing when I should
aspire,
From faltering when I should
climb higher,
From silken self, O Captain, free
Thy soldier who would follow
Thee.

From subtle love of softening
things,
From easy choices, weakenings,
Not thus were spirits fortified,
Not this way went the Crucified,
From all that dims Thy Calvary,
O Lamb of God, deliver me.
—Amy Carmichael

2342. No person has ever been honored
for what he received. One is honored for
what he gives. —Calvin Coolidge

2343. Sacrifice or sacrilege? God still
looks for the costly gift—not in terms of
monetary value but in relation to what we
have left. —Robert H. Cowles

2344. Love is pure when self is slain.
—Harold R. Crosser

2345. O, grant me this, dear God,
Through tears or loss—
To know the joyous secret
Of thy cross!
—Ralph Spaulding Cushman

2346. It's the life you live after "death"
that counts. If you haven't died [to self and
sin] the life you are now living is not counting. —Charles E. DeVol

2347. God makes His ministers a flame
of fire. Am I ignitable? God, deliver me
from the dread asbestos of "other things."
Saturate me with the oil of Thy Spirit that
I may be a flame. Make my thy fuel, Flame
of God. —Jim Elliot

2348. Why do we set our hearts on
health and honor? The Calvary thread is
often missing from the Christian skein of
life. We do not see God at work in priva-
tion, sickness, poverty, and death. We believe, superficially, that God purposes for
each of us only health, wealth, honor, and
happiness. (What more could a sinner
wish?) But the true measure of life's worth
is the willingness to suffer worthily and to
die for Christ, if need be. Good health and
good pay are not salvation; they may be
only narcotics that help souls exist after
they have "died." —George E. Failing

2349. Life is not genuinely our own until
we can renounce it. —Hermann Feifel

2350. As soon as we cease to bleed, we
cease to bless. —John Henry Jowett

2351. Those looking for the deluxe
brand of salvation without a cross are more
in search of salve than salvation. You can
have a religion without crucifixion—but
not Christianity. Life in Christ begins with
the death of self. —Cecil B. Knight

2352. To have what we want, is riches; but to be able to do without, is power.

—George MacDonald

2353. Everyone that gets to the throne must put their foot upon the thorn. The way to the crown is by the cross. We must taste gall if we are to taste glory.

—Robert Murray McCheyne

2354. There are many activities I must cut out simply because I desire to excel in my pursuit after God and holiness.

—Wendell W. Price

2355. The captain of a Coast Guard rescue crew ordered his craft out to rescue a ship floundering on the reefs. The first mate protested, "The gale is terrific and the reefs are terribly treacherous. We probably could get out ther, but we could never get back.;; The captaqin replied, "Launch the boat! We don't have to get back. But we have to go out!"   —Alvin Rogness

2356. To a world which . . . harbors unjust inequalities and unfair social roles, Jesus gives us not, "Fulfill yourself," but "Deny yourself."   —David C. Shultz

2357. Once there lived another man within me,
Child of earth and slave of Satan he;
But I nailed him to the cross of Jesus,
And that man is nothing now to me.

—A. B. Simpson

2358. If Jesus be God and died for me, then no sacrifice can be too great for me to make for Him.   —C. T. Studd

2359. I have never made a sacrifice in my life.   —James Hudson Taylor

2360. For though I knew His love Who followed,
Yet was I sore adread
Lest, having Him, I must have naught beside.

—Francis Thompson

2361. When a man forgets himself, he usually does something that everyone else remembers.

2362. Not I, but Christ, be honored, loved, exalted;
Not I, but Christ, be seen, be known, be heard;
Not I, but Christ, in every look and action;
Not I, but Christ, in every thought and word.

2363. Unhappy over your sacrifice? Take a new look at His.

2364. To hold life only for the sake of giving,
To find in loss a gain, in gain a loss,
This is the paradox of Christian living,
Venture of the contemporary Cross.

2365. You deny Christ when you fail to deny yourself for Christ.

2366. Material plenty and Christian passion have seldom, if ever, been working partners. If you ignore your plenty, you may not long have it. If you don't ignore it, Christian passion will die.

2367. Socrates said: Know thyself; Freud said: Be thyself; Jesus said: *Give* thyself.

(see also: Cross-Bearing; Discipleship; Surrender)

SELF-EXAMINATION

2368. There are only two people who can tell you the truth about yourself—an enemy who has lost his temper and a friend who loves you dearly.   **—Antisthenes**

2369. O wad some Power the giftie gie
  us
  To see ourselves as others see us!
     —Robert Burns

2370. People, people everywhere,
  Pushing, rushing here and there.
  Laughing, talking, wasting time,
  Playing, basking in sunny clime.
  Where are you going?
  What is your goal?
  Where is your heart?
  Where is your soul?
  Time's swiftly passing,
  Judgment is near.
  People are wailing
  In sorrow and fear.
  Precious moments
  So fruitless and lost.
  What have you gained?
  What has it cost?
     —Stephen J. Earle

2371. In Nathanael
  No cunning nor deceit could Jesus
   see:
  Which makes me pause and
   ponder
  What does Jesus see in me?
     —Clare M. Gilmore

2372. Most of us use weak threads when we mend our ways.   **—Arnold Glasow**

2373. I have had more trouble with myself than with any other man.
     —Dwight L. Moody

2374. An enemy I had whose mien
  I stoutly strove to know,
For hard he dogged my steps,
  unseen
Wherever I might go.

My plans he balked, my aims he
  foiled,
He blocked my onward way.
When for some lofty goal I toiled
He grimly said me nay.

"Come forth!" I cried, "Lay bare
  thy guise!
Thy features I would see."
But always to my straining eyes
He dwelt in mystery.

One night I seized and held him
  fast
The veil from him did draw,
I gazed upon his face at last—
And lo! myself I saw.
     —Edwin L. Sabin

2375. The unexamined life is not worth living.   **—Socrates**

2376. Everybody thinks of changing humanity and nobody thinks of changing himself.   **—Leo Tolstoy**

2377. I pitied him in his blindness;
  But can I boast "I see"?
  Perhaps there walks a spirit
  Close by, who pities me.

2378. How many of us will ever sit down, open our Bibles, bow our heads, and pray, "Lord, show me where I'm wrong"?

2379. What you are when you're alone is alone what you are.

2380. Whatever the pastime
  In which you engage,
  For the cheering of youth
  Or the solace of age,
  Turn away from each pleasure
  You'd shrink from pursuing

Were God to look down and say, "What are you doing?"

2381. Cease the race to save your face and start to conquer inner space.

2382. It is not what a man thinks he is; but what a man *thinks*—he is!

2383. You may be tempted to think that rough treatment by others stands you in good stead with Him who endured the roughness of the Cross. And the sharp sword of criticism will tempt you to fly in the face of your critics with panic defense. So you lash back with, "Well, they criticized and crucified my Lord, too." But what we forget is that three men were crucified on Calvary's hill that day and two of them deserved it. So the odds are at least two to one that you are a criminal figure instead of a Christ figure, that the criticism is valid, and your "crucifixion" deserved.

SELF-IDENTITY

2384. Within my earthly temple there's a crowd:
There's one of us that's humble, one that's proud;
There's one that's broken-hearted for his sins,
There's one who, unrepentant, sits and grins;
There's one who loves his neighbor as himself,
And one who cares for naught but fame and self—
From much corroding care I should be free,
If once I could determine which is me.
—**Edward Sanford Martin**

2385. The best challenges force you to identify yourself.   —**Chaim Potok**

2386. You find that your self emerges more quickly if you do not keep asking the question. If you lose your life, you find it, or it could be that it will find you. You will then say: "Now that seems to be what I am, or what I'd like to do." I don't think you go to some sterile, barren land filled with sagebrush and gaze at your navel to find out who you are.   —**Joseph Sittler**

2387. Who I am is what I think—not the other way around.   —**William Stringfellow**

2388. We are all handicapped. It's just that some of us can pretend better than others.

SELF-INDULGENCE

(see also: Materialism and Hedonism; Pride)

SELFISHNESS

2389. Milton has carefully marked in his Satan, the intense selfishness which would rather reign in hell than serve in heaven.
—**Samuel Taylor Coleridge**

2390. Usually he is most empty who is most full of himself.   —**A. G. Lawson**

2391. To set up self is to deny Christ; to exalt Christ is to reject self.
—**Henry Sandham**

(see also: Pride; Self-Deception, Self-Examination; Self-Indulgence; Self Pity; Self-Righteousness)

SELF-PITY

2392. Self-pity is a death that has no resurrection, a sinkhole from which no rescuing hand can drag you because you have chosen to sink.   —**Elisabeth Elliot**

2393. There is only one way to end a self-pity cycle—stop comparing yourself to others and simply follow Christ.

—Linda Harry

2394. The opposite of having faith is having self-pity. —Leslie Parrott

2395. Pouting is a sin,
But if you think you must,
Try it with grin,
Forgetting why you fussed.

—Lydia Regehr

2396. Jonah sulking under his withered gourd, Elijah bitter under the juniper, Job complaining on the ash pile—what is all that but this: God owes me some extras in life and He's not producing. . . . The cure for self-pity is the mind of Christ, who . . . emptied Himself and took the form of a servant. Wherefore God highly exalted Him. —William Vander Hoven

2397. When a man has a pet peeve, it's remarkable how often he pets it.

2398. I've taught a class for many years;
Borne many burdens—toiled
through tears;
But folks don't notice me a bit,
I'm so discouraged—I'll just quit.

Sometime ago I joined the choir
That many souls I might inspire;
But folks do not seem moved a bit,
And I won't stand it. I'll just quit.

I've led young people day and
night
And sacrificed to lead them right,
But folks won't help me out a bit;
And I'm so tired, I think I'll quit.

Christ's cause is hindered
everywhere,
And folks are dying in despair;

The reason why? Just think a bit;
The church is full of folks who
quit.

SELF-RIGHTEOUSNESS

2399. You can always tell when a man is a great way from God—when he is always talking about himself, how good he is.

—Dwight L. Moody

2400. The worst form of badness is human goodness when that human goodness becomes a substitute for the new birth.

—Adrian Rogers

(see also: Pharisaism)

SEPARATION

2401. Christians must be personally alongside the lost without compromising the truth. —Elwood D. Bass

2402. Jesus prayed that we be "in the world but not of it." In theory, we may have this straight. It is in practice that many of us still do not have the hang of it.

—J. D. Eppinga

2403. The early Christians did not transform the world, they transcended it. It was only in later years, when Constantine made a Christian profession easy and the church ceased looking for the Lord to return and began trying to build heaven on earth, that Christians became "reasonable" and the world could live comfortably with them. But let it not be forgotten that a twice-born, Spirit-filled Christian is always a contradiction to this old world.

—Vance Havner

2404. Schism is splitting, putting apart that which belongs together. It is to divide where God does not divide. . . . But it is no less wicked to run together that which in the mind of God is diverse.

—Leonard Verduin

(see also: Nonconformity)

SERVICE

2405. Jesus deliberately turned His back on all the ideas of power held in the world and proposed something new: *servanthood.*

—Arthur Merrihew Adams

2406. He who labors as he prays lifts his heart to God with his hands.

—Bernard of Clairvaux

2407. The greatest among men is always ready to serve and yet is unconscious of the service. —H. P. Blavatsky

2408. Some folk are poor spellers. They think "service" is spelled "serve us."

—Robert C. Cunningham

2409. Love's secret is to be always doing little things for God and not to mind because they are so little.

—Frederick W. Faber

2410. I'd rather see a sermon than hear
one any day;
I'd rather one should walk with
me than merely tell the way.
The eye's a better pupil and more
willing than the ear;
Fine counsel is confusing, but
example's always clear;
And the best of all the preachers
are the men who live their
creeds,
For to see good put in action is
what everybody needs.

—Edgar Guest

2411. There is a treasury of blessing to be found in sharing with shut-ins; they have much to give and often no one to give it to.

—William J. Johnston

2412. Sick or well, blind or seeing, bond or free, we are here for a purpose, and however we are situated, we please God better with useful deeds than with many prayers of pious resignation. —Helen Keller

2413. The fact that when we are "in Christ" there is no condemnation for our sins, does not mean there is no examination of our works. —Samuel Leith

2414. A Christian man is the most free, lord of all, and subject to none; he is also the most dutiful servant to all and subject to everyone. —Martin Luther

2415. Put a world in my heart, Lord
Jesus.
Give me eyes to see it with care.
Give me hands that will offer the
fruit of my work.
Give me feet that will go
anywhere.

Put a world in my heart, Lord
Jesus.
Give me lips to tell the Good
News.
Give me the will for denial of self
And the courage to do as You
choose.

—Robin McGregor

2416. The measure of a man is not the number of his servants, but the number of people whom he serves. —Paul D. Moody

2417. My life must be Christ's broken
bread,
My love, His outpoured wine;
A cup o'erfilled, a table spread
Beneath His name and sign,
That other souls, refreshed and
fed,
May share His life through
mine.

—Albert Orsborn

2418. Servanthood is only redemptive when it can be taken advantage of.
—John Oswalt

2419. A man dreamed he visited a celestial museum. No crown or scepters were there, no miters or thrones, no Pope's rings, or even Martin Luther's inkpot. A handful of thorns was there, a seamless robe, and a cup of cold water. "Have you a towel and basin?" the man asked. "No," said the guardian angel, "you see, they are in perpetual use." The man knew then he was in the Holy City. —Calvin L. Phillips

2420. We must realize that the symbol of Christianity is not a beautifully polished cross, but a lopsided, crude, splintery cross over which is draped a towel—not the lush plush kind of towel we buy for our guest bathroom, but a dirty old rag, wet with the sweat and dirt of men's feet.
—Norman Schouten

2421. In the kingdom of God there are no score sheets. Menial tasks rank as high as glamorous ones. Things are measured by the spiritual way in which they are done.
—Carolyn Schultz

2422. The only people who will be really happy are those who have sought and found how to serve. —Albert Schweitzer

2423. It has taken me half of my life to discover that my business in the world is not to try to make something of myself, but rather to find a job worth doing and lose myself in it. —Benjamin Tenney

2424. The simplest and shortest ethical precept is to be served as little as possible . . . and to serve others as much as possible.
—Leo Tolstoy

2425. There is not one single passage in the Old Testament or the New Testament where the filling with the Holy Spirit is spoken of and not connected with the testimony of service. —R. A. Torrey

2426. There are two great divisions among religious people: those who serve God legally, and those who serve Him lovingly. —George D. Watson

2427. Shamgar had an oxgoad,
David had a sling,
Samson had a jawbone,
Rahab had a string,
Mary had some ointment,
Aaron had a rod,
Dorcas had a needle—
All were used for God.

2428. The immediate payment [for Christian service] may not be great, but the retirement plan is out of this world.

2429. Service is love made visible.

2430. A noble life is not a blaze
Of sudden glory won,
But just an adding up of days
In which good work is done.

2431. He has no hands but our hands
To do His work today;
He has no feet but our feet
To lead men in His way;
He has no voice but our voice
To tell men how He died;
He has no help but our help
To lead them to His side.

(see also: Christian Action; Goodness)

SEX

2432. The freedom of the sexual revolution is physiological; it certainly is not emotional or spiritual. . . . Who do you think in the beginning made them male and female, Hugh Hefner?
—Stephen Board

2433. Modern man speaks of intercourse as "having sex." However, the Scriptures never speak this way. In Biblical language a man "knows" his wife. It is not an act; it is a relationship.   —Paul Bubna

2434. Everyone, presumably, knows what the content of the movement for sexual liberation is. Such a profound change in popular morality seems to require some kind of rationale. One simple and crude one is that pleasure is good and that whatever doesn't "hurt" anybody else is all right. There is a sublime simplicity in the assumption that the hurtful is something any fool can recognize and use as a criterion. But this is notoriously an argument people fall back on when they haven't anything left to say.   —James Munro Cameron

2435. The Hugh Hefner Curve: You start a magazine proclaiming that sex, so far from being dirty, isn't even serious; it's just good, clean fun. A few decades later you have massive abortions, vast numbers of illegitimate children born to teenagers from the poorest strata of society, and a delightful organization named the North American Man-Boy Love Association going on national TV to explain that your basic pedophile . . . is not a pervert and child molester, but rather a lonely boy's best friend.   —David R. Carlin, Jr.

2436. Usually any one or all of the sexual difficulties that a person experiences stem from inadequate functioning of the most important sexual organ of them all—the *head*, which controls the mind, the attitudes, and the emotions influencing behavior.   —Barbara Chesser

2437. Cheap sex and precious love; you can't have one if you have the other.   —Jim Conway

2438. The sex drive in the young is a river of fire that must be banked and cooled by a hundred restraints if it is not to consume in chaos both the individual and the group.   —Will Durant

2439. There is a difference between the sexes. Of all the crazy things in today's world, surely the denial of such difference is the craziest.   —Medford Evans

2440. Sexuality is what I am and sensuality is how I use it.   —Sandy Flanigan

2441. We build a solid foundation for love by moving toward commitment at the same rate we move toward physical intimacy. . . . All along the way the privileges of growing intimacy carry with them the responsibilities of growing commitment, so that the ultimate intimacy in sexual intercourse coincides with the ultimate commitment in the covenant of marriage.   —Richard J. Foster

2442. Where reason does not control because it cannot, the result is shame; where reason can control but does not, the result is sin; and where reason can control and habitually does so, the result is chastity, otherwise describable as rational sex, moderate sex, or virtuous sex.   —James Gaffney

2443. People being what they are, it is no great achievement to woo some unstable person into a short-lived intimacy. It takes a great deal more character and finesse to make a long-term marriage into a romantic, glowing love affair. And the depth of affection and the freedom of total emotional expression that marriage provides is something experimenters can never know.   —M. P. Horban

2444. The truth is that wherever a man lies with a woman, there, whether they

185

like it or not, a transcendental relation is set up between them which must be eternally enjoyed or eternally endured.

—C. S. Lewis

2445. Modern people are always saying, "Sex is nothing to be ashamed of." They may mean one of two things. They may mean, "There is nothing to be ashamed of in the fact that the human race reproduces itself in a certain way, nor in the fact that it gives pleasure." If they mean that, they are right. . . . But, of course, when people say, "Sex is nothing to be ashamed of," they may mean that "the state into which the sexual instinct has now got is nothing to be ashamed of." If they mean that . . . I think it is everything to be ashamed of.

—C. S. Lewis

2446. The sexual impulse is God-given, and it must be God-guided.

—James Earl Massey

2447. If you ever discover that you are truly unhappy, and that being a virgin has caused your unhappiness, then you can always change it. But you sure can't say that for being a nonvirgin.

—Mary Jane Meyer

2448. Homosexuality is the sexual plague of a monogamous society gone promiscuous. Those societies that sow the winds of heterosexual freedom ironically reap the whirlwind of homosexual perversion.

—John W. Miller

2449. Sex is the only mysticism materialism offers, and so to sex the pursuers of happiness address themselves with an avidity and dedication, seldom, if ever surpassed. Who among posterity will ever be able to reconstruct the resultant scene? Who for that matter can convey it today? The vast, obsessive outpouring of erotica

in every shape and form; in book and film and play and entertainment, in body and word and deed, so that there is no escape for anyone.

—Malcolm Muggeridge

2450. This society has no more chance of surviving than the proverbial snowball in Hell unless it repents of its perversions of the relationship between man and woman.

—Donald Nicholl

2451. Sex is good. But don't jump from that to saying that bad sex is better than no sex.

—Eugene O'Sullivan

2452. Sex, like personality, requires intimacy; it calls for veiling. There is no way that we can turn it into just another public "fact."

—Bruce Shelley

2453. There is no such thing as casual sex, no matter how casual people are about it. . . . After intercourse, a couple's relationship is somehow not what it was before.

—Lewis Smedes

2454. Sex may be redeemed in our secular age not by denying it and not by indulging it but integrating it into our quest for depth, loyalty, and permanence in interpersonal relationships.

—Edward E. Thornton

2455. Sex is no test of love, for it is precisely the very thing that one wants to test that is destroyed by the testing.

—Walter Trobisch

2456. The energy which holds a society together is sexual in nature. When a man is devoted to one woman and one family, he is motivated to build, save, protect, plan, and prosper on their behalf. However, when his sexual interests are dispersed and generalized, his effort is invested in the gratification of sensual desires. Any human society is free to display great energy or to enjoy sexual license; but they cannot do both for more than one generation.   **—J. D. Unwin**

2457. "Free sex" merely delays the payment.

2458. Only a passionate love of purity can save a person from impure passion.

(see also: Chastity)

SIN

2459. Sin: a thought, a form, a fascination, a fall.   **—Augustine**

2460. The question is not how sin looks to us, or to worldly people, or to liberal theologians. The question is: how does sin appear to a holy God?   **—Kenneth D. Barney**

2461. Human reason is never the measure of sin's severity.   **—Michael P. Barrett**

2462. If a man will depart from iniquity, he must depart from his darling sin first; for as long as that is entertained, the others, at least those that are most suiting with that darling, will always be haunting him.   **—John Bunyan**

2463. Sin that damns is a mindset which means awareness and conscious choice of self-worship instead of God-worship.
   —Hugh Calkins

2464. Sin is not doing wrong; it is wrong being—deliberate, emphatic independence of God. It is the saint, not the sinner, who knows what sin is.
   —Oswald Chambers

2465. When you have finished committing sin, sin is not finished with you. The first cost is high, but it is only the down payment. You keep paying in your conscience, in your body, in the suffering you produce for your family, your friends, and your community. And finally, you will have to pay in hell.   **—Ruth Copeland**

2466. Sin is simply wanting one's own way above all else.   **—Ralph Earle**

2467. The most devastating effect of sin is that by it we are blinded to it.
   —Billy Graham

2468. The Spirit convinceth of the fact of sin, that we have done so and so; of the fault of sin, that we have done ill in doing so; of the folly of sin, that we have acted against right reason and our true interest; of the filth of sin, that by it we are become odious to God; of the foundation of sin, the corrupt nature; and lastly, of the fruit of sin, that the end thereof is death.
   —Matthew Henry

2469. God may forgive your sins but your nervous system won't.   **—Alfred Korzybski**

2470. I hate sin when I see what it does to human beings. I hate sin most when I see what it did to Christ! It turned the fairest face that ever was into a bruised and bloody thing. When sin did that to the Son of God . . . how can you ever play with it again?   **—Ian MacPherson**

2471. Recognition of the reality of sin offers . . . real hope.   **—Karl Menninger**

2472. All human sin seems so much worse in its consequences than in its intentions.   **—Reinhold Niebuhr**

2473. Denying sin has not freed us from it any more than hiding death has kept us alive. It has only made us unable to deal with it. . . . If we dare not admit to any sin, in the end we dare not admit that anything is sinful.   **—Malcolm Nygren**

2474. Sin is not misfortune; sin is not error or ignorance. Sin is a choice against what you know pleases God. If you lose this meaning of sin, you lose the beauty of forgiveness. —Robert H. O'Bannon

2475. Sin is a failure of men to live in right relationships of love, first with God and then with other persons.
—Norman Pittenger

2476. It is a grave mistake to underestimate sin and strive for no-fault moralities.
—Cornelius Plantinga

2477. Sin means that our reason is warped by our pride. —Robert Raines

2478. A little fire is quickly trodden out which, by being suffered, rivers cannot quench. —William Shakespeare

2479. Sin itself is hell, and death, and misery to the soul. . . . Avoid sin, therefore, as you would avoid being miserable.
—Samuel Shaw

2480. Christ most certainly is not the Saviour of anyone who continues to practice sin. Do you claim to have Jesus as your Saviour? I remind you that He came to save His people from their sins.
—Lehman Strauss

2481. Sinners cannot find God for the same reason that criminals cannot find a policeman: They aren't looking!
—Billy Sunday

2482. The abuse of a harmless thing is the essence of sin. —A. W. Tozer

2483. There is nothing wrong in this world except for sin. —C. M. Ward

2484. God, we may be sure, is not a God who can deal with sinners as if they were not sinners. —B. B. Warfield

2485. Remember there can be no little sin till we can find a little God.
—John Wesley

2486. Whatever weakens your reason, impairs the tenderness of conscience, obscures your sense of God, takes the relish off spiritual things, this is sin to you.
—Susanna Wesley

2487. By God's law, whatever evil the heart wants to do, the hand has already done. —Otto Whittaker

2488. You cannot win, who play with sin, in the gaming house of shame.
—Oscar Wilde

2489. He that falls into sin is a man. He that boasts of sin is a devil. He that grieves over sin is a saint. He that forgives sin is God.

2490. When you steal a penny the devil makes a fortune.

2491. The difference between the saved sinner and the unsaved sinner is that the former sins by default while the latter sins by design.

2492. Sins, like weeds, seem to get started where nothing else is growing.

2493. The heart of the problem is a problem of the heart.

SOCIAL CONCERNS

2494. The soul of reform is the reform of the soul. —Horace Bushnell

2495. It is since Christians have largely ceased to think of the other world that they have become so ineffective in this one. —C. S. Lewis

(see also: Alcoholic Beverages; Abortion; Brotherhood; Gambling; Morality)

SOCIALISM

2496. No nation, now or ever, was rich enough to feed all its idle people. When Rome began its welfare state, the end of Rome was near. —**Thomas J. Anderson**

2497. Socialism will work only in two places: In heaven where it's not needed, and in hell where they already have it. Capitalism is the unequal distribution of wealth. Socialism is the equal distribution of poverty. —**Winston Churchill**

2498. I'm against a homogenized society because I want the cream to rise.
—**Robert Frost**

(see also: Communism)

SOLITUDE

2499. If from society we learn to live, it is from solitude we should be taught how to die. —**George Gordon Byron**

2500. An old Danish peasant on his deathbed asked of his son only one promise: that he should sit alone for a half-hour each day in the best room in the house. The son did this and became a model citizen for the whole district.

(see also: Meditation)

SORROW

2501. The soul would have no rainbow had the eye no tears. —**John Vance Chency**

2502. You cannot cure your sorrow by nursing it; but you can cure it by nursing another's sorrow. —**George Matheson**

2503. Earth has no sorrow that Heaven cannot heal. —**Thomas Moore**

2504. The Lord gets His best soldiers out of the highlights of affliction.
—**Charles H. Spurgeon**

2505. My life is but the weaving
Between my God and me.
I only choose the colors,
He weaveth steadily.
Sometimes He weaveth sorrow
And I in foolish pride,
Forget He sees the upper
And I the under side.

(see also: Trouble)

SPORTS

2506. When a brutal team wins a game by strong physical measures, it has not won a game of basketball so much as destroyed it. —**Leon Morris**

2507. For when the One Great Scorer
comes
To write against your name,
He writes—not that you won or
lost,
But how you played the game.
—**Grantland Rice**

2508. Came the time for the county basketball tournament! The season had been wet, and because our school was on mud roads, we hadn't played many games; we were practically an unknown quantity in basketball. But we drove through the mud to a neighboring town where the tournament was to be played. For the first round we drew a bye. We went into round two. The team against whom we were paired for round two had gone home for supper and had become stuck in the mud. We won by their failure to appear on the floor. That put us into the third round—the semifinals. For that game our opponents ran six men onto the floor—a violation of the rules, and we won again by a forfeiture because of that team's carelessness. Now we were in the finals. The gym was packed. It was a tough game. The score was 83 to nothing. We lost. —**John Schmidt**

2509. And in the world as in the school,
You know how Fate may turn and
shift;
The prize be sometimes to the
fool,
The race not always to the swift.

Who misses or who gains the
prize,
Go, lose or conquer as you can;
But if you fall or if you rise,
Be each, pray God, a gentle man.
—**William M. Thackeray**

2510. I define football as 22 men on the field desperately in need of rest and 76,000 people in the stands desperately in need of exercise. —**Bud Wilkinson**

STEWARDSHIP

2511. One verse in every six in the first three Gospels relates, either directly or indirectly, to money. Sixteen of our Lord's forty-four parables deal with the use or misuse of money. A loving, joyful, liberal giving to the Lord's work is an acid test of a spiritual heart, pleasing to God.
—**William E. Allen**

2512. If you do not give the tenth part to God, He will take the nine parts.
—**Ambrose**

2513. Tithes ought to be paid, whatever your occupation. He who has given to us the whole has thought it meet to ask a tenth. It is not for His benefit, but for ours.
—**Augustine**

2514. I fail or succeed in my stewardship of life in proportion to how convinced I am that life belongs to God. —**Pearl Bartel**

2515. If each church member in America were to suddenly go on welfare, and if each would then begin to give the Lord the 10 percent He asks for, the income of America's churches would be 35 percent higher than it is now. —**Louis Cassels**

2516. Stewardship is the practice of our religion. —**W. H. Greener**

2517. Stewardship is what I do after I say, "I believe." —**Max R. Hickerson**

2518. Ever wish you were more concerned about the things of God? Put your money there. The interest will naturally follow. —**M. P. Horban**

2519. Someday, all that we will have is what we have given to God.
—**M. P. Horban**

2520. Give according to your income lest God make your income according to your giving. —**Peter Marshall**

2521. To meet Jesus is to look yourself in the pocketbook, which is the most unmistakable way of looking yourself in the heart. —**J. Robert Ross**

2522. The ultimate tragedy is the poor fool who clings to his pittance until it becomes eternal poverty. —**Forrest Smith**

2523. He who needs least is most like the gods. —**Socrates**

2524. When a man becomes a Christian, he becomes industrious, trustworthy and prosperous. Now, if that man, when he *gets* all he can and *saves* all he can, does not *give* all he can, I have more hope for Judas Iscariot than for that man! —**John Wesley**

2525. John Wesley refused to raise his living standard when the Lord prospered him. He continued to live as simply as when he first began his ministry, giving the increase in salary to the Lord's work.

2526. It is a spiritual tragedy when God's stewards feel free to lavish what has been entrusted to them on needless and even harmful luxuries, while the interests of God's kingdom in many lands are declining for lack of means.

2527. It is true that you can't take it with you, but you can send it on ahead.

(see also: Charity; Giving; Materialism and Hedonism; Money; Time)

STRENGTH

2528. Of Thee, dear Lord, I do not ask
That you would lighten any task,
But rather
Make me adequate.

I do not ask for lighter loads
Nor do I ask for smoother roads,
But rather
Make me adequate.

I do not ask for greater rest
From fears and failures that
oppress,
But rather
Make me adequate.
　　　　　　　—James L. Flick

2529. Strength without gentleness is tyranny.　　　**—Joanne D. Holland**

2530. If you'll put yourself at the feet of Jesus, He'll set you *on your feet*. And you'll never be *on your feet* unless He puts you there.

(see also: Power)

SUCCESS

2531. The closer one gets to the top, the more one finds there is no "top."
　　　　　　　—Nancy Barcus

2532. Build a better mousetrap and the world will beat a path to your door.
　　　　　　　—Ralph Waldo Emerson

2533. Before everything else, getting ready is the secret of success. **—Henry Ford**

2534. If a man wakes up famous he hasn't been sleeping.　　**—Wes Izzard**

2535. It is abundantly clear that success tends to negate humility.
　　　　　　　—Landrum P. Leavell

2536. Some aspects of success seem rather silly as death approaches.
　　　　　　　—Donald A. Miller

2537. The successful person is the individual who forms the habit of doing what the failing person doesn't like to do.
　　　　　　　—Donald Riggs

2538. On earth we have nothing to do with success or results, but only with being true to God and for God. Defeat in doing the right is nevertheless victory.
　　　　　　　—F. W. Robertson

2539. A man can do only what he can do. But if he does that each day he can sleep at night and do it again the next day.
　　　　　　　—Albert Schweitzer

2540. God may allow His servant to succeed when He has disciplined him to a point where he does not need to succeed to be happy. The man who is elated by success and is cast down by failure is still a carnal man. At best his fruit will have a worm in it.　　**—A. W. Tozer**

2541. Success is relevant to coping with obstacles. . . . But no problem is ever solved by those, who, when they fail, look for someone to blame instead of something to do.　　**—Fred Waggoner**

2542. Success is to be measured not so much by the position that one has reached in life as by the obstacles which he has overcome. —Booker T. Washington

2543. A winner never quits and a quitter never wins.

2544. The road to success is always under construction.

2545. *Make* yourself indispensable and you'll be moved up. *Act as if* you're indispensable and you'll be moved out.

SUFFERING

2546. God washes the eyes by tears until they can behold the invisible land where tears shall come no more.
—Henry Ward Beecher

2547. It is infinitely easier to suffer publicly and honourably than apart and ignominiously. —Dietrich Bonhoeffer

2548. Only the willingness to suffer can conquer suffering. —David J. Bosch

2549. Pain is pain and sorrow is sorrow. It hurts. It limits. It impoverishes. It isolates. It restrains. It works devastation deep within the personality. It circumscribes in a thousand different ways. There is nothing good about it. But the gifts God can give with it are the richest the human spirit can know. —Margaret Clarkson

2550. It is absurd for Christians to constantly seek new demonstrations of God's power, to expect a miraculous answer to every need, from curing ingrown toenails to finding parking places; this only leads to faith in miracles instead of faith in God.
—Charles W. Colson

2551. If God is in charge and loves us, then whatever is given is subject to His control and is meant ultimately for our joy.
—Elisabeth Elliot

2552. Blessed is any weight, however overwhelming, which God has been so good as to fasten with His own hands upon our shoulders. —Frederick W. Faber

2553. The true measure of life's worth is the ability to worthily suffer and die. Good health and good housing are not salvation; they may only be narcotics that help poor souls to exist, even though they are "dead."
—George E. Failing

2554. God prepares great men for great tasks by great trials. —J. K. Gressett

2555. If you can suffer without a hint of self-pity, without a hint of self-preoccupation, then this develops an almost limitless capacity for compassion for everyone everywhere. —John Howard Griffin

2556. Suffering tempers our easy optimism and checks our prejudices. You can often recognize those who have suffered. They are slow to give opinions when some issue is being discussed. They are patient with those caught in some sin. They withhold judgment because they have felt its sting. —Gordon Houser

2557. When through fiery trials thy
 pathway shall lie,
 My grace, all sufficient, shall be
  thy supply;
 The flame shall not hurt thee; I
  only design
 Thy dross to consume and thy
  gold to refine.
—George Keith

2558. We are not in this world simply to enjoy God's gifts. We are here to use them in the building of His kingdom, which calls for some kind of suffering.

—Arnold G. Kuntz

2559. The security we crave would teach us to rest our hearts in this world and pose an obstacle to our return to God. . . . Our Father refreshes us on the journey with some pleasant inns, but will not encourage us to mistake them for home. —C. S. Lewis

2560. The problem of reconciling human suffering with the existence of a God who loves, is only insoluble so long as we attach a trivial meaning to the word "love." —C. S. Lewis

2561. C. S. Lewis has estimated that four-fifths of human suffering is caused by human beings being wicked to one another.

2562. How often we look upon God as our last and feeblest resource. We go to Him because we have nowhere else to go. And then we learn that the storms of life have driven us, not upon the rocks, but into the desired haven.

—George MacDonald

2563. Teach me, dear God. the glory of my cross; teach me the value of my "thorn." Show me that I have climbed to Thee by the path of pain. Show me that my tears have made my rainbow.

—George Matheson

2564. It is suffering and then glory. Not to have the suffering means not to have the glory. —Robert C. McQuilkin

2565. Indeed, the truth that many people never understand until it is too late, is that the more you try to avoid suffering, the more you suffer, because smaller and more insignificant things begin to torture you, in proportion to your fear of being hurt. —Thomas Merton

2566. Great souls suffer in silence.

—Schiller

2567. There are four things you can do with the hurts that come into your life, nurse them; curse them; rehearse them; or reverse them. —Patrick Shaughnessy

2568. The fear of suffering and the drive to explain other people's pain are closely connected. . . . In the drama of life the need to play the friends of Job is fueled by our fear of playing Job himself. —John Shea

2569. It is remarkable with what Christian fortitude and resignation we can bear the suffering of other folks.

—Jonathan Swift

2570. The presence of Christ puts pain in perspective. —David L. Thompson

2571. It is by those who have suffered that the world has been advanced.

—Leo Tolstoy

2572. Each time we have some pain to go through, we can say to ourselves quite truly that it is the universe, the order and beauty of the world and the obedience of creation to God that are entering our body. After that, how can we fail to bless with tenderest gratitude the Love that sends us this gift? —Simone Weil

2573. One ship drives east and another
    drives west
With the selfsame winds that
    blow.
'Tis the set of the sails and not
    the gales
Which tells us the way to go.

Like the winds of the sea are the
    ways of fate,
As we voyage along through life:

'Tis the set of the soul that
decides its goal,
And not the calm or the strife.
—Ella Wheeler Wilcox

2574. Who would complain if God allowed one hour of suffering in an entire lifetime of comfort? Why complain about a lifetime that includes suffering when that lifetime is a mere hour of eternity?
—Philip Yancy

2575. God giveth the shoulder according to the burden.

2576. He who would have nothing to do with thorns must never attempt to gather flowers.

2577. The will of God will not take you where the grace of God cannot keep you.

2578. Suffering does two things for the Christian that could not otherwise be so well accomplished: It cultivates humility and develops strength.

(see also: Trouble)

SUNDAY

2579. Instead of a holy day, the sabbath is to millions nothing more than a holiday. . . . But man was made for fellowship with his Creator. One of his essential needs is to worship God. . . . Let us remember the Christian sabbath is a spiritual bulwark to the individual and to the nation.
—L. Nelson Bell

2580. From a moral, social and physical point of view, the observance of Sunday is a duty of absolute consequence.
—William E. Gladstone

2581. There is a plant in the corner of my heart called reverence, and it needs watering at least once a week.
—Oliver Wendell Holmes

2582. If the Sabbath goes, everything else goes with it.   —Marion Lawrence

2583. There is probably no more accurate test of one's Christian devotion than one's attitude toward, and conduct on, the Lord's Day.   —Richard Taylor

2584. Sunday honors God the Father by being the day of the dawn of creation; honors the Son by being the day the work of redemption was sealed by His resurrection; and honors the Holy Spirit by being the day the Spirit descended on the 120 in the Upper Room.

2585. It's very strange that heat on
Sunday
Seems so much hotter than on
Monday;
And weekday pains that we
ignore,
On Sundays seem to hurt much
more.
So we decide to stay in bed
When we should be in church
instead.

SURRENDER

2586. The surrendered life is the careful life. The sanctified steward uses what belongs to Another and handles it very carefully against the day of accounting. On the other hand, the surrendered life is a carefree life. Losses that devastate the natural man are endured with amazing calm by the sanctified man, for how can he really lose what he has already relinquished?
—R. B. Acheson

2587. There is only one way to bring peace to the heart, joy to the mind, and beauty to the life; it is to accept and do the will of God.   —William Barclay

2588. If God would only use His fingers, and make us broken bread and poured-out wine in a special way! But when He uses someone whom we dislike, or some set of circumstances to which we said we would never submit, and makes those the crushers, we object. We must never [try to] choose the scene of our own martyrdom.
—Oswald Chambers

2589. Resolved, never, henceforward, till I die, to act as if I were my own, but entirely and altogether God's.
—Jonathan Edwards

2590. When you follow Christ it must be a total burning of all your bridges behind you. —Billy Graham

2591. If Jesus Christ is not Lord *of all*, He is not Lord *at all*. —Vance Havner

2592. All of life submits to us if we submit to Christ. —Virgil Hurley

2593. I ordered the Lord:
Get right with me;
My will be done,
And instantly!

And I don't know why,
But prayers fell numb,
Till I learned to pray
In Jesus' way:
Thy Kingdom come;
Thy Will be done.
—Henry Hubert Hutto

2594. Lay down thy life, thy selfish aims,
ambitions,
Thy many plans, the wishes of
thine heart;
The way thy mind hath purposed,
'tis but folly;
Then lay it down and come with
Me apart.
—Elza Levensalor

2595. Wherever the will conferred by the Creator is perfectly offered back in delighted and delighting obedience by the creature, there, most undoubtedly, is heaven, and there the Holy Ghost proceeds. —C. S. Lewis

2596. Life is the gift of God to those who choose to let the divine will transcend theirs. Death is the state of those who do not. —Frances O'Neill

2597. By ingenious means we will gerrymander through the different areas of life, willing to surrender lordship in one province in order to maintain it in others. Or we will set up puppet kingdoms, denying that we are in control when, in fact, we are still maintaining subtle sovereignty. But . . . the true Sovereign exposes our false sense of sovereignty for what it is—a delusion. —Millard Reed

2598. To take all that we are and have, and hand it over to God, may not be easy; but it can be done, and when it is done, the world has in it one less candidate for misery. —Paul Scherer

2599. God never comes through the door that I hold open for Him, but always knocks at the one place which I have walled up with concrete. But if I do not let Him in there, He turns away altogether.
—Helmut Thielicke

2600. The altar is not a bargain counter where you haggle with God. With Him it is all or nothing. —Lance Zavitz

2601. God will only mend a broken heart when He is given all the pieces.

2602. Disappointment—His
appointment;
Change one letter, then I see

That the thwarting of my purpose
Is God's better choice for me.

All my life's plan in His molding,
Not one single choice be mine;
Let me answer, unrepining,
"Father, not my will, but Thine."

(see also: Commitment, Self-Denial)

SYMPATHY

2603. The truest help we can render an afflicted man is not to take his burden from him, but to call out his best strength that he may be able to bear the burden.

—**Phillips Brooks**

2604. Sympathy is a thing to be encouraged apart from humane consideration, because it supplies us with the materials for wisdom. —**Robert Louis Stevenson**

(see also: Interpersonal Relations; Love)

TEACHING

2605. A teacher affects eternity; he can never tell where his influence stops.

—**Henry Adams**

2606. That if you become a teacher,
By your pupils you'll be taught.
—**Oscar Hammerstein II**

2607. The great teacher must not only give the best that is in his subject, but what is even more important, the best that is in himself. —**Herman Kelly**

2608. Teaching is a partnership with God. You are not molding iron nor chiseling marble; you are working with the Creator of the universe in shaping human character and determining destiny.

—**Ruth Vaughn**

2609. A builder builded a temple;
He wrought with care and skill.
Pillars and groins and arches
Were fashioned to meet his will;
And men said when they saw its
beauty:
"It shall never know decay.
Great is thy skill, O builder,
Thy fame shall endure for aye."

A teacher builded a temple;
She wrought with skill and care,
Forming each pillar with
patience,
Laying each stone with prayer.
None saw the unceasing effort;
None knew of the marvelous plan;
For the temple the teacher
builded
Was unseen by the eyes of man.

Gone is the builder's temple;
Crumbled into the dust,
Pillar and groin and arches
Food for consuming rust;
But the temple the teacher
builded
Shall endure while the ages roll;
For that beautiful, unseen temple
Was a child's immortal soul.

TELEVISION

2610. Television is the supreme child molester in our society. A few sesame seeds cannot disguise the fact that the loaf is poisoned with artificial preservatives. . . . TV encourages self-indulgence through its commercials, and induces through its programming a glazed passivity and a shortened attention span that depend on regular injections of [super excitement]. Even the healthy fun of what used to be called comics is now corroded by wise-guy dialogue and self-mockery.

—**James H. Billington**

2611. To the commercials on television are given the loudest, most far-reaching voice ever enjoyed by a communicator. They are based and designed on the most thorough and sophisticated research into the motivation of human personality . . . and are produced with the most capable, expert talent available. After two years of detailed research into their content, I have concluded that commercials represent an insidious assault on the Christian view of life. —Kenneth Curtis

2612. Television is a religion beyond the dreams of emperors and priests because its ministrations are subsidized by a levy on the price of all goods and are invited to entertain in every home in the land.
—George Gerbner

2613. I think television is having a detrimental effect on Christians. They are no longer sensitive to sin. . . . TV has brought the night club into the home along with violence and sex—things which Christians looked upon ten years ago with abhorrence. . . . Christians are generally becoming desensitized, and I can cite case after case where they now watch these things on TV without feeling any tinge of conscience. —Billy Graham

2614. Our permissive society has affected me: I watch things on television today I would not have tolerated in my life twenty years ago. Am I being slowly brainwashed by Satan's forces, by the very culture about which the Lord says, "Come out from among them and be ye separate and touch not the unclean thing?"
—Billy Graham

2615. I can assure you that these same network officials [who deny that violence on TV causes some viewers to act violently] do not say this to advertisers. They don't tell advertisers that TV will not motivate people [to ape what they see and] buy products. —Harry N. Hollis, Jr.

2616. Eighty percent of American homes have a Bible; ninety-six percent have a television set. —Russell Holt

2617. Television is a teaching instrument that brings to viewers experiences and ideas which are gradually integrated into one's own view of life. —Stewart M. Hoover

2618. Television is educational. It's driving people to reading. —Kae Jaworski

2619. Suppose someone invented an instrument, a convenient little talking tube which, say, could be heard over the whole land. . . . I wonder if the police would not forbid it, fearing that the whole country would become mentally deranged if it were used. —Soren Kierkegaard
(1813–1855)

2620. Only the family can rival television's power to shape attitudes, communicate values, and form consciences.
—Ellwood Kieser

2621. If you actually lived in an environment that contained as much violence and perversion as television depicts, you would try to move, wouldn't you?
—Cecil B. Knight

2622. Discriminating use of television may depend more on what you are doing with your life than on whether you have the will power to turn off the set.
—David Kucharsky

2623. Television makes people stagnant.
—Norman Lear

2624. Television is a cultural wasteland.
—Newton Minow

2625. Western man has made a graven image—a terrible graven image . . . of himself. —Malcolm Muggeridge

2626. The first step in devotional Bible study is to walk over to the television set and turn the switch to the "off" position. If this doesn't quiet the beast, find the cord . . . and pull the plug. —Walt Neufeld

2627. Family life stagnates while we watch the tube, vicariously living the vexations and glamour of others.
—Kevin Perrotta

2628. Television is not in itself sinful. It cannot sin; it is an inanimate object. . . . There won't be one TV set brought before the judgment seat of Christ to give an account of its behavior. The question we must face is this: "Is television our master or our servant?" —Everek R. Storms

2629. When you send a boy to a good Christian school, you are in one sense pressuring him to become a Christian without forcing him. This is exactly the kind of compulsion television programs apply to shape the thinking of our children.
—Philip Teng

2630. Television acts as a drug, rendering inert the minds of all those forlorn souls addicted to its doses. If another generation or two of Americans is exposed to this odious medium, all will be living at the intellectual level of brussels sprouts. TV is rapidly driving intelligent conversation and even sociability out of our lives.
—R. Emmett Tyrrell

2631. Children who ask for the wholesome bread of parental interaction and guidance are too often given a plugged-in pacifier, a mechanical nipple void of human touch or feeling.
—James Vanden Bosch

2632. A family watching television is a way of doing nothing together.

2633. A TV repair service ad: We can fix anything wrong with your television set—except the lousy programs.

2634. The titillated masses scramble aboard this pre-routed cattle car that transports them into an intellectual Auschwitz.

2635. The Television Age began around 1947. It is estimated that a person born since then will, by the time he is sixty-five, spend nine years of his life—that's about 80,000 hours—sitting in front of the TV! By contrast, if a newborn infant were taken to Sunday school the first week of his life and never missed a Sunday until he was sixty-five, he would spend less than four months in Sunday school.

(see also: Mass Media)

TEMPERANCE

2636. Temperance is to the body what religion is to the soul—the foundation of health, strength and peace.
—Tryon Edwards

2637. Abstinence is as easy to me as temperance would be difficult.
—Samuel Johnson

(see also: Alcoholic Beverages; Balance; Self-Control)

TEMPTATION

2638. Temptation is the tempter looking through the keyhole into the room where you are living; sin is your drawing back the bolt and making it possible for him to enter. —J. Wilbur Chapman

2639. In every sense the crisis of the moment is decided only by the tenor of life; nor, since the world began has any man

been dragged over into the domain of evil, who had not strayed carelessly or gazed curiously or lingered guiltily beside its verge.
—Marshall Hayden

2640. Temptation is the appeal of the emotions to control the will in opposition to the truth. —J. W. Jepson

2641. What you do in the hour of temptation will depend upon what you were the day before. —Bob Jones

2642. Temptation discovers what we are.
—Thomas à Kempis

2643. You can't keep the birds from flying over your head; but you can keep them from building a nest in your hair.
—Martin Luther

2644. The devil comes without invitation but leaves only when commanded.
—W. E. McCumber

2645. Bolt that door!
Each sin has its door of entrance.
Keep that door closed!
Bolt it tight!
Just outside the wild beast
Crouches in the night.
Pin the bolt with a prayer,
God will fix it there.
—John Oxenham

2646. It is one thing to be tempted, another thing to fall. —William Shakespeare

2647. And oftentimes, to win us to our harm,
The instruments of darkness tell us truths,
Win us with honest trifles, to betray us
In deepest consequence.
—William Shakespeare

2648. Learn to say no; it will be of more use to you than to be able to read Latin.
—Charles H. Spurgeon

2649. At every fork in the road the devil is dangling the carrot down the wrong path. —William Vander Hoven

2650. A thief will not assault an empty house, but only where he thinks there is treasure. Though to be tempted [by Satan] is a trouble, yet to think why you are tempted is a great comfort.
—Thomas Watson

2651. To a greater or lesser degree, if you are alive you are tempted.
—Bruce Wideman

2652. In all thy temptations be not discouraged. Those surges may be, not to break thee, but to heave thee off thyself, onto the Rock of Christ.
—Thomas Wilcocks

2653. No degree of temptation justifies any degree of sin. —Nathaniel Parker Willis

2654. Every temptation is, among other things, an opportunity for getting closer to God.

2655. Calling on Jesus to help you overcome temptation may look weak to men. But the demons know it is their undoing.

2656. Temptations are like tramps. Treat them kindly and they will return bringing others with them.

THANKSGIVING

2657. Be on the lookout for mercies. The more we look for them, the more of them we will see. Blessings brighten when we count them. Out of the determination of the heart the eyes see. If you want to be gloomy, there's gloom enough to keep you glum; if you want to be happy, there's gleam enough to keep you glad. Better to lose count while naming your blessings than to lose your blessings by counting your troubles.   —**Maltbie D. Babcock**

2658. The unthankful heart, like my finger in the sand, discovers no mercies; but let the thankful heart sweep through the day, and as the magnet finds the iron, so it will find, in every hour, some heavenly blessings; only the iron in God's sand is gold!   —**Henry Ward Beecher**

2659. You say grace before meals. All right. But I say grace before the concert and the opera, and grace before the play and pantomime, and grace before I open a book, and grace before sketching, painting, swimming, fencing, boxing, walking, playing, dancing and grace before I dip the pen in the ink.   —**G. K. Chesterton**

2660. Chrysostom . . . had the curious thought that a Christian could even give thanks for Hell, because Hell was a threat and a warning to keep him in the right way.

2661. A thankful heart is not only the greatest virtue, but the parent of all other virtues.   —**Cicero**

2662. Thanksgiving is a sure index of spiritual health.   —**Maurice Dametz**

2663. A hundred times every day I remind myself that my life depends on the labors of other men, living and dead, and that I must exert myself in order to give, in the measure as I have received, and am still receiving.   —**Albert Einstein**

2664. It is always possible to be thankful for what is given rather than to complain about what is not given. One or the other becomes a habit of life.   —**Elisabeth Elliot**

2665. I thank Thee, Lord, for blessings,
   big and small;
For spring's warm glow and
   songbird's welcome call;
For autumn's hue and winter's
   white snow shawl.

I thank Thee for the harvest rich
   with grain;
For tall trees and the quiet
   shadowed lane;
For rushing stream, for birds that
   love to fly;
My country's land, the mountains
   and the plain.

I thank Thee for each sunset in
   the sky,
For sleepy nights, the bed in
   which I lie;
A life of truth and peace; a
   woman's hand,
Her hand in mine until the day I
   die.

I thank Thee, Lord, for all these
   things above;
But most of all I thank Thee for
   Thy love.
      —**Ralph Gaither (written while
      a POW in North Vietnam)**

2666. If you would enter deeply into the meaning of thanksgiving, cultivate the mood of expectant love, the attitude of awe before the marvelous, and the open-heartedness that turns in confidence to that source from whence we sprung.
      —**Henry David Gray**

2667. On the night Matthew Henry was robbed he prayed this prayer: "I thank Thee first because I was never robbed before; second, because although they took my purse they did not take my life; third, although they took my all, it was not much; and fourth, because it was I who was robbed and not I who robbed."

2668. Thou who has given so much to
me,
Give one thing more—a grateful
heart;
Not thankful when it pleaseth
me,
As if Thy blessings had spare days,
But such a heart whose pulse may
be Thy praise.
—**George Herbert**

2669. Normal day, let me be aware of the treasure you are. —**Mary Jean Irion**

2670. Many live in dread of what is coming. Why should we? The unknown puts adventure into life. It gives us something to sharpen our souls on. The unexpected around the corner gives a sense of anticipation and surprise. Thank God for the unknown future. —**E. Stanley Jones**

2671. The greatest saint in the world is not he who prays most or fasts most; it is not he who gives alms, or is most eminent for temperance, chastity or justice. It is he who is most thankful to God, and who has a heart always ready to praise Him.
—**William Law**

2672. Jesus, please teach me to appreciate what I have before time forces me to appreciate what I had. —**Susan L. Lenzkes**

2673. Gratitude is the memory of the heart. —**Massieu**

2674. Not what we say about our blessings but how we use them is the true measure of our thanksgiving. —**W. T. Purkiser**

2675. Were there no God we would be in this glorious world with grateful hearts and no one to thank. —**Christina Rossetti**

2676. The beginning of men's rebellion against God was, and is, the lack of a thankful heart. —**Francis Schaeffer**

2677. I thank Thee for Thy keeping
power
Through every day and every
hour.
I thank Thee that Thou lovest me
Despite the times I stray from
Thee.
I thank Thee for Thy watchful
care,
The blessed privilege of prayer,
The joy in knowing Thou art
near,
The love of those to me most dear.
For Thy supply that has no end,
I thank Thee, Lord, my Savior,
Friend.
—**Helen Mary Sees**

2678. Let never day nor night
unhallowed pass,
But still remember what the Lord
hath done.
—**William Shakespeare**

2679. For all the blessings of the year;
For sunshine and for showers,
For seedtime and for harvest rich,
For bird songs and for flowers,
From hearts o'erflowing with Thy
praise,
Accept, O Lord, the thanks we
raise.

And for the gift of Thy dear Son
From sin to set us free,
No tongue can tell, no words
express
The praise we offer Thee.
For Christ, who came for us to
die,
Accept out thanks, O God on
high.
—**A. E. Sherwood**

2680. God gave you the gift of 86,400 seconds today. Have you used one to say "thank you"?   —William A. Ward

2681. The Pilgrims made seven times more graves than huts. No Americans have been more impoverished than those—who, nevertheless, set aside a day of thanksgiving.   —H. W. Westermeyer

2682. Thank God for dirty dishes;
They have a tale to tell.
While other folks go hungry,
We're eating pretty well.

With home, and health, and
        happiness,
We shouldn't want to fuss;
For by this stack of evidence,
God's very good to us.

2683. Seeds of discouragement will not grow in the thankful heart.

2684. Were thanks for every gift
        expressed,
    Each day would be
        thanksgiving;
Were gratitude its very best,
    Each life would be
        thanksliving.

2685. For grief unsuffered, tears unshed,
    For clouds that scattered
        overhead;
For pestilence that came not nigh,
For dangers great that passed me
        by;
For sharp suspicion smoothed,
        allayed,
For doubt dispelled that made
        afraid;
For fierce temptation well
        withstood,
For evil plot that brought forth
        good;

For weakened links in friendship's
        chain
That, sorely tested, stood the
        strain;
For harmless blows with malice
        dealt,
For base ingratitude unfelt;
For hatred's sharp unuttered word,
For bitter jest unknown, unheard;
For every evil turned away,
Unmeasured thanks I give today.

2686. Most of us don't realize how much we have to be thankful for until we have to pay taxes on it.

2687. We do not always get what we ask from God, but we always have reason to thank Him.

2688. Even though we can't have all we want, we ought to be thankful we don't get all we deserve.

(see also: Praise)

THEOLOGY

2689. Theology is faith seeking understanding.   —Karl Barth

2690. It is the task of theology not to get drunk with foreign ideas and beat up on God's children, but to feed and strengthen them.   —Klaus Bockmuhl

2691. I am more and more impressed with the fact that it is never the ink of the theologian but always the blood of the martyr that is the seed of the church. Let's not despise the ink. . . . But let's not pretend it's blood.   —Elwyn Davies

2692. I would rather feel contrition than know how to define it. —Thomas à Kempis

2693. Modern theology is in the position that medicine would be in if it lost confi-

dence in the germ theory. . . . Either Scripture speaks unequivocally of God, or the death of theology is a dead certainty. When will the [modern] theologian learn that a reliable Bible is his only survival kit?
—John Warwick Montgomery

2694. Whoever pries into God's hidden motivations,
And gains naught for his pains but doubts and speculations,
Is like a man who combs the bottom of the sea
For strange and curious things he thinks therein may be,
And who, when coming up, holds nothing in his hands
But sand, that drifts away before he ever lands.
—Jacobus Revius

2695. If German theologians saw two doors, one marked "Heaven" and the other "Discussion On Heaven," they would go into the second.
—Helmut Thielicke

2696. The Bible is God's Word about man; theology is man's word about God.

(see also: Doctrine; God; Truth)

THOUGHT

2697. The relationship of a man's soul to God is best evidenced by those things that occupy his thoughts. —Kenneth L. Dodge

2698. A man is not what he thinks he is, but what he thinks, he is.
—Max R. Hickerson

2699. A wise man will be master of his mind, a fool will be its slave.
—Publilius Syrus

2700. Though man a thinking being is defined,

Few use the grand prerogative of mind.
How few think justly of the thinking few!
How many never think, who think they do!
—Jan Taylor

2701. I believe that the mind can be permanently profaned by the habit of attending to trivial things, so that all our thoughts shall be tinged with triviality.
—Henry David Thoreau

2702. We build our fortune thought by thought,
For so the universe was wrought,
Thought is another name for fate:
Choose then the destiny and wait,
For love brings love and hate brings hate.
—Henry Van Dyke

2703. You can lead a man to college, but you can't make him think.

(see also: The Mind)

TIME

2704. Time wasted is a theft from God.
—Henri Frederic Amiel

2705. I know well enough what [time] is, provided that nobody asks me; but if I am asked what it is and try to explain, I am baffled. —Augustine

2706. Time isn't a commodity, something you pass around like cake. Time is the substance of life. When anyone asks you to give your time, they're really asking for a chunk of your life. —Antoinette Bosco

2707. Would we know the value of the present? Ask the past. Would we learn the

preciousness of time? Ask the aged, rocking in their chairs of regret.
—Charles G. E. Chilton

2708. Time goes, you say? Ah, no! Alas, time stays, we go! —Henry A. Dobson

2709. All my possessions for a moment of time. —Queen Elizabeth I

2710. Guard well your spare moments. They are like uncut diamonds. Discard them and their value will never be known. Improve them and they will become the brightest gems in a useful life.
—Ralph Waldo Emerson

2711. The highest value in life is found in the stewardship of time.
—Robert M. Fine

2712. Dost thou love life? Then do not squander time, for that's the stuff life is made of. —Benjamin Franklin

2713. Look not mournfully into the past, it comes not back again. Wisely improve the present, it is thine. Go forth to meet the shadowy future without fear and with a manly heart.

—Henry Wadsworth Longfellow

2714. As every thread of gold is valuable, so is every moment of time. —John Mason

2715. Minutes are worth more than money. Spend them wisely.
—Thomas P. Murphy

2716. Clocks are corrected by astronomy! What good is a clock unless it is set by the stars? Without a sense of eternity you don't even know what time it is.
—R. Eugene Sterner

2717. Time is but the stream I go a-fishing in. —Henry David Thoreau

2718. Though I am always in haste, I am never in a hurry; because I never undertake any more work than I can go through with perfect calmness of spirit. —John Wesley

2719. No time for God?
What fools we are. . .
No time for God?
As soon to say no time
To eat, to sleep, to live, to die.
Take time for God,
Or a poor misshapen thing you'll
be
To step into eternity,
And say, I had no time for Thee.

2720. When as a child, I laughed and
wept,
Time crept.
When as a youth, I dreamed and
talked,
Time walked.
When I became a full-grown man,
Time ran.
And later, as I older grew,
Time flew.
Soon I shall find while traveling
on,
Time gone.

2721. What I do today is important because I'm exchanging a day of my life for it.

2722. The hourglass of this age is nearly out of sand.

2723. Time is the dressing room for eternity.

2724. Yesterday is already a dream, and tomorrow is only a vision; but today, well lived, makes every yesterday a dream of happiness and every tomorrow a vision of hope.

(see also: The Future; History; The New Year; The Past; The Present)

TITHING

(see: Stewardship)

THE TONGUE
(see: Censoriousness; Gossip)

TRIBULATION
(see: Suffering; Trouble)

THE TRINITY
2725. Tell me how it is that in this room there are three candles and but one light, and I will explain to you the mode of the divine existence. —**John Wesley**

TROUBLE
2726. Better is poverty at the hand of God than riches in the storehouse.
—**Amenemapt**

2727. If sorrow makes us shed tears, faith in the promises of God makes us dry them.
—**Augustine**

2728. In the day of prosperity we have many refuges to resort to; in the day of adversity, only one. —**Horatius Bonar**

2729. As we cry to God, He hears, and dares us to look at things from His perspective. —**Karen Bosch**

2730. Our antagonist is our helper. He that wrestles with us strengthens our muscles, sharpens our skill. —**Edmund Burke**

2731. With patient mind by course of
    duty run;
God nothing does or suffers to be
    done
But thou wouldst do thyself, if
    thou couldst see
The end of all events as well as
    He.
—**George Gordon Byron**

2732. Winds have ne'er uprooted
    timber

Growing deep beneath the sod;
Strife has never conquered
    mortals
Who are rooted deep in God.
—**Byron E. Debolt**

2733. Reverses cannot befall that fine
    prosperity
Whose sources are interior.
—**Emily Dickinson**

2734. No greater tragedy can be found than that of a soul crying out, "It's not fair!" and allowing the cold waters of cynicism to overflow and drown him. On the other hand, no greater victory can be won than by the person who has been plunged into those same waters and says, "I cannot feel the bottom, but I'll swim until I can!"
—**Doris E. Dougherty**

2735. Shadows can only be
Where light surrounds,
And storms can only come
Where power abounds.

Then know that shadows pass;
The sun remains.
The storm will cease,
God's power sustains.

Some things are seen best
In shadow and storm.
And oft when life is pressed
Faith is born.
—**John Drescher**

2736. Job didn't get an answer to his questions. He had to accept the fact that a relationship with the One who knows the answers is better than the answers themselves. —**David W. Dyke**

2737. Every experience of trial puts us to this test: "Do you trust God or don't you?"
—**Elisabeth Elliot**

2738. Refuse self-pity. Refuse it absolutely. It is a deadly thing with power to destroy you. Turn your thoughts to Christ who has already carried your griefs and sorrows. —**Elisabeth Elliot**

2739. 'Tis not in the high stars alone,
Nor in the redbreast's mellow tone,
But in the mud and scum of things,
There always, always something sings.
—**Ralph Waldo Emerson**

2740. Adversity is God's university.
—**Paul Evans**

2741. When God would make a pearl, He allows a grain of sand to hurt the oyster. When God would make a saint, He buries a sorrow in the life. —**George E. Failing**

2742. A time of disarray is also a moment of opportunity. —**Frederick Ferre**

2743. Man's extremity is God's opportunity. —**John Flavel**

2744. Have you come to the Red Sea place in your life,
Where, in spite of all you can do,
There is no way out, there is no way back,
There is no other way but through?
Then wait on the Lord with a trust serene
Till the night of your fear is gone;
He will send the wind, He will heap the floods,
When He says to your soul, "Go on."
—**Annie Johnson Flint**

2745. God may not prevent tragedy, but He enables us to move beyond it.
—**Kenneth Gibble**

2746. How could history record victories if there were no battles? How could we define light if there were no darkness? How could we describe a mountain if there were no valleys? How could we appreciate shelter if there were no storms? How could we enjoy a cool drink if there were no thirst? How could there be faith if there were no doubts? How could we hope for a glorious resurrection if there were no grave?
—**J. K. Gressett**

2747. As trees must be pruned, gold refined, grain sifted, and pearls polished, so the Lord tests and tries His children that they may develop their true potential and reflect their Maker's glory.
—**George Gritter**

2748. Christianity may not always offer supernatural deliverance from earth's problems, but it always offers supernatural use for them. It is likely that Peter, who was delivered from prison, learned less than Paul, who stayed there.
—**L. Thomas Holdcroft**

2749. This life of mine so strange it seems,
So empty are its fairest dreams;
And disappointments crowd so fast,
Well, there's the next, but ne'er the last.
Am I a pioneer in care?
Has no one else but me been there?
Ah, yes, indeed Christ knows this road;
He trod it with a heavy load.

So as I walk with footsteps sore,
It's great to know He's gone
  before.
  —William Houghton

2750. Our religion, no matter how orthodox, will be salt to no one unless when it
rains it pours.　　—Keith E. Huttenlocker

2751. You can rescue out of every unjust,
impossible situation something that makes
that situation not confining, but contrib-
uting.　　　　　　　—E. Stanley Jones

2752. Keep your face to the sunshine and
you cannot see the shadow. —Helen Keller

2753. No one ever would have crossed
the ocean if he could have gotten off the
ship in the storm.　　—C. F. Kettering

2754. In this life, the Lord allows His
saints to enjoy many sweet blessings, but
none are more precious than those which
occur deep in the valleys of disappointment, pain and heartache, where He without fail draws near. —George S. Lauderdale

2755. It is certain that whatever seeming
calamity happens to you, if you thank and
praise God for it, you will turn it into a
blessing.　　　　　　　—William Law

2756. We must use every situation in life,
whether good or bad, as building blocks for
our spiritual and emotional well-being,
never giving thanks for the bad things that
come our way, but thanking God for bringing us through them.　　—James N. Layne

2757. Say not, my soul, "From whence
    Can God relieve my care?"
  Remember that Omnipotence
    Hath servants everywhere.

  His help is always sure,
    His methods seldom guessed;
  Delay will make our pleasure pure:
    Surprise will give it zest.

His wisdom is sublime,
  His heart profoundly kind;
God never is before His time,
  And never is behind.

Hast thou assumed a load
  Which none will bear with
    thee?
And art thou bearing it for God,
  And shall He fail to see?

Be comforted at heart,
  Thou art not left alone;
Now thou the Lord's companion
    art—
  Soon thou shalt share His
    throne.

  —J. J. Lynch

2758. The greatest good and the most
profitable gain come when we are up
against a blank wall. . . . Then we learn to
pray in plain language.　　—Arthur Lynip

2759. No man ought to lay a cross upon
himself, or to adopt tribulation . . . ; but if a
cross or tribulation come upon him, then
let him suffer it patiently, and know that it
is good and profitable for him.
　　　　　　　　　　—Martin Luther

2760. The bitterest cup with Christ is
better than the sweetest cup without Him.
　　　　　　　　　—Ian MacPherson

2761. Crises bring us face to face with
our inadequacy and our inadequacy in turn
leads us to the inexhaustible sufficiency of
God.　　　　　　　—Catherine Marshall

2762. Justin Martyr was roasted to death
on a huge griddle. After they had cooked
him over a slow fire for some time, he
looked at his torturers and said with a
smile, "Turn me over; this side is done."

2763. Earthly prosperity is no sign of the
special love of heaven; nor are sorrow and

care any mark of God's disfavor, but the reverse. God's love is robust and true and eager—not for our own comfort, but for our lasting blessedness.　　—F. B. Meyer

2764. A great many people seem to embalm their troubles. I always feel like running away when I see them coming.
　　　　—Dwight L. Moody

2765. His love in time past forbids me to
　　　think
　　　He'll leave me at last in trouble to
　　　　sink;
　　　Each sweet Ebenezer I have in
　　　　review
　　　Confirms His good pleasure to
　　　　carry me through.
　　　　—John Newton

2766. God, give us grace to accept with serenity the things that cannot be changed, courage to change the things which should be changed, and the wisdom to distinguish the one from the other.
　　　　—Reinhold Niebuhr

2767. I believe there is nothing that honours God more, or that God more honours, than praising Him in tribulation.
　　　　—Brownlow North

2768. I think as I look back over my life, that there was hardly a single . . . instance where things seemed to go against me, in which I cannot even now see that by God's profound mercy they really went for me all the while.　　—Francis Paget

2769. It is a distrust of God, to be troubled about what is to come; impatience against God, to be troubled with what is present; and anger at God to be troubled for what is past.　　—Simon Patrick

2770. There are lessons which cannot be learned in a dress parade. Only the firing line puts the mettle in the soldier.
　　　　—Bill Popejoy

2771. I thank Thee more that all my joy
　　　　Is touched with pain;
　　　That shadows fall on brightest
　　　　hours,
　　　　That thorns remain;
　　　So that earth's bliss may be my
　　　　guide,
　　　And not my chain.
　　　　—Adelaide Ann Proctor

2772. When God sorts out the weather,
　　　　and sends rain;
　　　Why, rain's my choice.
　　　　—James Whitcomb Riley

2773. Life isn't always fair. But neither was the Cross. God took that Cross—an instrument of execution—and transformed it into the hope of the world. He will do that with your cross, too, if you will let Him.　　—Robert Russell

2774. In sickness let me not so much say, "Am I getting better of my pain?" but, "Am I getting better for it?"
　　　　—William Shakespeare

2775. Underneath us—Oh, how easy!
　　　We have not to mount on high,
　　　But to sink into His fullness
　　　And in trustful weakness lie.

　　　And we find our humbling failures
　　　Save us from the strength that
　　　　harms;
　　　We may fail, but underneath us
　　　Are the everlasting arms.
　　　　—A. B. Simpson

2776. Would you like to be there [heaven] and see yourself pointed at as the one saint who never knew a sorrow? Oh,

no! For you would be an alien in the midst of the sacred brotherhood.
—**Charles H. Spurgeon**

2777. The Lord gets His best soldiers out of the highlands of affliction.
—**Charles H. Spurgeon**

2778. At the profoundest depths in life men talk not about God, but with Him.
—**Elton Trueblood**

2779. Life need not be easy to be joyful. Joy is not the absence of trouble but the presence of Christ.
—**William Vander Hoven**

2780. People who escape trouble miss growth. —**C. M. Ward**

2781. Don't shun the valley! It never need be the symbol of disgrace. Jesus descended! He came *down* to *walk* with men. I know this much: I have some walking to do before I'm ready to *climb*. —**C. M. Ward**

2782. God could keep us from the furnace,
From our paths each trial turn;
But he'd have us know the rapture
Of the flame that does not burn.

2783. The brook would lose its song if you removed the rocks.

2784. The pessimist says of trouble: "It's enough to make a person *lose* his religion," while the optimist says: "It's enough to make a person *use* his religion."

2785. God has not promised us a quiet journey—only a safe arrival.

2786. Whenever God gives us a cross to bear, it is a prophecy that He will also give us strength.

2787. As a knot appears unexpectedly in a thread, so disappointment blocks the smoothness of life. If a few deft strokes can untangle the skein, life continues evenly; but if it cannot be corrected, then it must be quietly woven into the design. Thus the finished piece can still be beautiful—though not as perfect as planned.

2788. Sorrow touched by love grows bright,
With more than rapture's ray;
And darkness shows us worlds of light
We never saw by day.

2789. Nations and men are much alike. They seldom appeal to God unless they are getting licked.

2790. Our problems and troubles are really a gracious sharing with us by God of His cross. In a sense He is allowing us to take part in the redemption of the world through Christ by letting us carry small—very small—splinters of His cross.

(see also: Suffering)

TRUSTING GOD

2791. Relying on God has to begin all over again every day as if nothing yet had been done. —**C. S. Lewis**

2792. I suppose living from day to day ("take no thought for the morrow") is precisely what we have to learn—though the Old Adam in me sometimes murmurs that if God wanted me to live like the lilies of the field, I wonder He didn't give me the same lack of nerves and imagination as they enjoy! Or is that just the point, the precise purpose of this Divine paradox and audacity called Man—to do with a mind what other organisms do without it?
—**C. S. Lewis**

2793. When you have no helpers, see all your helpers in God. When you have many helpers, see God in all your helpers. When you have nothing but God, see all in God; when you have everything, see God in everything. Under all conditions, stay thy heart only on the Lord.

—Charles H. Spurgeon

(see also: Faith; Peace of Mind; Trouble)

TRUTH

2794. All truths are equally true, but not all truths are equally important.

—Ermal Allen

2795. The standard to which we should march today . . . ought to banner this slogan: Truth before friendship, truth before unity, and truth before success.

—Robert C. Bateman

2796. Let us be true to truth, loving it not because it is pleasant or picturesque or ancient, but because it is true and divine.

—Horatius Bonar

2797. Truth and duty are always wedded. There is no duty which has not its corresponding truth.   —Phillips Brooks

2798. Truth has nothing ultimately to fear from opposition, but has reason for concern when believers fear putting their understanding of it to the test.

—Lester DeKoster

2799. Though love repine, and reason chafe,
There came a voice without reply—
'Tis man's perdition to be safe,
When for the truth he ought to die.

—Ralph Waldo Emerson

2800. It is easier to perceive error than to find truth, for the former lies on the surface and is easily seen, while the later lies in the depth, where few are willing to search for it. —Johann Wolfgang von Goethe

2801. If an offense comes out of the truth, it is better that the offense come than that the truth be concealed.

—Jerome

2802. Truth is always narrow, but error goes off in all directions. —Paul E. Johnson

2803. It is more from carelessness about truth than from intentional lying, that there is so much falsehood in the world.

—Samuel Johnson

2804. "Making us free" means "making us truthful." The truthful community is the free community. The truthful person is the free person. And when we are made free and truthful, we are united.

—Kosuke Koyama

2805. Though the cause of Evil prosper,
Yet the truth alone is strong;
Truth forever on the scaffold,
Wrong forever on the throne—
Yet that scaffold sways the future,
And, behind the dim unknown,
Standeth God within the shadow,
Keeping watch above His own.

—James Russell Lowell

2806. Modern man's pattern for determining what is true goes something like this: "How do you *feel* about it?"

—W. F. Lown

2807. The most dangerous fault in American life today is the lack of interest in truth.   —Henry Luce

2808. Seek not greatness, but seek truth and you will find both.   —Horace Mann

2809. The reason we do not see truth is not that we have not read enough books or do not have enough academic degrees, but that we do not have enough courage.
—Rollo May

2810. Everything can be imitated except the truth.
—Menachem Mendel

2811. What was relevance and truth a million years ago will be so a million years hence. Truth is not a thing that is subject to fashion.
—Malcolm Muggeridge

2812. David Hume boasted he was the greatest among skeptics and had diligently searched for truth. Later he confessed he had not given the New Testament one proper reading.
—Bartlett Peterson

2813. Open minds like open windows need screens to keep the bugs out.
—Robert K. Rudolph

2814. If the truth be not diffused, error will be.
—Daniel Webster

2815. God cannot bear witness to a lie. The Gospel therefore which He confirms, must be true in substance. There may be opinions maintained at the same time which are not exactly true; and who can be secure from these? When I was much younger . . . I thought myself almost infallible; but I bless God, I know better now.
—John Wesley

2816. Witness to the truth you already know and more will be given to you.

2817. The problem with most people is not in finding the truth, but in facing it.

2818. Agnosticism doubts truth. Rationalism questions truth. Infidelity scoffs at truth. Logic dissects truth. Education searches for truth. But Jesus said, "I am the Truth."

U—NBELIEF

2819. Nobody talks so constantly about God as those who insist that there is no God.
—Heywood Broun

2820. "There is no God," the foolish saith,
But none, "There is no sorrow":
And nature oft the cry of faith
In bitter need will borrow.
Eyes, which the preacher could not school,
By wayside graves are raised;
And lips say, "God be pitiful,"
Who ne'er said, "God be praised."
—Elizabeth Barrett Browning

(see also: Atheism; Doubt)

UNITED STATES

2821. This is the only country where it takes more brains to prepare the income tax return than it does to earn the income.
—William Dettle

2822. You can't explain free government in any other terms than religious. The Founding Fathers had to refer to the Creator in order to make their revolutionary experience make sense; it was because "all men are endowed by their Creator with certain inalienable rights" that man could dare to be free. They wrote their religious faith into our founding documents, stamped their trust in God upon the faces of our coins and currency, and put it boldly at the base of our institutions. And when they drew up their bold Bill of Rights, where did they put freedom of worship? First, in the cornerstone position. That was no accident.
—Dwight D. Eisenhower

2823. America is another name for opportunity. Our whole history appears like a last effort of divine providence in behalf of the human race. —**Ralph Waldo Emerson**

2824. The American dream will end when the American people fall asleep as surely as other dreams end when people wake up. —**J. Kesner Kahn**

2825. The four cornerstones of character on which the structure of this nation was built are: Initiative, Imagination, Individuality and Independence.
—**Edward Rickenbacker**

2826. You are told by your leaders that power without any attempt at conciliation will lead to a world conflict. But I would say that power with continual compliance, continual retreat, is no power at all.
—**Alexander Solzhenitsyn**

2827. I sought for the greatness and genius of America in fields and boundless forests; it was not there. I sought for it in her free schools and her institutions of learning; it was not there. I sought for it in her matchless Constitution and democratic congress; it was not there. Not until I went to the churches and temples of America and found them aflame with righteousness did I understand the greatness and genius of America. America is great because America is good. When America ceases to be good, America will cease to be great. —**Alexis de Tocqueville**

(see also: The Nation; United States/Moral Climate)

UNITED STATES/MORAL CLIMATE

2828. Americans seem able to temper their distaste for depravity in proportion to the amount of elegance in which it is conducted. —**Russell Baker**

2829. We live in an age of nuclear giants and spiritual dwarfs. —**Omar Bradley**

2830. We live in a day of perfect means and confused goals. —**Albert Einstein**

2831. A whole nation sits glued to the tube watching all sorts of violence and adultery, night after night, and calls it entertainment! Meanwhile, others sit at the movies and eat popcorn while being sprayed with sex, profanity, and violence. When the lights go on again and the customers file out, the management fields a complaint. The popcorn was too salty.
—**J. D. Eppinga**

2832. We are a nation with crises, but we only dully perceive their import. We spend much of our time in government today debating whether to travel first or second class on the Titanic. —**Edgar J. Fredricks**

2833. The modern tendency is to consult your attorney instead of your conscience.
—**Arnold Glasow**

2834. America reminds me of a mental institution where the patients have taken over and locked up all the doctors.
—**Billy Graham**

2835. It is too late in our history to restore order or reestablish authority: The American temperament has passed the point where self-interest can subordinate itself to citizenship. —**Andrew Hacker**

2836. In the United States, separation of church and state has become the framework for militating against reflections of the Christian world-life view in the public schoolroom, for sanctioning abortion on demand, and for increasingly tolerating re-

ligion only as an inner private concern that is without public importance.
—Carl F. H. Henry

2837. Our professed love of freedom is increasingly shown to be a sophistry that replaces wisdom and righteousness with self-gratification.   —Carl F. H. Henry

2838. The typical American has developed a remarkable capacity for being serious about religion without taking religion seriously.   —Will Herberg

2839. One of America's biggest problems is not simply bad people who do wrong, but good people who do nothing.
—Ted Lindman

2840. We have tried so hard, we meant so well, and we failed so terribly.
—Walter Lippmann

2841. The most dangerous fault in American life today is the lack of interest in truth.   —Henry Luce

2842. Catering to a sex craze across our world, authors, publishers, and movie moguls continue to reap the commercial benefits of their selfish pursuits. Gratification and graft have a hammer-lock on many, many minds and lives, and have choked out needed spiritual awareness. Evil is out in the open. Sin has gained the privileged position.   —James Earl Massey

2843. Just because treason has become institutionalized does not mean it ceases to be treason.   —Lawrence P. McDonald

2844. That's one of the jobs of the church—to shake up our present population. To do that you'd have to preach nothing but hellfire.   —Marshall McLuhan

2845. For what more oft, in peoples grown corrupt

Than to love bondage more than liberty,
Bondage with ease than strenuous liberty?
—John Milton

2846. I thought of a rather cruel trick I once played on a wasp. He was sucking jam on my plate, and I cut him in half. He paid no attention, merely went on with his meal, while a tiny stream of jam trickled out of his severed oesophagus. Only when he tried to fly away did he grasp the dreadful thing that had happened to him. It is the same with modern man. The thing that has been cut away is his soul, and there was a period—twenty years, perhaps—during which he did not notice it.   —George Orwell

2847. We have now sunk to a depth at which the restatement of the obvious is the first duty of intelligent men.
—George Orwell

2848. Are your children growing up in a "permissive" society? Not on your life! An "insistent" society is the word for it. Ours is a society that practically *insists* that teenagers (and now even preteens) become "sexually active."   —Paul Ramsey

2849. Open immorality can now accurately be called a characteristic of contemporary Western culture. —W. Stanford Reid

2850. What this country needs is dirtier fingernails and cleaner minds.
—Will Rogers

2851. Today self-reliance is a sin; state-reliance is a virtue.   —E. Merrill Root

2852. Let there be spiritual adultery [the turning away from Jehovah God to the idols of modern man] and it will not be long until physical adultery sprouts like toadstools in the land. —Francis Schaeffer

2853. America's impotence comes from living a life of ease; people are unwilling to risk their comforts.

—Alexander Solzhenitsyn

2854. Fights between husbands and wives are now so numerous and so bloody that sociologist Murray Strauss comments, "The streets have become far safer than the home; the company of strangers safer than relatives."

2855. Of the twenty-two civilizations that have appeared in history, nineteen of them collapsed when they reached the moral state the United States is in now.

—Arnold Toynbee

2856. Any human society is free to choose either to display great energy, or to enjoy sexual freedom; the evidence is that they cannot do both for more than one generation. —J. D. Unwin

2857. We've had our fling. We've allowed our politicians to mortgage huge chunks of the future. We haven't said no to very much. It's been a fast ride toward a far country. —C. M. Ward

2858. We live in a "fast food" culture. We are overfed and undernourished on almost every level of existence: physical, emotional, intellectual and spiritual.

UNITY

2859. Christians are people who are drawn together because they owe a common debt to the goodness and the grace of God. —William Barclay

2860. What have we if we have not life together? —T. S. Eliot

2861. Unity comes from mutual recognition of virtue. —Medford Evans

2862. Unity must be according to God's Holy Word, or else it were better war than peace. —Hugh Latimer

2863. I am quite sure that the best way to promote union is to promote truth. It will not do for us to be all united together by yielding to one another's mistakes.

—Charles H. Spurgeon

Values

2864. Of all the masters the soul can choose, there are at last only two—God and mammon. All choices, however small, however the alternatives may be disguised, are but variants of this choice.

—George A. Buttrick

2865. Although mass starvation and the threat of nuclear war are monumental concerns, the ultimate issue confronting people of every generation is how one comes to know God. —Bruce Demarest

2866. As a young boy Benjamin Franklin invested all his savings in a whistle which he purchased from one of his friends. He was overjoyed and blew it incessantly until his family informed him he had paid ten times as much for the whistle as it was worth. The joy disappeared. Later in life he reflected: "As I grew up and observed the actions of men, I thought I met with many, far too many, who paid too much for their whistles."

2867. If a man does not really think that there is a distinction between virtue and vice, why, sir, when he leaves our house let us count our spoons. —Samuel Johnson

2868. God in His wisdom has ordained that man should ally himself absolutely to the Absolute, and only relatively to the relative. But, man in his finite wisdom has rather allied himself only relatively to the Absolute, and absolutely to that which is relative. —Soren Kierkegaard

2869. All that is not eternal is eternally out of date. —C. S. Lewis

2870. It is better to fail in a cause that will ultimately succeed than to succeed in a cause that will ultimately fail. —Peter Marshall

2871. What we obtain too cheap, we esteem too lightly; it is dearness only that gives everything its value. —Thomas Paine

2872. Let my heart be broken with the things that break the heart of God. —Robert W. Pierce

2873. The world as we live in it, is like a shop window in which some mischievous person has got in overnight and shifted all the price labels round, so that the cheap things have high price labels on them and the really precious things are priced low. —William Temple

2874. Read not the times. Read the eternities. —Henry David Thoreau

2875. The man who has God for his treasure has all things in one. —A. W. Tozer

(see also: Priorities)

VANITY

(see: Pride)

VICTORY

2876. What God expects us to attempt, He also enables us to achieve. —Stephen Olford

2877. Defeat in doing the right is nevertheless victory. —F. W. Robertson

2878. If life is a comedy to him who thinks, and a tragedy to him who feels, it is a victory to him who believes.

2879. Your outcome in life doesn't depend on your income, but on how you overcome.

(see also: Faith; Success)

VISION

2880. The health of the eye seems to demand a horizon. We are never tired so long as we can see far enough. —Ralph Waldo Emerson

2881. The Christians who have turned the world upside down for God have been men and women with a vision in their hearts, and the Bible in their hands. —T. B. Matson

2882. Looking forward strains the eyesight; looking upward opens heaven. —F. B. Meyer

WAR

2883. The Vietnam War was one which Americans were afraid to win and ashamed to lose. —Paul Harvey

2884. There are several things worse than war and they all come with defeat. —Ernest Hemingway

2885. All killing is not murder any more than all sexual intercourse is adultery. —C. S. Lewis

2886. War is an ugly thing, but not the ugliest thing: the decayed and degrading state of moral and patriotic feeling which thinks that nothing is worth a war is worse. . . . A man who has nothing for which he is willing to fight, nothing which he cares about more than his personal safety, is a miserable creature who has no chance of being free, unless made and kept so by the exertions of better men than himself. **—John Stuart Mill**

2887. The only men who do not serve in some army are those who are ruled by someone else's army. Without power you must do as you are told. When you lay down your arms, it's not the saints that come marching in.

WIFEHOOD

2888. Wives are young men's mistresses, middle-aged men's companions, and old men's nurses. **—Francis Bacon**

2889. I wanted to be a star. I ruined two marriages because of it and I know it. Well—I gave it all up. I gave it up to the Lord, this selfish ambition, and now I have a husband who adores me. So I tell my daughters (and we've got six of them), "You do like the Bible says. You submit. You submit to your husband. If he tells you to get down and scrub floors, buddy, you hit it! On all fours if necessary!"

—June Carter Cash

2890. The primary responsibility for a good relationship in a marriage lies with the wife. If the wife is submissive to her husband, they'll have a good relationship. I'll tell you why: submission is simply the acceptance of reality. **—Marvin DeHaan**

2891. As Christ is the Head of the mystical body, so the husband is the head of the wife. . . . One woman may be a corporation lawyer in the world, a devoted wife at home, and a humble communicant at church without violating the design of the Designer. But if in church and home she

ignores the revealed design which gives authority to men, she is like the Auca who uses a film for an earplug. **—Elisabeth Elliot**

2892. Four hands on a steering wheel spell disaster. One person has to do the driving. Somewhat arbitrarily, God himself has told us who is to back off. He makes the rules, not us. **—Earl Jaby**

2893. A wife's rebellion for her child's sake will result in a lost closeness with her husband and in a child who is determined to go his own way. **—Patty Peres**

2894. It is the submissive wife who generally gets most of her own way.

—Publilius Syrus

2895. One thing I had to learn was to understand goals. My husband's goal was to get the job done. My goal was to be a supplier—a supporter—and to give to my husband without keeping score.

—Leilani Watt

2896. Treat a dog with kindness, pet him often, feed him well, and he'll never leave you. The same system usually works with husbands.

(see also: Marriage)

WISDOM

2897. Wisdom in this world is serenity of spirit. . . . It is a refusal to question the ways, the machinations, and the divine purposes of God. It is contentment. It is the willingness to abide cheerfully by the verdict of any court, of any jury, knowing full well that the *true* decision was handed down by God. **—Charles Doss**

2898. The wisest person is not the one who has the fewest failures but the one who turns failures to best account.

—Richard R. Grant

2899. True perfection consists in having but one fear, the loss of God's friendship.
—Gregory of Nyssa

2900. It is open to all to know themselves and be wise. —Heraclitus

2901. The wise learn from tragedy; the foolish merely repeat it. —Michael Novak

2902. The wisest man is he who knows his own ignorance. —Socrates

2903. The wise man must remember that while he is a descendant of the past, he is a parent of the future. —Herbert Spencer

2904. Wisdom is oftentimes nearer when we stoop than when we soar.
—William Wordsworth

WITNESSING

(see: Christian Witness)

WOMEN

2905. Woman is the salvation or destruction of the family. She carries its destinies in the folds of her mantle.
—Henry Frederic Amiel

2906. The relative positions to be assumed by man and woman in the working out of our civilization were assigned long ago by a higher intelligence than ours.
—Grover Cleveland

2907. Marriage, real marriage as distinct from the new "arrangement" called coupledom, is not heaven and not even in the neighborhood of heaven. But those, especially those women, who think they have willed themselves or contracted themselves or argued themselves into a more reasoned and more just alternative to marriage have done themselves little good. And those men who have jumped at the

chance to reap their own special benefits from the situation have done themselves even less. —Midge Decter

2908. The best thing that a woman can do for a man is to be a woman.
—Elisabeth Elliot

2909. What I can't understand is that she (the modern married woman) looks for meaning everywhere but in the life she shared with her husband and children, that life she built with her years and moments. . . . What is the point of freeing ourselves in self-discovery if not to serve freely that world which we served bound?
—Margery Frisbie

2910. Woman is physically inferior to man, intellectually his equal, socially his superior, morally more susceptible and religiously more devotional. —W. L. Hayden

2911. Much of what we as women do is in a supportive role, but imagine what would happen to a building if its support pillars were removed. —Judy Hubbell

2912. I'll bet the time ain't far off when a woman don't know any more than a man.
—Will Rogers

2913. Women once had great power for good. Then they decided they wanted to be like men. —Adela Rogers St. John

2914. Women crave novelty, they dread a consistent world. —Vladimir Solovyev

2915. The women's liberation movement reminds me of the basic psychological attitude of the remotest African bush. There it is a declared fact that a woman is inferior and secondary; she is just dung, a nobody. And with a surprising naivete the women's liberation movement has accepted this presupposed position, telling the woman that as long as she is a woman, she is inferior. Therefore, in order to be superior she has to be like a man.

—Walter Trobisch

2916. In this twentieth century, womanhood has become overshadowed by "equalhood" as we wear his pants, strive for his job, and imitate his language and drinking habits.   —Patricia Young

2917. Here's to women: Once our superior; now our equal.

2918. Men will be as immoral as women will let them be.

2919. Men and women are equal before God—equally sinners and equally saved. Given this profound and ultimate equality, further debate seems rather unnecessary.

(see also: Motherhood; Wifehood)

WORDS

2920. A word is dead when it is said,
      some say.
   I say it just begins to live that day.
                    —Emily Dickinson

2921. Glibness is the curse that most often afflicts those with a natural talent for expressing themselves in words. When the words come too easily, they often come off the top of the head, and not from the center of the heart.   —Roy Larson

2922. Speak, that I may see thee.
                    —Socrates

(see also: Censoriousness)

WORK
(see: Labor)

WORKS
(see: Goodness; Service)

WORLDLINESS

2923. We have been offered in the church, all too often, a watered-down gospel in willy-nilly fashion, and so we go through the motions of being faithful while turning to a secular world for the stimulus and satisfaction we seek.

—James Armstrong

2924. Farewell, vain world; my soul can
      bid adieu;
   My Saviour taught me to abandon
      you.
   Your charms may gratify a sensual
      mind;
   But not please a soul wholly for
      God designed.
   Forbear to entice, cease then my
      soul to call:
   'Tis fixed through grace; my God
      shall be my all.
                    —David Brainerd

2925. We cannot capitulate to the spirit of the age, or accommodate ourselves to what the public is said to want. "The public" is notoriously fickle; if we could ascertain what it wants this week, it would still be impossible to predict what it might want next week.   —Elisabeth Elliot

2926. I grew up in the Pentecostal church. I know what it means to be laughed at. But none of those experiences of the past were any more uncomfortable than the humiliation I feel when I hear the guffaws of the ungodly ridiculing a Christian who is trying to talk about the world above, while she looks like she belongs to the one below.   —W. W. Griffin

2927. He that carries the love of the world in his heart will faint by the way and never come to Christ. The over-valuing of the world makes the doctrine of the gospel a sorrowful doctrine and man's endeavor to come to Christ unfruitful.

—Alexander Grosse

2928. Worldliness is a spirit, a temperament, an attitude of the soul. . . . It is a gaze always horizontal and never vertical.

—John Henry Jowett

2929. The weakness of so many modern Christians is that they feel too much at home in the world. In their effort to achieve restful "adjustment" to unregenerate society they have lost their pilgrim character and become an essential part of the very moral order against which they are sent to protest. —A. W. Tozer

2930. Worldliness is an accepted part of our way of life. Our religious mood is social instead of spiritual. We have lost the art of worship. We are not producing saints. Our models are successful businessmen, celebrated athletes and theatrical personalities. Our homes have been turned into theatres. Our literature is shallow and our hymnody borders on sacrilege. And scarcely anyone appears to care.

—A. W. Tozer

2931. Anything that you love and do that keeps you from enjoying God's love and doing God's will is worldly and must be avoided. —Warren W. Wiersbe

2932. The reason the church is failing to effectively invade the world is because the world has invaded the church.

(see also: Materialism and Hedonism; Secularism)

WORLD MISSIONS

2933. When the tide of missionary impulse comes in, it lifts "all the boats."

—Gerald Ensley

2934. It is not in our choice to spread the gospel or not. It is our death if we do not.

—Peter Taylor Forsyth

2935. If God's love is for anybody anywhere, it's for everybody everywhere.

—Edward Lawlor

2936. God had only one Son and He made that Son a missionary.

—David Livingstone

2937. Never pity missionaries. Envy them. They are where the real action is, where life and death, sin and grace, Heaven and Hell converge.

—Robert C. Shannon

2938. The supreme task of the church is the evangelization of the world. No one has the right to hear the gospel twice until everyone has had an opportunity to hear it at least once. —J. Oswald Smith

2939. 'Tis the churches' great
         commission,
    'Tis the Master's last command;
    Christ has died for every creature,
    Tell it out in every land.

2940. Every person in the world is either a missionary or a mission field.

WORLD PEACE
(see: Peace)

WORRY
2941. The misfortunes hardest to bear are those which never happen.

—James Russell Lowell

2942. A day of worry is more exhausting than a week of work. —John Lubbuck

2943. Worry is the interest paid by those who borrow trouble. —George Lyons

2944. Worry affects the circulation, the heart, the glands, the whole nervous system, and profoundly affects the health.
—Charles Mayo

2945. What worries you masters you.
—Haddon W. Robinson

2946. All worry is atheism, because it is a want of trust in God.   —Fulton Sheen

2947. Worry does not empty tomorrow of its sorrow; it empties today of its strength.
—Corrie ten Boom

2948. I am an old man and have known a great many troubles, but most of them never happened.   —Mark Twain

2949. I have nothing to do with
          tomorrow;
    It's sunlight I never may see.
    So today, with the plow in the
          furrow,
    In the vineyard I faithful would
          be.

    I have nothing to do with
          tomorrow;
    My Savior will make that His
          care,
    Its grace and its strength I can't
          borrow—
    So why should I borrow its care?
—D. W. Whittle

2950. Never borrow from the future. If you live in dread of what may happen and it doesn't happen, you have worried in vain. Even if it does happen, you have to worry twice.

2951. Worry is a futile thing,
    It's somewhat like a rocking chair.
    Although it keeps you occupied,
    It doesn't get you anywhere.

2952. Worry never climbed a hill, worry
          never paid a bill,
    Worry never dried a tear, worry
          never calmed a fear,
    Worry never darned a heel, worry
          never cooked a meal,
    It never led a horse to water, nor
          ever did a thing it "oughter."

2953. One cannot change the past, but one can ruin the present by worrying over the future.

2954. Worry is the sin we're not afraid to commit.

2955. The way to worry about nothing is to pray about everything.

2956. Worry happens when we assume responsibility God never intended us to have.

(see also: Anxiety; Peace of Mind)

WORSHIP

2957. When men worship Jesus Christ, they do not fall at His feet in broken submission, but in wondering love. A man does not say, "I cannot resist a might like that." He says, "Love so amazing, so divine, demands my life, my soul, my all." A man does not say, "I am battered into surrender." He says, "I am lost in wonder, love and praise."   —William Barclay

2958. I have never known a man, who habitually and on principle absented himself from the public worship of God, who did not sooner or later bring sorrow upon himself or his family.
—Henry Whitney Bellows

2959. More tender than we can
          imagine,
    More faithful than we can
          conceive,

Stronger than we can envision,
Wiser than we can believe—
What loss through our blindness
we suffer
When God's boundless love we
ignore;
But when we just taste of its
sweetness,
'Tis then we fall down and adore!
—Laurie H. DuBose

2960. Without the Holy Spirit we worship what we do not know. —Larry Graybill

2961. We leave our places of worship and no deep and inexpressible wonder sits upon our faces.... There is nothing to suggest that we have been looking at anything stupendous and overwhelming.
—John Henry Jowett

2962. To worship God vicariously through the medium of program is ineffective. There must be heart-to-heart communication daily. —Raymond Kitchen

2963. In the process of worshiping God He communicates His Spirit to us.
—C. S. Lewis

2964. The whole you needs worship— and the part of you that will live forever needs it most. —Robert W. McIntyre

2965. Worship is an inward reverence, the bowing down of the soul in the presence of God, an awesome dependence on Him, ... a solemn consciousness of the Divine, a secret communion with the unseen. —J. H. Morrison

2966. Worship is one thing and entertainment is another, and it is dangerous business to play lightly with holy things, to tickle the senses in place of calling men to bow their hearts in faith and repentance.
—John C. Neville

2967. We who worship the true, living God would be better, if not completely different, if we worshiped Him better. For to worship Him as we ought is to become what we ought. —Ben Patterson

2968. Everyone has a first love, present tense. —Bill Popejoy

2969. I worshiped in the hills today
Where God in greatness stood
Revealing all His majesty
In water, stone, and wood.

I heard His voice speak from the
brook,
Saw mountains He had made;
His aspen trees clapped golden
hands—
I rested in their shade.

I saw the graceful trees He made,
The balsam and the birch;
But all the while my conscience
cried,
"You should have gone to
church." —Clessen K. Scoles

2970. We are often so caught up in our activities that we tend to worship our work, work at our play and play at our worship. —Charles Swindoll

2971. To worship is to quicken the conscience by the holiness of God, to feed the mind with the truth of God, to purge the imagination by the beauty of God, to open the heart to the love of God, to devote the will to the purpose of God.
—William Temple

2972. We have become so engrossed in the work of the Lord that we have forgotten the Lord of the work. —A. W. Tozer

2973. Sing lustily and with a good courage. Beware of singing as if you were half dead, or half asleep; but lift up your voice with strength. —John Wesley

(see also: Reverence)

WRATH

2974. The divine wrath is slow indeed in vengeance, but it makes up for its tardiness by the severity of the punishment.
—Valerius Maximus

2975. So fond are mortal men
Fall'n into wrath divine,
As their own ruin on themselves
to invite.
—John Milton

(see also: God's Judgment)

YOUTH

2976. The most important thing in the world that makes young people civilized is good old people. —William D. Poe

2977. The "now generation" often wants today what only tomorrow can give them.
—W. T. Purkiser

2978. We must view young people not as empty bottles to be filled, but as candles to be lit. —Robert H. Shaffer

2979. If we wish to scale a mountain, or go down in a diving dress, or up in a balloon, we must be about it while we are still young. It will not do to delay until we are dogged with prudence. . . . Youth is the time to see the sun rise in town or country. Youth is the time to be converted at a revival. It is the time of venture.
—Robert Louis Stevenson

2980. The young prophesy by their very existence—they *are* the future.
—Paul Valery

2981. The personal crisis for students during the university years is to change from external to internal resources for the enterprise of life. —Roger Van Harn

2982. You are young at any age if you're planning for tomorrow.

2983. All that steam you see is caused by young people trying to set on fire a world that is all wet.

2984. Half the world's population is under thirty. The other half is trying to act that way.

2985. There is a super myth going around that young people today know more than their elders. The fact is that everything young people know, they have learned from their elders.

ZEAL

2986. Most great men and women are not perfectly rounded in their personalities, but are instead people whose one driving enthusiasm is so great it makes their faults seem insignificant. —Charles A. Cerami

2987. Nazism would never have established so firm a grip if, from the outset, it had been faced by Christians as enthusiastic for what is true as the Nazis were for what is false. —Edward Halifax

(see also: Ambition; Initiative; Involvement)

AUTHOR INDEX

225

SOURCE LIST

1. *Church Herald* Feb. 20 70 p2
2. *Pentecostal Testimony* Feb. 85 p21
3. *America* Dec. 27 75 p456
4. *Christian Standard* Jan. 11 76 p9
5. Editor's Files
6. *Presbyterian Journal* July 22 81 p10
7. *Pentecostal Evangel* Jan. 13 85 p5
8. *Pentecostal Evangel* Mar. 16 75 p7
9. *Wesleyan Advocate* Apr. 14 75 p13
10. *American Opinion* Dec. 75 p45
11. *Wesleyan Advocate* June 20 77 p13
12. *American Opinion* Dec. 76 p23
13. *Banner* Sept. 10 76 p11
14. *Alliance Witness* May 4 77 p7
15. *American Issue* Mar.–Apr. 75 p1
16. *Church Herald* Oct. 3 76 p14
17. Editor's Files
18. *American Issue* Nov.–Dec. 75 p4
19. *Baptist Bulletin* Nov. 76 p5
20. *Presbyterian Journal* Oct. 23 74 p11
21. *Moody Monthly* Feb. 78 p63
22. *American Opinion* Jan. 71 p75
23. *Christianity Today* Jan. 27 78 p25
24. *Faith For The Family* Nov.–Dec. 76 p22
25. *Faith For The Family* Nov.–Dec. 76 p22
26. *Link* Apr. 70 p59
27. *Herald Of Holiness* Jan. 15 79 p10
28. Editor's Files
29. *Vital Christianity* Nov. 30 75 p14
30. *Wesleyan Advocate* Feb. 2 76 p9
31. *The Christian Example* Nov. 11 84 p10
32. *Wesleyan Advocate* Mar. 3 75 p7
33. *America* Oct. 11 75 p208
34. *Presbyterian Journal* July 22 81 p11
35. *Presbyterian Journal* July 22 81 p15
36. *Evangel* Apr. 28 75 p22
37. *Lutheran* Sept. 19 79 p3
38. *American Opinion* Oct. 76 p37
39. *Christian Standard* July 6 75 p9
40. *Christian Life* Dec. 75 p53
41. *Congregationalist* June 77 p6
42. *Wesleyan Advocate* Jan. 3 77 p5
43. *Wesleyan Advocate* Oct. 19 81 p2
44. *Christian Reader* Feb.–Mar. 74 p44
45. *Wesleyan Advocate* July 4 77 p2
46. *A.D.* May 75 p40
47. *Presbyterian Journal* Jan. 22 75 p9
48. *Presbyterian Journal* Oct. 24 73 p13
49. *Wesleyan Advocate* Jan. 31 76 p9
50. *Pentecostal Evangel* Mar. 9 75 p13
51. *Preacher's Magazine* June 81 p23
52. *Link* Dec. 74 p46
53. *Christian Standard* Aug. 8 76 p4
54. *Presbyterian Journal* Nov. 29 78 p8
55. *Christian Standard* Oct. 2 83 p15
56. *American Opinion* Dec. 76 p23
57. *Herald Of Holiness* Sept. 15 78 p18
58. *Herald Of Holiness* Apr. 15 79 p20
59. *Alliance Witness* Mar. 24 76 p10
60. *Link* Dec. 66 p57
61. *Christian Standard* Feb. 22 76 p5
62. *Congregationalist* Jan. 77 p6
63. Editor's Files
64. *Herald Of Holiness* Apr. 15 79 p20
65. *Jewish Frontier* Feb. 80 p3
66. *Wesleyan Advocate* Oct. 1 79 p3
67. *Alliance Witness* Jan. 1 75 p7
68. *Christian Herald* June 76 p28
69. Editor's Files
70. Editor's Files
71. *Preacher's Magazine* Mar. 75 p9
72. *Church Herald* July 75 p41
73. *Pentecostal Evangel* Sept. 7 75 p2
74. *Banner* Jan. 20 78 p21
75. *Jewish Spectator* Fall 82 p34
76. *Emphasis On Faith and Living*
    Oct. 1 80 p3
77. *Pentecostal Evangel* Feb. 10 80 p2

78. *Christian Century* Mar. 9 77 p239
79. *Church Herald* Sept. 2 77 p5
80. Editor's Files
81. *Congregationalist* Dec. 70 p5
82. *Faith For The Family* Sept.–Oct. 75 p5
83. *Herald Of Holiness* Jan. 15 79 p9
84. *Encyclopedia Of Religious Quotations* 1965 p12
85. *Encyclopedia Of Religious Quotations* 1965 p12
86. *Encyclopedia Of Religious Quotations* 1965 p12
87. *Encyclopedia Of Religious Quotations* 1965 p13
88. *Herald Of Holiness* Apr. 1 82 p7
89. *Wesleyan Advocate* Nov. 22 76 p5
90. *Wesleyan Advocate* Oct. 13 75 p6
91. *Pentecostal Evangel* July 15 79 p14
92. *Flashlight* Mar. 76 p3
93. Editor's Files
94. *Alliance Witness* Sept. 19 79 p4
95. *Alliance Witness* Mar. 12 75 p5
96. *Christian Standard* Apr. 7 85 p15
97. *Pentecostal Evangel* June 1 80 p3
98. *Alliance Witness* June 2 76 p19
99. *Christian Herald* Nov. 76 p50
100. Editor's Files
101. Editor's Files
102. *Christian Herald* Oct. 78 p60
103. *Lutheran* May 77 p3
104. Editor's Files
105. *Christian Herald* Apr. 71 p29
106. *Alliance Witness* Aug. 4 82 p6
107. Editor's Files
108. *Christian Reader* 1952 p56
109. *Christian Reader* 1952 p438
110. *Encyclopedia Of Religious Quotations* 1965 p15
111. *Encyclopedia Of Religious Quotations* 1965 p15
112. *Christian Century* Apr. 2 80 p380
113. *Alliance Witness* July 11 79 p5
114. *Banner* Mar. 11 77 p5
115. *Banner* Apr. 25 80 p8
116. *Christian Reader* July–Aug. 79 p100
117. *Encyclopedia Of Religious Quotations* 1965 p23
118. *Encyclopedia Of Religious Quotations* 1965 p23
119. *Christian Reader* July 84 p32
120. *Christian Herald* June 81 p46
121. *Banner* Nov. 5 76 p5
122. *His* May 71 p5
123. *Christian Reader* Mar. 79 p75
124. *Lutheran* Nov. 2 77 p3

125. *Presbyterian Journal* Dec. 12 79 p13
126. *Lutheran Witness* Jan. 16 77 p7
127. *Lutheran Witness* May 18 75 p11
128. *Christianity Today* Oct. 24 80 p29
129. *Presbyterian Journal* Nov. 3 76 p9
130. *Presbyterian Journal* Jan. 1 75 p8
131. *Christian Standard* Sept. 28 75 p16
132. *Presbyterian Journal* Sept. 15 76 p12
133. *Pentecostal Evangel* Dec. 8 74 p2
134. *Good News Broadcaster* Mar. 78 p17
135. *Moody Monthly* May 77 p76
136. *Pentecostal Evangel* Jan. 15 84 p14
137. Editor's Files
138. *Presbyterian Journal* Mar. 31 76 p11
139. *Pentecostal Evangel* June 27 76 p31
140. *Pentecostal Evangel* Dec. 31 72 p12
141. *Christian Educators' Journal* Feb. 86 p16
142. Editor's Files
143. *Christianity Today* July 2 76 p10
144. *Lutheran Witness* Oct. 5 75 p4
145. *Christian Herald* June 77 p22
146. *Episcopal Recorder* Apr. 78 p8
147. *Alliance Witness* Oct. 15 80 p6
148. *His* Dec. 75 p19
149. *Baptist Bulletin* Oct. 76 p12
150. *Evangel* Feb. 9 76 p25
151. *Pentecostal Evangel* Jan. 15 84 p14
152. *Pentecostal Evangel* Dec. 8 74 p2
153. *Pentecostal Evangel* Apr. 11 76 p19
154. *Episcopal Recorder* June 76 p1
155. *Herald Of Holiness* Oct. 1 79 p11
156. *Evangel* July 26 76 p27
157. *Emphasis On Faith And Living* Oct. 15 79 p3
158. *American Opinion* May 75 p22
159. Editor's Files
160. *Pentecostal Evangel* Dec. 10 78 p2
161. *Herald Of Holiness* Sept. 15 82 p10
162. *His* May 77 p29
163. *Christian Herald* Feb. 76 p67
164. *Christian Reader* July 84 p32
165. *Herald Of Holiness* Dec. 4 74 p18
166. *Herald Of Holiness* Dec. 4 74 p13
167. *Pentecostal Evangel* Oct. 9 83 p6
168. *Pentecostal Evangel* Oct. 9 83 p4
169. Editor's Files
170. *Pentecostal Evangel* Jan. 15 84 p14
171. Editor's Files
172. *Herald Of Holiness* Dec. 1 82 p11
173. *Christian Herald* Oct. 75 p70
174. *Christian Standard* Sept. 12 76 p11
175. *Moody Monthly* June 75 p89
176. *Keep Christmas In Your Heart* 1984 p782
177. *Treasury of Courage And Confidence* 1985 p177

178. *Christian Reader* 1952 p356
179. *Encyclopedia Of Religious Quotations* 1965 p35
180. *Encyclopedia Of Religious Quotations* 1965 p36
181. *Moody Monthly* Oct. 76 p49
182. *Presbyterian Journal* Nov. 3 76 p9
183. *Wesleyan Advocate* Oct. 27 75 p15
184. *Christian Educator's Journal* Oct. 83 p13
185. *Episcopal Recorder* Feb. 77 p10
186. *Wesleyan Advocate* Oct. 27 75 p15
187. *Pentecostal Evangel* Jan. 30 88 p11
188. *Mennonite* May 31 77 p365
189. *Vital Christianity* Aug. 6 78 p24
190. *Alliance Witness* June 30 76 p31
191. *Daily Study Bible*
192. *Christian Standard* Jan. 18 76 p13
193. *Link* Mar. 71 p37
194. *Baptist Bulletin* June 83 p7
195. *American Opinion* Dec. 76 p24
196. *American Opinion* Apr. 76 p22
197. *Presbyterian Journal* May 11 77 p12
198. *Banner* Mar. 14 80 p9
199. *Baptist Bulletin* Feb. 84 p5
200. *Banner* July 81 p15
201. Editor's Files
202. *Wesleyan Advocate* Oct. 10 77 p7
203. *Wesleyan Advocate* Feb. 28 77 p13
204. *If* p46
205. *Wesleyan Advocate* Mar. 3 75 p7
206. *Jewish Frontier* Feb. 76 p4
207. *Chelsea Journal* Sept.–Oct. 78 p262
208. *Herald Of Holiness* July 1 83 p7
209. *Wesleyan Advocate* Mar. 27 78 p10
210. *Christian Standard* Sept. 23 79 p10
211. *Wesleyan Advocate* Sept. 1 75 p8
212. *Pentecostal Evangel* Nov. 25 79 p4
213. *Evangel* Jan. 26 76 p25
214. *Herald Of Holiness* Apr. 1 76 p11
215. *Herald Of Holiness* Sept. 1 79 p7
216. *American Scholar* Spring 77 p166
217. *Presbyterian Journal* July 6 77 p13
218. *Vital Christianity* Sept. 7 75 p10
219. Editor's Files
220. *Wesleyan Advocate* Feb. 16 76 p5
221. *Christian Herald* Sept. 75 p16
222. *Christian Herald* Feb. 77 p49
223. *Link* Sept. 70 p58
224. *Christian Herald* Feb. 71 p47
225. *Christian Herald* Dec. 78 p71
226. *Christian Herald* May 79 p41
227. *Pentecostal Evangel* Oct. 1 79 p2
228. *Pentecostal Evangel* Oct. 1 78 p2
229. *Wesleyan Advocate* Sept. 1 75 p8
230. *Christian Standard* Oct. 28 84 p10

231. *Christian Standard* Dec. 21 75 p14
232. *Religion In Life* Spring 78 p79
233. *Commentary* Oct. 81 p67
234. Editor's Files
235. *Pentecostal Evangel* Dec. 4 77 p7
236. *Christian Herald* Oct. 75 p24
237. Editor's Files
238. *Link* Dec. 74 p54
239. *Herald Of Holiness* May 1 76 p7
240. *Banner* May 5 78 p9
241. *Christian Herald* May 77 p48
242. *Christian Herald* Dec. 78 p46
243. *Herald Of Holiness* May 1 76 p17
244. Editor's Files
245. *Wesleyan Advocate* Feb. 3 75 p1
246. *Christian Home* June 81 p6
247. *Herald Of Holiness* Jan. 1 79 p13
248. *Christian Herald* Mar. 80 p54
249. *Evangel* July 28 80 p31
250. *Daedalus* Fall 74 p300
251. *American Opinion* May 77 p29
252. *Evangel* Oct. 12 81 p15
253. *Emphasis On Faith And Living* May 86 p14
254. *Vital Christianity* Jan. 18 76 p6
255. *Christian Herald* May 78 p89
256. *Herald Of Holiness* May 1 76 p7
257. *American Opinion* Feb. 83 p39
258. Editor's Files
259. *Good News Broadcaster* Mar. 85 p6
260. *Wesleyan Advocate* Feb. 19 79 p1
261. *Christian Herald* Sept. 76 p58
262. *Emphasis On Faith And Living* Aug. 15 80 p7
263. *Emphasis On Faith And Living* Mar. 81 p7
264. *Herald Of Holiness* July 2 75 p19
265. *Christian Herald* Nov. 75 p24
266. *Daily Study Bible*
267. *Presbyterian Journal* Jan. 22 86 p19
268. *Christian Herald* Feb. 83 p23
269. *Daily Study Bible*
270. *Christianity Today* July 16 76 p9
271. *Banner* Oct. 13 78 p19
272. *Evangel* Jan. 26 76 p25
273. *U.S. Catholic* Oct. 83 p16
274. *Alliance Witness* Mar. 10 76 p4
275. Editor's Files
276. *Christian Herald* Nov. 79 p55
277. *Herald Of Holiness* Apr. 9 75 p19
278. *Encyclopedia Of Religious Quotations* 1965 p43
279. *Chelsea Journal* Jan.–Feb. 76 p20
280. *Christian Standard* Apr. 7 85 p14
281. *These Times* Oct. 75 p3

282. *Christianity Today* Feb. 19 82 p18
283. *Treasury of Courage And Confidence* p188
284. *Vital Christianity* Feb. 5 78 p1
285. Editor's Files
286. *Christian Herald* Nov. 78 p78
287. *Presbyterian Journal* Jan. 22 75 p7
288. Editor's Files
289. *Lutheran* Feb. 6 80 p3
290. *Evangel* Feb. 28 77 p27
291. *Wesleyan Advocate* Sept. 25 78 p20
292. *Daily Study Bible*
293. *Salvation Army News Letter* Aug. 29 78 p1
294. *Vital Christianity* Oct. 16 77 p6
295. *Daily Study Bible*
296. *Christian Herald* Sept. 77 p18
297. *Christian Standard* Oct. 2 83 p15
298. Editor's Files
299. *Lutheran* July 78 p5
300. *Christian Standard* Feb. 17 80 p14
301. *His* Oct. 79 p19
302. *Evangel* Feb. 28 77 p27
303. *Alliance Witness* May 11 83 p5
304. *Pentecostal Evangel* Apr. 17 77 p9
305. *Emphasis On Faith And Living* Feb. 15 79 p3
306. *His* June 79 p4
307. *Christian Standard* Jan. 14 79 p9
308. *Christian Ministry* Sept. 81 p19
309. *Christianity Today* Feb. 4 82 p41
310. *North Star Baptist* Apr. 78 p29
311. *Christianity Today* Jan. 16 76 p9
312. *Vital Christianity* Sept. 11 77 p11
313. Editor's Files
314. *His* Oct. 80 p32
315. *Presbyterian Journal* Oct. 6 82 p10
316. *Christian Reader* May–June 75 p32
317. *Link* Feb. 72 p59
318. *War Cry* Aug. 3 85 p15
319. Editor's Files
320. *Congregationalist* Jan. 77 p26
321. *Christianity Today* Oct. 2 81 p34
322. *Pentecostal Evangel* Mar. 8 81 p17
323. *Pastoral Psychology* May 71 p51
324. *Herald Of Holiness* May 1 76 p17
325. *Christian Home* Sept. 80 p33
326. *Presbyterian Journal* Mar. 22 78 p12
327. Editor's Files
328. *Evangel* Nov. 8 82 p13
329. *Christian Standard* Apr. 18 76 p6
330. *Episcopal Recorder* Apr. 78 p19
331. *Evangel* Feb. 23 76 p25
332. *Daily Study Bible/Colossians/p157*
333. *Banner* Mar. 7 75 p8

334. *Christian Ministry* July 76 p33
335. *Preacher's Magazine* June 81 p23
336. *Christian Home* Oct. 75 p3
337. *Church Herald* Feb. 24 78 p9
338. *Presbyterian Journal* Mar. 26 75 p12
339. *His* June 73 p33
340. *Pentecostal Evangel* June 27 76 p23
341. *Vital Christianity* Nov. 19 78 p16
342. *Catholic Mind* Sept. 78 p53
343. *Catholic Mind* Dec. 78 p15
344. *Christian Standard* Dec. 21 75 p9
345. *Wesleyan Advocate* Sept. 16 74 p9
346. *Wesleyan Advocate* Sept. 3 79 p3
347. *Vital Christianity* Aug. 1 76 p13
348. *Moody Monthly* May 77 p76
349. Editor's Files
350. *Christian Herald* Jan. 77 p14
351. Editor's Files
352. *Christian Standard* Sept. 3 78 p4
353. *Banner* Feb. 13 76 p11
354. *Daily Study Bible*
355. *Daily Study Bible/Ephesians/p105*
356. *Daily Study Bible/Corinthians/p186*
357. *Daily Study Bible/Philippians/p80*
358. *Moody Monthly* Feb. 86 p37
359. *Messenger* June 75 p26
360. *Alliance Witness* Apr. 20 77 p5
361. Editor's Files
362. Editor's Files
363. *Wesleyan Advocate* Jan. 30 78 p12
364. *These Times* Dec. 75 p19
365. *Faith For The Family* July–Aug. 75 p21
366. *Banner* June 24 77 p6
367. *Christian Home* Jan. 79 p28
368. Editor's Files
369. *Wesleyan Advocate* Feb. 3 86 p13
370. *Presbyterian Journal* Apr. 23 75 p8
371. *Emphasis On Faith And Living* Mar. 1 79 p3
372. *Christian Reader* Sept.–Oct. 76 p5
373. *These Times* Oct. 75 p5
374. *Christian Century* Dec. 1 82 p1229
375. *Pentecostal Evangel* June 7 70 p10
376. *Christian Herald* May 81 p54
377. *Herald Of Holiness* May 15 80 p19
378. *Wesleyan Advocate* June 20 77 p13
379. *Episcopal Recorder* Sept. 76 p18
380. *War Cry* Sept. 28 85 p22
381. *Emphasis On Faith And Living* May 15 80 p3
382. *Wesleyan Advocate* Mar. 3 75 p1
383. *Lutheran* June 18 80 p3
384. *Christian Herald* Jan. 81 p26
385. *His* Oct. 75 p19
386. *Wesleyan Advocate* Oct. 11 76 p14

387. *Mennonite* Nov. 18 75 p663
388. *Banner* July 20 81 p13
389. *Christian Century* Oct. 21 81 p1055
390. Editor's Files
391. Editor's Files
392. *Herald Of Holiness* Apr. 1 78 p15
393. *Pentecostal Evangel* Nov. 30 75 p31
394. *Herald Of Holiness* June 1 80 p16
395. Editor's Files
396. Editor's Files
397. *Herald Of Holiness* Nov. 5 75 p6
398. *Daily Study Bible/Galatians/p11*
399. *Daily Study Bible/Corinthians/p87*
400. *Alliance Witness* Nov. 20 74 p3
401. *Christian Standard* Oct. 9 83 p10
402. *Presbyterian Journal* Apr. 16 75 p9
403. *Herald Of Holiness* Mar. 1 78 p3
404. *Alliance Witness* Apr. 9 75 p5
405. *Christian Ministry* May 85 p34
406. *Herald Of Holiness* Mar. 1 82 p17
407. *Messenger* Oct. 75 p1
408. *Christian Herald* Nov. 79 p55
409. *Good News Broadcaster* Mar. 72 p5
410. *Christian Standard* June 19 83 p9
411. *Presbyterian Journal* Apr. 6 77 p13
412. *Vital Christianity* Sept. 3 78 p17
413. *Lutheran Standard* Apr. 18 86 p12
414. *Presbyterian Journal* Feb. 4 76 p7
415. *His* Nov. 78 p28
416. *Alliance Witness* Sept. 8 76 p6
417. *Vital Christianity* Feb. 8 70 p6
418. *Wesleyan Advocate* Mar. 27 78 p10
419. *Wesleyan Advocate* Sept. 19 83 p4
420. *Christian Ministry* Mar. 75 p13
421. *Emphasis On Faith And Living*
     Apr. 82 p23
422. *Christian Standard* Aug. 4 85 p14
423. *Presbyterian Journal* Mar. 10 76 p8
424. *Wesleyan Advocate* Dec. 6 76 p9
425. *Alliance Witness* Aug. 9 78 p31
426. *Church Herald* Nov. 14 75 p9
427. *Presbyterian Journal* Oct. 13 76 p20
428. *Moody Monthly* Jan. 79 p59
429. *Good News Broadcaster* June 83 p35
430. *Presbyterian Journal* June 7 78 p1
431. *Christian Standard* Dec. 25 83 p4
432. *Central Visitor* Jan. 19 77 p2
433. *Christian Herald* Nov. 75 p23
434. *Banner* June 7 74 p3
435. *Congregationalist* Dec. 74 p3
436. *Pentecostal Evangel* Dec. 19 76 p31
437. *Christian Century* Dec. 8 76 p1101
438. *Herald Of Holiness* Dec. 15 82 p15
439. *Presbyterian Journal* Dec. 14 83 p8
440. *Christian Standard* Dec. 25 83 p4

441. *Congregationalist* Dec. 75 p18
442. *Christian Ministry* Nov. 76 p37
443. *Evangel* Dec. 8 76 p5
444. *Herald Of Holiness* Dec. 17 75 p19
445. *Christianity Today* Dec. 22 72 p5
446. *Christianity Today* Dec. 16 83 p26
447. *Pentecostal Evangel* Dec. 6 70 p12
448. *Lutheran* Dec. 82 p3
449. *Lutheran* Dec. 77 p5
450. *U.S. Catholic* Dec. 74 p13
451. *Lutheran Witness* Dec. 15 74 p4
452. *Pentecostal Evangel* Dec. 5 76 p2
453. *Presbyterian Journal* Dec. 24 75 p8
454. *American Opinion* Dec. 73 p29
455. *American Opinion* Dec. 73 p75
456. *Church Herald* Dec. 26 75 p8
457. *Vital Christianity* Dec. 14 75 p14
458. *Presbyterian Journal* Dec. 24 75 p12
459. *Wesleyan Advocate* Dec. 8 75 p20
460. *Mennonite* Nov. 4 75 p632
461. *Lutheran* Dec. 82 p3
462. *Presbyterian Journal* Dec. 20 78 p1
463. *Christian Ministry* Jan. 79 p17
464. *Mennonite* Dec. 23 75 p732
465. *Banner* July 30 76 p17
466. *Banner* Feb. 13 76 p17
467. *Daily Study Bible/Ephesians/p177*
468. *Christian Herald* Dec. 77 p21
469. *Presbyterian Journal* Oct. 29 75 p9
470. *Presbyterian Journal* Apr. 23 75 p18
471. *Moody Monthly* Mar. 77 p29
472. *Wesleyan Advocate* Jan. 30 78 p12
473. *Vital Christianity* Aug. 6 78 p2
474. *Pentecostal Evangel* July 27 75 p3
475. *American Opinion* Mar. 77 p37
476. *Nazarene Preacher* Feb. 75 p8
477. *America* Oct. 10 81 p197
478. *Banner* Aug. 19 77 p9
479. *American Opinion* Oct. 80 p21
480. *Herald Of Holiness* Mar. 1 76 p8
481. *Church Herald* Sept. 5 75 p9
482. *Encounter* Autumn 78 p365
483. *Alliance Witness* Sept. 21 77 p28
484. *His* May 77 p19
485. *Mennonite* Dec. 3 74 p718
486. *Vital Christianity* Sept. 21 75 p8
487. *Evangel* Mar. 8 76 p25
488. *Evangel* Oct. 13 75 p16
489. *Banner* Jan. 21 85 p19
490. *U.S. Catholic* Jan. 77 p9
491. *Lutheran* Apr. 21 82 p3
492. *Banner* May 4 81 p12
493. *Emphasis On Faith And Living*
     Oct. 82 p2
494. *Vital Christianity* Jan. 18 76 p7

495. *Wesleyan Advocate* Dec. 8 75 p9
496. *Presbyterian Journal* Apr. 16 75 p12
497. Editor's Files
498. *Evangel* Mar. 23 81 p16
499. *Pentecostal Testimony* Aug. 84 p30
500. *Christian Standard* July 6 75 p10
501. *Banner* Feb. 28 75 p13
502. *Alliance Witness* June 29 77 p3
503. *Presbyterian Journal* Mar. 4 81 p11
504. *Lutheran Standard* Sept. 16 83 p17
505. Editor's Files
506. *Good News Broadcaster* Jan. 82 p5
507. *Pentecostal Evangel* Oct. 11 81 p6
508. *United Evangelical Action* Fall 78 p13
509. Editor's Files
510. Editor's Files
511. *Presbyterian Journal* Apr. 28 82 p9
512. Editor's Files
513. *Herald Of Holiness* Oct. 7 70 p8
514. *American Opinion* Dec. 73 p75
515. *Vital Christianity* July 18 76 p9
516. *Declaration Of Independence*
517. *A.D.* Feb. 76 p32
518. *Vital Christianity* June 24 79 p4
519. *Christian Standard* Jan. 22 84 p6
520. *Christianity Today* Feb. 28 75 p17
521. *Moody Monthly* June 76 p97
522. Editor's Files
523. *Christian Standard* Feb. 20 83 p8
524. *Mennonite* June 1 76 p380
525. *Christian Standard* Sept. 2 84 p3
526. *Emphasis On Faith And Living*
      Aug. 83 p18
527. Editor's Files
528. *American Opinion* Sept. 79 p21
529. *American Opinion* Feb. 80 p31
530. *American Opinion* Apr. 77 p31
531. *New American* Feb. 3 86 p43
532. *America* Sept. 17 77 p145
533. *American Opinion* Apr. 76 p21
534. *American Opinion* Jan. 76 p22
535. *United Evangelical Action* Spring 76 p13
536. *American Opinion* Jan. 83 p29
537. *American Opinion* July–Aug. 74 p19
538. *Presbyterian Journal* Oct. 8 75 p12
539. *American Opinion* Oct. 72 p91
540. *American Opinion* Nov. 76 p39
541. *Banner* Feb. 27 76 p11
542. *American Opinion* Oct. 80 p21
543. *Church Herald* Aug. 22 75 p9
544. *Presbyterian Journal* July 30 75 p10
545. *Pentecostal Evangel* Apr. 15 85 p5
546. *Catholic Mind* Mar. 80 p40
547. *Chelsea Journal* Jan.–Feb. 75 p3
548. *Good News Broadcaster* Nov. 76 p24
549. *American Opinion* Nov. 83 p21
550. *Eternity* Mar. 75 p50
551. *Daily Study Bible/John*/p183
552. *Wesleyan Advocate* Jan. 31 77 p15
553. *America* Mar. 13 76 p195
554. *Christian Herald* Oct. 78 p46
555. Editor's Files
556. *Daily Study Bible/Hebrews*/p77
557. *Mennonite* June 10 75 p374
558. Editor's Files
559. *American Opinion* Mar. 76 p16
560. *Christianity Today* Apr. 7 78 p33
561. *Presbyterian Journal* Feb. 14 79 p9
562. *Link* July 68 p58
563. *Christian Standard* May 15 83 p16
564. *Encyclopedia Of Religious Quotations*
      1965 p83
565. *Encyclopedia Of Religious Quotations*
      1965 p83
566. *As Touching The Holy* 1980 p141
567. *Link* Nov. 66 p58
568. *Mennonite* Feb. 8 77 p104
569. *Mennonite* July 6 76 p430
570. *Link* Nov. 71 p39
571. *Presbyterian Journal* Apr. 19 78 p13
572. *Wesleyan Advocate* Oct. 1 79 p3
573. *Lutheran* Dec. 15 76 p3
574. *Jewish Spectator* Fall 75 p10
575. *Pentecostal Evangel* Dec. 8 74 p16
576. *Encounter* Spring 75 p123
577. *Presbyterian Journal* Mar. 26 86 p30
578. *American Opinion* Feb. 75 p35
579. *Vital Christianity* Aug. 24 80 p6
580. *Wesleyan Advocate* Feb. 2 76 p1
581. *Wesleyan Advocate* Sept. 30 74 p20
582. *Pentecostal Evangel* Feb. 27 77 p31
583. *Wesleyan Advocate* Feb. 2 76 p4
584. Editor's Files
585. *Daily Study Bible/John*/p205
586. *Alliance Witness* June 8 83 p6
587. *Faith For The Family* Feb. 77 p13
588. *Episcopal Recorder* Jan. 77 p17
589. *Episcopal Recorder* Jan. 78 p6
590. *Church Herald* Feb. 10 78 p17
591. *Christian Herald* Nov. 78 p78
592. *Good News Broadcaster* Nov. 83 p16
593. *Lutheran* Sept. 21 77 p3
594. *Pentecostal Evangel* Mar. 31 85 p3
595. *Pentecostal Evangel* Feb. 17 85 p5
596. *Daily Study Bible/John*/p191
597. *Pentecostal Evangel* June 1 80 p15
598. Editor's Files
599. *New Catholic World* Mar.–Apr. 76 p61
600. *Herald Of Holiness* Sept. 10 75 p10
601. *Alliance Witness* Dec. 15 76 p9

602. *Presbyterian Journal* Apr. 6 77 p13
603. *Christian Standard* July 13 75 p13
604. Editor's Files
605. *Presbyterian Journal* Sept. 8 76 p13
606. Editor's Files
607. Editor's Files
608. *Christian Century* Mar. 85 p29
609. *Herald Of Holiness* Nov. 1 85 p6
610. *Christian Home* Nov. 77 p25
611. *Soundings* Fall 80 p331
612. Editor's Files
613. *Daily Study Bible*
614. *American Opinion* June 75 p17
615. *Mennonite* June 10 75 p374
616. *Mennonite* June 10 75 p374
617. *Mennonite* June 10 75 p374
618. *Vital Christianity* May 21 78 p1
619. *Vital Christianity* Nov. 29 70 p3
620. *Christian Home* Oct. 77 p30
621. *Religious Humanism* Winter 86 p9
622. *Vital Christianity* Sept. 6 81 p13
623. *Presbyterian Journal* Apr. 6 77 p13
624. *American Opinion* Feb. 75 p35
625. *Banner* June 14 82 p21
626. *Messenger* Oct. 15 71 p22
627. *American Opinion* Apr. 73 p75
628. *Presbyterian Journal* May 11 77 p12
629. *Vital Christianity* Nov. 2 75 p2
630. *Lutheran* Nov. 5 75 p17
631. *Ecclesiastes 8:11* (NEB)
632. *Baptist Bulletin* Nov. 76 p13
633. *American Opinion* Dec. 75 p45
634. *Daily Study Bible/Colossians*/p147
635. *Evangel* Mar. 14 77 p27
636. *Pentecostal Evangel* Nov. 29 81 p6
637. *Pentecostal Evangel* Mar. 27 83 p30
638. *Presbyterian Journal* Sept. 16 70 p11
639. Editor's Files
640. *A.D.* Feb. 76 p32
641. *U.S. Catholic* Mar. 76 p40
642. *Banner* June 11 76 p11
643. *A.D.* Apr. 75 p46
644. *Episcopal Recorder* Sept. 76 p18
645. *Presbyterian Journal* Apr. 7 76 p1
646. *Cross Currents* Spring 78 p29
647. *Pentecostal Evangel* May 27 79 p2
648. *U.S. Catholic* Nov. 75 p42
649. *Presbyterian Journal* Feb. 19 86 p10
650. *Eternity* Jan. 75 p27
651. *Wesleyan Advocate* June 9 75 p12
652. *Wesleyan Advocate* Jan. 31 77 p20
653. *Journal Of Religion And Health* July 78 p184
654. *Christian Standard* Apr. 19 81 p3
655. *Christian Standard* Apr. 15 84 p6
656. *Journal Of Religion And Health* July 78 p170
657. *Vital Christianity* Apr. 27 75 p5
658. *Herald Of Holiness* Sept. 1 83 p13
659. *Pentecostal Testimony* Feb. 86 p17
660. *Mennonite* Mar. 4 75 p141
661. Editor's Files
662. *Christian Standard* Apr. 15 84 p6
663. Editor's Files
664. Editor's Files
665. *Christian Standard* Apr. 15 84 p5
666. *Presbyterian Journal* Mar. 10 82 p9
667. Editor's Files
668. *Banner* Oct. 26 79 p7
669. *Herald Of Holiness* Oct. 1 79 p15
670. *American Opinion* Dec. 80 p37
671. *Daily Study Bible*
672. *Good News Broadcaster* Jan. 83 p13
673. *Baptist Bulletin* Sept. 84 p12
674. *Pentecostal Evangel* Sept. 23 84 p6
675. *Wesleyan Advocate* Jan. 18 82 p13
676. *Alliance Witness* Sept. 16 81 p23
677. Editor's Files
678. Editor's Files
679. *Mennonite* Feb. 8 77 p104
680. *Encounter* Summer 76 p256
681. *Christian Herald* June 82 p18
682. Editor's Files
683. Editor's Files
684. *Presbyterian Journal* May 5 82 p9
685. *Christian Ministry* Nov. 74 p24
686. *Presbyterian Journal* Mar. 17 76 p11
687. *Christianity Today* May 6 77 p24
688. *Presbyterian Journal* May 5 82 p8
689. *Herald Of Holiness* Aug. 1 78 p19
690. *U.S. Catholic* Dec. 75 p49
691. *Critic* Sept.–Oct. 73 p28
692. *Wesleyan Advocate* Feb. 16 76 p5
693. *Christian Standard* Aug. 8 82 p3
694. Editor's Files
695. *Encyclopedia Of Religious Quotations* 1965 p114
696. *Midstream* Nov. 75 p59
697. Editor's Files
698. *Presbyterian Journal* Sept. 8 76 p12
699. *Daily Study Bible/Hebrews*/p136
700. *Christian Standard* Jan. 26 75 p12
701. *Vital Christianity* Sept. 3 78 p14
702. *A.D.* June 81 p23
703. *Vital Christianity* Jan. 30 77 p17
704. *Christian Reader* July 84 p81
705. *Christian Standard* May 25 75 p9
706. *His* Jan. 74 p17
707. *Christianity Today* Apr. 9 82 p80
708. *Alliance Witness* June 23 82 p36

709. *Herald Of Holiness* Mar. 12 75 p16
710. *Today's Education* Nov.–Dec. 74 p17
711. *These Times* Oct. 75 p5
712. *American Opinion* Apr. 74 p77
713. *Theology Today* July 80 p232
714. *United Evangelical Action* Fall 75 p27
715. *Link* Nov. 71 p39
716. Editor's Files
717. *Christian Standard* June 17 78 p8
718. *Christianity Today* Nov. 7 75 p17
719. *Episcopal Recorder* Apr. 77 p14
720. *His* June 76 p22
721. *Christianity Today* Feb. 18 77 p32
722. *Pentecostal Evangel* Apr. 24 77 p2
723. *Christian Herald* Jan. 76 p36
724. *Wesleyan Advocate* July 5 76 p9
725. *Wesleyan Advocate* May 26 75 p10
726. *Vital Christianity* Apr. 13 86 p7
727. *Banner* Mar. 21 75 p12
728. Editor's Files
729. *U.S. Catholic* June 1 79 p6
730. *Lutheran Witness* Apr. 25 76 p8
731. *Alliance Witness* May 4 77 p9
732. *Christian Century* June 20 79 p669
733. *Church Herald* Apr. 29 77 p16
734. *Presbyterian Journal* Sept. 10 75 p9
735. *Encyclopedia Of Religious Quotations* 1965 p115
736. *Encyclopedia Of Religious Quotations* 1965 p115
737. *His* Mar. 86 p30
738. Editor's Files
739. *Banner* Nov. 5 65 p9
740. *His* Oct. 76 p31
741. *His* Mar. 79 p11
742. *Zygon* Dec. 76 p372
743. *Daily Study Bible*/Hebrews/p138
744. *Episcopal Recorder* July 78 p19
745. *Banner* Jan. 13 78 p8
746. *Faith For The Family* Sept. 83 p9
747. *American Opinion* Apr. 76 p21
748. *Pentecostal Evangel* Nov. 14 82 p14
749. *Christian Standard* Mar. 21 82 p13
750. *Emphasis On Faith And Living* Apr. 1 80 p3
751. *Lutheran* Apr. 2 80 p3
752. *Christian Herald* Mar. 75 p20
753. *Herald Of Holiness* Mar. 26 75 p19
754. *Alliance Witness* Oct. 5 77 p7
755. *Evangel* Apr. 12 76 p8
756. *Alliance Witness* Mar. 23 77 p3
757. *Vital Christianity* Apr. 18 76 p1
758. *Herald Of Holiness* Oct. 1 79 p16
759. *War Cry* Mar. 29 86 p10
760. *Christianity Today* Sept. 26 69 p36

761. *American Opinion* Jan. 76 p21
762. *Link* Aug. 69 p58
763. *Commonweal* Feb. 28 75 p420
764. *Religious Education* May 81 p307
765. *Presbyterian Journal* Mar. 23 77 p13
766. *Episcopal Recorder* Aug. 77 p9
767. *Catholic Mind* Dec. 80 p28
768. *Jewish Spectator* Spring 85 p22
769. *Church Herald* Dec. 18 70 p5
770. *Wesleyan Advocate* Jan. 31 76 p9
771. *Church Herald* Feb. 21 75 p11
772. *Zygon* Sept. 76 p248
773. *U.S. Catholic* Dec. 80 p15
774. *Banner* Sept. 12 75 p17
775. *Soundings* Fall 75 p363
776. *Theological Educator* Spring 77 p49
777. Editor's Files
778. *Daily Study Bible*/Galatians/p53
779. *Eternity* Feb. 75 p50
780. *Link* Oct. 71 p62
781. *Encyclopedia Of Religious Quotations* 1965 p121
782. *Encyclopedia Of Religious Quotations* 1965 p122
783. *Herald Of Holiness* Mar. 12 75 p13
784. *Lutheran* Mar. 4 81 p3
785. *Christianity Today* Mar. 12 76 p37
786. *Daily Study Bible*/Corinthians/p44
787. *Daily Study Bible*/Colossians/p129
788. *Herald Of Holiness* July 1 83 p17
789. *Vital Christianity* Feb. 16 75 p10
790. *Herald Of Holiness* Dec. 15 82 p7
791. *Pentecostal Evangel* Jan. 10 82 p6
792. *Christian Standard* Sept. 18 83 p3
793. *Christian Standard* May 25 86 p3
794. *Christian Standard* Dec. 7 75 p13
795. *Faith For The Family* Oct. 82 p30
796. *Evangel* June 9 75 p18
797. *Banner* Jan. 26 79 p7
798. *Mennonite* July 6 76 p432
799. *Evangel* June 13 83 p18
800. *Herald Of Holiness* Mar. 15 83 p3
801. Editor's Files
802. *Emphasis On Faith And Living* Nov. 84 p3
803. *Evangel* Nov. 28 77 p17
804. Editor's Files
805. *Encyclopedia Of Religious Quotations* 1965 p125
806. *Encyclopedia Of Religious Quotations* 1965 p126
807. *Encyclopedia Of Religious Quotations* 1965 p126
808. *Baptist Bulletin* Feb. 84 p37
809. *Christianity Today* Jan. 23 81 p18

810. *Pentecostal Testimony* Feb. 85 p14
811. Editor's Files
812. *Link* Dec. 67 p56
813. *Link* Nov. 71 p39
814. *Christianity Today* Nov. 21 75 p28
815. *Vital Christianity* Aug. 10 80 p7
816. *Vital Christianity* Nov. 18 79 p8
817. *Christian Standard* Mar. 7 76 p15
818. *American Opinion* Mar. 75 p35
819. *American Opinion* June 75 p17
820. Editor's Files
821. *Pentecostal Evangel* May 15 77 p2
822. Editor's Files
823. *Pentecostal Evangel* Apr. 25 76 p5
824. *Christian Home* Nov. 74 p16
825. *Evangel* Jan. 12 76 p25
826. *Daily Study Bible/John/*p175
827. *Daily Study Bible/John/*p45
828. *His* Mar. 75 p32
829. *Evangel* Jan. 12 76 p25
830. *Lutheran* Nov. 4 81 p3
831. *Lutheran* Nov. 17 82 p3
832. *Link* Nov. 66 p58
833. *Journal Of Psychology And Theology* Spring 78 p125
834. *A.D.* Mar. 75 p68
835. *Alliance Witness* Apr. 21 76 p7
836. *Alliance Witness* Sept. 17 80 p9
837. *Good News Broadcaster* Mar. 85 p51
838. *Alliance Witness* Sept. 26 84 p31
839. *Wesleyan Advocate* Apr. 28 75 p7
840. *Christian Standard* Dec. 23 79 p6
841. *Encounter* Autumn 76 p371
842. *Christian Reader* Nov.–Dec. 74 p7
843. Editor's Files
844. *Christianity Today* Nov. 8 74 p16
845. *Herald Of Holiness* Nov. 1 84 p3
846. *His* May 76 p32
847. *U.S. Catholic* Oct. 80 p29
848. *His* Jan. 82 p31
849. *Alliance Witness* Sept. 8 76 p7
850. *Alliance Witness* June 23 82 p29
851. *Pentecostal Evangel* July 17 77 p2
852. *Pentecostal Evangel* Mar. 21 82 p5
853. *Wesleyan Advocate* Dec. 6 76 p13
854. *His* Apr. 77 p7
855. *Journal Of Psychology And Judaism* Fall 78 p43
856. Editor's Files
857. *Daily Study Bible/Hebrews/*p175
858. *Mennonite* Apr. 29 75 p266
859. Editor's Files
860. *Banner* May 18 81 p17
861. *Mennonite* Apr. 22 86 p192
862. *The Complete Toastmaster* 1960 p252
863. *Moody Monthly* July–Aug. 77 p92
864. *Herald Of Holiness* May 7 75 p19
865. *Commonweal* Feb. 27 76 p140
866. *Link* Oct. 67 p58
867. *Christian Home* June 77 p3
868. *Christian Home* Fall 83 p22
869. *Evangel* Aug. 22 77 p2
870. *Mennonite* May 8 73 p301
871. *Herald Of Holiness* Aug. 15 78 p15
872. *Wesleyan Advocate* Jan. 19 76 p9
873. *Christian Reader* Mar.–Apr. 78 p46
874. *Encyclopedia Of Religious Quotations* 1965 p141
875. *Encyclopedia Of Religious Quotations* 1965 p142
876. *Christian Reader* Mar.–Apr. 75 p86
877. *Banner* June 17 77 p16
878. *Daily Study Bible/Ephesians/*p153
879. *Mennonite* June 23 81 p403
880. *New Catholic World* July–Aug. 75 p170
881. *Christian Standard* June 13 76 p7
882. *Herald Of Holiness* Oct. 1 76 p7
883. *Herald Of Holiness* Apr. 15 76 p14
884. *Christian Reader* Sept.–Oct. 76 p51
885. *Banner* Sept. 12 75 p13
886. *Presbyterian Journal* Dec. 16 81 p3
887. *Wesleyan Advocate* June 9 75 p6
888. *Christian Home* June 77 p23
889. *Christianity Today* Nov. 17 78 p28
890. *American Opinion* Jan. 74 p77
891. *These Times* June 79 p33
892. *Christian Herald* June 75 p22
893. *These Times* June 79 p33
894. *Alliance Witness* May 28 80 p5
895. *Alliance Witness* May 28 80 p3
896. *Vital Christianity* Aug. 1 76 p3
897. *Christian Herald* Feb. 79 p58
898. *Pentecostal Evangel* June 13 77 p8
899. *Herald Of Holiness* Oct. 15 69 p11
900. *War Cry* Apr. 19 69 p22
901. *Christian Herald* Nov. 11 77 p16
902. *Pentecostal Evangel* Nov. 14 76 p13
903. *His* Jan. 83 p34
904. Editor's Files
905. *American Opinion* Mar. 75 p35
906. *Christian Life* May 86 p50
907. *Christian Century* Feb. 19 75 p161
908. *Good News Broadcaster* May 84 p7
909. *Christian Standard* Jan. 7 79 p4
910. *War Cry* Nov. 11 72 p8
911. *Pentecostal Evangel* June 1 80 p2
912. *His* Jan. 75 p32
913. *Daily Study Bible*
914. *Daily Study Bible/Hebrews/*p120
915. *Lutheran Standard* Nov. 19 82 p6

916. *Catholic Weekly* June 26 81 p4
917. *Evangel* May 24 76 p3
918. *Moody Monthly* Mar. 76 p41
919. *Wesleyan Advocate* July 7 75 p5
920. Editor's Files
921. Editor's Files
922. *Good News Broadcaster* Apr. 80 p14
923. *Evangel* May 24 76 p4
924. *American Opinion* Dec. 79 p23
925. *Religious Humanism* Spring 85 p64
926. *Eternity* Feb. 77 p67
927. *Commentary* Dec. 75 p60
928. *Christian Standard* Mar. 22 81 p1
929. Editor's Files
930. *Commonweal* Apr. 9 76 p241
931. *American Opinion* Sept. 76 p37
932. *American Opinion* Oct. 76 p37
933. *American Opinion* June 76 p39
934. *Christianity Today* Apr. 23 76 p58
935. *Presbyterian Journal* Oct. 13 76 p7
936. *American Opinion* Oct. 80 p21
937. *America* May 8 82 p356
938. Editor's Files
939. *Christian Standard* Sept. 12 76 p10
940. *American Issue* July–Aug. 76 p1
941. Editor's Files
942. *Banner* Nov. 8 74 p3
943. *Pentecostal Evangel* June 11 72 p23
944. *American Scholar* Autumn 78 p442
945. *Pentecostal Evangel* July 6 75 p10
946. *Herald Of Holiness* Mar. 12 75 p11
947. *Christian Herald* Dec. 78 p46
948. *Moody Monthly* May 77 p65
949. *Link* Dec. 74 p54
950. *Christian Herald* Apr. 78 p42
951. *American Opinion* Mar. 75 p35
952. *Church Herald* Jan. 12 79 p12
953. *Alliance Witness* May 7 86 p11
954. *American Scholar* Spring 85 p160
955. *Eternity* Apr. 77 p23
956. *Christian Standard* Nov. 11 84 p3
957. Editor's Files
958. *U.S. Catholic* Oct. 70 p38
959. *American Opinion* Nov. 76 p39
960. *Link* July 68 p58
961. *Christian Herald* Nov. 78 p78
962. *Evangel* Nov. 10 80 p21
963. *Episcopal Recorder* Jan. 78 p7
964. *Church Herald* Mar. 18 83 p6
965. *Good News Broadcaster* Mar. 86 p12
966. *Christian Reader* Nov.–Dec. 76 p7
967. *Church Herald* Nov. 26 76 p11
968. *Christian Reader* May–June 79 p26
969. *His* Feb. 76 p32
970. *Emphasis On Faith And Living*
       Sept. 15 79 p3
971. *Christian Herald* June 78 p41
972. *American Opinion* Nov. 72 p91
973. *Emphasis On Faith And Living*
       Sept. 15 76 p19
974. *Christian Century* Aug. 6–13 75 p703
975. *Christian Century* Mar. 13 85 p270
976. *Alliance Witness* Mar. 10 76 p10
977. *Pentecostal Evangel* Oct. 16 83 p12
978. Editor's Files
979. *American Opinion* Nov. 79 p37
980. *Encyclopedia Of Religious Quotations*
       1965 p160
981. *Christian Herald* Apr. 78 p42
982. *Encyclopedia Of Religious Quotations*
       1965 p159
983. *Encyclopedia Of Religious Quotations*
       1965 p161
984. *War Cry* Mar. 18 85 p9
985. *Mennonite* May 22 73 p330
986. *Church Herald* Nov. 17 78 p8
987. *Link* July 74 p23
988. *Herald Of Holiness* July 2 75 p4
989. *Christian Home* Sept. 78 p13
990. *Daily Study Bible/Ephesians*/p151
991. *Banner* May 14 76 p11
992. *Banner* Nov. 22 74 p3
993. *Evangel* Aug. 11 75 p25
994. *Jewish Frontier* Oct. 74 p24
995. *Church Herald* June 28 74 p2
996. *Link* Dec. 66 p31
997. *Vital Christianity* Aug. 6 78 p23
998. *Lutheran* June 7 78 p3
999. *Alliance Witness* Oct. 9 74 p3
1000. *Daily Study Bible/Ephesians*/p86
1001. Editor's Files
1002. *Pentecostal Evangel* Apr. 2 78 p7
1003. Editor's Files
1004. *Daily Study Bible/Colossians*/p183
1005. *Mennonite* Mar. 25 86 p127
1006. *Herald Of Holiness* Mar. 12 75 p19
1007. Editor's Files
1008. *Vital Christianity* Aug. 1 76 p10
1009. *Emphasis On Faith And Living*
       Feb. 86 p10
1010. *Presbyterian Journal* May 14 80 p14
1011. *Lutheran* Jan. 17 79 p3
1012. *Wesleyan Advocate* June 20 83 p3
1013. *Vital Christianity* Mar. 5 78 p8
1014. *Wesleyan Advocate* July 19 76 p12
1015. *Preacher's Magazine* Mar.–Apr. 78 p13
1016. *Together* June 65 p23
1017. *Christian Standard* Sept. 5 76 p14
1018. Editor's Files
1019. *Pulpit* Apr. 69 p23
1020. *Pentecostal Evangel* Oct. 13 74 p15
1021. *Vital Christianity* Dec. 29 68 p3

1022. *Christianity And Crisis* Oct. 5 81 p268
1023. *His* Jan. 73 p1
1024. *Wesleyan Advocate* June 20 77 p13
1025. Editor's Files
1026. *Encyclopedia Of Religious Quotations* 1965 p193
1027. *Encyclopedia Of Religious Quotations* 1965 p193
1028. *Herald Of Holiness* Dec. 17 75 p19
1029. *Presbyterian Journal* Mar. 26 75 p12
1030. *Church Herald* Oct. 21 83 p18
1031. *Christian Standard* Apr. 18 76 p6
1032. *Lutheran* May 21 80 p3
1033. *Encyclopedia Of Religious Quotations* 1965 p197
1034. *Encyclopedia Of Religious Quotations* 1965 p198
1035. *Encyclopedia Of Religious Quotations* 1965 p199
1036. *A.D.* Feb. 76 p32
1037. *Evangel* June 27 77 p13
1038. *Christian Ministry* Jan. 79 p13
1039. *Evangel* Mar. 8 76 p15
1040. *Banner* Feb. 11 85 p5
1041. *Herald Of Holiness* July 15 76 p7
1042. *Daily Study Bible/John/*p66
1043. *Lutheran Witness* Oct. 31 76 p6
1044. *Christian Reader* July–Aug. 76 p55
1045. *Presbyterian Journal* June 11 75 p11
1046. *Presbyterian Journal* Feb. 4 76 p11
1047. *Mennonite* Jan. 8 74 p32
1048. *Christian Standard* June 15 75 p11
1049. *Christian Reader* Feb.–Mar. 72 p31
1050. *Encyclopedia Of Religious Quotations* 1965 p205
1051. *Herald Of Holiness* Apr. 1 85 p17
1052. *Banner* June 21 82 p21
1053. *Encyclopedia Of Religious Quotations* 1965 p206
1054. *Banner* Mar. 28 80 p11
1055. *Vital Christianity* Mar. 2 75 p15
1056. *Herald Of Holiness* Sept. 26 73 p3
1057. *Daily Study Bible/Philippians/*p17
1058. *War Cry* May 22 71 p24
1059. *Episcopal Recorder* May 78 p14
1060. *Christian Herald* Nov. 64 p64
1061. *Baptist Bulletin* Sept. 82 p17
1062. *Lutheran Witness* Nov. 3 74 p6
1063. *Evangel* Mar. 27 78 p32
1064. *Pentecostal Evangel* June 28 81 p6
1065. *U.S. Catholic* July 78 p41
1066. *Link* May 66 p58
1067. *Link* Nov. 66 p58
1068. *Evangel* Dec. 8 75 p5
1069. *American Opinion* Feb. 83 p39
1070. *Congregationalist* Mar. 76 p16
1071. *Christian Herald* June 76 p31
1072. *Pentecostal Evangel* Oct. 17 82 p21
1073. *American Opinion* Sept. 76 p37
1074. *Christian Reader* Mar.–Apr. 75 p48
1075. *Christian Standard* May 16 76 p11
1076. Editor's Files
1077. *Herald Of Holiness* Jan. 15 76 p18
1078. *Christian Herald* Sept. 79 p46
1079. *Lutheran Standard* Sept. 5 72 p35
1080. Editor's Files
1081. *Presbyterian Journal* Nov. 17 76 p13
1082. *Wesleyan Advocate* Feb. 3 75 p9
1083. *Presbyterian Journal* Jan. 1 75 p11
1084. *Pentecostal Evangel* Sept. 19 76 p31
1085. *Christian Home* Summer 84 p51
1086. *Evangel* May 22 78 p17
1087. *His* Apr. 77 p34
1088. *U.S. Catholic* Nov. 77 p9
1089. *U.S. Catholic* Nov. 75 p8
1090. *Wesleyan Advocate* June 19 78 p7
1091. *Presbyterian Journal* Oct. 15 75 p7
1092. *Pentecostal Evangel* Aug. 15 76 p11
1093. *Eternity* Feb. 86 p25
1094. *Presbyterian Journal* Dec. 11 74 p7
1095. *Presbyterian Journal* July 3 74 p12
1096. *Christian Herald* Apr. 79 p53
1097. *Christian Herald* Jan. 79 p44
1098. *U.S. Catholic* Nov. 77 p9
1099. *Christianity Today* Aug. 6 76 p14
1100. *Banner* Oct. 24 75 p3
1101. Editor's Files
1102. *Presbyterian Journal* Apr. 21 82 p11
1103. *Daily Study Bible/Ephesians/*p98
1104. *America* Nov. 26 83 p335
1105. *Christian Standard* June 6 76 p6
1106. *Daily Study Bible/Barclay*
1107. *American Opinion* May 76 p27
1108. *Soundings* Fall 83 p296
1109. Editor's Files
1110. *Daily Study Bible/Hebrews/*p223
1111. *Today's Education* Sept. 72 p64
1112. *Commentary* Dec. 76 p34
1113. *American Opinion* Oct. 76 p37
1114. *Episcopal Recorder* Apr. 78 p19
1115. *Evangel* Apr. 11 83 p19
1116. *Daily Study Bible/Colossians/*p150
1117. *His* May 75 p34
1118. *Moody Monthly* Jan. 85 p18
1119. *Pentecostal Testimony* Feb. 85 p19
1120. *Christian Standard* Apr. 7 85 p14
1121. *Pentecostal Testimony* Mar. 85 p19
1122. *Evangel* Apr. 28 80 p26
1123. *These Times* Jan. 76 p17
1124. *America* Mar. 1 75 p151
1125. *Presbyterian Journal* July 22 81 p2
1126. *Christian Standard* Aug. 31 80 p3

1127. *Herald Of Holiness* July 15 76 p8
1128. *Wesleyan Advocate* Aug. 4 75 p4
1129. Editor's Files
1130. *Wesleyan Advocate* Apr. 26 76 p15
1131. *Alliance Witness* Jan. 10 79 p4
1132. *Pentecostal Evangel* June 7 81 p4
1133. *War Cry* May 25 85 p15
1134. *Moody Monthly* Jan. 85 p19
1135. *War Cry* May 25 85 p14
1136. *Wesleyan Advocate* Jan. 2 78 p1
1137. *Emphasis On Faith and Living*
       July 84 p7
1138. *Pentecostal Evangel* Oct. 3 76 p15
1139. *Banner* May 27 77 p6
1140. *Pentecostal Evangel* Aug. 12 79 p4
1141. *Alliance Witness* June 2 76 p4
1142. *Presbyterian Journal* May 11 83 p11
1143. *Alliance Witness* Feb. 11 76 p5
1144. *Banner* May 4 81 p12
1145. *Wesleyan Advocate* Nov. 25 74 p2
1146. *Alliance Witness* Feb. 11 76 p5
1147. *Pentecostal Evangel* Aug. 18 74 p2
1148. *Christian Herald* July–August 77 p52
1149. *Christian Herald* Nov. 76 p50
1150. *Lutheran* Mar. 5 80 p3
1151. *Link* Jan. 74 p14
1152. *Christian Century* Dec. 3 75 p1111
1153. *Evangel* Jan. 14 85 p32
1154. *Christian Life* Oct. 76 p30
1155. *America* Dec. 20 75 p441
1156. *Herald Of Holiness* Jan. 1 75 p19
1157. *Critic* Nov.–Dec. 70 p1
1158. *Evangel* Jan. 14 85 p32
1159. *Mennonite* Nov. 15 77 p678
1160. *Pentecostal Evangel* Mar. 14 76 p2
1161. *Mennonite* Sept. 30 75 p538
1162. *Judaism* Summer 83 p331
1163. *Christian Standard* Dec. 17 78 p11
1164. *Christian Reader* Dec.–Jan. 71 p61
1165. *Presbyterian Journal* July 26 78 p12
1166. Editor's Files
1167. *Alliance Witness* Feb. 17 82 p24
1168. *Herald Of Holiness* Apr. 15 78 p9
1169. *Daily Study Bible/Barclay*
1170. *United Evangelical Action* Spring 78
       p18
1171. *Humanist* Sept.–Oct. 78 p43
1172. *A.D.* Mar. 75 p29
1173. *Presbyterian Journal* Mar. 24 76 p13
1174. *Christian Century* Dec. 1 82 p1230
1175. *Christian Century* Dec. 1 82 p1230
1176. *Emphasis On Faith And Living*
       Apr. 15 79 p3
1177. *Lutheran* June 6 79 p3
1178. *Herald Of Holiness* Apr. 15 78 p9

1179. *Christian Ministry* May 86 p28
1180. *Christian Herald* June 78 p41
1181. *Pentecostal Evangel* Feb. 26 78 p2
1182. *Good News Broadcaster* Oct. 83 p31
1183. *Christian Standard* Aug. 29 82 p13
1184. *Pentecostal Evangel* Feb. 26 78 p2
1185. *Presbyterian Journal* Mar. 14 79 p15
1186. *Pentecostal Evangel* Sept. 14 80 p2
1187. *Banner* Aug. 18 78 p11
1188. Editor's Files
1189. *Church Herald* Sept. 16 77 p9
1190. *Banner* Aug. 18 78 p11
1191. *Christian Herald* Oct. 81 p66
1192. *Lutheran* Dec. 2 81 p3
1193. *American Opinion* Mar. 79 p35
1194. Editor's Files
1195. *Moody Monthly* June 79 p1
1196. Editor's Files
1197. *Episcopal Recorder* July 76 p4
1198. *Christianity Today* July 6 73 p39
1199. *American Opinion* May 75 p21
1200. *Christianity Today* Jan. 29 71 p6
1201. *Chelsea Journal* May–June 77 p156
1202. *Vital Christianity* Oct. 3 76 p8
1203. Editor's Files
1204. Editor's Files
1205. *Vital Christianity* June 30 74 p1
1206. *Christian Herald* Dec. 78 p46
1207. *Encyclopedia Of Religious Quotations*
       1965 p243
1208. *Episcopal Recorder* Dec. 80 p5
1209. *Moody Monthly* Jan. 84 p39
1210. *Christianity Today* Sept. 22 78 p18
1211. *Christian Century* Apr. 16 80 p441
1212. Editor's Files
1213. *Today's Education* Mar.–Apr. 74 p26
1214. *American Opinion* Nov. 70 p71
1215. *American Opinion* June 73 p77
1216. Editor's Files
1217. *Pentecostal Evangel* Nov. 20 77 p32
1218. *Pentecostal Evangel* Apr. 25 76 p8
1219. *Christian Century* Apr. 14 76 p364
1220. *Vital Christianity* Apr. 8 79 p12
1221. *His* Apr. 80 p12
1222. *Christianity Today* Dec. 19 75 p22
1223. *Christianity Today* Dec. 19 75 p22
1224. *Daily Study Bible/Corinthians/*p85
1225. *American Opinion* May 77 p29
1226. *Daily Study Bible/Corinthians/*p168
1227. *Herald Of Holiness* Jan. 18 74 p8
1228. *Vital Christianity* Nov. 18 84 p21
1229. *Mennonite* June 7 77 p383
1230. *Herald Of Holiness* May 1 76 p10
1231. *Wesleyan Advocate* Feb. 2 76 p9
1232. Editor's Files

1233. *Pentecostal Evangel* June 19 83 p2
1234. Editor's Files
1235. *Christian Standard* Apr. 6 75 p11
1236. *American Opinion* Jan. 72 p77
1237. Editor's Files
1238. *Christian Herald* Oct. 75 p14
1239. *Wesleyan Advocate* Sept. 29 75 p3
1240. *Link* July 70 p66
1241. *Wesleyan Advocate* Feb. 2 76 p9
1242. Editor's Files
1243. *Daily Study Bible/Barclay*
1244. *Christian Herald* July 83 p57
1245. *American Opinion* Mar. 73 p95
1246. Editor's Files
1247. *Link* Apr. 70 p12
1248. *Link* Dec. 67 p58
1249. *Commonweal* Feb. 27 76 p140
1250. *Christian Herald* Apr. 75 p1
1251. Editor's Files
1252. *Wesleyan Advocate* Aug. 4 75 p2
1253. *Christian Standard* Aug. 6 78 p13
1254. Editor's Files
1255. *Christian Home* Dec. 75 p6
1256. *War Cry* Feb. 2 85 p3
1257. *Church Herald* Jan. 12 79 p13
1258. *Link* Oct. 67 p58
1259. *Presbyterian Journal* Jan. 7 76 p8
1260. *Mennonite* Nov. 9 82 p548
1261. *Congregationalist* Apr. 75 p7
1262. *U.S. Catholic* Jan. 75 p22
1263. *Jewish Spectator* Fall 75 p10
1264. *Presbyterian Journal* Jan. 9 80 p18
1265. *His* Feb. 77 p18
1266. *Alliance Witness* Oct. 14 81 p22
1267. *Mennonite* May 31 77 p354
1268. *Detroit Free Press* Sept. 25 78 p4B
1269. *American Opinion* Feb. 75 p35
1270. *Center Magazine* May–June 75 p29
1271. *His* Nov. 75 p32
1272. *Christian Herald* Mar. 81 p58
1273. *Presbyterian Journal* Nov. 16 77 p7
1274. *Pentecostal Evangel* Dec. 4 77 p3
1275. *Moody Monthly* Jan. 75 p29
1276. *American Opinion* Jan. 75 p33
1277. *Herald Of Holiness* Sept. 1 79 p16
1278. *Today's Education* Mar.–Apr. 75 p57
1279. *Alliance Witness* Oct. 28 81 p23
1280. *Lutheran* Sept. 17 75 p13
1281. *Christian Century* Aug. 6–13 75 p707
1282. *War Cry* Jan. 14 78 p11
1283. *Vital Christianity* Mar. 25 79 p9
1284. *Mennonite* Nov. 9 71 p675
1285. *Church Herald* Jan. 12 79 p12
1286. *Christian Standard* Mar. 9 75 p10
1287. *Lutheran* Nov. 3 82 p3
1288. *War Cry* Feb. 4 84 p10
1289. *Pentecostal Evangel* Nov. 26 78 p2
1290. *Christian Herald* Jan. 76 p36
1291. *His* Mar. 82 p32
1292. *Presbyterian Journal* May 16 79 p13
1293. *Vital Christianity* Dec. 3 78 p17
1294. *Pentecostal Evangel* Dec. 20 81 p21
1295. *Christian Reader* Sept. 80 p6
1296. *Lutheran* Feb. 16 77 p3
1297. *Moody Monthly* Feb. 78 p57
1298. *Christian Herald* Mar. 79 p67
1299. *Christian Standard* May 23 76 p8
1300. *Link* Oct. 74 p61
1301. *American Opinion* Dec. 75 p45
1302. *Vital Christianity* Mar. 25 79 p16
1303. *American Opinion* Dec. 76 p23
1304. Editor's Files
1305. *Mennonite* Oct. 9 73 p572
1306. *Link* May 66 p58
1307. *American Opinion* Apr. 73 p75
1308. *Christian Herald* Feb. 77 p49
1309. *Christian Herald* May 81 p54
1310. *Daily Study Bible/Corinthians/p196*
1311. *Religion In Life* Autumn 78 p353
1312. *Christian Reader* May–June 76 p54
1313. *Pentecostal Evangel* Mar. 2 86 p5
1314. *Lutheran* June 17 81 p3
1315. *Presbyterian Journal* Jan. 1 75 p8
1316. *Moody Monthly* Apr. 76 p134
1317. *Pentecostal Evangel* Mar. 2 86 p5
1318. *Pentecostal Evangel* Nov. 30 75 p6
1319. Editor's Files
1320. *Pentecostal Evangel* Oct. 24 76 p11
1321. *Pentecostal Evangel* Apr. 11 76 p8
1322. *Episcopal Recorder* Apr. 76 p15
1323. *Evangel* Dec. 9 74 p9
1324. *Vital Christianity* May 30 71 p3
1325. *Episcopal Recorder* Mar. 78 p15
1326. *Herald Of Holiness* Aug. 13 75 p15
1327. *Christianity Today* Dec. 19 75 p20
1328. *Alliance Witness* Feb. 21 79 p5
1329. *Presbyterian Journal* June 17 81 p11
1330. *Episcopal Recorder* July 78 p19
1331. *Banner* Sept. 5 75 p3
1332. *Presbyterian Journal* Mar. 3 71 p9
1333. *Presbyterian Journal* Aug. 27 75 p13
1334. *Christian Standard* Dec. 14 75 p9
1335. *A.D.* Nov. 74 p53
1336. *Christianity Today* Dec. 19 75 p22
1337. *Evangel* Mar. 24 75 p11
1338. *Daily Study Bible/Philippians/p88*
1339. *Pentecostal Evangel* May 22 77 p2
1340. *Banner* June 6 75 p8
1341. *Banner* Apr. 13 81 p12
1342. *Christianity Today* Aug. 27 76 p9

1343. *Pentecostal Evangel* Nov. 30 75 p10
1344. *Wesleyan Advocate* Nov. 8 76 p6
1345. *Pentecostal Evangel* Sept. 8 74 p3
1346. *Moody Monthly* Jan. 75 p65
1347. *Banner* Oct. 24 75 p3
1348. *Pentecostal Evangel* Dec. 31 72 p11
1349. *Vital Christianity* Jan. 15 78 p1
1350. *Encyclopedia Of Religious Quotations* 1965 p261
1351. *Encyclopedia Of Religious Quotations* 1965 p262
1352. *Encyclopedia Of Religious Quotations* 1965 p262
1353. *Religious Quotes* 1976
1354. *A Reader's Notebook*/Kennedy p153
1355. *A Reader's Notebook*/Kennedy p153
1356. *Christian Reader*/Association Press 1952 p487
1357. *Lutheran Standard* Mar. 4 83 p15
1358. *Church Herald* Mar. 18 77 p9
1359. *One Thousand Inspirational Things*/ Spencer Press p363
1360. *Christian Reader* Sept. 80 p9
1361. *Congregationalist* Feb. 76 p3
1362. *Christian Educator's Journal* Feb. 82 p20
1363. *Wesleyan Advocate* Oct. 25 76 p14
1364. *Wesleyan Advocate* Mar. 27 78 p10
1365. Editor's Files
1366. *Lutheran* Jan. 5 77 p3
1367. *American Opinion* Dec. 79 p22
1368. *American Opinion* Jan. 77 p35
1369. *Soundings* Fall 78 p308
1370. *American Opinion* Jan. 75 p33
1371. *American Opinion* Apr. 80 p37
1372. Editor's Files
1373. *Evangel* Jan. 10 77 p25
1374. *Link* Dec. 67 p58
1375. *Evangel* Feb. 28 77 p27
1376. *Wesleyan Advocate* July 5 76 p7
1377. *Link* Jan. 71 p33
1378. *American Opinion* May 76 p27
1379. *Herald Of Holiness* Aug. 15 84 p5
1380. Editor's Files
1381. *Alliance Witness* Sept. 2 81 p31
1382. *American Opinion* Sept. 83 p39
1383. *American Opinion* Feb. 83 p39
1384. *Link* Dec. 67 p58
1385. *Christian Herald* May 83 p47
1386. *Christian Standard* Sept. 5 76 p6
1387. *American Opinion* Dec. 76 p23
1388. *Christian Standard* Aug. 31 80 p3
1389. *Congregationalist* Feb. 74 p7
1390. *Christianity Today* May 4 79 p36
1391. *Wesleyan Advocate* Sept. 3 79 p16
1392. *Presbyterian Journal* Mar. 10 76 p13

1393. *Pentecostal Evangel* June 29 69 p10
1394. *Evangel* July 26 76 p31
1395. *Emphasis On Faith And Living* Oct. 1 80 p7
1396. *New Catholic World* Sept.–Oct. 80 p224
1397. *American Opinion* Jan. 81 p37
1398. *Motivational Quotes*/Graphicenter/ 1984 p5
1399. *Presbyterian Journal* Aug. 2 78 p11
1400. *Wesleyan Advocate* Jan. 5 76 p20
1401. *Daily Study Bible*/John/p18
1402. *Christianity Today* June 20 75 p20
1403. *Vital Christianity* Feb. 21 71 p5
1404. *Christianity Today* Feb. 27 76 p46
1405. *America* Mar. 26 83 p228
1406. *Presbyterian Journal* Jan. 21 76 p7
1407. Editor's Files
1408. *American Opinion* Sept. 75 p29
1409. *American Opinion* May 77 p29
1410. *American Opinion* Nov. 76 p39
1411. *Wesleyan Advocate* June 20 83 p7
1412. *Pentecostal Evangel* June 27 76 p31
1413. *Daily Study Bible*/John/p222
1414. *Herald Of Holiness* July 1 82 p5
1415. *American Opinion* Mar. 77 p37
1416. *American Opinion* Apr. 83 p39
1417. *Church Herald* June 26 81 p10
1418. *Christian Ministry* Jan. 79 p26
1419. *Herald Of Holiness* May 7 75 p5
1420. *Banner* Jan. 12 81 p11
1421. *Daily Study Bible*/John/p193
1422. *Christianity Today* Sept. 23 77 p14
1423. *Church Herald* Sept. 7 79 p15
1424. *Wesleyan Advocate* Feb. 2 81 p4
1425. *Wesleyan Advocate* Dec. 8 75 p9
1426. *Wesleyan Advocate* Nov. 8 76 p6
1427. *Journal Of Medicine And Philosophy* June 78 p135
1428. *Banner* Mar. 11 77 p5
1429. *Emphasis On Faith And Living* Aug. 81 p5
1430. Editor's Files
1431. *Pentecostal Evangel* Aug. 24 75 p21
1432. *Christian Home* Sept. 71 p14
1433. *Presbyterian Journal* Aug. 15 79 p14
1434. *Pentecostal Evangel* Aug. 10 75 p10
1435. Editor's Files
1436. *Christian Ministry* Nov. 76 p31
1437. *Zygon* Dec. 84 p445
1438. Editor's Files
1439. *Link* Dec. 67 p40
1440. *Herald Of Holiness* May 7 75 p5
1441. *Christian Herald* Nov. 75 p24
1442. *Alliance Witness* Sept. 5 79 p5

1443. *Pentecostal Evangel* Aug. 26 84 p14
1444. Editor's Files
1445. *American Opinion* Apr. 77 p31
1446. *His* Oct. 71 p32
1447. *Lutheran Standard* Oct. 7 80 p26
1448. *Presbyterian Journal* Oct. 17 79 p10
1449. *Chelsea Journal* Nov. Dec. 77 p292
1450. *Vital Christianity* Sept. 21 75 p11
1451. Editor's Files
1452. Editor's Files
1453. *These Times* Dec. 70 p5
1454. *Emphasis On Faith And Living* Feb. 1 79 p3
1455. *War Cry* Aug. 11 84 p3
1456. *Emphasis On Faith And Living* Nov. 1 80 p3
1457. *Pentecostal Evangel* Oct. 8 78 p6
1458. *Emphasis On Faith And Living* Nov. 15 79 p3
1459. *Theology Today* July 79 p162
1460. Editor's Files
1461. *Banner* May 6 77 p7
1462. *American Opinion* Mar. 77 p112
1463. *Presbyterian Journal* Apr. 30 75 p13
1464. *The Complete Toastmaster/ H. V. Prochnow* p254
1465. *Preacher's Magazine* Mar. 86 p18
1466. *Herald Of Holiness* Jan. 1 76 p7
1467. *Pentecostal Evangel* Aug. 2 70 p4
1468. Editor's Files
1469. *Presbyterian Journal* Mar. 15 78 p3
1470. *Banner* Apr. 20 79 p9
1471. *Christian Home* Oct. 77 p23
1472. *Christian Home* Aug. 77 p8
1473. *Christian Home* July 78 p6
1474. *Lutheran* Feb. 16 77 p3
1475. *Church Herald* Feb. 4 77 p14
1476. *Link* Apr. 69 p13
1477. *Pentecostal Evangel* Oct. 30 77 p2
1478. Editor's Files
1479. *Alliance Witness* July 28 76 p10
1480. *American Opinion* Oct. 75 p27
1481. Editor's Files
1482. *Christian Standard* Aug. 13 78 p3
1483. *Christian Home* Sept. 78 p19
1484. *Eternity* Apr. 77 p39
1485. *Lutheran* May 3 78 p3
1486. *American Opinion* Dec. 75 p45
1487. *Christian Home* Aug. 77 p23
1488. *Vital Christianity* Sept. 21 75 p11
1489. Editor's Files
1490. *Christian Ministry* Sept. 80 p27
1491. *Christian Herald* June 77 p26
1492. *Lutheran* Jan. 5 77 p3
1493. *Lutheran* July 14 76 p3
1494. *Lutheran* Mar. 2 77 p3
1495. *America* Oct. 6 79 p173
1496. *Link* Aug. 69 p58
1497. *Link* July 72 p55
1498. Editor's Files
1499. *Link* Dec. 72 p63
1500. *Pentecostal Evangel* Sept. 18 77 p2
1501. Editor's Files
1502. Editor's Files
1503. *Michigan Catholic* Feb. 13 81 p4
1504. *Lutheran* Oct. 3 79 p3
1505. *Emphasis On Faith And Living* Oct. 15 79 p3
1506. *Lutheran* Jan. 17 79 p3
1507. *Preacher's Magazine* Mar. 78 p44
1508. *Preacher's Magazine* Mar. 78 p45
1509. *Daedalus* Winter 75 p278
1510. Editor's Files
1511. *Ecumenical Review* Jan. 76 p66
1512. *American Opinion* Mar. 74 p96
1513. *Link* Dec. 74 p47
1514. Editor's Files
1515. Editor's Files
1516. *Vital Christianity* Feb. 1 76 p3
1517. *American Opinion* Mar. 79 p35
1518. *Lutheran* Oct. 5 77 p3
1519. *Link* Apr. 72 p43
1520. *Christian Advocate* Feb. 17 72 p11
1521. *Presbyterian Journal* Jan. 10 79 p15
1522. Editor's Files
1523. *Good News Broadcaster* Mar. 80 p4
1524. *Christian Reader* Mar. 77 p21
1525. *American Opinion* Nov. 71 p48
1526. *Lutheran* Dec. 1 76 p3
1527. *American Opinion* Nov. 70 p70
1528. Editor's Files
1529. *Pentecostal Evangel* Oct. 16 77 p7
1530. Editor's Files
1531. *Pentecostal Evangel* Sept. 18 77 p2
1532. Editor's Files
1533. *Emphasis On Faith And Living* Apr. 15 80 p3
1534. Editor's Files
1535. *American Opinion* Jan. 81 p37
1536. *Moody Monthly* July 74 p63
1537. *His* Jan. 86 p4
1538. *Link* Dec. 71 p37
1539. Editor's Files
1540. Editor's Files
1541. Editor's Files
1542. *Encyclopedia Of Religious Quotations* 1965 p273
1543. *Encyclopedia Of Religious Quotations* 1965 p273
1544. Editor's Files

1545. Editor's Files
1546. *Evangel* Dec. 22 75 p25
1547. *Lutheran Standard* Jan. 19 71 p7
1548. *Daily Study Bible/Ephesians*/p164
1549. Editor's Files
1550. *Christianity Today* Sept. 23 77 p14
1551. Editor's Files
1552. *Vital Christianity* Dec. 11 77 p6
1553. *Moody Monthly* Jan. 75 p47
1554. *U.S. Catholic* June 79 p6
1555. *Journal Of Religion And Health* Apr. 79 p139
1556. *Mennonite* Sept. 23 75 p525
1557. *Christian Herald* June 75 p20
1558. *Religious Humanism* Winter 80 p37
1559. Editor's Files
1560. *1001 Inspirational Things*/p131
1561. *Emphasis On Faith And Living* Feb. 15 79 p8
1562. Editor's Files
1563. *Chelsea Journal* Sept.–Oct. 78 p262
1564. Editor's Files
1565. *Chelsea Journal* Jan.–Feb. 76 p19
1566. *Christian Standard* Dec. 19 82 p10
1567. *Vital Christianity* Feb. 11 79 p12
1568. *Eternity* May 75 p27
1569. *Church Herald* Apr. 20 79 p17
1570. Editor's Files
1571. *Vital Christianity* Feb. 11 79 p14
1572. *Lutheran* Nov. 15 78 p9
1573. *Humanist* Jan.–Feb. 79 p43
1574. *Secret Country of C. S. Lewis*/p109
1575. Editor's Files
1576. *Preachers's Magazine* Sept. 78 p63
1577. *Christian Standard* Nov. 14 76 p9
1578. *Pentecostal Evangel* July 20 80 p2
1579. *Congregationalist* July–Aug. 77 p21
1580. *Messenger* Sept. 1 71 p21
1581. *Wesleyan Advocate* Apr. 26 76 p19
1582. *Pentecostal Evangel* Feb. 1 81 p14
1583. *Christian Herald* Apr. 78 p42
1584. *His* Jan. 80 p8
1585. *Lutheran* May 18 77 p12
1586. *U.S. Catholic* Nov. 75 p19
1587. *Herald Of Holiness* Mar. 1 86 p9
1588. *Christian Ministry* May 78 p17
1589. *Wesleyan Advocate* Jan. 16 84 p9
1590. Editor's Files
1591. Editor's Files
1592. *Wesleyan Advocate* Nov. 19 79 p10
1593. *Evangel* Feb. 9 81 p27
1594. *Church Herald* Sept. 8 78 p3
1595. Editor's Files
1596. *Christian Herald* Feb. 82 p48
1597. *Link* Nov. 66 p58
1598. *Christian Standard* Feb. 16 86 p16
1599. Editor's Files
1600. *Moody Monthly* Feb. 78 p57
1601. *Christian Standard* Aug. 13 78 p14
1602. *Link* Dec. 73 p39
1603. *Pentecostal Evangel* May 25 75 p7
1604. Editor's Files
1605. Editor's Files
1606. *Pentecostal Evangel* Oct. 12 80 p2
1607. *Wesleyan Advocate* July 5 76 p6
1608. *Presbyterian Journal* Aug. 29 79 p11
1609. *Christian Reader* Mar.–Apr. 75 p72
1610. *A Reader's Notebook/Kennedy* p168
1611. Editor's Files
1612. *Presbyterian Journal* Mar. 10 76 p8
1613. *Daily Study Bible/John*/p45
1614. *Good News Broadcaster* Apr. 71 p26
1615. *Pentecostal Evangel* June 11 78 p31
1616. *Daily Study Bible/Barclay*
1617. *Soundings* Spring 80 p7
1618. *Chelsea Journal* Jan.–Feb. 76 p19
1619. *Wesleyan Advocate* Feb. 2 76 p13
1620. *Moody Monthly* Sept. 75 p132
1621. *Moody Monthly* Nov. 76 p58
1622. *His* Nov. 75 p32
1623. *United Evangelical Action* Spring 76 p15
1624. *Christian Reader* Jan. 85 p76
1625. *Worldview* June 76 p32
1626. *Herald Of Holiness* July 15 82 p12
1627. *Daedalus* Spring 78 p61
1628. *Critic* Fall 76 p31
1629. *American Opinion* Dec. 75 p45
1630. Editor's Files
1631. *Christian Ministry* Mar. 86 p27
1632. Editor's Files
1633. *Moody Monthly* Feb. 76 p46
1634. Editor's Files
1635. *Theology Today* July 79 p175
1636. *Daily Study Bible/Corinthians*/p110
1637. *Christian Home* Spring 85 p60
1638. *Christian Home* Winter 85 p57
1639. *Banner* Mar. 17 86 p13
1640. *Journal Of Religion And Health* Jan. 79 p39
1641. *Pentecostal Evangel* Oct. 12 75 p19
1642. *Pentecostal Evangel* Oct. 12 75 p19
1643. *Christian Standard* June 5 83 p3
1644. Editor's Files
1645. *Pentecostal Evangel* Sept. 5 76 p4
1646. *Pentecostal Evangel* June 1 80 p2
1647. *Moody Monthly* June 75 p86
1648. *These Times* Oct. 75 p8
1649. *Moody Monthly* Sept. 75 p74
1650. *Pentecostal Evangel* Feb. 29 76 p2
1651. *Pentecostal Testimony* Sept. 84 p19

1652. *Journal Of Psychology And Theology* Fall 75 p246
1653. *Emphasis On Faith And Living* Apr. 85 p6
1654. *Jewish Spectator* Spring 75 p48
1655. *Church Herald* Oct. 13 72 p13
1656. *American Scholar* Winter 75–76 p807
1657. *Christian Standard* June 5 83 p3
1658. *Christianity Today* Mar. 26 76 p46
1659. *Commonweal* Feb. 27 76 p140
1660. *Lutheran* Oct. 20 76 p15
1661. *Commonweal* Feb. 27 76 p140
1662. *Christian Home* Sept. 77 p23
1663. *America* Aug. 25 79 p81
1664. *Lutheran* Nov. 5 75 p15
1665. *Church Herald* Nov. 26 76 p10
1666. *Alliance Witness* Oct. 19 77 p9
1667. Editor's Files
1668. *Banner* July 23 76 p16
1669. Editor's Files
1670. *Zygon* June 78 p151
1671. *Christian Reader* May 85 p21
1672. *Christian Century* Sept. 26 79 p916
1673. *Church Herald* Sept. 17 82 p10
1674. *U.S. Catholic* Oct. 81 p11
1675. *Christian Century* June 9 76 p555
1676. *Christian Standard* Nov. 14 82 p8
1677. Editor's Files
1678. Editor's Files
1679. Editor's Files
1680. *Liguorian* Dec. 80 p65
1681. *Alliance Witness* Jan. 10 79 p31
1682. *These Times* Oct. 75 p4
1683. *Canadian Catholic Review* Feb. 85 p21
1684. *Canadian Catholic Review* Feb. 85 p19
1685. *United Evangelical Action* Summer 78 p6
1686. *Congregationalist* Jan. 79 p5
1687. *American Scholar* Winter 75–76 p767
1688. Editor's Files
1689. *Pentecostal Evangel* Aug. 14 83 p16
1690. *Catholic Mind* May 75 p14
1691. *Daily Study Bible/Barclay*
1692. *Christian Reader* Nov. 79 p19
1693. *Encounter* Spring 75 p131
1694. *Daily Study Bible/John/p211*
1695. *Wesleyan Advocate* July 4 77 p15
1696. *Pentecostal Evangel* July 15 79 p14
1697. *Eternity* Mar. 75 p50
1698. *Mennonite* July 6 76 p430
1699. *Wesleyan Advocate* Oct. 3 83 p3
1700. *Vital Christianity* Jan. 18 76 p3
1701. *Christian Standard* July 20 80 p13
1702. *Moody Monthly* June 74 p29
1703. *Church Herald* Mar. 21 75 p9
1704. *Pentecostal Evangel* July 30 78 p2

1705. *American Opinion* Feb. 80 p31
1706. *Link* Dec. 71 p45
1707. *Pentecostal Evangel* Oct. 11 81 p30
1708. *United Evangelical Action* Summer 79 p23
1709. *These Times* July 80 p23
1710. *Presbyterian Journal* Feb. 18 76 p9
1711. *Christianity Today* June 6 75 p12
1712. *Lutheran* Apr. 18 79 p3
1713. *Preacher's Magazine* Sept. 78 p63
1714. *Church Herald* May 4 84 p5
1715. *Herald Of Holiness* Apr. 23 75 p12
1716. *Christian Century* Feb. 19 75 p161
1717. *Pentecostal Evangel* July 11 76 p32
1718. *Christianity Today* 4 77 p24
1719. *War Cry* Mar. 30 85 p9
1720. *Christianity Today* Oct. 10 75 p34
1721. *Humanist* Jan.–Feb. 79 p35
1722. Editor's Files
1723. *Wesleyan Advocate* Nov. 24 75 p16
1724. *Church Herald* Jan. 21 83 p6
1725. Editor's Files
1726. Editor's Files
1727. *Christian Standard* Apr. 28 85 p16
1728. *Pentecostal Evangel* July 15 79 p14
1729. Editor's Files
1730. Editor's Files
1731. *Presbyterian Journal* Aug. 29 79 p11
1732. *Pentecostal Evangel* Oct. 9 83 p2
1733. *Christian Reader* Nov. 79 p18
1734. *Christian Herald* July 83 p57
1735. *Episcopal Recorder* June 78 p9
1736. Editor's Files
1737. Editor's Files
1738. *Wesleyan Advocate* Apr. 7 86 p6
1739. *Lutheran Standard* Apr. 18 86 p13
1740. *Banner* Aug. 13 84 p7
1741. Editor's Files
1742. *Daily Study Bible/Ephesians/p162*
1743. Editor's Files
1744. *War Cry* Nov. 9 85 p11
1745. *Christian Herald* June 77 p48
1746. *Link* Dec. 71 p31
1747. Editor's Files
1748. *Presbyterian Journal* June 20 79 p21
1749. *1001 Inspirational Things/p258*
1750. *Good News Broadcaster* June 75 p40
1751. *Pentecostal Evangel* Aug. 17 75 p32
1752. *Christian Century* Apr. 7 76 p328
1753. *Herald Of Holiness* Apr. 10 74 p13
1754. *Christianity Today* Nov. 11 83 p40
1755. *Mennonite* Feb. 17 76 p106
1756. *Evangel* Mar. 8 76 p7
1757. *Preacher's Magazine* Sept. 79 p30
1758. *Psychology Today* Sept. 80 p33

1759. *Pentecostal Evangel* Aug. 10 75 p10
1760. *Presbyterian Journal* Mar. 10 76 p7
1761. *Mennonite* Feb. 17 76 p106
1762. *War Cry* Feb. 23 85 p8
1763. *Lutheran* May 77 p3
1764. *America* Mar. 13 76 p197
1765. *Christian Standard* Feb. 16 86 p16
1766. *Ministry* Jan. 80 p21
1767. *Alliance Witness* June 15 77 p5
1768. *Link* Dec. 67 p56
1769. *Lutheran* July 78 p5
1770. Editor's Files
1771. Editor's Files
1772. *Daily Study Bible/Corinthians/*p95
1773. *Christian Standard* Mar. 20 83 p10
1774. *Christian Standard* Mar. 20 83 p10
1775. *Christian Reader* Mar. 83 p59
1776. *Evangel* Mar. 12 79 p13
1777. *Herald Of Holiness* Sept. 25 74 p18
1778. *Vital Christianity* June 4 78 p1
1779. *Good News Broadcaster* Feb. 81 p5
1780. *Presbyterian Journal* Aug. 16 78 p12
1781. *Episcopal Recorder* Apr. 77 p7
1782. *Baptist Bulletin* May 76 p17
1783. *His* Feb. 75 p24
1784. Editor's Files
1785. *His* June 85 p32
1786. *Pentecostal Evangel* Nov. 20 77 p9
1787. *American Opinion* Mar. 77 p37
1788. *Christian Standard* Sept. 8 85 p14
1789. *Light From Many Lamps/Watson* p18
1790. *Pentecostal Evangel* Nov. 20 77 p9
1791. *His* June 85 p32
1792. *His* June 79 p22
1793. *Pentecostal Evangel* Nov. 20 77 p10
1794. Editor's Files
1795. *Vital Christianity* Sept. 16 73 p3
1796. *Journal Of Ecclesiastical History* Jan. 78 p87
1797. Editor's Files
1798. *U.S. Catholic* Apr. 70 p33
1799. Editor's Files
1800. *Christianity Today* Aug. 8 75 p22
1801. *Christian Reader* Mar. 86 p10
1802. *American Opinion* Mar. 77 p37
1803. *American Opinion* Dec. 76 p24
1804. *United Evangelical Action* Spring 75 p8
1805. *New Catholic World* Nov.–Dec. 77 p283
1806. *Christian Herald* May 76 p86
1807. *Christian Home* Mar. 77 p13
1808. *Christian Standard* June 13 76 p8
1809. *Evangel* Apr. 27 81 p5
1810. *Christian Standard* Sept. 5 76 p12
1811. *Pentecostal Evangel* May 9 82 p3
1812. *Good News Broadcaster* May 71 p20
1813. Editor's Files

1814. *U.S. Catholic* Nov. 77 p8
1815. Editor's Files
1816. *Baptist Bulletin* Sept. 78 p13
1817. *Christian Century* Oct. 1 75 p863
1818. Editor's Files
1819. *Pentecostal Testimony* Mar. 86 p12
1820. *Evangel* Aug. 25 75 p25
1821. *Banner* Sept. 3 76 p17
1822. *Lutheran* Nov. 17 76 p3
1823. *Christianity Today* June 18 76 p14
1824. *Pentecostal Evangel* Sept. 1 85 p5
1825. *Pentecostal Evangel* Jan. 8 78 p31
1826. *Mennonite* Mar. 27 79 p240
1827. *Pentecostal Evangel* Jan. 8 78 p31
1828. *Religion In Life* Autumn 76 p296
1829. *Banner* Oct. 11 82 p23
1830. *Banner* June 6 75 p15
1831. *Christian Standard* Sept. 3 78 p7
1832. *Good News Broadcaster* Nov. 82 p38
1833. Editor's Files
1834. *These Times* Oct. 70 p33
1835. *U.S. Catholic* July 75 p6
1836. Editor's Files
1837. *Link* Dec. 71 p31
1838. *Faith For The Family* Nov.–Dec. 76 p5
1839. *American Opinion* Apr. 83 p39
1840. *Presbyterian Journal* Feb. 18 76 p9
1841. *Vital Christianity* June 13 76 p16
1842. *Presbyterian Journal* Feb. 18 76 p16
1843. *American Opinion* Oct. 76 p37
1844. Editor's Files
1845. *Presbyterian Journal* Oct. 31 79 p10
1846. *Presbyterian Journal* Jan. 13 82 p15
1847. *Worldview* Nov. 82 p7
1848. *Presbyterian Journal* Mar. 10 76 p11
1849. *Christian Herald* Nov. 75 p24
1850. *Presbyterian Journal* Aug. 13 75 p7
1851. *Herald Of Holiness* Dec. 3 75 p3
1852. *Christian Standard* Jan. 28 79 p2
1853. *American Issue* July–Aug. 76 p1
1854. *Jewish Spectator* Fall 82 p55
1855. *Presbyterian Journal* Aug. 20 75 p12
1856. *New Catholic World* Mar.–Apr. 76 p60
1857. *Alliance Witness* July 11 79 p5
1858. *Banner* May 26 78 p13
1859. *Christian Reader* Apr.–May 71 p29
1860. *Pentecostal Evangel* Sept. 28 75 p21
1861. *War Cry* Feb. 19 72 p24
1862. *American Opinion* Apr. 75 p76
1863. *Episcopal Recorder* June 76 p4
1864. Editor's Files
1865. *Religious Humanism* Winter 75 p24
1866. *Pentecostal Evangel* July 16 78 p15
1867. *Christian Century* Dec. 30 81 p1375
1868. Editor's Files
1869. *Pentecostal Evangel* Jan. 6 74 p2

1870. *Wesleyan Advocate* Dec. 20 76 p1
1871. *Vital Christianity* Feb. 15 76 p10
1872. *Presbyterian Journal* Dec. 29 82 p13
1873. *Pentecostal Evangel* Dec. 28 75 p4
1874. Editor's Files
1875. *Evangel* Jan. 14 80 p27
1876. *Christian Herald* Jan. 79 p15
1877. *Christian Herald* May 77 p48
1878. *Mennonite* Nov. 1 77 p627
1879. *Herald Of Holiness* Apr. 9 75 p14
1880. *Lutheran* Mar. 16 77 p3
1881. *Pentecostal Evangel* Dec. 28 75 p12
1882. *Emphasis On Faith And Living*
      Apr. 15 79 p3
1883. *Daily Study Bible/Hebrews/*p206
1884. *Herald Of Holiness* June 4 75 p10
1885. *Alliance Witness* Nov. 26 80 p6
1886. *Daily Study Bible/Barclay*
1887. *Herald Of Holiness* Feb. 1 81 p11
1888. *Daily Study Bible/Barclay*
1889. *Pentecostal Evangel* Aug. 1 76 p14
1890. *Wesleyan Advocate* Sept. 17 79 p4
1891. *Moody Monthly* July 80 p53
1892. *Presbyterian Journal* June 2 76 p13
1893. Editor's Files
1894. *A Reader's Notebook/Kennedy* p197
1895. *Link* Oct. 72 p63
1896. *War Cry* June 29 85 p9
1897. *Wesleyan Advocate* Mar. 15 76 p9
1898. *Alliance Witness* July 28 76 p10
1899. Editor's Files
1900. *Pentecostal Evangel* Jan. 14 79 p31
1901. *Pentecostal Evangel* Jan. 14 79 p13
1902. *Evangel* Jan. 9 78 p13
1903. *Christianity Today* Apr. 21 78 p15
1904. *Vital Christianity* Aug. 29 76 p17
1905. *American Scholar* Winter 77–78 p52
1906. *Wesleyan Advocate* May 12 75 p10
1907. *Link* Nov. 71 p39
1908. *Christian Herald* Oct. 80 p70
1909. *Motivational Quotes/Graphicenter/*p85
1910. *Motivational Quotes/Graphicenter/*p16
1911. *War Cry* Feb. 1 86 p9
1912. *Motivational Quotes/Graphicenter/*p11
1913. *Quiet Hour Echoes* July 85 p3
1914. *American Opinion* Oct. 70 p73
1915. *Christianity Today* Jan. 13 78 p31
1916. *American Opinion* Sept. 76 p37
1917. *Banner* Sept. 28 81 p8
1918. *A Reader's Notebook/Kennedy* p201
1919. *Banner* May 7 76 p17
1920. *Christian Reader* Nov.–Dec. 75 p78
1921. *Journal Of Psychology And Theology*
      Spring 77 p145
1922. *Catholic Mind* Oct. 78 p39
1923. *Theology Today* July 75 p380

1924. *Pentecostal Evangel* July 12 81 p4
1925. *Christian Home* Aug. 77 p5
1926. *Presbyterian Journal* Jan. 10 79 p12
1927. *Christian Reader* Sept. Oct. 76 p51
1928. *Alliance Witness* Nov. 30 77 p9
1929. *Herald Of Holiness* June 15 83 p12
1930. *Ministry* Dec. 78 p6
1931. *Presbyterian Journal* Apr. 5 72 p8
1932. *Baptist Bulletin* Jan. 76 p13
1933. *Pentecostal Evangel* June 27 76 p19
1934. *Link* Apr. 69 p58
1935. *Church Herald* Aug. 8 75 p12
1936. *Pentecostal Evangel* June 12 83 p30
1937. *Vital Christianity* Dec. 14 75 p16
1938. *Daedalus* Fall 81 p145
1939. *Eternity* Aug. 76 p43
1940. *Good News Broadcaster*
      June 78 p9
1941. *War Cry* Feb. 15 86 p22
1942. *Episcopal Recorder* Oct. 77 p3
1943. *Banner* Sept. 8 80 p15
1944. *Moody Monthly* June 76 p28
1945. *Pentecostal Evangel* May 7 78 p15
1946. *Wesleyan Advocate* Sept. 27 76 p6
1947. *Pentecostal Evangel* June 12 77 p8
1948. *Christianity Today* May 9 75 p5
1949. *Banner* Sept. 5 75 p5
1950. *Wesleyan Advocate* Jan. 6 86 p6
1951. *Christian Home* May 74 p11
1952. *Pentecostal Evangel* June 13 76 p2
1953. Editor's Files
1954. Editor's Files
1955. *Moody Monthly* June 81 p43
1956. Editor's Files
1957. Editor's Files
1958. Editor's Files
1959. Editor's Files
1960. Editor's Files
1961. *American Opinion* Mar. 76 p15
1962. *Pentecostal Evangel* Oct. 1 78 p2
1963. *Wesleyan Advocate* Mar. 15 76 p9
1964. *Today's Education* Sept. 72 p64
1965. *Theology Today* July 76 p168
1966. *Mennonite* May 31 77 p368
1967. *Pentecostal Evangel* Sept. 30 79 p10
1968. *Presbyterian Journal* June 8 83 p13
1969. *Cross Currents* Winter 75 p413
1970. *Cross Currents* Winter 75 p411
1971. Editor's Files
1972. *Christianity Today* May 8 81 p21
1973. Editor's Files
1974. *Pentecostal Evangel* July 27 75 p11
1975. *Pentecostal Evangel* May 26 85 p8
1976. *Lutheran Witness* July 79 p3
1977. *American Opinion* Jan. 83 p29
1978. *Christian Herald* July–Aug. 76 p48

1979. *Wesleyan Advocate* Feb. 13 78 p1
1980. *Presbyterian Journal* Jan. 16 80 p10
1981. *Lutheran* Jan. 16 80 p3
1982. *Humanist* Mar.–Apr. 78 p37
1983. *Pentecostal Evangel* Nov. 16 75 p3
1984. *Wesleyan Advocate* June 23 75 p8
1985. *Daily Study Bible/John/*p136
1986. *Presbyterian Journal* Dec. 4 74 p13
1987. *Christian Standard* Feb. 17 80 p13
1988. *Pentecostal Evangel* Jan. 28 79 p2
1989. *Christian Herald* June 77 p48
1990. *Emphasis On Faith And Living*
      Mar. 83 p14
1991. *Herald Of Holiness* Feb. 1 85 p9
1992. *Herald Of Holiness* Nov. 6 74 p4
1993. *Alliance Witness* June 8 84 p6
1994. *Christian Herald* May 76 p76
1995. *Herald Of Holiness* Feb. 1 84 p6
1996. *Nazarene Preacher* Oct. 64 p11
1997. Editor's Files
1998. *Christian Standard* Oct. 7 79 p3
1999. *Episcopal Recorder* July 78 p19
2000. *Banner* Apr. 15 85 p17
2001. *Daily Study Bible/Hebrews/*p160
2002. *His* Feb. 81 p26
2003. *Banner* Feb. 27 76 p3
2004. *Banner* Mar. 31 78 p20
2005. *Presbyterian Journal* Mar. 17 76 p11
2006. *A.D.* Feb. 76 p32
2007. *Good News Broadcaster* Nov. 76 p24
2008. *Presbyterian Journal* Dec. 11 74 p11
2009. *Pentecostal Testimony* Mar. 86 p3
2010. Editor's Files
2011. *Baptist Bulletin* Nov. 75 p8
2012. *Wesleyan Advocate* Mar. 27 78 p10
2013. *Episcopal Recorder* July 78 p19
2014. *Baptist Bulletin* Mar. 72 p18
2015. *Mennonite* Apr. 11 78 p245
2016. Editor's Files
2017. *1001 Inspirational Things* p258
2018. *Christian Home* Mar. 78 p24
2019. Editor's Files
2020. *America* Mar. 29 75 p233
2021. *American Opinion* Nov. 74 p21
2022. *Christian Herald* Nov. 70 p33
2023. *Presbyterian Journal* Dec. 8 82 p11
2024. *Christian Herald* Mar. 75 p12
2025. *Presbyterian Journal* Mar. 9 77 p23
2026. Editor's Files
2027. *Pentecostal Evangel* Oct. 24 76 p7
2028. *American Opinion* Feb. 75 p36
2029. *American Opinion* Sept. 75 p29
2030. *Evangel* Apr. 12 76 p11
2031. *Vital Christianity* Nov. 2 75 p10
2032. *These Times* May 71 p5

2033. *American Opinion* Jan. 83 p29
2034. *Daedalus* Fall 81 p1
2035. *American Opinion* Dec. 79 p35
2036. *Lutheran* Mar. 16 77 p3
2037. *American Opinion* Apr. 73 p75
2038. *American Opinion* Nov. 76 p39
2039. *American Opinion* Feb. 80 p31
2040. *Daedalus* Fall 78 p57
2041. *Christian Standard* Oct. 27 75 p8
2042. Editor's Files
2043. *Center Magazine* May–June 75 p3
2044. *Good News Broadcaster* July–Aug.
      78 p4
2045. *Encounter* Spring 77 p96
2046. *Link* Apr. 69 p41
2047. *American Opinion* May 76 p29
2048. *Commentary* June 75 p70
2049. *American Opinion* Oct. 75 p27
2050. *Wesleyan Advocate* Oct. 11 76 p14
2051. *Eternity* Apr. 84 p36
2052. *American Opinion* May 77 p30
2053. *American Opinion* Jan. 81 p37
2054. *American Opinion* Nov. 75 p29
2055. *American Opinion* Dec. 76 p23
2056. *Presbyterian Journal* Oct. 16 74 p10
2057. *American Opinion* Nov. 83 p110
2058. *Christian Standard* Feb. 8 81 p7
2059. *Banner* Sept. 12 75 p17
2060. *American Opinion* Mar. 76 p15
2061. *Banner* Sept. 22 78 p17
2062. *Christian Century* Dec. 11 74 p1164
2063. *Christianity Today* Sept. 7 84 p13
2064. *Midstream* Jan. 78 p27
2065. *Zygon* Dec. 76 p361
2066. Editor's Files
2067. *Christian Century* Feb. 26 75 p196
2068. *American Opinion* July–Aug. 75 p159
2069. *American Opinion* Oct. 75 p40
2070. Editor's Files
2071. *Christianity Today* Oct. 10 75 p21
2072. *Christian Standard* Dec. 21 75 p7
2073. *U.S. Catholic* Aug. 76 p14
2074. *Christian Standard* Oct. 17 76 p8
2075. *Emphasis On Faith And Living*
      July 84 p7
2076. *Vital Christianity* Aug. 15 76 p1
2077. *Presbyterian Journal* Jan. 12 77 p8
2078. *Moody Monthly* Feb. 76 p82
2079. *Lutheran* Apr. 2 80 p6
2080. *Pentecostal Evangel* Nov. 28 76 p7
2081. Editor's Files
2082. *Faith For The Family* Feb. 81 p13
2083. Editor's Files
2084. *Wesleyan Advocate* Sept. 29 75 p10
2085. *Pentecostal Evangel* Nov. 18 79 p5

2086. *His* Mar. 77 p4
2087. Editor's Files
2088. *Mennonite* June 21 83 p293
2089. *Herald Of Holiness* Apr. 15 78 p12
2090. *Wesleyan Advocate* Feb. 28 77 p3
2091. *Christian Reader* Sept.–Oct. 76 p6
2092. *Evangel* Apr. 28 75 p17
2093. *Herald Of Holiness* Jan. 15 76 p17
2094. *Herald Of Holiness* Aug. 1 80 p7
2095. *Pentecostal Evangel* Sept. 27 81 p30
2096. *Wesleyan Advocate* Feb. 6 84 p7
2097. *Wesleyan Advocate* Mar. 14 77 p13
2098. *His* Nov. 80 p32
2099. *Presbyterian Journal* June 28 78 p19
2100. *Evangel* Jan. 13 86 p7
2101. *Moody Monthly* Nov. 75 p155
2102. *Pentecostal Evangel* July 1 73 p11
2103. *Christian Life* Jan. 74 p70
2104. *U.S. Catholic* Nov. 83 p37
2105. *Pentecostal Testimony* Jan. 86 p12
2106. *Wesleyan Advocate* May 4 81 p15
2107. *A.D.* Mar. 75 p28
2108. *Herald Of Holiness* Dec. 15 78 p14
2109. *Wesleyan Advocate* July 19 76 p12
2110. *Alliance Witness* Apr. 6 77 p3
2111. *Pentecostal Evangel* Jan. 6 85 p5
2112. *Vital Christianity* Oct. 5 75 p25
2113. *Christian Herald* Apr. 79 p53
2114. *His* Apr. 80 p18
2115. *Pentecostal Evangel* Jan. 4 76 p2
2116. *Presbyterian Life* Apr. 1 65 p2
2117. *Lutheran Standard* Apr. 3 81 p28
2118. *Wesleyan Advocate* Oct. 6 80 p6
2119. *U.S. Catholic* Oct. 78 p16
2120. Editor's Files
2121. *Lutheran* Apr. 5 78 p3
2122. Editor's Files
2123. *Alliance Witness* July 2 75 p5
2124. *Pentecostal Testimony* Jan. 86 p13
2125. *Christian Herald* Jan. 83 p22
2126. *Christian Standard* Jan. 11 76 p6
2127. *America* Mar. 15 80 p208
2128. *Church Herald* Oct. 28 77 p10
2129. *Christianity Today* Nov. 19 76 p21
2130. *Pentecostal Evangel* July 1 84 p4
2131. *Presbyterian Journal* Aug. 14 74 p10
2132. *Emphasis On Faith And Living* May 82 p23
2133. *Alliance Witness* Feb. 23 77 p7
2134. *Wesleyan Advocate* July 31 78 p14
2135. *Christian Herald* Jan. 83 p22
2136. *Alliance Witness* Mar. 12 86 p16
2137. *Wesleyan Advocate* May 16 83 p12
2138. *Pulpit* Oct. 64 p14
2139. *Wesleyan Advocate* Mar. 17 86 p13

2140. *Good News Broadcaster* June 81 p3
2141. *Herald Of Holiness* Oct. 25 67 p11
2142. *Church Herald* July 26 74 p6
2143. *Banner* Nov. 28 75 p3
2144. *Christian Herald* Feb. 78 p58
2145. *Pentecostal Evangel* Aug. 26 79 p31
2146. *U.S. Catholic* Oct. 78 p14
2147. *War Cry* Feb. 2 85 p3
2148. *Pentecostal Evangel* Dec. 28 75 p8
2149. *Christian Herald* Aug. 75 p38
2150. *Wesleyan Advocate* Feb. 13 78 p4
2151. *Lutheran* Nov. 2 77 p3
2152. Editor's Files
2153. Editor's Files
2154. Editor's Files
2155. *A.D.* Jan. 75 p32
2156. *Good News Broadcaster* Mar. 80 p9
2157. *Christianity Today* Sept. 23 77 p19
2158. *Christian Ministry* Mar. 75 p24
2159. *Vital Christianity* Oct. 19 75 p10
2160. *Christian Standard* May 20 84 p15
2161. *Christian Ministry* Mar. 75 p6
2162. *Herald Of Holiness* Dec. 3 75 p4
2163. *Pentecostal Testimony* Apr. 83 p7
2164. *Presbyterian Journal* Jan. 26 72 p17
2165. *Religious Humanism* Winter 76 p34
2166. *Moody Monthly* July–Aug. 76 p93
2167. *Wesleyan Advocate* Nov. 21 77 p14
2168. *Pentecostal Testimony* May 83 p4
2169. *Presbyterian Journal* Nov. 17 76 p11
2170. *Wesleyan Advocate* May 17 71 p10
2171. *Emphasis On Faith And Living* Sept. 81 p15
2172. *Congregationalist* Feb. 75 p11
2173. *Faith For The Family* Apr. 77 p9
2174. *Wesleyan Advocate* Mar. 14 77 p15
2175. *Banner* May 16 75 p11
2176. *Mennonite* Nov. 11 75 p648
2177. *Congregationalist* Feb. 75 p11
2178. *Christian Standard* Mar. 10 85 p6
2179. *Wesleyan Advocate* Sept. 11 78 p6
2180. Editor's Files
2181. *Pentecostal Evangel* May 9 76 p3
2182. *Alliance Witness* May 11 83 p2
2183. *Eternity* Jan. 85 p28
2184. *Change* Sept. 78 p36
2185. Editor's Files
2186. *Alliance Witness* Jan. 14 76 p4
2187. *Link* May 66 p58
2188. *Evangel* Dec. 27 76 p21
2189. *Herald Of Holiness* July 15 80 p13
2190. *Eternity* Apr. 84 p35
2191. *Wesleyan Advocate* Oct. 11 76 p14
2192. *Preacher's Magazine* Dec. 79 p32
2193. *Vital Christianity* Feb. 1 76 p4

2194. *Episcopal Recorder* Oct. 79 p1
2195. *Christian Herald* July 83 p57
2196. *Mere Christianity*
2197. *Christian Herald* July 83 p57
2198. Editor's Files
2199. *Vital Christianity* Oct. 2 77 p15
2200. *Herald Of Holiness* June 18 75 p18
2201. *Pentecostal Evangel* June 19 77 p20
2202. *Alliance Witness* June 27 79 p4
2203. *Wesleyan Advocate* July 5 76 p7
2204. Editor's Files
2205. Editor's Files
2206. *Herald Of Holiness* June 18 75 p18
2207. *Lutheran Standard* Dec. 8 70 p12
2208. Editor's Files
2209. *Alliance Witness* Sept. 5 79 p5
2210. *Banner* July 7 78 p15
2211. *His* May 78 p32
2212. *His* Apr. 77 p33
2213. *Christian Herald* Jan. 77 p49
2214. *Presbyterian Journal* Jan. 12 72 p13
2215. *American Opinion* Mar. 75 p35
2216. Editor's Files
2217. *Pentecostal Evangel* Mar. 23 75 p5
2218. *Journal Of The American Scientific Affiliation* June 75 p60
2219. *Christian Standard* Sept. 26 76 p11
2220. *Daily Study Bible/Corinthians/*p99
2221. *Christian Standard* Oct. 24 76 p6
2222. *Mennonite* Feb. 8 77 p85
2223. *Daily Study Bible/Corinthians/*p95
2224. *America* Dec. 15 73 p463
2225. *Moody Monthly* Feb. 75 p3
2226. *Christianity Today* Jan. 21 77 p14
2227. *Wesleyan Advocate* Oct. 27 75 p15
2228. *Wesleyan Advocate* Oct. 27 75 p15
2229. *Herald Of Holiness* Jan. 15 80 p3
2230. *Wesleyan Advocate* Nov. 22 76 p6
2231. *Mennonite* Jan. 11 77 p31
2232. *Soundings* Winter 75 p497
2233. *Christian Century* Sept. 19 79 p888
2234. *His* Mar. 75 p32
2235. Editor's Files
2236. *Religious Humanism* Winter 76 p23
2237. Editor's Files
2238. *Christian Standard* Mar. 20 83 p3
2239. *Church Herald* Jan. 23 81 p11
2240. *Christianity Today* Oct. 19 79 p18
2241. *Congregationalist* Dec. 75 p18
2242. *Alliance Witness* Aug. 11 76 p8
2243. *Congregationalist* June 71 p7
2244. *Pentecostal Evangel* Sept. 14 80 p7
2245. Editor's Files
2246. *Christian Standard* July 15 84 p3
2247. *Herald Of Holiness* May 15 85 p15

2248. *Presbyterian Journal* Aug. 20 75 p7
2249. *Wesleyan Advocate* Mar. 14 77 p14
2250. Editor's Files
2251. *Episcopal Recorder* Sept. 76 p17
2252. *Pentecostal Evangel* June 27 76 p21
2253. *Eternity* May 71 p15
2254. *Pentecostal Evangel* July 23 72 p5
2255. *United Brethren* Feb. 77 p32
2256. *Herald Of Holiness* Jan. 15 78 p5
2257. Editor's Files
2258. *Christian Ministry* May 75 p30
2259. Editor's Files
2260. *Vital Christianity* Nov. 30 75 p14
2261. *Presbyterian Journal* Dec. 10 75 p9
2262. *Christian Standard* Oct. 17 76 p13
2263. *Herald Of Holiness* June 7 67 p11
2264. *Evangel* Aug. 8 77 p17
2265. *Evangel* Apr. 28 75 p16
2266. *Faith For The Family* May 81 p4
2267. *Pentecostal Evangel* Dec. 14 75 p7
2268. *Presbyterian Journal* Nov. 17 71 p19
2269. *Presbyterian Journal* Oct. 22 80 p11
2270. Editor's Files
2271. *Baptist Bulletin* June 83 p7
2272. Editor's Files
2273. Editor's Files
2274. Editor's Files
2275. Editor's Files
2276. *Moody Monthly* Jan. 78 p93
2277. Editor's Files
2278. *Christian Herald* Sept. 79 p43
2279. *Good News Broadcaster* Nov. 78 p10
2280. *Christian Reader* July–Aug. 79 p100
2281. *Christian Standard* Feb. 20 83 p14
2282. *Presbyterian Journal* Aug. 2 78 p8
2283. *Pentecostal Evangel* Sept. 19 76 p13
2284. Editor's Files
2285. *Evangel* Sept. 8 75 p32
2286. *Evangel* Apr. 12 76 p27
2287. *Banner* May 27 77 p6
2288. *Evangel* Jan. 26 76 p32
2289. *Christian Reader* Jan. 81 p18
2290. Editor's Files
2291. Editor's Files
2292. *Wesleyan Advocate* June 7 76 p3
2293. *Herald Of Holiness* May 15 78 p18
2294. *Vital Christianity* Jan. 13 85 p8
2295. *Alliance Witness* June 4 75 p3
2296. *Wesleyan Advocate* Feb. 2 76 p13
2297. *Alliance Witness* Apr. 24 85 p5
2298. *War Cry* Feb. 2 85 p3
2299. *Presbyterian Journal* May 5 82 p9
2300. *Presbyterian Journal* May 5 82 p9
2301. *Preacher's Magazine* Sept. 79 p45

2302. *War Cry* Nov. 5 83 p24
2303. *Christian Ministry* Nov. 74 p24
2304. *Alliance Witness* Jan. 25 78 p8
2305. Editor's Files
2306. Editor's Files
2307. *Christian Standard* Feb. 3 85 p5
2308. Editor's Files
2309. *Lutheran* Nov. 18 81 p3
2310. *Christian Scholar's Review* Vol. 14, No. 2, p138
2311. *Daedalus* Spring 78 p61
2312. *Banner* Jan. 11 82 p14
2313. *Episcopal Recorder* Feb. 78 p1
2314. *Vital Christianity* Oct. 5 75 p5
2315. *Pentecostal Evangel* June 29 75 p22
2316. *Vital Christianity* Aug. 25 85 p14
2317. *Vital Christianity* Dec. 2 79 p17
2318. *Christian Century* Feb. 22 84 p198
2319. *Mennonite* Oct. 16 79 p624
2320. *Presbyterian Journal* Oct. 7 81 p9
2321. *Religious Humanism* Winter 71 p29
2322. Editor's Files
2323. *Pentecostal Evangel* May 22 77 p2
2324. *Episcopal Recorder* May 78 p14
2325. *Pentecostal Evangel* Oct. 3 76 p2
2326. Editor's Files
2327. Editor's Files
2328. *Encyclopedia Of Religious Quotations* 1965 p396
2329. *Encyclopedia Of Religious Quotations* 1965 p396
2330. *Encyclopedia Of Religious Quotations* 1965 p396
2331. *Encyclopedia Of Religious Quotations* 1965 p397
2332. *Encyclopedia Of Religious Quotations* 1965 p397
2333. *Vital Christianity* Aug. 15 76 p8
2334. *Banner* Oct. 17 83 p11
2335. *Christian Reader* July–Aug. 75 p14
2336. *Daily Study Bible/John*/p135
2337. *Link* Oct. 67 p58
2338. *Christian Herald* June 76 p35
2339. *Presbyterian Journal* Oct. 8 75 p11
2340. *War Cry* Sept. 7 85 p9
2341. *Good News Broadcaster* Oct. 23 p26
2342. *Wesleyan Advocate* June 20 77 p13
2343. *Alliance Witness* Dec. 13 78 p31
2344. *Wesleyan Advocate* Oct. 27 75 p12
2345. *Banner* June 6 75 p8
2346. *Wesleyan Advocate* Apr. 14 75 p3
2347. *Vital Christianity* June 24 79 p4
2348. *Wesleyan Advocate* July 3 77 p2
2349. *Theology Today* Oct. 75 p250
2350. *Evangel* Mar. 8 76 p25
2351. *Evangel* July 28 75 p14
2352. *1001 Inspirational Things*/p259
2353. *War Cry* Feb. 2 85 p3
2354. *Alliance Witness* Aug. 9 78 p4
2355. *Preacher's Magazine* Sept. 78 p63
2356. *Vital Christianity* July 13 75 p6
2357. *Alliance Witness* June 4 75 p4
2358. *Pentecostal Evangel* July 22 79 p2
2359. Editor's Files
2360. *Christian Century* Oct. 21 81 p1055
2361. *Link* Dec. 70 p53
2362. *Christian Standard* Mar. 18 84 p10
2363. *North Star Baptist* Aug. 80 p27
2364. *Herald Of Holiness* Feb. 12 75 p17
2365. Editor's Files
2366. Editor's Files
2367. Editor's Files
2368. *Daily Study Bible/Barclay*
2369. *Wesleyan Advocate* Oct. 11 76 p13
2370. *Pentecostal Evangel* July 27 75 p2
2371. *Pentecostal Evangel* Oct. 30 77 p2
2372. *Link* May 66 p58
2373. *Christian Ministry* Sept. 78 p38
2374. *Good News Broadcaster* Sept. 77 p8
2375. *Change* Nov. 76 p22
2376. *His* Oct. 74 p33
2377. *Christian Standard* Feb. 3 85 p6
2378. *Christian Standard* Mar. 25 79 p12
2379. Editor's Files
2380. Editor's Files
2381. Editor's Files
2382. Editor's Files
2383. Editor's Files
2384. Editor's Files
2385. *Christianity Today* Sept. 8 78 p15
2386. *Christian Century* Sept. 26 79 p917
2387. Editor's Files
2388. Editor's Files
2389. *Encyclopedia Of Religious Quotations* 1965 p399
2390. *Encyclopedia Of Religious Quotations* 1965 p399
2391. *Encyclopedia Of Religious Quotations* 1965 p399
2392. *Christianity Today* Feb. 27 76 p8
2393. *Moody Monthly* Jan. 82 p125
2394. Editor's Files
2395. *Mennonite* Apr. 17 79 p287
2396. *Banner* Dec. 26 75 p3
2397. *Emphasis On Faith And Living* Feb. 1 79 p3
2398. *North News* Aug. 79 p3
2399. *Encyclopedia Of Religious Quotations* 1965 p401
2400. *Pentecostal Evangel* Oct. 25 81 p12

2401. *Banner* July 30 76 p17
2402. *Banner* Sept. 13 82 p25
2403. *Presbyterian Journal* Feb. 25 76 p13
2404. *Banner* May 2 75 p3
2405. *Preacher's Magazine* Sept. 79 p1
2406. *Vital Christianity* Nov. 14 71 p14
2407. *Link* Apr. 70 p12
2408. *Pentecostal Evangel* Sept. 5 76 p15
2409. *Pentecostal Evangel* Feb. 13 77 p19
2410. *Evangel* Aug. 13 84 p8
2411. *Wesleyan Advocate* Mar. 15 76 p9
2412. *Christian Herald* Dec. 75 p30
2413. *Pentecostal Evangel* Mar. 16 75 p7
2414. *Christian Herald* Sept. 76 p58
2415. *Evangel* May 77 p27
2416. *Herald Of Holiness* Mar. 15 78 p16
2417. *War Cry* Sept. 18 71 p16
2418. *Wesleyan Advocate* Apr. 28 75 p5
2419. *Christian Standard* Nov. 27 83 p17
2420. *Church Herald* Feb. 10 78 p12
2421. *Mennonite* Nov. 29 77 p700
2422. *Christian Ministry* Jan. 79 p26
2423. *Pentecostal Evangel* Sept. 18 77 p5
2424. *Pentecostal Evangel* Apr. 29 84 p4
2425. *Evangel* Sept. 22 75 p5
2426. *Wesleyan Advocate* July 19 76 p12
2427. *Pentecostal Evangel* May 21 78 p7
2428. *Christian Herald* June 75 p22
2429. *Presbyterian Journal* Oct. 11 78 p15
2430. *Pentecostal Evangel* Sept. 5 76 p15
2431. *Daily Study Bible/Barclay*
2432. *His* Feb. 75 p5
2433. *Alliance Witness* Apr. 30 80 p10
2434. *Catholic Mind* Sept. 77 p20
2435. *Commonweal* May 20 83 p295
2436. *Journal Of Religion And Health* Jan. 79 p38
2437. *Christian Reader* Sept.–Oct. 76 p33
2438. *Christianity Today* Feb. 19 82 p17
2439. *American Opinion* May 75 p21
2440. *His* Feb. 76 p7
2441. *War Cry* Mar. 1 86 p8
2442. *New Catholic World* Nov.–Dec. 77 p278
2443. *Pentecostal Evangel* Sept. 17 78 p2
2444. *Christianity Today* Oct. 10 75 p5
2445. *These Times* Oct. 75 p4
2446. *Vital Christianity* Jan. 15 78 p14
2447. *These Times* May 75 p33
2448. *Mennonite* June 6 78 p372
2449. *Banner* Feb. 3 86 p7
2450. *Catholic Mind* Jan. 78 p42
2451. *Catholic Mind* May 75 p15
2452. *Church Herald* May 30 75 p9
2453. *Mennonite* Nov. 10 81 p629
2454. *Link* Dec. 66 p31

2455. *Herald Of Holiness* May 7 75 p17
2456. *Herald Of Holiness* Oct. 1 76 p23
2457. *Christian Reader* May–June 79 p24
2458. Editor's Files
2459. *Faith For The Family* Feb. 77 p17
2460. *Pentecostal Evangel* Jan. 18 81 p5
2461. *Faith For The Family* Jan. 86 p7
2462. *War Cry* Feb. 2 85 p3
2463. *U.S. Catholic* Nov. 75 p9
2464. *Emphasis On Faith And Living* Oct. 1 80 p3
2465. *Pentecostal Evangel* Feb. 8 76 p32
2466. Editor's Files
2467. Editor's Files
2468. *Episcopal Recorder* Mar. 77 p6
2469. *Christian Century* May 21 75 p525
2470. *Pentecostal Evangel* Feb. 2 86 p9
2471. *Mennonite* Feb. 17 76 p118
2472. *Lutheran* May 21 80 p3
2473. *Church Herald* Mar. 21 75 p7
2474. *Evangel* July 9 79 p17
2475. *Religion In Life* Winter 75 p430
2476. *Banner* Feb. 17 86 p15
2477. Editor's Files
2478. *American Opinion* Oct. 76 p37
2479. *Wesleyan Advocate* Dec. 8 75 p9
2480. *Good News Broadcaster* June 85 p12
2481. *Good News Broadcaster* Dec. 82 p7
2482. *The Best Of Tozer*
2483. *Pentecostal Evangel* Feb. 23 75 p6
2484. *The Watchman* Jan. 85 p5
2485. *Wesleyan Advocate* July 19 76 p12
2486. *Christian Ministry* May 81 p35
2487. *Presbyterian Journal* May 28 75 p13
2488. *Christianity Today* May 7 76 p14
2489. *Christian Herald* Dec. 75 p56
2490. *Banner* Oct. 24 75 p10
2491. Editor's Files
2492. *Christian Reader* Feb.–Mar. 71 p38
2493. Editor's Files
2494. *His* June 82 p27
2495. *Christian Standard* Oct. 2 83 p15
2496. *American Opinion* May 76 p27
2497. *Presbyterian Journal* Feb. 28 73 p8
2498. *American Opinion* Nov. 74 p21
2499. *Encyclopedia Of Religious Quotations* 1965 p411
2500. *Encyclopedia Of Religious Quotations* 1965 p410
2501. *Encyclopedia Of Religious Quotations* 1965 p412
2502. *Christian Standard* Jan. 27 85 p6
2503. *Encyclopedia Of Religious Quotations* 1965 p413
2504. *Encyclopedia Of Religious Quotations* 1965 p414

2505. *Encyclopedia Of Religious Quotations* 1965 p412
2506. *Christianity Today* Mar. 12 76 p64
2507. *These Times* Mar. 70 p34
2508. *A Reader's Notebook/Kennedy*/p289
2509. Editor's Files
2510. *Banner* Oct. 1 76 p21
2511. *Alliance Witness* Apr. 20 77 p7
2512. *Alliance Witness* Apr. 20 77 p7
2513. *Alliance Witness* Apr. 20 77 p7
2514. *Mennonite* May 10 83 p218
2515. *Christian Standard* Apr. 6 80 p3
2516. *Christian Standard* May 24 81 p9
2517. *Christian Standard* Jan. 4 76 p9
2518. *Pentecostal Evangel* Nov. 12 78 p2
2519. *Pentecostal Evangel* Oct. 19 75 p2
2520. Editor's Files
2521. *Christian Standard* Aug. 1 76 p11
2522. *Pentecostal Evangel* June 11 78 p12
2523. Editor's Files
2524. *United Evangelical Action* Winter 76 p19
2525. Editor's Files
2526. *Presbyterian Journal* Dec. 17 75 p13
2527. Editor's Files
2528. *Wesleyan Advocate* Jan. 31 77 p20
2529. Editor's Files
2530. Editor's Files
2531. *Eternity* Sept. 78 p32
2532. *Banner* Nov. 5 76 p4
2533. *American Opinion* Mar. 73 p95
2534. *American Opinion* Sept. 75 p29
2535. *Theological Educator* Fall 76 p114
2536. *Presbyterian Journal* Nov. 5 75 p8
2537. *Wesleyan Advocate* Apr. 11 77 p12
2538. *Wesleyan Advocate* July 5 76 p2
2539. *Pulpit* Feb. 69 p25
2540. *Moody Monthly* May 79 p65
2541. *Christian Standard* Aug. 8 76 p8
2542. *Wesleyan Advocate* July 7 75 p7
2543. Editor's Files
2544. *Link* Dec. 74 p55
2545. Editor's Files
2546. *Encyclopedia Of Religious Quotations* 1965 p431
2547. *A.D.* Apr. 75 p46
2548. *Church Herald* May 13 77 p12
2549. *Banner* Nov. 19 84 p13
2550. *Herald Of Holiness* Nov. 1 85 p11
2551. *Christian Herald* Jan. 78 p40
2552. *Wesleyan Advocate* Jan. 3 77 p5
2553. *Wesleyan Advocate* Oct. 3 83 p3
2554. *Pentecostal Evangel* Nov. 30 75 p10
2555. *U.S. Catholic* Nov. 77 p25
2556. *Mennonite* Jan. 14 87 p24
2557. *Pentecostal Evangel* Apr. 20 80 p3

2558. *Lutheran Witness* Nov. 3 74 p6
2559. *Presbyterian Journal* July 26 78 p9
2560. *Christian Herald* July 75 p26
2561. *Pentecostal Evangel* June 26 77 p2
2562. *Christian Herald* May 81 p54
2563. Editor's Files
2564. *Encyclopedia Of Religious Quotations* 1965 p431
2565. *Vital Christianity* Nov. 9 80 p16
2566. Editor's Files
2567. *Herald Of Holiness* Mar. 1 79 p15
2568. *U.S. Catholic* Feb. 85 p7
2569. *Christian Herald* July 82 p28
2570. *Wesleyan Advocate* July 13 81 p11
2571. *Encyclopedia Of Religious Quotations* 1965 p432
2572. *Encounter* Winter 78 p38
2573. *War Cry* Aug. 24 74 p1
2574. *Christianity Today* Mar. 24 78 p16
2575. *Alliance Witness* Jan. 20 82 p23
2576. *Christian Herald* July–Aug. 76 p48
2577. *Wesleyan Advocate* July 5 76 p9
2578. Editor's Files
2579. *Link* Nov. 66 p58
2580. *Presbyterian Journal* June 3 81 p10
2581. *Presbyterian Journal* Dec. 10 75 p9
2582. *Episcopal Recorder* Aug. 76 p5
2583. *Herald Of Holiness* Nov. 15 78 p7
2584. *Vital Christianity* May 30 76 p9
2585. *Emphasis On Faith And Living* Sept. 15 76 p3
2586. *Wesleyan Advocate* Jan. 31 77 p9
2587. *Herald Of Holiness* Apr. 23 75 p18
2588. *Christian Herald* May 81 p54
2589. *Faith For The Family* Nov.–Dec. 76 p13
2590. *Church Herald* May 13 77 p9
2591. Editor's Files
2592. *Christian Standard* July 2 78 p5
2593. *Christian Herald* June 76 p24
2594. *Pentecostal Evangel* July 18 76 p2
2595. *Presbyterian Journal* May 25 77 p9
2596. *A.D.* May 78 p17
2597. *Herald Of Holiness* Dec. 17 75 p8
2598. *Vital Christianity* Sept. 7 75 p3
2599. *Wesleyan Advocate* Mar. 27 78 p10
2600. *War Cry* Oct. 10 70 p3
2601. *Christian Herald* Dec. 70 p34
2602. *Faith For The Family* Feb. 77 p13
2603. *Encyclopedia Of Religious Quotations* 1965 p433
2604. *Encyclopedia Of Religious Quotations* 1965 p434
2605. *American Scholar* Autumn 75 p642
2606. *Religious Education* Mar. 79 p135
2607. Editor's Files
2608. *Pentecostal Evangel* June 13 76 p2

2609. *Good News Broadcaster* Sept. 83 p53
2610. *Theology Today* July 76 p133
2611. *Eternity* Nov. 76 p15
2612. *Eternity* Nov. 76 p13
2613. *Emphasis On Faith And Living* Nov. 82 p3
2614. *Christianity Today* Nov. 17 78 p22
2615. *Christian Standard* July 13 75 p7
2616. *These Times* Feb. 76 p31
2617. *A.D.* May 78 p24
2618. *American Opinion* Sept. 75 p29
2619. *Eternity* Sept. 81 p58
2620. *America* May 6 78 p359
2621. *Evangel* Mar. 28 77 p5
2622. *Christian Herald* Sept. 78 p50
2623. *American Scholar* Autumn 79 p455
2624. *American Scholar* Autumn 78 p449
2625. *Pentecostal Evangel* July 1 79 p13
2626. *Mennonite* Jan. 17 78 p37
2627. *Christianity Today* Apr. 18 80 p17
2628. *Emphasis On Faith And Living* Sept. 15 76 p3
2629. *Alliance Witness* June 11 80 p25
2630. *Detroit News* Aug. 2 84 p11-A
2631. *Banner* Sept. 14 79 p5
2632. Editor's Files
2633. *Link* July 73 p63
2634. *Christian Herald* Oct. 80 p31
2635. *Emphasis On Faith And Living* Aug. 81 p5
2636. *Encyclopedia Of Religious Quotations* 1965 p435
2637. *Encyclopedia Of Religious Quotations* 1965 p436
2638. *His* Mar. 77 p34
2639. *Christian Standard* Aug. 27 78 p5
2640. *Pentecostal Evangel* Oct. 23 77 p4
2641. *Faith For The Family* May 77 p22
2642. *Herald Of Holiness* July 30 75 p11
2643. Editor's Files
2644. *Herald Of Holiness* Aug. 1 78 p19
2645. *Christian Standard* Sept. 26 76 p16
2646. Editor's Files
2647. *Christian Herald* July–Aug. 77 p52
2648. Editor's Files
2649. *Banner* Nov. 14 75 p3
2650. *Episcopal Recorder* Mar. 76 p21
2651. *Presbyterian Journal* July 30 75 p7
2652. *Episcopal Recorder* July 78 p19
2653. *His* Mar. 77 p34
2654. *Christian Example* Oct. 28 84
2655. Editor's Files
2656. *His* Mar. 77 p34
2657. *Pentecostal Evangel* Nov. 18 84 p5
2658. *Evangel* May 26 75 p5

2659. *Christian Ministry* July 83 p27
2660. *Daily Study Bible/Ephesians/*p197
2661. *Lutheran* Nov. 15 78 p3
2662. *Emphasis On Faith And Living* Nov. 15 80 p5
2663. *Emphasis On Faith And Living* Nov. 15 80 p5
2664. *Christian Herald* Jan. 78 p40
2665. *Pentecostal Evangel* June 27 76 p2
2666. *Congregationalist* Nov. 75 p5
2667. *Banner* Nov. 22 74 p12
2668. *Herald Of Holiness* Nov. 15 85 p5
2669. *Reader's Digest* July 82 p2
2670. *Treasury of Courage And Confidence* p243
2671. *Evangel* Nov. 24 75 p25
2672. *Christian Life* May 76 p70
2673. *Presbyterian Journal* Aug. 5 81 p11
2674. *Herald Of Holiness* Nov. 7 73 p18
2675. *Lutheran* Nov. 17 82 p3
2676. *Wesleyan Advocate* Apr. 20 81 p9
2677. *Christian Home* Oct. 77 p8
2678. *Banner* Nov. 26 76 p8
2679. *Pentecostal Evangel* Nov. 18 84 p16
2680. *Pentecostal Evangel* Aug. 8 76 p2
2681. *Pentecostal Evangel* Nov. 19 78 p3
2682. *Christian Herald* Feb. 79 p58
2683. Editor's Files
2684. *Christian Home* Nov. 77 p31
2685. *Alliance Witness* Nov. 15 78 p8
2686. Editor's Files
2687. Editor's Files
2688. *Emphasis On Earth And Living* Nov. 82 p23
2689. *Theology Today* Jan. 80 p540
2690. *Christianity Today* Feb. 27 76 p46
2691. *His* Feb. 81 p26
2692. *Christian Century* Mar. 23 77 p270
2693. *Christianity Today* May 9 75 p51
2694. *Banner* Aug. 24 81 p12
2695. *Pentecostal Testimony* Mar. 85 p18
2696. Editor's Files
2697. *Herald Of Holiness* July 1 84 p3
2698. *Christian Standard* Dec. 28 75 p8
2699. *American Opinion* Oct. 72 p91
2700. *Good News Broadcaster* May 79 p4
2701. *Good News Broadcaster* June 75 p29
2702. Editor's Files
2703. *Banner* Sept. 15 78 p8
2704. *American Scholar* Autumn 78 p449
2705. *Christian Century* Dec. 30 81 p1374
2706. *Mennonite* June 24 75 p408
2707. *Alliance Witness* Jan. 14 76 p3
2708. *Church Herald* Dec. 31 71 p10
2709. Editor's Files

2710. *Christian Herald* June 78 p41
2711. *Wesleyan Advocate* June 9 75 p12
2712. *Good News Broadcaster* Jan. 81 p5
2713. *Presbyterian Journal* Feb. 15 78 p9
2714. *American Opinion* June 76 p39
2715. *Emphasis On Faith And Living* Jan. 81 p9
2716. *Vital Christianity* Nov. 2 75 p9
2717. *Herald Of Holiness* Jan. 1 78 p2
2718. *Preacher's Magazine* May–June 78 p11
2719. Editor's Files
2720. *Episcopal Recorder* Feb. 78 p14
2721. *Christian Herald* Nov. 75 p24
2722. Editor's Files
2723. Editor's Files
2724. *Lighted Pathway* Aug. 70 p25
2725. *Encyclopedia Of Religious Quotations* 1965 p446
2726. *Journal Of Biblical Literature* Dec. 79 p489
2727. *Lutheran* Aug. 82 p3
2728. *Wesleyan Advocate* Jan. 3 77 p5
2729. *Church Herald* Mar. 19 76 p15
2730. *Christian Standard* Mar. 16 75 p6
2731. *Eternity* June 76 p50
2732. *Pentecostal Evangel* Aug. 22 76 p2
2733. *American Opinion* Sept. 71 p71
2734. *Vital Christianity* July 27 75 p17
2735. *Wesleyan Advocate* Jan. 17 77 p15
2736. *Eternity* Jan. 75 p48
2737. *Pentecostal Evangel* Oct. 22 78 p2
2738. *Moody Monthly* May 77 p127
2739. *Christian Standard* Dec. 5 76 p14
2740. Editor's Files
2741. *Wesleyan Advocate* Feb. 28 77 p2
2742. *Religion In Life* Spring 78 p6
2743. *Herald Of Holiness* Aug. 1 78 p3
2744. *Christian Herald* Dec. 77 p21
2745. *Church Herald* Mar. 18 83 p8
2746. *Pentecostal Evangel* Nov. 30 75 p11
2747. *Banner* May 23 75 p8
2748. *Pentecostal Evangel* July 17 77 p2
2749. *Moody Monthly* Sept. 85 p75
2750. *Vital Christianity* Sept. 3 78 p17
2751. *Wesleyan Advocate* July 4 77 p15
2752. *Evangel* Sept. 22 75 p25
2753. *American Opinion* Nov. 74 p21
2754. *Presbyterian Journal* Jan. 11 78 p11
2755. *Christian Reader* Sept.–Oct. 75 p70
2756. *Evangel* Nov. 13 78 p5
2757. *Alliance Witness* Jan. 1 86 p9
2758. *Wesleyan Advocate* June 20 77 p13
2759. *Lutheran* Mar. 15 78 p3
2760. *Pentecostal Evangel* June 7 70 p10
2761. *Alliance Witness* July 16 75 p8

2762. *Pentecostal Evangel* June 22 80 p7
2763. *Evangel* Apr. 14 75 p16
2764. *War Cry* Feb. 2 85 p3
2765. *Pentecostal Evangel* Dec. 26 76 p31
2766. *Christian Century* Dec. 19 84 p1195
2767. *Episcopal Recorder* Aug. 77 p18
2768. *Presbyterian Journal* July 16 75 p10
2769. *Encyclopedia Of Religious Quotations* 1965 p447
2770. *Pentecostal Evangel* June 8 75 p7
2771. *Pentecostal Evangel* Aug. 16 81 p5
2772. *Pentecostal Evangel* Dec. 28 80 p12
2773. *Christian Standard* June 14 81 p7
2774. *Good News Broadcaster* Oct. 75 p11
2775. *Alliance Witness* June 28 78 p5
2776. *Vital Christianity* Feb. 16 75 p25
2777. *Herald Of Holiness* Dec. 15 78 p17
2778. *Eternity* June 70 p50
2779. *Banner* Oct. 24 75 p3
2780. *Alliance Witness* Aug. 10 77 p3
2781. *Pentecostal Evangel* Dec. 12 76 p21
2782. *Herald Of Holiness* May 15 76 p14
2783. *Banner* Feb. 27 76 p9
2784. Editor's Files
2785. *Banner* May 25 79 p23
2786. *Encyclopedia Of Religious Quotations* 1965 p446
2787. *Christian Herald* July–Aug. 77 p52
2788. *Pentecostal Evangel* Oct. 20 74 p4
2789. *Encyclopedia Of Religious Quotations* 1965 p446
2790. *Presbyterian Journal* Sept. 1 82 p15
2791. *Lutheran* May 6 81 p3
2792. *Letters To An American Lady*
2793. *Banner* Feb. 10 78 p8
2794. *Christian Standard* Mar. 16 86 p11
2795. *Presbyterian Journal* Apr. 20 77 p10
2796. *His* May 75 p34
2797. *War Cry* Feb. 2 85 p3
2798. *Church Herald* May 16 75 p9
2799. Editor's Files
2800. *American Opinion* Jan. 76 p22
2801. *American Opinion* Dec. 80 p37
2802. *Wesleyan Advocate* Feb. 7 72 p2
2803. *Daily Study Bible/Barclay*
2804. *Ecumenical Review* July 75 p201
2805. *Daily Study Bible/Barclay*
2806. *Christian Standard* July 20 80 p11
2807. *Herald Of Holiness* Apr. 1 76 p13
2808. *Pentecostal Evangel* Sept. 25 77 p5
2809. *Herald Of Holiness* Apr. 1 76 p13
2810. *Catholic Mind* Jan. 78 p27
2811. *Catholic Mind* Dec. 78 p17
2812. *Pentecostal Evangel* Jan. 12 86 p21
2813. *Episcopal Recorder* July 76 p10

2814. *Episcopal Recorder* Feb. 77 p10
2815. *Preacher's Magazine* May 78 p11
2816. *Presbyterian Journal* Feb. 26 75 p13
2817. Editor's Files
2818. Editor's Files
2819. *Encyclopedia Of Religious Quotations* 1965 p456
2820. *Encyclopedia Of Religious Quotations* 1965 p456
2821. Editor's Files
2822. Editor's Files
2823. *Wesleyan Advocate* June 16 80 p18
2824. *American Opinion* Sept. 71 p73
2825. *American Opinion* Feb. 75 p35
2826. *Wesleyan Advocate* Feb. 2 76 p9
2827. *Episcopal Recorder* Aug. 76 p1
2828. *Wesleyan Advocate* Sept. 27 76 p12
2829. *Pentecostal Evangel* June 1 73 p15
2830. *Christianity Today* Nov. 7 80 p27
2831. *Banner* Dec. 3 76 p9
2832. *Banner* May 27 77 p9
2833. *American Opinion* Nov. 76 p39
2834. *Vital Christianity* Jan. 5 75 p14
2835. *United Evangelical Action* Spring 76 p7
2836. *Christianity Today* Jan. 21 77 p30
2837. *Christianity Today* Oct. 10 75 p33
2838. *Religion In Life* Summer 76 p146
2839. *Church Herald* Sept. 16 77 p13
2840. *Evangel* Aug. 8 77 p16
2841. *Herald Of Holiness* Apr. 1 76 p13
2842. *Vital Christianity* July 16 78 p16
2843. *American Opinion* May 76 p27
2844. *U.S. Catholic* Jan. 77 p9
2845. *Daedalus* Summer 76 p143
2846. *Worldview* Oct. 76 p41
2847. *Commentary* Dec. 80 p39
2848. *Theology Today* Apr. 79 p10
2849. *Presbyterian Journal* Nov. 18 77 p10
2850. *Pentecostal Evangel* Sept. 5 76 p15
2851. *American Opinion* Mar. 77 p37
2852. *Presbyterian Journal* Nov. 3 76 p9
2853. *Christian Standard* Mar. 13 83 p13
2854. *Mennonite* Dec. 2 80 p708
2855. *Emphasis On Faith And Living* June 15 79 p3
2856. *Evangel* June 9 75 p18
2857. *Pentecostal Evangel* May 25 75 p10
2858. *New Catholic World* Mar.–Apr. 76 p50
2859. *Daily Study Bible/Philippians/*p21
2860. *Mennonite* Apr. 22 86 p192
2861. *American Opinion* Dec. 75 p45
2862. *Church Herald* Jan. 22 71 p7
2863. *Christian Standard* Sept. 26 76 p5
2864. *Good News Broadcaster* Apr. 78 p6
2865. Editor's Files

2866. *War Cry* Feb. 1 86 p7
2867. *American Opinion* Oct. 83 p43
2868. *Wesleyan Advocate* May 24 76 p5
2869. *Eternity* June 73 p20
2870. Editor's Files
2871. *American Opinion* July–Aug. 75 p159
2872. *Christian Herald* Feb. 79 p58
2873. *Pentecostal Evangel* Feb. 29 76 p5
2874. *Good News Broadcaster* June 75 p29
2875. Editor's Files
2876. *Moody Monthly* Feb. 76 p82
2877. *Wesleyan Advocate* July 5 76 p2
2878. *Link* Mar. 71 p37
2879. *Link* Apr. 74 p63
2880. *Religious Humanism* Autumn 76 p155
2881. Editor's Files
2882. *Alliance Witness* Apr. 31 76 p31
2883. Editor's Files
2884. *Presbyterian Journal* Jan. 16 80 p15
2885. *Center Magazine* Sept. 79 p63
2886. *American Opinion* Mar. 77 p38
2887. Editor's Files
2888. *His* Feb. 76 p28
2889. *Christian Herald* July–Aug. 77 p60
2890. *Good News Broadcaster* Mar. 82 p47
2891. *United Evangelical Action* Fall 75 p28
2892. *Church Herald* Aug. 8 75 p13
2893. *Moody Monthly* May 77 p31
2894. *Theological Educator* Spring 83 p79
2895. *Pentecostal Evangel* Nov. 25 84 p11
2896. *Emphasis On Faith And Living* Apr. 81 p3
2897. *Church Herald* Apr. 1 77 p10
2898. *Vital Christianity* Nov. 18 79 p8
2899. Editor's Files
2900. *Change* Nov. 76 p22
2901. Editor's Files
2902. *American Scholar* Autumn 83 p504
2903. *American Opinion* July–Aug. 75 p159
2904. *Pentecostal Evangel* Sept. 18 77 p2
2905. Editor's Files
2906. *Lutheran* Nov. 17 76 p3
2907. *Commentary* Mar. 84 p36
2908. *His* Jan. 78 p21
2909. Editor's Files
2910. *Christian Standard* Apr. 20 75 p6
2911. *Messenger* Nov. 75 p31
2912. *American Opinion* Apr. 85 p43
2913. *American Opinion* Jan. 75 p33
2914. *His* Jan. 75 p7
2915. *His* Feb. 75 p25
2916. *Presbyterian Journal* Aug. 16 78 p13
2917. *American Opinion* Sept. 79 p112
2918. Editor's Files
2919. Editor's Files

2920. *Jewish Frontier* Feb. 76 p4
2921. *U.S. Catholic* Feb. 77 p31
2922. *Pentecostal Evangel* Oct. 30 77 p2
2923. *Christian Ministry* Jan. 79 p17
2924. *Pentecostal Testimony* Aug. 83 p31
2925. *Christianity Today* June 6 75 p12
2926. *Pentecostal Testimony* Feb. 83 p2
2927. *Episcopal Recorder* May 78 p14
2928. *Moody Monthly* Oct. 75 p38
2929. *Presbyterian Journal* May 24 78 p13
2930. *Presbyterian Journal* Aug. 24 83 p15
2931. *Alliance Witness* May 7 75 p25
2932. Editor's Files
2933. *Wesleyan Advocate* Oct. 23 78 p8
2934. *Herald Of Holiness* Mar. 26 75 p19
2935. Editor's Files
2936. *Christian Standard* July 11 82 p14
2937. *Christian Standard* Jan. 2 83 p15
2938. *Vital Christianity* June 24 79 p3
2939. *Presbyterian Journal* Mar. 26 75 p13
2940. *Presbyterian Journal* Feb. 4 76 p7
2941. *Mennonite* Jan. 31 78 p79
2942. Editor's Files
2943. *Preacher's Magazine* Oct. 76 p21
2944. *Herald Of Holiness* Jan. 1 79 p9
2945. *Good News Broadcaster* Apr. 78 p7
2946. *Lutheran* Mar. 1 78 p3
2947. *Christian Herald* June 81 p46
2948. *Lutheran* July 76 p3
2949. *Pentecostal Evangel* May 21 78 p3
2950. *Pentecostal Evangel* Aug. 17 75 p32
2951. Editor's Files
2952. *Emphasis On Faith And Living* July 15 79 p3
2953. *Presbyterian Journal* Feb. 15 78 p9
2954. Editor's Files

2955. Editor's Files
2956. *Christian Herald* Mar. 80 p54
2957. *Daily Study Bible/Philippians*/p48
2958. *Vital Christianity* June 24 79 p8
2959. *Alliance Witness* June 6 84 p2
2960. *Messenger* Mar. 75 p14
2961. *Christian Standard* May 25 75 p9
2962. *War Cry* Nov. 16 74 p3
2963. *Pentecostal Testimony* Mar. 85 p17
2964. *Wesleyan Advocate* Apr. 7 86 p3
2965. *Preacher's Magazine* Oct. 76 p21
2966. *Presbyterian Journal* June 6 73 p22
2967. *Christianity Today* Feb. 1 85 p15
2968. *Pentecostal Evangel* Dec. 29 74 p3
2969. *Herald Of Holiness* Sept. 1 83 p9
2970. *Christian Standard* Jan. 22 84 p9
2971. *Banner* Dec. 4 70 p2
2972. *Banner* Dec. 14 73 p16
2973. *Christian Standard* Oct. 9 83 p8
2974. *Encyclopedia Of Religious Quotations* 1965 p481
2975. *Encyclopedia Of Religious Quotations* 1965 p480
2976. *Christian Century* Sept. 19 73 p916
2977. Editor's Files
2978. *Herald Of Holiness* Apr. 1 76 p16
2979. *Pentecostal Evangel* Dec. 26 76 p9
2980. *Catholic Mind* Apr. 75 p36
2981. *Banner* May 30 75 p12
2982. *American Opinion* May 77 p29
2983. *Lighted Pathway* Feb. 72 p8
2984. Editor's Files
2985. Editor's Files
2986. Editor's Files
2987. *American Opinion* Oct. 70 p74